Women in the World

of the

Earliest Christians

Women in the World

of the

Earliest Christians

Illuminating
Ancient Ways of Life

Lynn H. Cohick

Baker Academic
a division of Baker Publishing Group
Grand Rapids, Michigan

Published by Baker Academic
a division of Baker Publishing Group
P.O. Box 6287, Grand Rapids, MI 49516-6287
www.bakeracademic.com

Printed in the United States of America

Library of Congress Cataloging-in-Publication Data

Cohick, Lynn H.
      Women in the world of the earliest Christians : illuminating ancient ways of life / Lynn H.
  Cohick.
          p.   cm.
      Includes bibliographical references (p.   ) and indexes.
      ISBN 978-0-8010-3172-4 (pbk.)
      1. Christian women—Rome—Social life and customs. 2. Jewish women—Rome—Social
  life and customs. 3. Women—Rome—Social life and customs. I. Title.
  BR195.W6C63 2009
  274′.01082—dc22   2009029934

09   10   11   12   13   14   15   7   6   5   4   3   2   1

To my children
Charles James Cohick
and
Sarah Bloom Cohick

Contents

Illustrations

Acknowledgments

Many people have provided encouragement and inspiration for this project. I am indebted to Ross Kraemer, who challenged me to think broadly and clearly about women's lives in the ancient world. I am grateful for my Wheaton College colleagues Michael Graves, who tirelessly offered his insight into the topic of women in the rabbinic corpus, and George Kalantzis, who sharpened my own thinking on Roman women. I am deeply thankful for my associate dean, Jeffrey Greenman, and dean, Jill Peláez Baumgaertner, who encouraged me in this project and provided release time to write. Many thanks as well to Emily Bergen, my teaching assistant, whose research aid made the entire process smoother. I owe a considerable debt of gratitude to Jim Kinney, editorial director of Baker Academic, who provided unstinting support for this book and assistance in seeing the project to completion.

And for my husband, Jim, I am forever thankful—your belief in me and this project is a treasure beyond price.

Abbreviations

Bibliographic and General

b.	Babylonian Talmud
BBR	*Bulletin for Biblical Research*
BGU	*Aegyptische Urkunden aus den Königlichen Staatlichen Museen zu Berlin, Griechische Urkunden*, 15 vols. (Berlin, 1895–1983)
BJS	Brown Judaic Studies
CD	Damascus Document
CIG	*Corpus inscriptionum graecarum*, edited by A. Boeckh, 4 vols. (Berlin, 1828–77)
CIJ	*Corpus inscriptionum judaicarum*, edited by J. B. Frey, 2 vols. (Rome, 1936–52)
CIL	*Corpus inscriptionum latinarum* (Berlin, 1863–1959)
CLE	*Carmina Latina Epigraphica*, edited by F. Buecheler (Leipzig, 1895–97)
Cowley	*Aramaic Papyri of the Fifth Century B.C.*, by A. E. Cowley (Oxford, 1923)
CPJ	*Corpus papyrorum judaicorum*, edited by V. Tcherikover, 3 vols. (Cambridge, 1957–64)
EPE	*Elephantine Papyri in English*, edited by B. Porten (Leiden, 1996)
FGH	*Die Fragmente der griechischen Historiker*, edited by F. Jacoby (Leiden, 1923–58)
fr.	fragment
GRBS	*Greek, Roman and Byzantine Studies*
HTR	*Harvard Theological Review*

13

ILLRP	*Inscriptiones Latinae Liberae Rei Publicae*, by A. Degrassi, I² (Florence, 1965), II (Florence, 1963)
ILS	*Inscriptiones Latinae Selectae*, edited by H. Dessau (Berlin, 1892–1916)
JBL	*Journal of Biblical Literature*
JIGRE	*Jewish Inscriptions of Graeco-Roman Egypt*, by W. Horbury and D. Noy (Cambridge, 1992)
JRS	*Journal of Roman Studies*
JSNT	*Journal for the Study of the New Testament*
Kaibel	*Epigrammata Graeca ex lapidibus conlecta*, edited by G. Kaibel (Berlin, 1878)
LCL	Loeb Classical Library
LSAM	*Lois sacrées de l'Asie Mineure*, edited by F. Sokolowski (Paris, 1955)
Lutz	"Musonius Rufus: 'The Roman Socrates,'" by Cora E. Lutz, *Yale Classical Studies* 10 (1947): 3–147
LXX	Septuagint
m.	Mishnah
MAMA	*Monumenta Asiae Minoris Antiqua* (Manchester and London, 1928–93)
OGIS	*Orientis graeci inscriptiones selectae*, edited by W. Dittenberger, 2 vols. (Leipzig, 1903–5)
P.	papyrus
P.Brem.	*Die Bremer Papyri*, edited by U. Wilcken (Berlin, 1936)
P.Coll.Youtie	*Collectanea papyrologica: Texts published in honor of H. C. Youtie*, edited by A. E. Hanson (Bonn, 1976)
P.Eleph.	*Elephantine-Papyri*, edited by O. Rubensohn (Berlin, 1907)
P.Fouad	*Les papyrus Fouad*, edited by A. Bataille et al. (Cairo, 1939)
PG	Patrologia graeca
PGM	*Papyri graecae magicae: Die griechischen Zauberpapyri*, edited by K. Preisendanz (Berlin, 1928)
P.Iand.	*Papyri Iandanae*, edited C. Kalbefleisch et al. (Leipzig, 1913–35)
Pleket	*Epigraphica II: Texts on the Social History of the Greek World*, by H. W. Pleket (Leiden, 1969)
P.Oxy.	*The Oxyrhynchus Papyri*, edited by B. P. Grenfell, A. S. Hunt, et al. (London, 1898–)
P.Se'elim	*Naḥal Ṣe'elim Documents*, by Ada Yardeni (Jerusalem, 1995)
P.Tebt.	*The Tebtunis Papyri*, edited by B. P. Grenfell, A. S. Hunt, et al. (London, 1902–35)

P.XHev/Se   *Aramaic, Hebrew and Greek Documentary Texts from Naḥal Ḥever and Other Sites, with an Appendix Containing Alleged Qumran Texts*, by Hannah M. Cotton and Ada Yardeni, Discoveries in the Judean Desert 27 (Oxford, 1997)

P.Yadin   *The Documents from the Bar Kochba Period in the Cave of Letters: Greek Papyri*, edited by N. Lewis (Jerusalem, 1989)

R.   Rabbi

SB   *Sammelbuch griechischer Urkunden aus Aegypten*, edited by F. Preisigke et al. (Strasbourg and Berlin, 1915–)

SBLEJL   Society of Biblical Literature Early Judaism and Its Literature

SBLMS   Society of Biblical Literature Monograph Series

SEG   *Supplementum epigraphicum graecum* (Leiden, 1923–71; Amsterdam, 1979–)

SNTSMS   Society for New Testament Studies Monograph Series

s.v.   *sub verbo* (under the word)

SVF   *Stoicorum veterum fragmenta*, edited by H. von Arnim, 4 vols. (Leipzig, 1903–24)

TAD   *Textbook of Aramaic Documents from Ancient Egypt*, edited by Bezalel Porten and Ada Yardeni, 2 vols. (Jerusalem, 1986)

t.   Tosefta

TP   *Documenti processuali dalle Tabulae Pompeianae di Murecine*, edited by L. Bove (Naples, 1979)

TPSulp.   *Tabulae Pompeianae Sulpicianae*, edited by G. Camodeca (Naples, 1992)

y.   Jerusalem Talmud

Old Testament Books

Gen.	Genesis	Esther	Esther
Exod.	Exodus	Job	Job
Lev.	Leviticus	Ps. (Pss.)	Psalms
Num.	Numbers	Prov.	Proverbs
Deut.	Deuteronomy	Eccles.	Ecclesiastes
Josh.	Joshua	Song	Song of Songs
Judg.	Judges	Isa.	Isaiah
Ruth	Ruth	Jer.	Jeremiah
1–2 Sam.	1–2 Samuel	Lam.	Lamentations
1–2 Kings	1–2 Kings	Ezek.	Ezekiel
1–2 Chron.	1–2 Chronicles	Dan.	Daniel
Ezra	Ezra	Hosea	Hosea
Neh.	Nehemiah	Joel	Joel

Amos	Amos	Hab.	Habakkuk
Obad.	Obadiah	Zeph.	Zephaniah
Jon.	Jonah	Hag.	Haggai
Mic.	Micah	Zech.	Zechariah
Nah.	Nahum	Mal.	Malachi

New Testament Books

Matt.	Matthew	1–2 Thess.	1–2 Thessalonians
Mark	Mark	1–2 Tim.	1–2 Timothy
Luke	Luke	Titus	Titus
John	John	Philem.	Philemon
Acts	Acts	Heb.	Hebrews
Rom.	Romans	James	James
1–2 Cor.	1–2 Corinthians	1–2 Pet.	1–2 Peter
Gal.	Galatians	1–3 John	1–3 John
Eph.	Ephesians	Jude	Jude
Phil.	Philippians	Rev.	Revelation
Col.	Colossians		

Jewish Writings

Ant.	Josephus, *Antiquitates judaicae* (*Jewish Antiquities*)
B.J.	Josephus, *Bellum judaicum* (*Jewish War*)
C. Ap.	Josephus, *Contra Apionem* (*Against Apion*)
Contempl.	Philo, *De vita contemplativa* (*On the Contemplative Life*)
Fug.	Philo, *De fuga et inventione* (*On Flight and Finding*)
Sir.	Sirach
Spec.	Philo, *De specialibus legibus* (*On the Special Laws*)
Sus.	Susanna
Tob.	Tobit

Rabbinic Tractates

B. Bat.	*Bava Batra*	*Mak.*	*Makkot*	*Shab.*	*Shabbat*
Hor.	*Horayot*	*Ned.*	*Nedarim*	*Sot.*	*Sotah*
Ker.	*Keritot*	*Nid.*	*Niddah*	*Yevam.*	*Yevamot*
Ket.	*Ketubbot*	*Qidd.*	*Qiddushin*		

Qumran/Dead Sea Scrolls

1QM	War Scroll	4Q184	Wiles of the Wicked Woman
1QpHab	Habakkuk Pesher	4QMMT	Halakhic Letter
1QSa	Rule of the Congregation	11QT	Temple Scroll

Classical Writings

Ann.	Tacitus, *Annales (Annals)*
Ars	Ovid, *Ars amatoria (Art of Love)*
Conj. praec.	Plutarch, *Conjugalia praecepta (Advice to the Bride and Groom)*
Ep.	Pliny the Younger, *Epistulae (Letters)*
Fact. dict. mem.	Valerius Maximus, *Factorum et dictorum memorabilium (Memorable Deeds and Sayings)*
Gyn.	Soranus, *Gynaecia (Gynecology)*
Hist.	Livy, *Historia (History of Rome)*
Hist. Rom.	Cassius Dio, *Historia Romana (Roman History)*
Inst.	Quintilian, *Institutio oratoria (Institutes of Oratory)*
Mor.	Plutarch, *Moralia*
Nat.	Pliny the Elder, *Naturalis historia (Natural History)*
Noct. att.	Aulus Gellius, *Noctes atticae (Attic Nights)*
Pol.	Aristotle, *Politica (Politics)*
Quaest. rom.	Plutarch, *Quaestiones romanae (Roman Questions)*
Sat.	Juvenal, *Satirae (Satires)*
Vit. phil.	Diogenes Laertius, *Vitae et sententiae philosophorum (Lives and Opinions of Eminent Philosophers)*

Introduction

"Claudia invited her friend Lepidina to her birthday party." Who doesn't like a party? Time to catch up with friends, hear about births, marriages, mutual friends. Time to complain or enthuse about work, kids, one's spouse or in-laws. Time to relax and enjoy good food and drink. This invitation sounds like it refers to a current event, but actually it is taken from a first-century Latin invitation:

> Claudia Severa to her Lepidina greetings. On 11 September, sister, for the day of the celebration of my birthday, I give you a warm invitation to make sure that you come to us, to make the day more enjoyable for me by your arrival, if you are present. Give my greetings to your Cerialis. My Aelius and my little son send him their greetings. I shall expect you, sister. Farewell, sister, my dearest soul, as I hope to prosper, and hail.[1]

The invitation, found in the ancient Roman fort of Vindolanda in northern Britain, highlights several important aspects of women's lives in the ancient world. Husbands and sons are named, indicating the importance of marriage and motherhood. Friendship between women of equal social rank highlights the social networks women formed. The last two sentences were written by Claudia herself, not the military scribe, highlighting women's educational possibilities. In fact, the invitation is the earliest known female Latin writing sample. Both Claudia and Lepidina are wives of military commanders, and are posted with their husbands, giving them informal access to military and hence political authority.[2] In short, within this brief invitation a world of real women's lives opens up and begs to be explored.

1. Translation in Hans-Josef Klauck, *Ancient Letters and the New Testament: A Guide to Context and Exegesis*, with Daniel P. Bailey (Waco: Baylor University Press, 2006), 107. The invitation is dated to AD 101–2.
2. For a discussion of wives traveling with their husbands to the provinces, including a picture of the Claudia Severa invitation, see Valerie A. Maxfield, "Soldier and Civilian: Life

Fragment of Claudia's letter to her friend Lepidina (Photo courtesy of Peter Long/flickr.com)

What did a day in the life of a first-century Jewish or Christian woman look like? Perhaps not much different from some women's lives today, especially women who live in areas with limited technology, much poverty, and oppressive government. But for those of us who enjoy the benefits of advanced technology and stable democracies—in other words, the benefits of a middle-class existence—a first-century woman's life is barely comprehendible, and yet intriguing.

To draw a portrait of a real woman's life is not easy because she left few literary or epigraphic clues. All we have are the occasional snippets of verse or lines on a tombstone, and the odd invitation or business receipt. Our evidence comes mainly from her father, brother, husband, lover, and owner—in other words, men. Moreover, the information is often polemical or rhetorical, or simply uninterested in women's activities. Literary documents are not purely objective, unbiased accounts of history, but come with supporting ideologies and agendas that can obscure historical evidence. That said, ancient texts are not irredeemably patriarchal or androcentric; a careful reading can yield authentic pictures of women's lives. Using insights from cultural anthropology and sociology about the importance of class and status in understanding religious communities, this study will rely on epigraphic, inscriptional, and archaeological remains as a supplement to, and perhaps a corrective for, interpreting the literary evidence.

Why Write This Book?

I was on a journey of discovery, looking for information about real women who lived during the time of Second Temple Judaism, during the Roman

---

beyond the Ramparts," in *Birthday of the Eagle: The Second Augustan Legion and the Roman Military Machine*, ed. Richard J. Brewer (Cardiff: National Museums and Galleries of Wales, 2002), 150–51.

Republic and Empire, during the birth of Christianity. I read arguments describing their daily life inside and outside the home. But the more I read, the less clear this "everywoman" became. The immediate impetus for writing this book was my frustration over the various analyses concerning New Testament women. Some approaches, sympathetic to canonical authority, ignored the rhetorical and stylized character portraits, envisioning the texts as requiring no interpretation or reading them with little historical sophistication. Other scholars tended to repudiate authoritative texts, but extreme skepticism toward discovering historical information within canonical works seemed an unnecessary reaction, one that assumed an apologetic or theological text cannot at the same time carry historical data. Instead of concluding that no reliable historical evidence is retrievable, I would suggest that the authors of the canonical works are not intentionally misrepresenting women, but rather are interested in communicating something else, and chose as a device the "woman" topos. In so doing, these writings likely contain something useful about real women's experiences or the world in which they lived.

Clearly, the lack of agreement in discerning what women did is due in no small part to scholars' theological and ideological convictions that inform their historical reconstruction. However, I do not intend to present here a theological argument that debates important issues concerning women in the contemporary church. Rather than make theological assessments about women's ordination, for example—I leave that to church polity makers—my more modest intention is to provide an engaging and accurate reconstruction of ancient women's way of life.

The theological piece, however, accounts for only part of the disagreement. Diverse pictures also emerge through improper or uncritical reading of sources, or failing to appreciate all the sources in answering the questions about women's lives. Misinformation about what actual women did at this time created blind spots. Claims ranged from placing women only within the confines of their homes, rarely seen in public, to women mixing freely among men in society. Some descriptions painted women as mere appendages of male family members, while others drew women as independent agents. To make matters more difficult, many of these arguments cited ancient sources, leading me to wonder how to judge between these mutually exclusive portrayals of women.

Some modern authors showed no curiosity about an ancient author's polemics or ulterior motives in describing women, uncritically taking the ancient work at face value. Seneca's tirade on divorce illustrates my point. In *De beneficiis* 3.15–16 he argues that divorce used to be frowned upon, but since divorce notices were published for all in Rome to see, the populace's senses were dulled to its serious nature and divorce became ubiquitous. Some might use Seneca's remarks to prove a high divorce rate in the first century AD. But a closer look at his argument reveals that divorce per se is hardly a concern.

Seneca is talking about benefaction, the system of patronage that was governed by strict honor codes rather than by the courts. Certain men abused the system by not showing proper gratitude to their patrons. To rectify the problem, some wanted to bring the institution under the purview of the legal system, but Seneca resists, claiming that eventually the shock of such deeds would wear off and the public would grow to accept such ungratefulness. At this point he picks up his claims about rising divorce rates, inferring that as women read about a few elite women's divorces, they are led to do the same. His claims are based on the social "fact" that women are prone to wantonness and immorality. He expects his audience to agree with him that because (as everyone knows) women are promiscuous and gullible, so "naturally" divorce is on the rise. He denigrates women's character by using divorce as a topos or literary device to speak about a different subject altogether. He makes the implicit comparison to ungrateful men. Even as on the playground today, the worst thing that can be said to a boy is that he is a girl, so too the ancient world humbled male opponents by identifying them as women. In the end, Seneca tells us virtually nothing about divorce rates, but speaks volumes on the social norms governing debt repayment and gratitude toward patrons.[3]

On the other end of the spectrum, an extreme posture of suspicion toward attaining any historical information from ancient texts often renders ancient women invisible—the very thing the modern author was hoping to avoid! I do not embrace an extreme hermeneutics of suspicion, which understands all texts written by men (and most were) to be irredeemably androcentric, patriarchal, and misogynistic. A careful reading that attends to rhetoric and polemic can isolate those points at which real historical evidence glimmers through the haze. For example, the story of Susanna in the additions to the book of Daniel (Dan. 13) is a highly stylized tale that tends to titillate rather than inform. Yet amidst its improbable story, the author notes that Susanna's mother and father educated her in the law of Moses. This detail is substantiated by other literature and inscriptions, and thus likely reflects historical reality for women in the upper classes.

The deeper I dug into women's lives, the more I became convinced that an important way forward to clarifying the modern picture's diverse and contradictory portrayal of women lies ironically in not focusing solely on women as a category. Gender is often trumped by status. Greco-Roman culture and Early Judaism were deeply penetrated by layers of social status. Not only legal categories of free, freed, and slave, but also relative wealth and pursuit of honor played major roles in determining the choices available for women. Thus a survey of women's lives in the Greco-Roman world must consider issues of gender, class, status, and ethnicity to fully appreciate how women negotiated their local worlds. These categories are sorted out within an honor/shame

---

3. This passage is discussed in chapter 2.

culture, which defined honor for men and women and publicly praised the attainment of this value and shamed those who rejected or failed to uphold this cultural ideal. While the Greco-Roman world was not monolithic in its definitions of honor, all groups used this system to define themselves and others. Status was the social currency in the honor/shame system.

To best understand the complexity of ancient women's lives, we must consider the crucial role the institution of patronage played in the broader culture, as well as be attentive to the construction of gender identity as it impacts the discussion of real women. As will be discussed in the final chapter, patronage extended the household into the public arena, allowing women to influence the politics and religions of their cities. Patronage provided women with an avenue for attaining public honor and for impacting society. Patronage bridged the gap between public and private, and clarified how public women were esteemed with "private" virtues of modesty and chasteness.

The Goals of This Book

This book attempts to tell the story of the average woman and her life passages, her opportunities and limits, the sorrows and joys that accompany her throughout her journey. It investigates the life of the ordinary Greco-Roman woman—the mother, daughter, wife, slave, midwife, shopkeeper, both Jew and gentile, as well as those from both categories who became Christians. Her roles as daughter, mother, and wife take shape through stories, inscriptions, and philosophical assertions. Attention will be paid to what real women did and said, what jobs they held, what activities occupied their time. Religious convictions and behaviors will be given close scrutiny. The evidence overall suggests that within paganism, Judaism, and Christianity in the Greco-Roman world, women were active at all levels within their social and religious communities. However, their influence was not always identified by leadership titles, nor did their gender permanently determine their level of participation.

This is not a biography of a specific woman, but rather a sketch of women as they lived out their opportunities in the various strata of society. Rather than focus on a single aspect of a woman's life, such as work or marriage or religion, I will touch on all those categories. As useful as studies are that focus solely on a particular aspect, often those studies are then used without fully appreciating how the various compartments of a woman's life impact the whole. Not enough attention is paid to the fact that her family life greatly impacts her religious choices or that her occupation might be germane to understanding her marriage. This book therefore sketches the family, work, and religious life of average women, taking in each area as important to understanding the whole.

This is also not a book on women in the Gospels or the Pauline churches. Numerous good studies have been written on those topics. Instead, this work is a prolegomena to the study of New Testament women, an introduction to the world of the first Christian century. My hope is to enliven the sights, sounds, and smells (well, maybe not smells) of the ancient Greco-Roman world so that the social and cultural fabric of the Jewish and gentile worlds will penetrate, inform, and even ignite the reader's imagination to explore in more depth individual women of this time.

I hope to correct the misconceptions about women's lives that have crept into our modern imagination, such as the notion that first-century AD women were cloistered in their homes. I counter the xenophobic claims that Jewish leaders of the day were misogynists (usually claimed as a foil for the portrait of Jesus as bucking Jewish culture). Studies on the earliest Christian communities often use women to bolster their claims that Jesus and his message brought freedom from Jewish oppression. I strive to offer a more candid analysis of Jewish women's opportunities, without comparing or contrasting them to a constructed view of "liberated" Christian women. Aside from the difficulties inherent in determining why a woman might convert or why she wanted to join a sectarian movement, I want also to draw accurate pictures of Jewish life for its own sake, not simply as a backdrop to Christianity.

To help those who wish to better understand the women of the New Testament, I will fill out the historical situations of women in the Greco-Roman world. Rather than living in hermetically sealed environments, these women lived out their lives as either Jews or gentiles (some of whom became followers of Jesus). No separate Christian culture or society in the first century existed; thus, every woman negotiated her roles within the fledgling church in terms of the larger Jewish or gentile society's options and expectations. In an effort to avoid a skewed or biased picture of these women who followed Jesus, it is first necessary to see them among their Jewish and gentile peers. It is important to understand them as their neighbors did, as well as their colleagues at work and their patrons and politicians.

To accomplish this task, I have looked most broadly at women in the Greco-Roman world, the gentiles who made up most of the population, as well as the Jewish community. Imagine the project as a bull's-eye target. The largest circle is the Greco-Roman world, which makes up the outermost target area. The middle circle is Early Judaism, the period in Jewish history that spans the Hellenistic and early Roman periods (fourth century BC to first century AD). Finally, the smallest circle, the bull's-eye, is the earliest Christian community. While elucidating the bull's-eye is my goal, the other two circles can be studied on their own merits. I resist using either as merely background for Christianity. Instead, only by fully appreciating the historical realities within both larger circles can the bull's-eye be accurately outlined.

One danger with the target analogy is that it is static and immovable. History is not that way. Life is dynamic, changing, constantly adjusting to new stimuli and situations. Thus, this book is not a "background" to women in the New Testament, for that implies a two-dimensional staging onto which certain literary women walk, say their lines, and exit stage right. I assume, rather, that women were dynamic participants in their environments, shaping and being shaped by it.

I should make one final comment. It is important to acknowledge the emphasis our twenty-first-century Western culture places on choice as a measure of happiness and success. One who has options is lucky and fortunate. The ancient cultures, however, did not place such a premium on choice; rather, they focused on honor as the key social goal, and thus honor and shame became the social currency of the day. The honor/shame culture focuses on ideal behavior and how closely a person matches that ideal. For women this means that male proscriptions of proper decorum governed social assessment of her worth. Yet ironically, honor also at times muted an individual's gender by focusing on the person's gift to the community. A related danger inherent in any historical reconstruction is the imposition of one's own ideas about what constitutes "the good life." In today's terms, freedom to pursue personal goals, individualism, democratic social structures, and the positive appraisal of change mark out a fulfilled life. But women in the Greco-Roman world and Early Judaism probably valued community over individualism, benevolent despotism, and tradition. This suggests the need for caution in speaking about relative deprivation motivating women's actions in Judaism or among Jesus's followers.

Why Women's History Matters

Cicero said, "History . . . bears witness to the passing of the ages, sheds light upon reality, gives life to recollection and guidance to human existence, and brings tidings of ancient days."[4] Cicero pinpoints the value of understanding history—it illumines our own time as much as it informs us where we have been. Memory is crucial for moving forward. People who suffer memory loss from an accident or head injury struggle to make sense of their world because they have no solid moorings from which to launch out into life. A proper reconstruction of history grounds our own actions and decisions, and conversely, a false picture can lead to incorrect assessments of our own society. Cicero also notes the value history provides in offering guidance in daily life. This book examines those fundamental categories of life: birth, death, family, work, religion. Most cultures negotiate these categories with some view to gender

4. Cicero, *De Oratore* ii.9 (trans. E. W. Stutton and H. Rackham, LCL).

differences; what I explore is how both the gender category as well as ancient women themselves shape and are shaped by society's forces.

In many circles today, Christian and Jewish sacred texts are used to chart a course for proper piety and religious attitudes and actions. The significant role that the canonical texts play in shaping the modern communities of faith is unquestionable, and thus a proper understanding of the women who populate those texts is vital to a full comprehension and thus a proper interpretation. Contemporary twenty-first-century debates about women in the workplace and in the synagogue or church often depend in some measure on a recon-struction of the community's past. I hope this book further illumines that past, becoming a tool for building a more accurate and substantial history of real women's lives.

Theoretical Models Used

The Historical Approach, the Historian's Task

My goal is to be rigorous in assessing the historical reliability of documents and other sources with the view to writing a coherent but broad survey of women's lives in the Greco-Roman period. This method accepts that texts and other sources are not simply open windows into a past era, but that authors shape their material to convey what happened, why they think it occurred, and why they believe it is important. Yet the historical approach does hold that actual deeds and events can be recovered from sources, after careful analysis. I therefore pay special attention to primary sources. This approach takes ad-vantage of the synergy between text and artifact, document and inscription, story and statue.[5] In so doing, new insights into the biblical characters emerge, such as when the Samaritan woman's story (John 4) is drawn next to those women witnessed in the Babatha archives. My goal is historical plausibility or possibility, not certainty, with a good measure of informed imagination seasoning the dish.

The Sociological Approach

Alongside the historical approach I use social science models, drawing data from sociological analyses in locating the average woman's actions and possible attitudes. Reconstructing the typical woman (or man, for that mat-ter) is difficult because for the most part our sources are interested in the celebrity, the ruler, the wealthy elite. These are the movers and shakers, the

---

5. Shelly Matthews cautions that ancient texts be read "against the grain and against other texts, paying close attention not only to what the text says about women, but also to how it constructs what it says and does not say" (*First Converts: Rich Pagan Women and the Rhetoric of Mission in Early Judaism and Christianity* [Stanford, CA: Stanford University Press, 2001], 9).

people that make things happen—that make history, literally. The questions and methodology of the sociologist help us discern what the average person was doing. They help us pick up the crumbs from the celebrities' banquet to at least make a small meal. They help us interpret letters and receipts that reveal daily life among families. When possible, I will put names to the faceless average woman as she appears on grave markers, in marriage contracts, or in business transactions.

Literary Critique

Given the diverse assortment of data in this study, it becomes imperative to attend to genre and rhetoric. Information about historical lives can be found in most, but not all, of these sources. Thus I will use sparingly the hermeneutics of suspicion, the interpretive approach that questions the objectiveness of the author's description—in this case, the description of women. Women's lives are recoverable from existing data, however dim the silhouette may be. This does not mean that each syllable written about women is a direct claim about historical women's activities and thoughts. Because texts were written by men, often with agendas far different from our purposes here (which is to fairly and accurately describe women's lives), we must tread carefully through the maze of misdirection that ancient authors configured along the way. Thus I will pay special attention to the genre of the evidence and will give less credence, for example, to a satire's presentation of reality than to that reconstructed from a business receipt. The former is by definition trying to critique and thus shape society, while the latter makes no comment other than to record a transaction.

Feminist Critique

The feminist critique provides important questions and observations, particularly for our project, in the area of gender construction. This approach asks, "what does it mean to be male and female?" which was a persistent question in the Greco-Roman world. It exposes how gender was used as a device to talk about other social or cultural issues, such as city governance, political corruption, or a philosophical take on virtue. That is, a story supposedly about a woman might actually be a narrative maneuver to persuade a jury of a male client's innocence and may bear no correlation to a real woman's life. A discussion about the ideals of marriage might serve as a trope for explaining the superiority of male (soul) to female (material). In some cases "woman" or "female" is treated as a foil for promoting a vision of social order. A fictional female character need not bear any direct connection to real life any more than the characters in the TV drama "Charlie's Angels" revealed typical aspects of the average American woman's life in the 1970s. The fictional characters offer entertainment, a flight of fancy, not a direct window into what real women were like. While I accept this important caution, I reject the postmodern conclusion that rhetoric is reality and the attending corollary that history is lost behind this veil. Although texts and even inscriptions follow customs of propriety, I maintain that these pieces of information are attached to retrievable history.

A Word about Terminology

I have struggled with how to explain adequately and fairly the historical realities of the ancient world by using terms that do not carry the weight of historical development. And this has proved very difficult. For example, earliest female followers of Jesus are not best labeled as Christian, for this descriptor implies a host of entailments that were yet to be accrued to the term itself. Instead, from a social and cultural standpoint, the earliest followers of Jesus were either Jew or gentile. From a theological standpoint, a case can be made that Paul, for example, was moving to describe these followers as something other than Jew or gentile, however; for our purposes, that move is not relevant. Thus while I might use the term "Christian" because it is less cumbersome than writing "follower of Jesus," in fact it is the latter sense that defines the use of "Christian" in this book. Indeed it is precisely because the earliest Christians would have been identified (and likely identified themselves) as gentile (and formerly pagan) or Jew that so much time is spent exploring Greco-Roman women's lives. It is precisely these women who would populate the early missionary churches of Paul and others.

I wrestled as well with how to avoid creating the sense that only gentiles lived in the Greco-Roman world while the Jews lived somewhere else. To try to get around this, I do not limit the category "Greco-Roman world" to gentiles only, for Jews were as much a part of the Hellenistic and imperial world around the Mediterranean as any other ethnic group. Thus I use equally the descriptive titles "Greco-Roman gentile" and "Greco-Roman Jew," with no religious or theological bias attached. In a related conversation, within the study of Hellenistic Judaism there exists a pervasive tendency to see Jews living in Judea as committed or pious and those living in the Diaspora as sold out to Hellenism. This is a false distinction, yet our terms carry this bias. In reality, we can expect some dissimilarity between Jewish women who lived in Judea and those who lived in Rome or Thessalonica. This is due to the differences between urban and rural settings, as well as the closer proximity of gentiles in Diaspora cities than in rural Galilee, and the Jews' minority status in Diaspora cities. However, Jewish women throughout the Greco-Roman world reflect a similar range of behaviors and attitudes.

The Time Frame of This Book

I will examine evidence for women in the Greco-Roman period, which begins at the time of Alexander the Great's conquests (330s BC). I will use as an end date the turn of the first century AD, although some evidence will be considered from later centuries. Alexander the Great's conquest of Asia Minor, Syria, Judea, and Egypt spread the Greek language, culture, political ideology, and philosophy in its wake. This phenomenon is called Hellenism. Classical Greek ideals surrounding matrons—that the wealthy elite remain secluded in their homes—slowly gave way to the Roman picture of a virtuous woman participating in certain public settings. As Rome's military conquered the Mediterranean, wealth poured into the city and some women's fortunes likewise rose. With this increased wealth came increased political influence, so that by the time of Augustus, women in the imperial family held much (informal) power. Developing legal rights to own and dispense property and freedom from a male guardian (under specific circumstances) allowed some women a measure of autonomy. An important shift in marriage practices occurred about 150 BC during the Roman Republic. The custom of a daughter being given by her father to the control of a husband and his family changed so that the daughter, when married, remained under the power of her father. At the same time, divorce laws relaxed so that by the first century BC, both women and men could initiate divorce, and no particular reason for the action was legally necessary. As with any shifting of societal views and customs, conservative social commentators decry the changes and long to return to an idealized past. Some male authors lament the perceived boldness of women speaking and acting in public while other writers praise certain women's public deeds and speeches—and this during the same basic time frame. Thus while we can trace through the Roman period a general increase in autonomy for women, we should not imagine this change as a straight-line trajectory.

My decision to use the first century AD as the end date of the Greco-Roman period has to do with religion. This project seeks not only to discover what Jewish women were doing in the Second Temple period, but also to draw a picture of earliest Christian women. The Second Temple period, also referred to in this book as Early Judaism, begins roughly with the return of the Jewish exiles from Babylon and the rebuilding of the Jerusalem Temple, discussed in the biblical books of Ezra and Nehemiah. This period was profoundly affected by Hellenism at all levels of society and culture, and Jews reacted and interacted with the philosophical and ideological forces of Hellenism in a variety of ways. One important outcome is the translation of the Hebrew Bible into Greek, known as the Septuagint. This translation was widely used in the first century AD, including by the writers of the New Testament. In the second century, with the rise of the Patristic period, the church expanded geographically and numerically, especially in terms of gentile participants, and as such, requires a separate study. Moreover, Judaism went through tremendous shifts after the Second Revolt, which ended in AD 135 with a devastating defeat for the Jews in Judea. Rabbinic Judaism was taking shape, and the split between Christianity and Judaism was becoming pronounced in many areas.

The Organization of This Book

This book attempts to offer an authentic, descriptive historical picture of women's lives in the Hellenistic and early Roman imperial period, with special attention to earliest Christianity. There are arguably several options for organizing the material; this book follows the rhythms of family life, starting with daughters, then examining wives and mothers, before looking closely at religions and occupations, and finishing with benefaction and patronage. This organization has the advantage of being faithful to the categories used in the Greco-Roman world, thereby reflecting how women might have understood themselves or been understood by male authors. Again, using ancient categories will help illumine the use of gender as a rhetorical motif, social convention, or vehicle for other interests, such as the political or social advancement of the family.

Chapters 1 through 4 look at familial relationships: daughter, wife, and mother. Chapter 1 addresses a woman's role as daughter, also examining the issue of infanticide, which affected female infants more often than males. This chapter explores the daughter's relationships with her parents and siblings and her place in the family as a member who through marriage potentially increases the family's social, political, or material standing. Because the concept of the ideal wife was so prevalent, chapter 2 examines the archetypal wife, complementing chapter 3 on the historical wife. The Roman matron was not only a historical figure, but also a literary trope serving to delineate society's moral tone. In chapter 2, I investigate how the ideal of the modest, chaste matron functioned amidst daily activities such as dining and bathing—two important Roman social activities. In chapter 3, I delve into the realities of married life for the wife. Daughters were groomed to marry, and most people assumed marriage would bring children. But social institutions such as citizenship and slavery complicated matters, limiting whom one could marry and the status of one's children. A woman's dowry and family wealth greatly shaped her influence with her husband and children.

Chapter 4 explores childbirth and motherhood. Unlike today's culture, which emphasizes a mother's relationship to her young children, in the Greco-Roman world a mother was likely closer to her adult children. Infanticide and infant exposure were accepted practices, while many babies raised by families did not survive their first few years. These statistics certainly deromanticized motherhood, as did the very real threat of the mother's death in childbirth. Most women remarried if their husbands died, and given the high mortality rate, women could expect to be widowed and remarried if they lived through their child-bearing years. In general, the data reveals that underneath the proscriptions for a dutiful daughter, submissive wife, and steadfast mother we find educated daughters, independent wives, and powerful mothers.

Chapters 5 through 9 explore what women did—their occupations, religious activities, and benefaction. Chapter 5 is devoted to gentile women's religious expressions, including religious responsibilities in the home and specific groups such as the Vestal Virgins and the cults of Dionysos and the Bona Dea. I also look into the important category of God-fearer, those gentiles who displayed an interest in the synagogue and, at times, the early church. In chapter 6, I examine the religious responsibilities and rites of Jewish women, including the intriguing Therapeutrides and Essenes. Christian women's life situations are fleshed out in relation to specific parallels. In general, the literary evidence gives an overall negative account of women's religious activities, condemning or mocking women's religious celebrations and downplaying their priestly and ritual duties. Epigraphic evidence balances the literary material and offers a brighter, less polemical picture. Women were active in religious cults at all levels, from a simple devotee to a high priestess or synagogue leader. They traveled on religious pilgrimages and presented votive offerings to their deities. They celebrated alongside men in religious festivals and joined small sects that offered a stricter, more focused religious lifestyle.

A similar mixing of men and women bent on comparable goals was found in the ancient marketplace. Here women worked side by side with men, busy earning a living. Chapter 7 examines the working lives of women, noting that most (along with men) struggled to feed their families. Hard labor was the lot of most rural and many urban women. Those fortunate to have some means were active in buying, selling, and loaning money. Two jobs were restricted to women only: midwifery and wet-nursing, and two jobs were off-limits: soldiering and holding an imperial office. An entire chapter is devoted to slavery and prostitution, because a slave woman's experience could be markedly different from that of her male counterpart, at least in terms of her abilities to earn money. Chapter 8 therefore looks at the female slave and the prostitute, often herself a slave.

The informal glue that held the Greco-Roman society together was patronage, and women participated freely in this social institution. Chapter 9 examines the patron/client relationship, which was in many cases gender-blind. What counted was influence; thus women of wealth and status had access to the porticoes of power. The patronage system and the public expression of benefaction, euergetism, drew on the images of an unpretentious, traditional matron in publicly portraying the patroness as a chaste "mother," whether of a city, trade guild, or personal client. Women had a voice and influence within society through the patronage system.

Throughout this book, surprises await the reader: women who acted with courage, fortitude, and confidence, who managed the conservative social protocols and yet achieved renown, who held fast to religious convictions despite the cost. Careful clarification of rhetorical bluster versus historical evidence helps create a clearer picture of real women doing actual activities.

The complexities of gender roles and expectations of women's behaviors are multifaceted and often assumed rather than articulated in the Hellenistic and early Roman periods—much as we find them today. I hope I have captured for the reader this complexity, and yet also made clear the enormous influence and opportunities for self-expression available to women whose social rank, wealth, or sheer good fortune paved a way.

1

Women as Daughters

In modern Western culture, a baby daughter often conjures up pictures of lacey pink dresses and ribbons and bows. For some ancient authors the birth of a daughter foretold a life of anxiety and fear of public shame. For others, daughters heralded the hope of a son-in-law. Raising daughters involved different goals and potential pitfalls than raising sons—most prominently, the family's concerted effort to keep her pure and chaste until marriage. Because marriage was so important to the social prestige of the two families involved, daughters played an important role in advancing their family's honor. Some literary evidence suggests that daughters could be tools in the family's pursuit of greater prestige, but it is unclear how complicit the daughters might be in their "exploitation."

Jewish literature such as *Joseph and Aseneth*[1] portrays indulgent parents acceding to their daughter's wishes. Pseudo-Philo's *Liber antiquitatum biblicarum* retells the story of Jephthah's daughter (Judg. 11) and invents a mother to care for her condemned daughter. In the apocryphal book of Tobit, Sarah's mother, Edna, sheds tears on her daughter's wedding night. From Egyptian papyri letters, we overhear common chitchat between mother and daughter. Jewish and gentile fathers show relative interest in their daughters' lives and mourn their deaths. The literary and documentary evidence reveals a range of attitudes toward daughters, most of which transcend a Jew/gentile divide,

1. The dating of this text is quite problematic. While most scholars date it to the first or second century AD, a compelling argument for the third century is made by Ross S. Kraemer (*When Aseneth Met Joseph: A Late Antique Tale of the Biblical Patriarch and His Egyptian Wife, Reconsidered* [New York: Oxford University Press, 1998], 225–44).

Second-century AD Roman monument of a girl with what looks to be a doll in the upper left edge (Photo courtesy of Mary Harrsch/ flickr.com)

except in the singular case of infant exposure. No evidence suggests that Jews participated in this common gentile practice.

In general, a work that is proscriptive and literary tends to be more negative about daughters, while funerary inscriptions and letters, written with a particular daughter in mind, generally are more positive about the girl and about daughters as a whole. This makes sense given the honor/shame culture that permeated the Greco-Roman world. In this cultural matrix, women carried the burden of potentially bringing shame to the family through their unchaste behavior. Thus, as a group, girls were a potential danger to the family's reputation. But individual daughters who acted within the social norms could be proudly praised, as they contributed to the social respect of the family.

Daughters and Fathers in Non-Jewish Sources

Not surprisingly, there is more evidence about fathers' relationships to their daughters and about sons' connections with their mothers than about mother/ daughter bonds. Roman writers comment on how daughters resemble their fathers. Cicero brags that his daughter has such family devotion, such modesty and intellect—she is "the image of my face and speech and mind."[2] Valerius Maximus, also from the first century BC, notes about the father Q. Hortensius that his daughter had her father's eloquence: "Quintus Hortensius lived again in the female line and breathed through his daughter's words."[3] Such sentiment underscores the family pride expressed by fathers about their daughters.

2. Cicero, *Epistulae ad Quintum fratrem* 3.1.3 (trans. D. R. Shackleton Bailey, LCL).
3. Valerius Maximus, *Fact. dict. mem.* 8.3.3. Translation in Mary R. Lefkowitz and Maureen B. Fant, *Women's Life in Greece and Rome: A Source Book in Translation*, 3rd ed. (Baltimore: Johns Hopkins University Press, 2005), 152. See chapter 9 below for a discussion of Hortensia.

Eulogies on inscriptions and in texts also reveal the affection and importance daughters held. In a letter to his friend Marcellinus, Pliny the Younger shares the bereavement of their mutual friend Fundanus, whose thirteen-year-old daughter died. He recalls with great sorrow how affectionately she would wrap her arms around her father's neck, how diligently she would study, in what a dignified manner she carried herself, even in her final illness. Invitations to her wedding had been sent, but instead of celebration, the family faced a funeral.[4] A first-century BC Latin inscription from Rome records a moving eulogy wherein a father memorializes his daughter, a young wife. "(The altar of) Minucia Suavis, wife of Publius Sextilis Campanus. She lived 14 years, 8 months, 23 days. Her father Tiberius Claudius Suavis (put this up)."[5] Notice that it is her father, not her husband, who erects the funeral bust in her honor. This likely reflects the predominant type of marriage at this time, the *sine manu* arrangement, in which the husband did not gain complete authority over his wife. She remained part of her father's family, and so it was not uncommon for her father (or his family) to take responsibility for her burial. Also of note is her age, just under fifteen years old. She likely died in childbirth, the killer of so many women at this time. The love of a daughter held public currency such that Quintilian could lament after the death of his wife (at age eighteen) that "her death was like the loss not merely of a wife, but of a daughter."[6]

The Power of the Father

The power of the father (*patria potestas*) is perhaps nowhere as apparent as in his role in accepting or rejecting his child at birth. In a quasi-official ceremony, the child would be placed before the father, and if he lifted it up from the ground, he signaled his willingness to accept responsibility for rearing the child.[7] If he did not pick up the newborn, it was cast out of the family. The same power was held by slave owners (male and female) over their slaves' children. Mothers who were not in a licit marriage (which meant the child was not legally the responsibility of the father) could decide themselves whether to raise their baby. If a wife was divorced or widowed while pregnant, the baby when born would be raised (or rejected) by her husband's family. If the newborn was rejected, it was either killed directly (infanticide) or exposed. If the latter, it might be rescued and raised by someone else (usually as their slave) or die from the elements and animals. The father himself did not actually place the child outside the house—that was done by another household member, perhaps a slave or the mother. There is no record as to how the person

4. Pliny the Younger, *Ep.* 5.16.1–7.
5. *CIL* VI.22560. Translation in Lefkowitz and Fant, *Women's Life in Greece and Rome*, 207.
6. Quintilian, *Inst.* 6.
7. Cicero, *Epistulae ad Atticum* 11.9.

abandoning the child would feel; we can only guess that the emotions would be at best neutral, at worst devastating. Although exposure was technically not the same as infanticide, historians debate how many exposed infants lived through their childhood. Certainly the risk was great that abandoning the child would lead to its death.

Both male and female children retained the legal status of their birth, if it could be proved; therefore, a freeborn exposed infant, though raised as a slave, was technically free.[8] Legal cases concerning status claims of exposed children were argued regularly. Generally, the father wished to reclaim a child (who might be an adult now) that he had earlier exposed, while the one who rescued the child wanted compensation. The law upheld the father's right of *patria potestas*, even though he had previously chosen to expose the infant; the rescuer was not owed money to cover expenses in raising the child. If the birth father was dead, the child's mother (or a female relative) could bring a claim against the rescuer to free the child. One curious case is that of Emperor Vespasian's wife, Flavia Domitilla. Suetonius tells us that she was originally of Latin rank, not a Roman citizen. She was later declared a freeborn citizen of Rome after her father, Flavius Liberalis, brought a suit before the court. It is possible that she was abandoned (or sold) at birth and raised as a slave until she was reclaimed by her father.[9] Suetonius also tells the story of the grammarian Gaius Melissus, who was exposed at birth due to a disagreement between his parents.[10] He was cared for and well educated by the man who retrieved him, and was given as a slave to a certain Maecenas, a kind owner who valued Melissus's work. Though his mother later claimed the boy was freeborn, he chose to remain Maecenas's slave. Subsequently he was freed and won Augustus's favor.[11] In a final example, the Christian author of the Shepherd of Hermas identifies himself as a foundling: "The master, who reared me, had sold me to one Rhoda in Rome."[12] In his next sentence, he implies that he was freed, for he notes that after many years he met her again.

The situation could get complex, as in the case of a man who divorced his pregnant wife and married another woman. The first wife apparently did not inform her ex-husband of their child but exposed their son, though (curiously) he was raised with his father's name (and thus was likely not a slave). When the father died, without any other children, the mother (his first wife) and

8. Pliny the Younger, *Ep.* 10.65–66, 72.
9. Suetonius, *Vespasianus* 3. See Judith Evans-Grubbs, "Hidden in Plain Sight: Expositi in the Community" (paper presented at the Fifth Roman Family Conference: Secrets de familles, familles secrètes: Mémoire et identité familiales, Université de Fribourg, June 15, 2007), 6n14.
10. The disagreement is not made explicit, but one guess is that the legitimacy of the child was in question.
11. Suetonius, *De grammaticis* 21; see also 7.
12. Shepherd of Hermas, *Vision* 1.1. Translation by J. B. Lightfoot, *The Apostolic Fathers*, 2nd ed. (London: Macmillan, 1898), 405.

the father's mother brought forth the child as the man's legitimate heir who was entitled to inherit the estate. Ironically, in this case the question was the status of the deceased man's slaves. They were freed at his death, but now with the heir present, their manumission was revoked, for they were part of the son's inheritance.[13]

Infant Exposure and Infanticide

The story of the divorced man and the son of his first wife highlights several complexities in the practice of infant exposure and its connection to other family customs and Roman law. First, note that the divorced wife apparently circumvented the father's prerogative of accepting the infant. Perhaps she guessed that he would charge her to expose it and decided to do so on her own terms. The fact that the paternal grandmother knew of the son's existence suggests that the women attempted both to conceal and control the child's upbringing until events were favorable for his paternity to be known. They probably benefited from the son's inheritance, assuming that he would care for them. That divorced wives were given permission to expose infants is found in an annulment contract from first-century BC Alexandria, Egypt. Here we read of a pregnant widow who has renounced claims on her deceased husband's family. They in turn give her permission to expose the child and to marry again.[14]

A second point is that parents might have expected to eventually reunite with their child. This implies both that they did not expect the child would die from being set out of their house and that they supposed someone would raise the child.[15] This expectation might be overly optimistic, but the fact that some children were left with tokens (rattles, for example) that could identify them suggests the parents hoped to reclaim them. More negatively, the token could be explained as a burial amulet, indicating that the family expected the child to die. Ironically, the apparent ease with which parents could reunite with exposed children might have encouraged the parents' decision, in the hope that when their situation improved, they would be reunited.[16] Presumably, if the parents wanted to reconnect with the child later, they would take care that he or she was rescued by a family who would not then sell the child.

Related to this is a third point, namely that for the parents to reunite with the child, they needed to know of their child's whereabouts. This implies that someone in the household (parent, relative, house slave) followed up on

---

13. Evans-Grubbs ("Hidden in Plain Sight," 1) recounts this story from Cervidius Scaevola (cited in *Digesta Justiniana* 40.4.29), jurist of the Antonine period (AD 138–80).

14. *BGU* IV.1104. Translation in Lefkowitz and Fant, *Women's Life in Greece and Rome*, 91.

15. Justin Martyr gives that impression (*Apologia i* 27, 29).

16. Evans-Grubbs, "Hidden in Plain Sight," 14.

the person who rescued the infant, suggesting that exposed infants might be raised fairly close to their birth homes.[17] The evidence, however, is meager. The rescuer's profile varies—he or she could be from a local family, or a slave dealer. The person who chose to raise the child usually had only the outlay of a wet nurse—less expensive than buying a slave. In a few years, the child would be able to help in the household, and if no one claimed him or her, the rescuer had secured a slave at low cost. We saw above that Melissus was highly trained by his rescuer, who likely profited when he gave (sold?) the child to Maecenas.[18] Frequently a slave dealer picked up the infant to raise and later sell, often as part of the sex trade.

Sometimes the infant was abandoned in an area that had traffic or was known as a place where unwanted infants were left. At other times a less-inhabited place was chosen, presumably so the child would die. The danger of the child dying was real in either case, for an unprotected newborn has no defenses. We should assume that even with the hope that the child would be found, a parent knew that death was a genuine possibility. Parenthetically, we should note that infant mortality rates for nonexposed children raised by their parents was extremely high; perhaps as many as 50 percent of children did not live beyond age five.[19]

Infant Exposure Defended and Defamed

What reasons might underpin the decision to expose or to kill a newborn? Ancient authors often point to the relative health of the infant, as a weak or deformed infant of either sex might be killed. Dionysius of Halicarnassus, writing in the first century BC about ancient Roman history, describes approvingly the decrees of Romulus, the first Roman king. The king enjoined that all male children and the first female child must be raised, and that all children up to the age of three should not be destroyed, unless they were deformed or maimed. The latter could be exposed by the parents, only after five nearest neighbors agreed with the assessment. For those who disobeyed these rulings, up to half their property would be confiscated.[20] We should not assume from this that Romans were in the habit of exposing children two and a half years old—the likely intent was that parents would be too attached by then to consider abandoning the child. In the following century, Seneca writes that parents when faced with a weak or deformed infant often chose to drown it,

---

17. Evans-Grubbs, "Hidden in Plain Sight," 15–16.

18. See chapter 9 on the patronage system; the gift or sale of this slave foundling could have connected these two owners.

19. Carolyn Osiek and David L. Balch, *Families in the New Testament World: Households and House Churches* (Louisville: Westminster John Knox, 1997), 67.

20. Dionysius of Halicarnassus, *Antiquitates romanae* 2.15. Whether Romulus actually decreed this is another matter. The point is that Dionysius believes that exposure is an ancient and acceptable Roman custom.

due not to anger but to wisdom, using reason to discern the harmful from the sound.[21]

While Seneca views the killing of deformed children as reasonable, Polybius suggests other motives behind exposing infants. He claims that men have become so indolent and greedy they are unwilling to support more than one or two children.[22] Other reasons could be an evil omen at birth, warning the father not to accept this child, as well as rape (interestingly, incest is not mentioned) and illegitimacy. Suetonius notes that the Emperor Claudius ordered the child of his ex-wife Urgulanilla cast out, most likely because she was accused of adultery with a freedman, Boter. Though initially Claudius raised the daughter (born five months after the divorce), he changed his mind and disowned her, placing her naked at her mother's door.[23] Some ancient authors indicate that poverty played a role. Appian, describing the turmoil during the republican period, notes that with the chaos over landownership, the poor were unable to raise their children.[24] Plutarch speaks of nature engendering love of offspring in both humans and animals, and then notes that people's minds can become crazy and choked with vice. He cites as an example those who have no money to educate their children properly and so decide not to raise them rather than condemn them to a life of poverty.[25] Likely these poor families assumed exposure would lead to the child's death. But family honor might also be behind their decision, for Plutarch writes that without education, the poor believed the child might be slavish and without any commendable virtue. If they exposed the child, who was then raised as a slave, the child's life would likely be very difficult, but the parents' honor would not be affected. And perhaps the child would be picked up by someone who would provide an education, and later the family could claim the child. In any case, Plutarch does not seem to approve of this decision; but because the text breaks off at this point, we cannot know for certain. Poverty is relative, of course, and some critics railed against fathers who, while claiming destitution, were really too stingy to use their money to raise the child.[26]

Arguing against the practices of the wealthy from a different angle, Juvenal (late first century AD) attacks aristocratic women, accusing them of not wanting the physical discomfort and unsightliness of pregnancy.[27] He contrasts them with poor women who bear children and nurse them, but who also might expose them at the city pools or reservoirs. From here, Juvenal sneers, the

21. Seneca, De ira 1.15.
22. Polybius, Historiae 36.17.5–8.
23. Suetonius, Divus Claudius 27.
24. Appian, Bella civilia 1.10.40.
25. Plutarch, De amore prolis 5.
26. Musonius Rufus, Dissertationes fr. 15 (Lutz). For a list of reasons, see William V. Harris, "Child-Exposure in the Roman Empire," JRS 84 (1994): 11–14.
27. Juvenal, Sat. 6.592–601.

wealthy wife takes a baby to fool her husband that it is his from her womb. While Juvenal's misogynistic polemic is against the habits of wealthy Roman wives, his casual comment that infants were exposed in certain well-known locations suggests an informal social convention that matched rescuers with infants whose parents hoped they would survive. It is difficult to determine whether any foundlings were presented to husbands as their own progeny—the wickedness and trickery of women was a well-worn trope. In sum, recognizing that infanticide and infant exposure can be a traditional theme within general social criticism, and thus literary evidence must be examined critically, still the overall impression is that the Greco-Roman authors offered coherent rationales (which matched general social consensus) for which infants should be raised and what characteristics led to exposure and infanticide.

The fate of a foundling was usually slavery, and when prices for slaves were high, presumably more exposed children were rescued. In many cases, the foundling was put into prostitution. Slave dealers raised foundlings to sell them later, or pimp them. Both boys and girls were used in this way, with the boys often made to look younger—even castrated. Pliny the Elder notes the special potions used to keep boys from growing body hair,[28] to make them more appealing to potential buyers. Justin Martyr, defending Christian rejection of the practice of abandoning infants, warns that a pagan who exposed his child (Justin says more girls than boys are exposed) might inadvertently commit incest later because the girl would be raised a slave and prostituted.[29] The evidence that most foundlings were prostituted may appear at odds with indications that parents hoped to be reunited with their children. One possibility is that the expectation of prostitution was not so onerous that such a fate dissuaded parents from reuniting. We might also wonder if in the cases where parents hoped to reunite, the child was carefully "exposed" to be raised by someone the parents knew. Finally, not all foundlings were made prostitutes. Some served as household slaves and were educated (predominantly the males).

It is commonplace to suggest that females were exposed more frequently than males. A fourth-century BC Greek comic poet opines, "Everyone raises a son even if he is poor, but exposes a daughter even if he is rich."[30] A note written in 1 BC from a husband to his pregnant wife reveals that this sentiment had not changed in the intervening three hundred years. The husband, working in Alexandria, reassures his wife that all is well with him and that he will send his pay home to her in Oxyrhynchus (about two hundred miles away, up the Nile River). Then he notes, "if you have the baby before I return,

---

28. Pliny the Elder, *Nat.* 32.47.135.

29. Justin Martyr, *Apologia i* 27.

30. Poseidippus, fr. 11E (cited by Stobaeus, *Florilegium* 77.7). Translation in Mark Golden, "Demography and the Exposure of Girls at Athens," *Phoenix* 35.4 [1981]: 316 (cited in J. Albert Harrill, *The Manumission of Slaves in Early Christianity*, 2nd ed. [Tübingen: Mohr Siebeck, 1998], 41).

if it is a boy, let it live; if it is a girl, expose it."[31] While literary and epigraphic evidence suggests that more girls were exposed than boys,[32] the ratio is difficult to determine. For example, both Suetonius[33] and Quintilian[34] note specific cases where boys are exposed, and do not mention girls directly (although they are likely included when the authors speak of groups of children). Yet few would argue that this evidence shows more boys than girls were exposed; more likely, the fate of boys was more interesting to ancient authors. Overall, it seems social sentiment indicated that sons were a better family investment for a host of reasons, and thus limited resources would be funneled in the direction of raising male children.

INFANTICIDE AMONG JEWS?

Though common among non-Jews, infanticide and exposure of infants are uniformly condemned in Jewish literature. Several sources distinguish the Jewish refusal to expose an unwanted baby from the wider social practice. Philo equates infanticide with exposure because the result is usually the same—death. He assumes exposure was done outside of the city in a deserted place, and there is no reason to doubt that he was aware of this practice. He announces that Jews do no such thing because Moses forbade it. Philo discusses the punishments of a man who strikes a pregnant woman such that she miscarries. If the miscarried fetus is completely formed, the man is guilty of murder. By implication, any Jew who discards a fully formed fetus will be guilty of murder.[35] Interestingly, Philo is here following the Septuagint (LXX), for the Hebrew text speaks about harm done to the woman, not the fetus (Exod. 21:22–25).[36] The shift might reflect a reaction against the Greco-Roman acceptance of infanticide. Josephus follows Philo's logic when he declares any mother who exposes her infant a murderer and associates this behavior with abortion.[37] It is interesting that Josephus speaks only of the

31. P.Oxy. 744. Translation in Jo-Ann Shelton, *As the Romans Did: A Sourcebook in Roman Social History* (New York: Oxford University Press, 1988), 28.

32. Sarah B. Pomeroy, "Infanticide in Hellenistic Greece," in *Images of Women in Antiquity*, ed. Averil Cameron and Amélie Kuhrt, 2nd ed. (London: Routledge, 1993), 207–22; William V. Harris, "The Theoretical Possibility of Extensive Infanticide in the Graeco-Roman World," *The Classical Quarterly* 32.1 (1982): 114–16. Harris disputes the claims of Donald Engels, "The Problem of Female Infanticide in the Greco-Roman World," *Classical Philology* 75.2 (1980): 112–20.

33. Suetonius, *Divus Claudius* 15; *De grammaticis* 7, 21.

34. Quintilian *Inst.* 7.1; *Declamationes* 278, 306, 338, 358, 372, 376. The *Declamationes minores*, cited here, while probably spurious, likely date from the first or second century AD.

35. Philo, *Spec.* 108–9.

36. Patrick Gray, "Abortion, Infanticide, and the Social Rhetoric of *The Apocalypse of Peter*," *Journal of Early Christian Studies* 9.3 (2001): 318.

37. Josephus, *C. Ap.* 2.202. See also *Sibylline Oracles* 2.281–82 and Pseudo-Phocylides 184–85. The dating of the *Sibylline Oracles* is difficult; it was likely compiled over centuries by an authorship community that was initially Jewish and later Christian.

mother doing away with the infant—the father is not mentioned. Josephus paints the Jewish male as the paragon of virtue, unlike his gentile counterpart. Thus to increase the polemical force of his statement, he has only the mother contemplate destroying the child—no Jewish male would even consider such a thing. Roman writers note with derision that Jews raise all children born to them.[38] Thus we have no evidence that Jews did practice infanticide, but we also cannot state categorically that they did not. But unlike Greco-Roman sensibilities, which accepted infanticide, the only reactions to this practice by Jewish writers, confirmed by Greco-Roman authors, are negative.

Inheritance Rights of Daughters

Of course, not all or even most daughters were exposed. Once the father agreed to raise his daughter, Roman law allowed her to benefit equally from her father's estate if he died intestate. If she was married under the *sine manu* (lit. "without hand") system, wherein her father retained legal authority (*manus*) over her (this was the most common form of marriage; see chap. 2), then she inherited an equal share of the family estate with her brothers. Once her father died, like her brothers, she was legally *sui iuris* or independent from his authority, no longer under the paterfamilias. If she or her brothers were children (below age twelve for girls, fourteen for boys) they were under the care of guardians. When her brothers came of age, they were released from that authority, but a girl continued under the supervision of a tutor, known as *tutela mulierum*. Her tutor was often a relative on her father's side, perhaps her uncle. He would supervise the sale of certain types of property or slaves and approve her will. Cicero recounts a case where a woman named Valeria, wife of Sextilius Andro, died intestate. Her husband wanted her fortune, but her guardian Flaccus (possibly her uncle, brother, or nephew) claimed it as well.[39] Sextilius Andro's camp argued that she was married *cum manu* (lit. "with hand") and so her husband's family had rights to her property. Cicero countered that his client would never have approved a *cum manu* marriage, and such a marriage needed the approval of all guardians. This meant that Valeria was still part of Flaccus's family, and thus her inheritance belonged to them. By the turn of the eras, several laws were in place that sought to prevent a wife from giving lavish gifts to her husband, as wives might try to circumvent their agnate tutor's wishes and give their inheritance to their husbands. Yet still with those laws in place, the wife could take on her husband's debt, unless the agnate guardian forbade it.

If the daughter had been emancipated by her father, he would have only the rights of the tutor, much more limited than his rights as a father. If the married daughter was a Roman citizen and had three live births (a freedwoman

38. Tacitus, *Historiae* 5.5; Strabo, *Geographica* 17.2.5.
39. Cicero, *Pro Flacco* 84, 86.

needed four live births) she was released from a tutor (under Augustus's *lex Papia Poppaea*; see chap. 3). During Claudius's reign, agnate guardianship was abolished. This opened the door for a woman to have as a tutor someone with no financial interest in her decisions, giving her more independence. For example, a woman's freedman could be counted on to show loyalty toward her business decisions and to approve a will that gave her estate to her children instead of her paternal relatives. Claudius's ruling also made it easier for a wife to take up her husband's debt, so in conjunction with abolishing agnate guardianship, the senate also enacted a law (*lex Velleianum*) that outlawed women from being the guarantor of debts. A woman could loan money or take out loans, but she could not stand as a third party to guarantee a loan. In the first century AD, then, daughters inherited equally with their brothers but had more legal restrictions on how to use their wealth. They therefore played an integral part in their family's financial situation.

This is not to say that daughters directed all their inheritance to their birth families. Cicero's letters to his wife, Terentia, written while he was in exile, reveal that they agreed she would help provide for her children from her property. "The separation of property did not entail a separation of interest. Terentia shared Cicero's assumption of . . . the availability of her fortune to their children in case of need."[40] After their divorce, she offered financial support for her son's career to be taken from part of her dowry. Convention suggests that all her money should eventually be returned, but perhaps the dotal pact indicated that her monies would be used to keep their son at the proper (high) social status required of a young man in the senate class. Moreover, during Cicero's exile, their married daughter needed financial help to pay some debts (and perhaps to pay part of the second installment of her dowry). She turned, not to her husband, and not to her father's representative, but to her mother. The latter was not obligated by law to assist, but apparently did so willingly. Cicero later repaid his wife. In sum, Suzanne Dixon concludes, "the financial separateness of the spouses was maintained much as the law required, but the maternal-child links apparently exceeded any legal definition of obligation."[41]

A second example is found in a eulogy to Murdia by her son for providing an inheritance for him. A fragmented marble inscription from Rome in the first century BC bears her firstborn son's praises. Murdia was widowed by his father, and she remarried and had other children, a daughter and other sons. Her first husband had given her property in addition to returning her dowry. She chose to will the property of her first husband to their firstborn son rather than combine it with her remaining dowry and then divide that total equally among her sons, after giving a bequest to her daughter. Her son pays tribute

40. Suzanne Dixon, "Family Finances: Terentia and Tullia," in *The Family in Ancient Rome: New Perspectives*, ed. Beryl Rawson (Ithaca, NY: Cornell University Press, 1987), 99.
41. Dixon, "Family Finances," 101–2.

to her decision, as well as to her character: "my dearest mother deserved greater praise than all others, since in modesty, propriety, chastity, obedience, wool-working, industry, and loyalty she was on an equal level with other good women, nor did she take second place to any woman in virtue, work and wisdom in times of danger."[42]

Several points should be noted, including her care for both her sons and her daughter. Like Terentia, Murdia used her dowry to support her children. And, like Terentia, Murdia remained closely connected to her son by a previous marriage. Maternal ties were strong. They survived widowhood and divorce. Both sons and daughters could depend upon mother's support through her dowry and other personal wealth as the society encouraged mothers' responsibility toward their children. This remained true even though the children were under the authority of their father.

Daughters and Mothers

Daughters, Mothers, Grandmothers

Daughters' relationships with their mothers have scant witness in the ancient world, both among Jews and non-Jews. Because the Jewish family was similar in this case to

Second-century BC funerary stele from Smyrna (modern Izmir) with the inscription: "Thalea [daughter of] Athenagoras, [from the city of] Oroanna, hail!" (Photo courtesy of PHGOM/Wikimedia Commons)

the prevailing Greco-Roman culture,[43] what evidence we do have from either group is important in building a picture of a daughter's life within Judaism and emerging Christianity. Interesting in this regard are nonliterary papyri from Egypt, including a letter from a non-Jewish mother to her daughter that provides a window into the world of upper class women. At the beginning of the second century AD, Eudaimonis writes to her daughter, Aline, who is married to Eudaimonis's son Apollonios.[44] The daughter had been with her

42. CIL VI.10230; ILS 8394. Translation in Lefkowitz and Fant, Women's Life in Greece and Rome, 17–18.

43. Ross S. Kraemer, "Jewish Mothers and Daughters in the Greco-Roman World," in The Jewish Family in Antiquity, ed. Shaye J. D. Cohen, BJS 289 (Atlanta: Scholars Press, 1993), 102.

44. P.Brem. 63. While scholars have long assumed that both Aline and Apollonios are children of Eudaimonis (marriage between siblings was common throughout Egypt), more recently Jane

mother just a few weeks before. Eudaimonis informs Aline that her sister, Souerous, had a baby, and expresses her hope that Aline's pregnancy will go well and that she will have a boy. Such sentiments reflect the wider Greco-Roman culture's valuation of boys; but since Aline already has a daughter, who is staying with Eudaimonis, it may be that Aline's mother is hoping that now she will have a boy.

Eudaimonis notes that Aline's daughter is busy with her studies, an interesting but frustratingly vague note about girls' education. Eudaimonis also complains about the extensive amount of weaving she must do, and she struggles even though Aline left her slaves to aid in the work. Weaving was a common task given to women throughout the Greco-Roman world. In fact, it was so ubiquitous that it became symbolic of what it meant to be a good wife—one who spins. In addition, Eudaimonis writes enigmatically about money that Aline sent her: "Why did you send me 20 drachmai when I have no leisure?"[45]

Several points from this letter are worth noting. First is the mobility of the women. Aline travels to her mother's house and back to her own home. Second, the women may be close emotionally, given that the mother informs Aline about her sister's baby. Third, this short letter reveals an intimate relationship between mother and daughter, who share news and even property. Aline leaves not only (some of) her slaves with her mother, but also her daughter. This latter act may be due to instability in Aline's area, as this letter was written during the Jewish revolt in Egypt (AD 115–17). Or perhaps Aline believes her mother can better educate her daughter. Perhaps Aline's own tutor was available to train her daughter. According to 2 Timothy 1:5, a similar mother/daughter team raised Timothy, Paul's coworker. Perhaps this indicates that women shared the child-rearing responsibilities across generational boundaries, and even traveled distances to make this work.

Alongside letters, the literature on Roman education also provides nuggets about mother/daughter relationships. The Roman matron influenced the earliest stages of education if the family employed an instructor, as wealthy families could afford to do. There are several statements—usually by sons—about their mothers' high level of education, which means that as daughters these women were educated. Pliny speaks of Corellia Hispulla who educated her son until he was fourteen years old.[46] Tacitus mentions both Caesar's mother, Aurelia,

---

Rowlandson has argued that Eudaimonis's address of Aline as "daughter" and similar familial language is figurative rather than literal (*Women and Society in Greek and Roman Egypt: A Sourcebook* [Cambridge: Cambridge University Press, 1998], 119–20). In either case, Aline is married to Eudaimonis's son and is therefore her daughter-in-law. For more letters by these two women, see Rowlandson, *Women and Society*, 118–24; and Roger S. Bagnall and Raffaella Cribiore, *Women's Letters from Ancient Egypt, 300 BC–AD 800* (Ann Arbor: University of Michigan Press, 2006), 139–63.

45. Translation in Kraemer, "Jewish Mothers and Daughters," 97.

46. Pliny, *Ep.* 3.3.

and Augustus's mother, Atia, as well educated.[47] Some women are praised for specific skills. As noted above, Hortensia, the daughter of the famous orator Hortensius, was praised by Quintilian for her oratory skills.[48] In this context, Quintilian praises parents who are both well educated. Writing in the late first century AD, Juvenal criticizes those women who know Greek and debate with men about issues of law, politics, literature, and rhetoric. In his sixth satire, he writes scathingly about women whose education is superior to that of their husbands or other men. "Really annoying is the woman who, as soon as she takes her place on the dining couch, praises Vergil, excuses Dido's suicide, compares and ranks in critical order the various poets and weighs Vergil and Homer on a pair of scales." He adds that there ought to be some things a woman does not understand, some things that are the purview of males only. He dismisses women who study grammar rules and then correct men. "Let her correct the grammar of her stupid girlfriend! A husband should be allowed an occasional 'I ain't'."[49] Though Juvenal does not approve of women's advanced education, his comments suggest that at least in some circles, women participated actively and learnedly in discussions with men.

Interestingly, it may be that mothers and daughters became closer as they got older. Especially if the mother was widowed and remarried, or divorced, she might not have seen her children when they were small. But when the children married, and were in need of financial help, her dowry money or personal wealth was expected to contribute to her child's well-being. It is possible that in elite circles, married daughters and their mothers (and even granddaughters) spent time together.

Slave Mothers and Their Daughters

Special complications might arise if the mother was previously a slave. Any children born to her were the property of her owner. But if she was a freedwoman at the time of the child's birth, her patron did not have rights over her child. Confusions arose if her date of manumission was contested. Exactly this sort of dilemma occurred in first-century AD Herculaneum, a city destroyed by the eruption of Vesuvius. We can piece together the story from wax tablets recording the lawsuit pursued by one of the parties.

Our story begins with a man, Gaius Petronius, who bought a slave woman, Vitalis. She was present in the home when the man married, perhaps purchased as a gift to his new wife, the freedwoman Calatoria Temidis. At some point, Vitalis gained her freedom (taking the name Petronia Vitalis) and bore a daughter, whom she named Justa. The daughter was illegitimate, and the rest of the story hinges on Vitalis's status at her birth. If Vitalis was a slave at

---

47. Tacitus, *Dialogus de oratoribus* 28.
48. Quintilian, *Inst.* 1.1.6.
49. Juvenal, *Sat.* 6.434–56. Translation in Shelton, *As the Romans Did*, 300–301.

that point, then Justa was also a slave. But if Vitalis was a freedwoman, then Justa had the status of freeborn. The girl's father was never named.

Justa was raised as part of the family, apparently accepted by Gaius Petronius as though she was his own. All was peaceful in the household for about ten years. Then Petronius and Calatoria had their own children. Apparently jealousies arose between Calatoria and Vitalis, and Vitalis decided to leave the household and establish her own residence. As a freedwoman, she would continue to serve Gaius Petronius as his client, and so would remain closely associated with the household. Petronius, however, did not want to relinquish Justa. Vitalis sued for custody of her daughter, claiming that the girl was freeborn. The case was brought to the local court, which decided in her favor and required only that she repay Petronius for the money spent in raising the daughter. That Vitalis could accommodate these demands suggests that she was a woman of means.

For a short time all was well, but then both Gaius Petronius and Vitalis died. Justa inherited her mother's sizable estate. It would be nice to end the story here, but human greed (apparently) enters the picture with Calatoria, who charged that Justa was a slave born in their house. Calatoria would gain Vitalis's estate if she could prove that Justa was born while Vitalis was a slave. In previous years, manumission was tightly monitored and regulated and a slave's freedom was recorded with the magistrates' office. But the slave population grew so quickly, it soon was possible for a slave to be freed based on a verbal contract of her owner in the presence of a few witnesses. This seems to be Vitalis's situation. The allegations were taken to the local court, which sent the case to Rome. Both sides presented their arguments, and Justa's defense seemed to be faltering.

Into the fray steps a freedman of Gaius Petronius named Telesforus. He was a longstanding member of the household, serving his patron in administrative roles. Before this, he was Calatoria's tutor, and so he was well acquainted with the household. Shockingly, Telesforus broke with standard practice of loyalty to his patroness and spoke eloquently for Justa's position, declaring that she was born after her mother was declared freed. Why did he take such a risk of publicly refuting Calatoria's position? Could it be that he was Justa's unnamed father? Such a supposition is not farfetched. He was a freedman in the household who had much power. He might have been influential in Vitalis gaining her freedom, especially if they were lovers. Telesforus might have put up the money to purchase her freedom. He helped negotiate the removal of Justa from Gaius Petronius's house to Vitalis's new house. Moreover, he identified Justa's mother as *"colliberta mea"* (his colleague in liberty), which may indicate a personal closeness with Vitalis. Taken on their own, these details do not confirm that Justa was his daughter. But the fact that he was willing to risk all for her sake, when added to the rest, best explains his actions. It would be surprising if a bond of slavery/manumission would prompt a man to denounce his living patroness for a dead freedwoman. But it is possible that a man would defend his living daughter and her property.

The case was heard in Rome, and Telesforus's information was duly noted. A verdict should have been rendered in favor of Justa. But instead, the courts decided to wait and placed the case under advisement. Were they waiting for a bribe? Vesuvius did its awful deed before Rome offered judgment. Justa spent her final years in legal limbo, and presumably Calatoria never enjoyed any of Vitalis's wealth.[50] This story offers modern readers a window into Roman society with its layered and interconnected social classes. It shows the love of mother and daughter, and even perhaps of father and daughter. It highlights the close bonds among slaves, freedmen/women, and owners. Living and working in close contact helped foster lasting relationships, and also allowed deep-seated resentments to deveop. It shows the slave woman and freedwoman beholden to owners/patrons, who wielded power and control over their futures. It also reveals that at least some former slaves, when the prize seemed worth it, were willing to take great risks. In this case, the prize was a daughter.

Daughters in Jewish Literature

As in Greco-Roman culture at large, so too in Jewish literature, the daughter is both praised and shamed. She plays key roles in marriage alliances, drawing families together. But she can also bring shame upon her family.

Daughters in Sirach

Jesus ben Sira has the unenviable reputation of being perhaps the most misogynistic Jewish writer in Early Judaism. In his second-century BC deuterocanonical work Ecclesiasticus (also called Ben Sira or Sirach), he blames the female sex for all the world's woes. "From a woman sin had its beginning, and because of her we all die" (Sir. 25:24). He does not spare daughters, lamenting their birth ("It is a disgrace to be the father of an undisciplined son, and the birth of a daughter is a loss," 22:3), and he cautions a father to watch over his daughter closely. Ben Sira's fear is public shame and dishonor, for honor was the currency of Greco-Roman culture, and no man could ascend the ladder of success if his family was disgraced. In a world in which so much was out of one's own control, Ben Sira exhorted his (male) readers to control what they could—their sexuality and that of their family. To this end, unmarried daughters were closely watched (7:24–25), and restricted from talking with married women, for the latter might discuss sex (42:12b–13). Fathers lost sleep

---

50. Some have argued that Vitalis was Jewish and/or that she and Telesforus converted to Christianity, but this is based on questionable claims; see Joseph Jay Deiss, *Herculaneum: Italy's Buried Treasure*, rev. ed. (Malibu, CA: J. Paul Getty Museum, 1989), 98–102.

because of their worries that sexual improprieties by their daughters (married or unmarried) or barrenness would bring ruin to the family (42:9–14). Ben Sira positions his final argument about women/daughters between his summary of moral injunctions that revolve around a discussion of two types of shame (41:14–42:8) and his praise of Yahweh (42:15–43:33) and famous men (44:1–50:21). This is hardly by accident, for the house of cards built by a young scribe eager for public honor can come crashing down with the sexual indiscretions of his family's women, including daughters over whom the father is to have control.

In a thinly veiled sexual allusion, he warns that even as a thirsty traveler will drink from any available water source, so too an unattended daughter will "sit in front of every tent peg and open her quiver to the arrow" (Sir. 26:12). Ben Sira's argument moves from a good wife to a bad wife and then to a daughter, following the pattern of 42:9–14. The lewd language, however, seems more apropos to harlots; so, although the text does read "daughter," some interpreters believe the content is speaking of unfaithful wives. It is possible that "daughter" was entered by a copyist to match this passage with one that has a similar opening line in 42:11, "keep strict watch over. . . ." Further evidence that 26:10 initially referred to adulterous wives is found in the descriptions that match characteristics of harlotry, such as the impudent eye (26:11a and 26:9), the verb "sin against you" (26:11 and 23:23), and the sexual postures (26:12 and 26:9).[51]

The assumptions underlying Ben Sira's injunctions are troubling for modern ears: women are greedy for men and will gallop off at the first chance they get. Girls are not discerning, nor do they (apparently) value their chastity and family honor enough to resist the pleadings of a would-be suitor. Ben Sira's paranoia about daughters' sexual purity reveals a well-attested belief in his day among both Jews and gentiles that women at any age are unable to practice virtues fully or adequately. For example, when a woman is brave, she is said to act with "manly" courage. What is at the heart of these railings? Like the current popular book series addressing "worst-case scenarios," Ben Sira, writing in the Wisdom genre, is offering advice and warnings to promising young scribes.[52] He wants them to be politically wise, economically stable, and socially skillful amidst the political and religious elite who governed Jerusalem. He recognized the scribes' precarious social level—they were of the retainer class, beholden to their employers/patrons for work and social advancement. That is why Ben Sira writes extensively about friendship, how to tell a true friend from someone who will use your skills and then toss you aside. And

51. Claudia V. Camp, "Understanding a Patriarchy: Women in Second Century Jerusalem through the Eyes of Ben Sira," in *"Women Like This": New Perspectives on Jewish Women in the Greco-Roman World*, ed. Amy-Jill Levine (Atlanta: Scholars Press, 1991), 22n45.

52. See Joshua Piven and David Borgenicht, *The Worst-Case Scenario Survival Guide* (San Francisco: Chronicle, 1999), and sequels.

Ben Sira also recognized that patrons would not tolerate improprieties of their clients/retainers. Any hint of shame or dishonor, and the young scribe would be looking for another employer.

Daughters in Jewish Novels

Ben Sira's harsh commentary does not match the portrait in some of the Jewish stories of the same period. These novels, such as Tobit, Judith, and *Joseph and Aseneth*, present a challenge to interpreters interested in exploring the lives of real women. No one argues that these novels are biographies, but can we read them for information on women's experiences? Making due allowances for literary propaganda and license, my approach will be to accept the stories as, to one degree or another, presenting values and life situations faced by women with various status levels within society. Less attractive is the approach that such works should be read as an allegory with no relation to real women.[53] A third option understands these novels as primarily conversations about gender, that is, meanings ascribed to male and female. This approach offers important correctives to the assumption that these novels present direct access to historical reality. It cautions that texts can use women not only to further a male-created female ideal but also as a stand-in for a male, noting that women may serve as "other" to the male "self." In sum, this theory prioritizes gender as the interpretive key, suggesting that these novels are best understood as classifying female and male, or what it means to be a masculine male.[54] While I will draw on insights gained through this theory, I primarily interpret these stories as fictionalized narratives representing possible experiences and life situations faced by real women. This multilevel approach assumes that woven together in these novels are both gender constructions and tropes that serve to define male and female, as well as glimpses of real women's experiences mediated through story. We will look at two novels below, Tobit and *Joseph and Aseneth*, as well as a first-century AD work that retells biblical stories, *Liber antiquitatum biblicarum*, to paint a fuller picture of Jewish daughters.

TOBIT

In the second-century BC apocryphal book of Tobit, Sarah, the daughter of Raguel and Edna, is well cared for and given every consideration. She is tormented by a demon that kills on their wedding night every man who marries her. After her maid mocks her, Sarah is in despair (Tob. 3:8–9). But her parents do not condemn her, and the narrator makes clear that Sarah's troubles are part of a divine plan preparing her to wed her close kin, Tobias. On the night

---

53. For a careful exposition of this type of reading, see Gideon Bohak, *Joseph and Aseneth and the Jewish Temple in Heliopolis*, SBLEJL 10 (Atlanta: Scholars Press, 1996).
54. An excellent example of this reading is Kraemer, *When Aseneth Met Joseph*, 191–222.

she is to marry Tobias, her mother, Edna, weeps when she enters the bridal chamber (probably Sarah's room) with her daughter. Did Edna sympathize with Sarah's pain at the deaths of her husbands and weep that the same situation would reoccur, causing her daughter yet more anguish? Or did she anticipate the pain of separation she would soon experience when her daughter moved to her husband's home? Yet in her later farewell speech, Edna is hopeful about seeing her daughter again, this time with grandchildren (10:12). Moreover, she asks Tobias, Sarah's new husband, to regard his wife as his sister, even as he regards Edna as his mother. Edna's language suggests that, from her perspective as narrated in Tobit, her family is enlarged, not diminished, with the marriage of her daughter. This fits well with Tobit's encouragement of endogamy, marriage within one's own people group.

Drying her tears, Edna shares words of comfort with Sarah: "Take courage, my daughter; the Lord of heaven grant you joy in place of your sorrow" (7:16). Ross Kraemer notes that the Greek verb for "take courage" (*tharsei*) is found on funerary inscriptions, both Jewish and non-Jewish, bidding the deceased to recognize that no one is immortal.[55] Is Edna equating marrying her daughter with burying her daughter? Not Sarah's death, but that of her former husbands, certainly hangs in the air. Perhaps Edna is afraid that this time, her daughter will succumb. Edna has an important role in Tobit, more active and verbal than the mother in the story of Isaac and Rebekah (Gen. 24), which likely served as a model for the entire story.[56] The differences between the stories might therefore highlight a social reality in Early Judaism.[57] For example, unlike the silent mother of Rebekah, Edna interacts with Sarah extensively and implores Tobias, "do nothing to grieve her all the days of your life" (Tob. 10:12). Is it possible that Jewish mothers in the Greco-Roman period had a stronger voice and presence?

LIBER ANTIQUITATUM BIBLICARUM

Writing probably in the first century AD, the author of the *Liber antiquitatum biblicarum* (*Biblical Antiquities*) was deeply troubled by the silence of one biblical character's mother. In the retelling of the story of Jephthah (Judg. 11), Pseudo-Philo provides Jephthah's daughter with a name, Seila, and with a mother and a nurse. The description of the nurse's part in wedding preparations might offer a glimpse into the social world of Pseudo-Philo. Moreover, the author emphasizes God's firm displeasure at Jephthah's vow: God declares that his daughter will serve as the sacrifice, punishing Jephthah for his unwise, un-

---

55. Kraemer, "Jewish Mothers and Daughters," 91n3.

56. There are several similarities between the stories: both fathers send for wives for their sons from within the clan, both searches are aided by angels, and both include formal blessings.

57. Ross Kraemer, "Jewish Mothers and Daughters," 92–93, notes that while Abraham sends a servant, Tobit sends his son; moreover, the "enhanced attention to mother-daughter relations so sparingly noted in Genesis 24" might also signal social reality.

holy vow. Seila accepts her
fate with great courage and
with the conviction that her
father must go through with
his vow to God. In this, Seila
represents the culture's highest ideals of piety
for women: submission to God's design and to
men's plans. Yet the text is also subversive in
at least two ways. First, Seila compares herself
favorably to Isaac's acceptance of his role as
sacrifice. Second, the narrator praises her as
displaying great wisdom, while her father is
explicitly condemned.[58]

Terra-cotta doll probably made in the third century BC (Photo courtesy of Marie-Lan Nguyen/Wikimedia Commons)

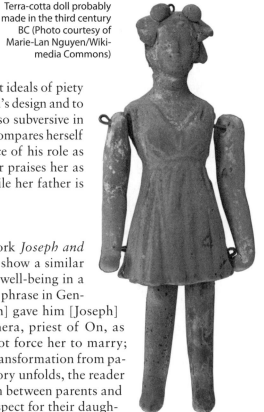

JOSEPH AND ASENETH

In the pseudepigraphic work *Joseph and
Aseneth*,[59] Aseneth's parents show a similar
concern for their daughter's well-being in a
story based on the enigmatic phrase in Genesis 41:45, "and he [Pharaoh] gave him [Joseph]
Asenath daughter of Potiphera, priest of On, as
his wife." Her parents do not force her to marry;
moreover, they support her transformation from paganism to Judaism. As the story unfolds, the reader
learns of the mutual affection between parents and
daughter and the parents' respect for their daughter's choices.

The story begins with Aseneth hearing that her parents have returned
from their fields to report on the healthy harvest they have taken that year.
With great joy, she dresses in white linen with all her jewels and greets them
as they enter the house. Her parents are also very pleased with their good
harvest, but they have even better news. Joseph, the Pharaoh's right-hand
man, is to stay with them, and her parents think he would make a good
match for their daughter. Her father seats Aseneth between himself and her
mother, and taking her hand, proceeds to sing Joseph's praises and recommends that "I will hand you over to him for (his) wife, and you will be a
bride to him" (4.8).[60] Aseneth is furious at this proposal, scorns Joseph as
a former slave and non-Egyptian, and takes great umbrage at her father's

---

58. *Liber antiquitatum biblicarum* 40.4.

59. Most date this anonymous work to the first century BC or first century AD. Kraemer
(*When Aseneth Met Joseph*) dates it to the third or fourth century AD.

60. Translation in James H. Charlesworth, ed., *Old Testament Pseudepigrapha* (Garden City,
NY: Doubleday, 1985), 2:177–247 (quotation, 207).

suggestion. In fact, she agrees to marry the king's son (who desires her) because "he is king of the whole land of Egypt" (4.11). The narrative describes her father as ashamed that he brought up the matter and silenced because of Aseneth's anger. He is hardly modeling Ben Sira's suggested firmness, nor does he act as though he is worried that she will compromise herself with any man.

We might pause here and reflect on Aseneth's outburst, for by uttering those words she steps outside the cultural norms of silent, obedient daughters. She angrily contradicts her father's description of Joseph, incautiously relies on "gossip" about Joseph, and even lies about his character. She claims Joseph slept with his master's wife, stressing his former status as slave and foreigner. Yet at this point, her father does not rebuke her. Instead, she becomes convicted of her error and confesses to God (13.12–14). In her "before" picture, Aseneth represents in her speech all that is immodest and inappropriate, and (from a Jewish perspective) pagan; in her "after" picture, the repentant Aseneth radiates holiness and speaks with great wisdom. She reinforces the feminine norms of chastity and devotion to the home by preserving peace among Joseph's brothers, her new brothers-in-law (28.7–14). The errant daughter becomes the obedient wife and faithful devotee of her husband's God.[61] It could also be argued that paganism has been feminized by associating Aseneth's unseemly womanly behavior with her pagan past. Women were notorious for their ill-mannered behavior; so too paganism feminizes the adherent. The Jewish (and Christian) audience affirmed their faith as the correct choice by identifying it with the culturally superior behavior exhibited by Aseneth after her transformation.

Interestingly, throughout *Joseph and Aseneth*, and in contrast to Edna's intimate involvement with her daughter Sarah in Tobit, Aseneth's mother plays a silent, supportive role. It is her husband, Aseneth's father, who speaks to Aseneth, and it is a male angel who prepares Aseneth for her wedding. Perhaps this is due to the narrator's emphasis on Aseneth's change of heart concerning Joseph and Judaism. The angel prepares her not only for marriage but for life in a new faith, as she abandons her days of idolatry. Because Aseneth's parents remain in their ancestral ways, the mother (perhaps) was understood by the author to be an insufficient guide for Aseneth in her new life. As noted above, a sensitivity to gender showed that Aseneth served as "other" in her paganism, and as "self" after her transformation, in part by conforming to social norms for upright women. Likewise, the mother's silence erases her from the drama, reinforcing the ideal of the active player on life's stage as male/masculine.

61. For a further discussion of images of the feminine in *Joseph and Aseneth*, see Sabrina Inowlocki, "Wisdom and Apocalypticism in *Aseneth*" (paper presented at the Society of Biblical Literature Annual Meeting, Toronto, Canada, November 2004).

Comparison between Sirach and Jewish Novels

Both Sarah's and Aseneth's parents act in ways that convey consideration toward their daughter's emotional well-being, a far cry from Ben Sira's overarching concern for the father's honor. Thus we should probably not assume that Ben Sira speaks for all families when he decries the birth and care of a daughter—with one exception. Ben Sira probably reflects the widespread conviction that a daughter's sexual purity is of paramount importance. Such convictions are evident in Tobit and *Joseph and Aseneth* in several telling details. Aseneth has her own room/tower, shielding her from the gaze of non–family members. Sarah is not mentioned as traveling outside her house until she is wedded to Tobias. Second Maccabees, written probably in the last quarter of the second century BC, intimates a similar arrangement when describing the reaction of Jewish women to the temple's defilement by Antiochus IV Epiphanes (see 2 Macc. 3:19). The author notes that unmarried women and daughters peeked from behind their courtyard walls at the public lamentation carried out by men and married women. In the same way 3 Maccabees 1:18 declares, "Young women who had been secluded in their chambers rushed out with their mothers, sprinkled their hair with dust, and filled the streets with groans and lamentations."[62] Most probably the authors of 2 and 3 Maccabees were presenting an idealized picture of Jewish piety, so we cannot assume that all daughters were sequestered indoors, as was the classical Greek ideal. But the detail does register the social sentiment among some (elites) that daughters are best kept away from men until safely married. Even more, the mention of unmarried daughters in the public arena signals to the reader the desperate danger faced by the Jews. The situation was so precarious that even young women put aside their bridal adornment to bring supplication to God against the pagan adversary.

Whereas Ben Sira presumes that daughters/girls are promiscuous and so must be separated from men, the novels of Tobit and *Joseph and Aseneth* reinforce the chastity ideal by portraying daughters who care deeply about their own purity and value their virginity. Aseneth clearly understands and even relishes her role within the family as the one who will further the family's fortunes through her marriage. Sarah cries out to God that she not hear reproaches, for "You know, O Master, that I am innocent of any defilement with a man, and that I have not disgraced my name or the name of my father in the land of my exile" (Tob. 3:14–15). Sarah recognizes that her behavior will reflect on her father, but she also treasures her "name" as distinct from and yet belonging to her father's family. Seila in the *Liber antiquitatum biblicarum* values her virginity and embraces the wider cultural expectation that sees virginity not as an end in itself but as the proper preparation for marriage.

---

62. Third Maccabees is difficult to date, but general consensus puts the composition in either the first century BC or first century AD.

The literary sources above all reflect the values of the upper class: Aseneth's family was quite wealthy; Tobit had piles of money stashed away; Ben Sira wanted his students to fit well with the elite who employed them.[63] Another literary source, Susanna, an addition to the book of Daniel found in the Apocrypha, tells of a daughter's education. Susanna is introduced as a daughter trained "according to the law of Moses" (Sus. 1:3). But we are left in the dark about what that means, although some speculate it refers to the injunctions in Deuteronomy 4:9 and 6:7 that encourage parents to "teach them [the commandments] diligently to your children" (6:7 RSV).

Daughters in Rabbinic Evidence

A famous saying from the rabbis should be mentioned at this point, though the dating is hotly contested and may fall outside our period of study. "Rabbi Eliezer says: 'If any man gives his daughter a knowledge of the Law it is as though he taught her lechery.'"[64] This maxim has been judged to forbid any education of the law to daughters, which would seem to contradict the injunctions in Deuteronomy 4:9 and 6:7. Elsewhere, fathers are enjoined to teach both sons and daughters the Scriptures.[65] Judith Romney Wegner argues persuasively that this saying cannot be taken beyond its limited context. As throughout the Mishnah, the sages when speaking of "the law" usually only refer to a specific law or set of laws under direct discussion. In this case, then, daughters are not to be taught the "law of jealousy," which states that good deeds might outweigh an occasional lapse.[66]

Before leaving the rabbinic evidence, we should also note an interchange between Pharisees and Sadducees, likely edited, which debates the inheritance rules for daughters.[67] The scene's characters include a father, his daughter, his son, and the son's daughter. Both men die; who inherits? The Sadducees advocate the two daughters (the father's daughter and granddaughter) splitting the inheritance. The Pharisees claim that the son's daughter should inherit along with any of the son's brothers; the father's daughter does not inherit.

---

63. Seila was raised by a nurse, but it is unclear how wealthy a family needed to be to afford a nurse. As seen below, many families, some apparently not at all wealthy, employed wet nurses.

64. *m. Soṭ.* 3:4. Translation in Herbert Danby, *The Mishnah* (Oxford: Oxford University Press, 1933). Rabbi Eliezer ben Hyrcanus, who taught ca. AD 80–120, had a reputation for being quite conservative and old-fashioned in his positions.

65. See *m. Ned.* 4:3.

66. Judith Romney Wegner, *Chattel or Person? The Status of Women in the Mishnah* (New York: Oxford University Press, 1988), 161.

67. *b. B. Bat.* 115b–116a. Jacob Neusner dates this text to second century AD, and thus outside our time frame (*Development of a Legend: Studies on the Traditions concerning Yohanan ben Zakkai* [Leiden: Brill, 1970], 205–6). But David Instone-Brewer believes "it is likely that the arguments originated at a time when the issues were still being discussed, [suggesting] a date before 70 CE" (*Techniques and Assumptions in Jewish Exegesis before 70 CE* [Tübingen: Mohr Siebeck, 1992], 98).

If this story preserves a historical debate, then Pharisees are standing over against the prevailing Roman norms followed by the Sadducees, which allowed a daughter to inherit. There is insufficient evidence to conclude whether the Pharisees' position carried influence among the greater Jewish population, but inscriptional and documentary evidence suggest that Roman/Sadducean protocols were normative.

Daughters in the New Testament

As we turn to the evidence about daughters in the New Testament writings, we discover that the Gospels reveal a variety of social classes and an overall positive view of daughters. In some cases, the love for daughters that is revealed in *Joseph and Aseneth* and in Tobit also shines forth from the pages of the Gospels. The synagogue leader begs Jesus to heal his sick daughter (Mark 5:21–24, 35–43), while the Canaanite woman pleads that Jesus might also heal her daughter (Matt. 15:21–28; cf. Mark 7:24–30). In both Matthew and Mark, the parent's overwhelming concern for the life of a daughter is palpable, which marginalizes further Ben Sira's remark that the birth of a daughter is a cause for mourning. In the book of Acts, there is a brief note about Philip and his four daughters, who are prophetesses (Acts 21:9). We know nothing about their background, their mother, or how they came to be prophetesses. Also we meet Paul's coworker, Timothy (Acts 16:1–3), who was brought up by his Jewish mother, Eunice, and his grandmother Lois (2 Tim. 1:5). This mother/daughter team worked together to raise Timothy and pass along to him their sincere faith. These daughters were important communicators of the gospel and the Jewish faith. Unfortunately, we know nothing about how Philip interacted with his daughters or how Lois related to her daughter, Eunice.

Daughters and Weddings

Most ancient communities assumed that a daughter would marry, but one wonders how this desire to see a daughter married, which included her leaving the house to live with her husband, impacted the emotional ties between mothers and daughters. The literature and nonliterary evidence gives precious little to go on. A few inscriptions by daughters eulogize their mothers, and parents, including mothers, express grief at the untimely death of their daughters. An example of the former comes from the Vigna Randanini catacomb on the Via Appia, where a daughter praises her mother who died at age twenty-nine.[68]

---

68. *CIJ* 141; Kraemer, "Jewish Mothers and Daughters," 95–96. The daughter, Dulcitia, praises her mother as being very sweet. For a lengthy discussion on inscriptions, see Ross Kraemer, "Jewish Women in Rome and Egypt," in *Feminism in the Study of Religion: A Reader*, ed. Darlene M. Juschka, (New York: Continuum, 2001), 223–27.

Kraemer cautions that social conventions are reflected in inscriptions, so we cannot be certain whether this mother felt a loss that her daughter did not marry or was simply reflecting social expectations in mourning her death as a virgin.[69] Similarly in Tobit, Edna's tears can be understood in a variety of ways, not merely that she is sorrowful her daughter is leaving the house.

Some scholars have suggested that because girls married young (between thirteen and twenty years of age), mothers resisted close emotional attachment, yet the evidence does not allow us to draw any firm conclusions. However, an interesting inscription from Egypt from a bit earlier than our period (fourth century BC), might shed light on the matter.[70] In this inscription, the mother, Artemisie, pleads with the god Oserapis and the gods with him to curse the father of her daughter. Artemisie claims that the father "robbed [the daughter] of the funeral gifts and tomb" and thus acted unjustly. She begs the gods to ignore any requests made by her daughter's father. While we cannot be certain that this petition reflects the mother's love toward her daughter, such a possibility exists.

Jewish Wedding Preparations

Though marriage was expected, the sources provide relatively little with which to paint a picture of wedding preparations. This might be due, in part, to a relative disinterest in weddings compared to the married state, or perhaps because such preparations were the responsibility of women and male authors had little interest in them. The information for Jewish wedding preparations comes primarily from three sources, including one inscription. None of the sources can be definitively labeled Jewish, but when taken together add up to a strong case. A funerary inscription discovered in Leontopolis, Egypt (second century BC to second century AD) records a young virgin bride asking passersby to look upon her sorry state. Speaking in the first person, the young woman pulls at the audience's emotions. Though not found in situ, the inscription shares several similarities with those found in the local Jewish graveyard, leading Susan Marks to posit a Jewish sponsorship of the stone. The text reads:

> Weep for me, stranger, a ripe maiden
> who formerly delighted
> in a great house.
> For, decked in fair bridal garments
> untimely, have I
> received this hateful tomb.

69. Cf. *CIJ/CPJ* 1509, discussed by Kraemer, "Jewish Mothers and Daughters," 96.

70. *PGM* XL.1–18. Translation by R. F. Hock in Ross S. Kraemer, ed., *Women's Religions in the Greco-Roman World: A Sourcebook*, rev. ed. (Oxford: Oxford University Press, 2004), 132.

For when a clatter of revelers at my door
announced that I was to leave
my father's house
like a luxuriant rose in a garden, wetted by dew,
suddenly Hades took me
and carried me away.
Stranger, I am twenty . . .[71]

Scholars debate the label "Jewish" for this inscription in part because of the term "Hades." If the inscription is Jewish, the term may be a generic reference to death and hell. Yet the reference also calls to mind the Persephone myth wherein the young "bride" Persephone was snatched from her mother by Hades and taken to the underworld. Nothing inherently prohibits a Jew from drawing on this myth, and the inscription strongly emphasizes the bridal status of the dead woman. Suggesting the inscription is likely Jewish, Marks does not believe the Hades reference is generic, but stresses the "*mythical* personification of death as a bridegroom and bridegroom as death."[72]

The gripping verses reveal several details about weddings and their preparation. Weddings provided an opportunity for families to display their wealth. This inscription draws attention to the father's large house where the deceased bride was raised. The wedding commences from this house, when revelers come to escort the bride to her new home. Moreover, the lengthy inscription itself highlights the family's wealth. We learn the age of this bride, twenty years. This conforms to the estimates made of first marriages. She apparently is entering her first marriage, for she is described as a "ripe maiden" implying her virginity. Whether second marriages would be celebrated with a wedding probably depended upon finances, as did first weddings.

The bride is met by members of the community hoping to celebrate what should be a wonderful day. As she comes from a "great house" we might expect that she was aided by servants. The verb translated as "decked out" is plural, suggesting she was helped to dress, and might reflect historical practice of brides attended by companions. Does this imply that she really did die on her wedding day, just as she was finishing her wedding toilette? We cannot be sure that she died exactly on the date set for her wedding. Young women who died before marriage were often lamented in funerary inscriptions. This inscription follows funerary conventions in presenting an unwed young woman as dying at the point of her wedding; that is, dying an untimely and thus grievous death. Perhaps she was betrothed? Or perhaps she had no suitor, as with Jephthah's daughter, discussed below, but was still mourned for the wedding she would

71. *JIGRE* 31 (*CIJ* 1508). Susan Marks's own translation in "Jewish Weddings in the Greco-Roman Period: A Reconsideration of Received Ritual" (PhD diss., University of Pennsylvania, 2003). Forthcoming from Georgias Press. See also Kraemer, *Women's Religions*, 121.
72. Marks, "Jewish Weddings," 144.

never have.[73] The inscription enjoins not only young women but all who pass by this monument to mourn the deceased. Twice the reader is addressed as "stranger." This convention both creates a distance from her local community and yet draws the young bride into the community of all humanity, for all will someday taste death.

In contrast to the inscription, two literary descriptions locate their brides more securely in a local community or family. In *Liber antiquitatum biblicarum*'s retelling of the story of Jephthah's daughter, Seila mourns her own death as a virgin; her mother bore her in vain as Sheol has become her bridal chamber. In her despair, she details all she will miss in dying before her wedding, including what was made and who prepared it. These additions to the biblical story probably reveal current practices or expectations about weddings. Seila grieves that she will not use the oil her mother prepared for her wedding, nor will she wear the white linen robe her mother wove for her. Her nurse's efforts were also in vain; she will not wear the crown of flowers plaited for her. Even her own work was fruitless, for she will not enjoy the dress/coverlet richly woven in hyacinth and purple (priestly colors). Her companions cannot perform their appointed task of rejoicing, but instead accompany her in grief.

What is implied in the inscription discussed above is expanded upon in this story: brides enjoyed the support of companions as they prepared for their special day. But more might be involved in this case, for in the biblical story of Jephthah's daughter, the narrator informs us that each year for four days young women mourn the loss of this young heroine (Judg. 11:40). It could be that Pseudo-Philo is reflecting a contemporary Jewish practice wherein young women mourn those who have died before their weddings. Perhaps the poetic form of the story reflects an ancient dirge sung in Seila's honor. If so, the song presents a surprisingly negative description of men, and a highly laudatory picture of women. Was the song subverting the status quo? Or did it provide a necessary "safety valve" to release hostile feelings generated by the oppressive culture? In fact, it is probably not as simple as an either-or question. Marks suggests the song provided "an integration of the gripes and fears of the women participants with the celebratory communal elements."[74]

Seila speaks with her own voice, as does the young bride in the inscription. Both highlight the special dress to be worn at the wedding, which now serves as funerary garb. Pseudo-Philo draws out the importance of companions, only hinted at in the inscription. And he notes garlands of flowers and anointing oils as part of the bride's preparation for her wedding. Seila's lament reveals that for some time her mother and nurse were planning and preparing for her wedding. As with the inscription, no mention is made of a specific groom,

---

73. See Marks, "Jewish Weddings," 145.
74. Marks, "Jewish Weddings," 153.

which might indicate that mothers and daughters went forward with wedding plans assuming that a marriage was in the future for every daughter.

Such is not the case with our final piece of evidence. In *Joseph and Aseneth* the groom is well known from the biblical story. We find not one, but two descriptions of wedding preparation in *Joseph and Aseneth* (3.1–4.2; 15.10). Before she meets Joseph, Aseneth dresses herself as might a bride, though at this point she is preparing herself to greet her parents just returned from the harvest. At the story's beginning, she is a pagan, the daughter of a pagan priest. Thus she wears precious stones engraved with the name of her Egyptian god and etched with pictures of idols. But in other respects her appearance is characteristic of weddings. First, it entails a great display of wealth. As one of the most important men in all Egypt, her father can afford to dress his daughter as befitted her status. She wears a gold girdle and gold trousers, bracelets on her hands and feet, and necklaces studded with jewels. On her head she wears a tiara and a diadem. Like Seila, her robe is the color of hyacinth, and she has maids to aid her. The text adds that she wore a veil, which was common for Greco-Roman brides. (The absence of a veil in Seila's story is likely due to the fact that corpses were not cremated or buried in a veil.) Aseneth's parents are pleased with her attire and proclaim she looks like the "bride of God" (4.1). A bit later in their conversation, they broach the topic of marriage to Joseph, and Aseneth vehemently rejects the idea. Then she meets him and repents of her rash decision.

When Aseneth dresses as a bride for a second time, it is with full knowledge that she will marry Joseph. Her attire is described briefly and is similar to what she wore to greet her parents, with two significant exceptions. While she does wear jewels, they do not evidence the name of the Egyptian god nor reflect idol carvings. Interestingly, she is commanded by the attending angel to remove her veil, "for you are a chaste virgin today, and your head is like that of a young man" (15.1).[75] The symbolism connected with the veil makes it problematic to determine if any historical judgment can be made about veils and weddings. The angel explains the veil's removal in terms of conversion, with no direct reference to marriage. Instead, he insists that Aseneth is now worthy, by virtue of her conversion to Judaism, to wed Joseph. We should not presume that Jewish women married without a veil, though the text is possibly hinting that a Jewish convert might. But the text's symbolism and metaphors suggest that historical practice and instructions for actual weddings are not the first priority (and might not be of interest at all). In fact, it is unclear that Aseneth knows Jewish wedding practices. It is uncertain whether, in fact, we can isolate any specific Jewish practices, aside from the absence of references to pagan deities. The text might be at home in certain Christian communities, and it was Christians who preserved the story.

75. Translation in Charlesworth, *Old Testament Pseudepigrapha*, 2:225–26.

The veil, however, was an important article of clothing for the Greco-Roman bride, tracing its roots back to ancient Greece. Plutarch assumes the bride will be veiled, as does Juvenal, but neither offers details about the ceremony.[76] While in ancient Greece it appears that the bride's face was initially covered, then unveiled during the wedding ceremony, in the Greco-Roman period the practice might have varied, with the bride's head but not face covered. The bridal veil was apparently the color of flame, a bright yellow or orange. After the wedding, the bride, now a matron, wore a stola (a sleeveless dress over her tunic) and a palla, a rectangular cloth that she wrapped around her shoulders and could pull up to cover her head.[77]

Weddings in Early Rabbinic Writings and the New Testament

Early rabbinic writings from the Tannaitic period contain no discussion about weddings. On the one hand, this is unfortunate because we could compare these explicitly Jewish texts with our ambiguous sources discussed above to determine more precisely whether they too were Jewish. On the other hand, the lack of interest shown in weddings by the Tannaitic rabbis could suggest that Jewish weddings were very similar to gentile weddings with little variation (except for explicit pagan references). The rabbis were much more interested in marriage, including what groups were suitable to marry each other. Like their Roman counterparts, it was marriage, not the wedding, that held their attention.

The wedding at Cana (John 2) unfortunately offers no picture of the bride or her preparations. We might draw historical precedents from the parable of the ten virgins, five of whom are ill prepared to meet the bridegroom when he comes to the celebration (Matt. 25:1–13). Still no bride is mentioned. But in Revelation, the church itself is presented as a bride, "adorned for her husband." This description supports other evidence that brides wore jewelry on their wedding day.

Daughters and Betrothal Practices

In the West today, most weddings are preceded by much planning during the engagement. Was there a betrothal stage during the Hellenistic period? Scholars are divided on how to read the evidence, but it seems that for the most part, among gentiles the custom of betrothal was minimal to nonexistent. Did Jews

---

76. Plutarch, Conj. praec. 138d; Juvenal, Sat. 2.119.

77. A brief description can be found in Everett Ferguson, Backgrounds of Early Christianity, 3rd ed. (Grand Rapids: Eerdmans, 2003), 96–97; a more lengthy description and discussion is found in Bruce W. Winter, Roman Wives, Roman Widows: The Appearance of New Women and the Pauline Communities (Grand Rapids: Eerdmans, 2003), 77–81; and Dale B. Martin, The Corinthian Body (New Haven: Yale University Press, 1999), 229–49.

in the Second Temple period follow betrothal practices? Later rabbinic material suggests that betrothals were an important part of the marriage negotiations, but only one other source provides any evidence of Jewish betrothals: the story of Joseph and Mary in the Gospel of Matthew. Tracing the history of the rise, fall, and subsequent rise of this practice sheds further light on early Jewish marriages.

In modern Western culture, the engagement is a time to prepare for the wedding, get to know each other as a couple, and decide if marriage is the right decision. If at any point the couple (or individual) decides that they should not marry, they simply separate; they do not need to divorce. In the Hebrew Bible, however, betrothal carried legal weight: the bride-to-be was considered married. The arrangement was called an inchoate marriage. The couple did not live together, but if the bride became pregnant with another man, she could be divorced as an adulteress. So too in classical Greek culture, the marriage was preceded by a time of betrothal.

A shift in language indicates that by the Greco-Roman period, both Jews and Greeks did not see betrothal as necessary for marriage. To illustrate, the ancient Greeks had a word for betrothal, *engyē*, and a word for the father handing the bride over to the husband, *ekdosis*. By the Hellenistic period, the betrothal had been collapsed into the *ekdosis*. The Septuagint also reveals the changed social setting.[78] When faced with translating the Hebrew term for betrothal ('rsh), the LXX used the Greek term *mnēsteuō* instead of the more natural term *engyē*. The new term does carry the sense of wooing or of being promised, but it lacks the legal weight of *engyē*. Satlow concludes, "Not fully understanding the biblical notion of inchoate marriage, the Septuagint's translators replace it with a word denoting a semiformal agreement that a marriage will take place."[79] A few other examples secure the point. In Deuteronomy 28:30, the Hebrew text reads "you will betroth a woman and another man will ravish her"[80] as an example of a curse that will befall Israel if it disobeys the law. The LXX, however, changes the text to read "you will *marry* a woman. . . ." The shift indicates a changed social situation that did not understand betrothal as binding, and so modified the text to explicitly identify the woman as a wife. In 2 Samuel 3:14, David demands Michal from her father, Saul, because David betrothed himself to her with a payment of one hundred Philistine foreskins. The LXX translates the Hebrew term for "betrothal" with the Greek for "married," presumably because its readers would not have considered "betrothal" to carry the necessary force.

---

78. In Tob. 6:13, some see a betrothal or inchoate marriage established. But in 7:12–13, the promise to give her in marriage and the act of handing her to Tobias occur at the same time, which suggests that 6:13 is not referring to an inchoate marriage.

79. Michael L. Satlow, *Jewish Marriage in Antiquity* (Princeton: Princeton University Press, 2001), 70.

80. Satlow's translation (*Jewish Marriage in Antiquity*, 70).

Outside of the LXX, both Philo and Josephus struggle to match contemporary practice with what happened in Israel's ancient past. Josephus uses the term "pledged" for the Hebrew term "betrothed." He discusses Deuteronomy 22:25 and its order to kill the man who raped an unmarried woman, and he substitutes "pledged" (katengyaō) for the biblical "betrothed." Josephus uses the same term when he talks about Agrippa's daughters' wedding plans. In one case, the daughter did not marry the man to whom she was pledged. Yet there was no discussion of divorce, which one would expect if it were an inchoate marriage.[81]

Philo reveals a tension within the Jewish community on the legal status of a betrothal. In a discussion about male violence against women, unmarried and/or virgins, he presents this scenario: a woman is raped or seduced the day before her wedding—is this adultery? Philo thinks it is because this imaginary couple has a mutual agreement that commits them to the marriage. Others disagree because the marriage has not been celebrated and presumably the financial arrangements have not been fulfilled. That takes place at the wedding; until then, the bride-to-be cannot be guilty of adultery.[82] Philo rejoins that a document has been signed indicating intent, and so the couple should be treated as married in terms of punishing the guilty man of undue violence or condemning the woman as an adulteress. Philo is likely advocating the combination of the Greek practice of betrothal, which carried no legal weight, and the Hebrew practice of inchoate marriage. The very fact that he has to argue for this suggests that at least some Jews were not observing inchoate marriage.

Another piece of evidence allegedly reflects the situation in Alexandria. A rabbinic statement attributed to Hillel refers to marriage practices in Hellenistic Alexandria.[83] Hillel is asked to judge whether the particular situation outlined counts as adultery. The scenario is that some Alexandrian Jews abduct betrothed Jewish women from the marketplace and take them as their wives. Hillel was asked, Should this be considered adultery, that is, stealing another man's wife? Hillel requested the Alexandrian marriage contract, which stipulated that the marriage is effective when the wife enters her husband's house: "When you enter my house you will be my wife according to the law of Moses and Israel."[84] He determined that until that condition was met, she was not legally his wife and had no claims on any prearranged pecuniary agreement he made to her until he was her husband. Hillel concluded that the couple was not legally married because the wife had not yet come into the

81. Josephus, Ant. 19.355; 20.143, 145, 147.
82. Philo, Spec. 3.72.
83. t. Ket. 4:9.
84. Satlow (Jewish Marriage in Antiquity, 72) writes, "the exceptional nature of the case, the attribution to the legendary Hillel, the assumption of 'rabbinic' power in the first century BCE, and some linguistic anachronisms all mitigate against the historical veracity of the account."

man's home. So the abductor was not guilty of the crime of adultery. Both Philo and the Tosefta indicate disagreement in their communities about the status of the woman (bride-to-be or wife). This suggests that perhaps within the Alexandrian Jewish community of the first century BC, lively discussion flourished about the binding nature of the betrothal agreement.

A final piece of evidence is from Matthew's birth narrative. In Matthew 1:18–19, Mary is pledged to marry Joseph (who is called her husband), and when she becomes pregnant, he decides he must divorce her. The decision to end this relationship through divorce indicates that the betrothal was seen as an inchoate marriage. Interestingly, Luke does not mention Joseph's decision to divorce (Luke 1:26–38). Was this because his Greek audience would not have understood that a man could divorce a woman when he was not yet married to her? The evidence suggests that some Jews practiced a form of inchoate marriage and others did not. The picture emerges that perhaps rural Galilean Jews followed the ancient biblical practice, while urban Jews and those in the Diaspora followed the patterns of the surrounding Greco-Roman culture.

Conclusion

The Greco-Roman daughter is a study in opposites. She is most beloved by her family, and is a cause of great anxiety. She is fully part of the family, receiving a share of the estate, and she is less desired than sons, more likely to face exposure than her brothers. Often she will receive some education, but she is also to remain confined in the home to preserve her chastity. The literary evidence leans toward a more negative picture of a daughter as a liability, while the epigraphic and epistolary evidence suggests that at the individual family level, many parents loved and cared for their daughters—if they chose to raise them. In most cases, a daughter was destined to marry; to die a virgin was to die having only half lived. It was a cause of great mourning, while the bride's wedding was a celebration. Once married, a daughter became a wife as well. As in many cultures today, the ideals of marriage did not match its realities. Before we look at the real world of daughters becoming wives, we will explore the ideals and controlling motifs that underpinned expectations about marriage and the model wife.

2

Marriage and Matron Ideals

"Like the sun rising in the heights of the Lord, so is the beauty of a good wife in her well-ordered home" (Sir. 26:16). So writes Jesus ben Sira in the second century BC. His words echo the general sentiment of his day, praising wives as the foundation of a good home. An inscription from Rome from the same time period endorses Ben Sira's thoughts: "Her parents gave her the name Claudia. She loved her husband in her heart. She bore two sons, one of whom she left on earth, the other beneath it. She was pleasant to talk with, and she walked with grace. She kept the house and worked in wool."[1] This theme resonates through varied sources as epitaphs and philosophers alike herald a diligent wife and her wool-working skills.

Dowry contracts and wedding celebrations do not exist in a social vacuum, then or now. Modern cultures reveal much about their

A married couple represented in a Thessalonican grave stele from the first century AD
(Photo courtesy of Todd Bolen/bibleplaces.com)

1. *ILLRP* 973; *ILS* 8403; *CLE* 52; *CIL* I².1211; *CIL* VI.15346. Translation by R. Lattimore in Mary R. Lefkowitz and Maureen B. Fant, *Women's Life in Greece and Rome: A Source Book in Translation*, 3rd ed. (Baltimore: Johns Hopkins University Press, 2005), 16.

values in their assumptions regarding what makes a good marriage. For example, the Western political climate privileges the individual as the fundamental unit of society. This works well for a democracy, translating into marriage expectations that include self-fulfillment and love. But in the ancient world, increasing family honor and avoiding shame were the chief motivating factors in influencing behavior, especially women's behaviors as portrayed by men. The individualistic motivators of passion and desire were treated with suspicion as disruptive to the social order.

The Views of Plato and Aristotle

Male and Female

Before discussing marriage, it is important to highlight two competing views of male and female, for they play a foundational role in the construction of family systems.[2] Plato's views on men and women were grounded in his belief in reincarnation of the soul. He argued that the soul was placed in a male or female body based on its relative strength of character, with weaker souls placed in female bodies. Through education, however, women could gain wisdom and virtue, because their soul is of the same nature as a man's soul. As they move further from their matter, or female mode, women progress closer to wisdom. In *Respublica* (*The Republic*), Plato writes that the man or woman's identity comes from the mind/soul, not the body. The soul is not matter, and so is not sexual. At the cosmic level, form is male, active, and superior, while matter is female, passive, and inferior.

Aristotle, Plato's student, rejected his views of reincarnation, believing that the soul cannot exist without the body. Moreover, Aristotle believed that the mother contributed nothing to the fetus. He sought consistency in determining sexual identity and offered the first comprehensive statement about sex polarity. By inextricably linking body and soul, and by determining the female body deficient, he concluded that the female soul (or mind) is likewise deficient. Aristotle declared that each man and woman as an individual substance is made up of matter and form (though in different degrees). Since women and men appear different in their bodies, they must also be different in their souls. The female has more matter, the male more form. Not only are they different, but they are opposites, with one being the privation of the other. Explaining woman as the privation of man, he declares that the female is incapable of becoming her opposite, which is male. Aristotle's conclusions on men and women proved most influential in the Hellenistic period.

2. For a useful discussion of the issues, see Prudence Allen, *The Concept of Woman: The Aristotelian Revolution, 750 B.C.–A.D. 1250*, 2nd ed. (Grand Rapids: Eerdmans, 1997), 57–95.

Marriage within the Society

Even as the forms of Western government, industry, commerce, and social customs shape today's expectations of marriage, so too in the ancient world philosophers and politicians drew on the forms of the larger society to create metaphors and topoi for marriage. The philosophical stance, that male was superior to female, played itself out in the cultural arena where women as a group were inferior to men. Moreover, this position played a key role in the social configuration of the ideals of marriage. From classical Greece up through the reign of imperial Rome, the subordination of women was understood as a moral issue, although it was also enforced by social and legal codes.

Plato's comparison of marriage and city (*polis*) was embraced by later Stoics. Aristotle suggests that the family is the smallest unit of social organization; upon this is built a village and then a colony.[3] In this picture of leadership, the husband rules his family (wife, children, and slaves) much as a king rules his colony. Aristotle distinguishes between this royal type of rule and a constitutional rule, in which leadership rotates among the community's members because they are equals. Aristotle declares that the father rules his children as a king would his subjects, but rules his wife from a constitutional position, suggesting that they are in some way equals. Aristotle then backs away the next logical step in his argument and qualifies himself: "the relation of the male to the female is of this kind [constitutional], but there the inequality is permanent."[4] These ideas remained current in the period we are examining, as evidenced by a quotation by Soranus (second century AD): "the female is by nature different from the male, so much so that Aristotle and Zenon the Epicurean say that the female is imperfect, the male, however, perfect."[5] Aristotle's expectations for the morality of women/wives differed from those concerning male virtue. Each gender has a special attribute, and so the courage or justice of a man is different in kind from a woman's courage—the former shows his courage in leading, the latter in obeying. Aristotle illustrates with a quotation from a contemporary poet: "silence is a woman's glory."[6]

Perhaps not all later philosophers agreed with Aristotle's classification of government leadership, but they did speak with one voice on the importance of a husband governing his wife, which served as the backbone of social stability.[7]

---

3. Aristotle, *Pol.* 1.2 (1252b.1–14).

4. Aristotle, *Pol.* 1.12 (1259a.35–1259b.9). For a translation and discussion, see Allen, *Concept of Woman*, 114–15.

5. Soranus, *Gyn.* 3.3. Translation in *Soranus' Gynecology*, trans. O. Temkin (Baltimore: Johns Hopkins University Press, 1991), 129.

6. Aristotle, *Pol.* 1.13 (1260b), quoting Sophocles, *Ajax* 293. Translation by Allen, *Concept of Woman*, 110.

7. For example, Diogenes Laertius, *Vit. phil.* 3.38–39 (third century AD), noted that males are natural rulers, and females are naturally ruled. Ironically, although he attributes this position to Plato, it actually reflects Aristotle's views; the point, however, is that this position is

Like Aristotle, they understood a husband's leadership and a wife's obedience to be "natural" or according to nature. It was essential, therefore, for the state to regulate the natural order between genders (and classes). Dionysius of Halicarnassus, writing in the first century BC, suggested that a virtuous married woman conforms obediently to the temperament of her husband, while the husband should rule his wife as an important and inseparable possession.[8] Writing a century later, Plutarch in his advice to a young couple writes, "if they [wives] subordinate themselves to their husbands, they are commended, but if they want to have control, they cut a sorrier figure than the subjects of their control. And control ought to be exercised by the man over the woman, not as the owner has control over a piece of property . . . it is possible to exercise care over the body without being a slave to its pleasures and desires, so it is possible to govern a wife and at the same time to delight and gratify her."[9] From the corpus of Pythagorean literature comes the sentiment that a wife must be in concert with her husband, so that what he calls sweet, she also calls sweet, and what he labels sour, she also labels sour. "Otherwise she will be out of tune with her whole universe."[10] Failure to manage the household was considered subversive, based on the Aristotelian view that a well-ordered household was the exemplar for a solid state.[11] If harmony is maintained, however, the wife enjoys high status within her home. In a Roman household, the wife acts as manager, overseeing the children, slaves, estate crops—in sum, all that comes under the umbrella of the home.

We can confidently conclude, then, that Aristotle's topos concerning household management permeated the discussions during the Hellenistic and imperial periods.[12] This has important ramifications for our understanding of the household codes in the New Testament.[13] For example, one term used to

---

understood to reflect social norms that could be traced back to classical Greece. For a careful discussion of the evidence, see David L. Balch, *Let Wives Be Submissive: The Domestic Code in 1 Peter*, SBLMS 26 (Chico, CA: Scholars Press, 1981), 23–49.

8. Dionysius of Halicarnassus, *Antiquitates romanae* 1.9–2.29 (trans. E. Cary, LCL). Quoted in Balch, *Let Wives Be Submissive*, 55.

9. Plutarch, *Conj. praec.* 33 (trans. F. C. Babbitt, LCL).

10. Stobaeus, *Florilegium* 4.28.10. Translation by Flora R. Levin in Sarah B. Pomeroy, *Goddesses, Whores, Wives, and Slaves: Women in Classical Antiquity* (1975; repr., New York: Schocken, 1995), 134–36 (quotation, 136). See also Holger Thesleff, ed., *The Pythagorean Texts of the Hellenistic Period* (Åbo: Åbo Akademi, 1965), 142–45. Dating these texts is problematic: the dates range from the fourth century BC to the second century AD.

11. Margaret Y. MacDonald notes: "historical investigation has revealed that the Aristotelian belief in the individual household as a paradigm of the state was widely held in Greco-Roman society" (*The Pauline Churches: A Socio-Historical Study of Institutionalization in the Pauline and Deutero-Pauline Writings* [Cambridge: Cambridge University Press, 2004], 189).

12. Balch, *Let Wives Be Submissive*, 34, notes that "the pattern of submissiveness (cp. the three pairs in Col. 3:18–4:1) was based upon an earlier Aristotelian topos 'concerning household management'; the discussion of these three relationships in a household was not a Jewish or Christian innovation."

13. The household codes include Eph. 5:21–6:9; Col. 3:18–4:1; 1 Pet. 2:18–3:7.

describe a wife is *oikodespotēs*, found in verb form in 1 Timothy 5:14 and translated as "to manage the household." A similar term (*proistēmi oikou*) is used earlier, in 1 Timothy 3:4–5, 12, to describe the role of the paterfamilias who manages his wife, children, slaves, and others connected to his household.[14] Thus within her sphere of influence, mediated by her husband, the wife had important responsibilities. Her active role in the household opens intriguing possibilities for important roles within the house church. Hospitality was highly valued, and women would have primary responsibilities in this arena (1 Tim. 5:10). A matron would also have opportunities to teach young men and women within the home setting (Titus 2:3–5). We should also note that the descriptions of a wife in the Pastorals serve an apologetic function, as failure to follow the dominant culture's expectations for wifely submission would cast a shadow over the early Christian movement (Titus 2:3–5; cf. 1 Tim. 5:14).[15]

Positive Portraits of Wives in Non-Jewish Literature

A Wife's Ideal Virtues

Laws establish a wife's proper sphere as her home with chastity as her most valued virtue, and poets laud her modesty as the highest good. From all around her, a wife in the Greco-Roman world heard a chorus of voices now entreating, now scolding her in the ideal virtues of modesty, chastity, and industry. Such characteristics were trumpeted publicly, but we must be cautious in accepting the prescriptions as reflecting daily life among women. Though we cannot assume that women themselves embraced these paradigms, these archetypes did play a role in larger debates about the proper behaviors and postures men should take, as well as discussions about politics. In our pursuit of historical women's lives, we must read the prescriptions and ideals of wives with an eye to the propaganda value such ideals might have in men's discussions about their world.

Stories carried these themes of a wife's industry in the home and her submission to her husband deep into the heart of the ancient Greco-Roman culture. Perhaps one of the most influential narratives capturing these ideas is that of the rape of Lucretia, as told by Livy.[16] He was repeating a legend that both

14. The literature on the household codes within the New Testament is extensive. See Balch, *Let Wives Be Submissive*; Carolyn Osiek and Margaret Y. MacDonald, *A Woman's Place: House Churches in Earliest Christianity*, with Janet H. Tulloch (Minneapolis: Fortress, 2006).

15. In this Christians were similar to Josephus and Philo, who defended Jewish marriages against Roman criticism by declaring that Jewish wives were submissive. See Josephus, *C. Ap.* 2.199, 206, 216; Philo, *Hypothetica* 7.2–5, 14. For a careful discussion, see Balch, *Let Wives Be Submissive*, 63–116.

16. Livy, *Hist.* 1.57.6–58.

memorialized the chaste, dutiful wife and her importance for family honor and, perhaps more importantly, introduced Lucius Brutus, the founder of the Roman Republic (ca. 509 BC), in his bid to overthrow the corrupt monarchy. The story begins with the king's sons and other soldiers laying siege to an enemy city, Ardea. After wine had flowed freely, the men began to brag about their wives' chaste deportment. They agreed that very night they would visit their wives to prove their claims. However, upon arriving at their homes, they discovered their wives preparing for a feast, with one notable exception: at the home of Tarquinius Conlatinus, they found his wife, Lucretia, still spinning into the night with her servants. Conlatinus clearly won the "bet" but ended up losing everything as one prince, Sextus Tarquinius, was aroused to jealousy. He returned a few days later and raped the defenseless Lucretia. Overcome with shame, she sent word to her absent husband and father that they must return home immediately. When they arrived, she described the terrible deed, despairingly asking, "How can anything go well for a woman who has lost her honor?"

The men declare that she is guiltless of any crime, but she maintains, "My body is greatly soiled, though my heart is still pure, as my death will prove." She believes that the only way to restore her honor is by her death, that "no woman shall use Lucretia as her example in dishonor." Her death proves her innocence, as she plunges a knife into her heart. It is Brutus who removes the knife, pledging to bring down the evil royal family that perpetrated this crime, and thus he launches his revolt against the monarchy. In what follows, three key elements from this story will surface repeatedly—a wife's chastity, her industry, and her loyalty to her family.

The Perfect Wife

Many ancient writers commented on the "perfect" marriage, the ideal wife, and the role of the household in securing a healthy society. These (male) writers often used marriage as a topos or a traditional theme on which to build a discussion about another topic, such as civic order or duty. To say a man had a good marriage was to compliment his social virtue and his faithful civic duty. These common attitudes include valuing marriage as the responsible action of a good citizen, the proper venue for procreation, and fitting with nature. Aristotle's words rang true in this period: "In the first place there must be a union of those who cannot exist without each other; namely, of male and female, that the race may continue . . . [for] mankind have a natural desire to leave behind them an image of themselves."[17] Antipater of Tarsus (second century BC) remarks that a high-born youth, as a civilized, political being, does his duty to the gods and his *polis* by marrying and producing children.

---

17. Aristotle, *Pol.* 1.2. Translation by Benjamin Jowett, *The Politics of Aristotle* (1885; repr., Charleston, SC: BiblioBazaar, 2008), 10.

Antipater argues that an unmarried man is incomplete; he must do as nature intended and have children.[18]

Often when men spoke of the virtuous wife, they described her as having *pietas*. By this they meant that she possessed a sense of duty, fidelity, and steadfastness to her family, her husband, the state, and the gods. Pliny the Younger, from the early decades of the second century AD, lauds a philosopher friend's wife, Fannia, who is fatally ill, describing her as having integrity and loyalty because she followed her husband twice into exile, rescuing his banned works as she fled.[19] Fannia was the granddaughter of Arria, wife of Caecina Paetus, who joined her husband in suicide after he was convicted of treason under Claudius. Pliny praises Arria for her steadfast devotion to her husband, remembering her last words as "Paetus, it does not hurt."[20]

Also from the second century AD, Plutarch continues to affirm the value of marriage.[21] In this work, he offers further examples of a proper wife. She should be educated and know philosophy. She must follow her husband's gods and support her in-laws. She should obey her husband in everything and refuse to listen to any negative comments about him. Eschewing fancy clothes and remaining silent in public reveal her noble character. In the bedchamber, she should show her affection and modesty in lovemaking. She must accept her husband's extramarital sexual activities with good grace and not let such behaviors push her toward divorce.

To the groom, Plutarch writes that he must allow his wife some personal expression, for she has her own personality (perhaps she is naturally austere, for example). He must control his own passions, thereby setting an example for his wife, for he is responsible to teach her. The husband may enjoy sex with others (except married women), but should avoid provoking his wife to jealousy. Plutarch reaches beyond the legal codes when he suggests that married couples have one purse, under the husband's control even if the wealth comes from the wife.

Emperor Augustus and Marriage

Because literary presentations run the risk of idealizing marriage without shedding light on the actual marriages experienced by real men and women, some scholars have turned to studying Roman laws concerning marriage. A flurry of legal activity criminalizing immorality and promoting marriage

18. *SVF* 3.254.23–257.10 (Stobaeus, *Florilegium* 4.507.6–512). Cited in Michael L. Satlow, *Jewish Marriage in Antiquity* (Princeton: Princeton University Press, 2001), 13–14.
19. Pliny the Younger, *Ep.* 7.19.1–6. For a discussion of this passage and translation, see Jo-Ann Shelton, *As the Romans Did: A Sourcebook in Roman Social History* (New York: Oxford University Press, 1988), 298.
20. Pliny the Younger, *Ep.* 3.16.3–6. See Shelton, *As the Romans Did*, 296.
21. Plutarch, *Mor.* 748e–771e; 138a–146a (= *Conj. praec.*).

occurred early in Augustus's reign (27 BC–AD 14). Augustus established the *lex Julia de maritandis ordinibus* and the *lex Julia de adulteriis coercendis* (both ca. 18 BC), and later the *lex Papia Poppaea* (AD 9). These laws allegedly targeted two specific issues: the former two addressed the lack of children produced by Roman citizens, and the latter focused on promiscuity. The laws' impact extended to inheritance practices and entered into what was previously private territory handled internally by families. The decrees mandated that a husband divorce his wife and prosecute her if he suspected her of adultery. If she was found innocent, he might remarry her. Augustus made marriage and inheritance more complex and more public. Said another way, as the father of the Empire, he chose to meddle in the private affairs of his "family," especially the elite Roman families of the senate.

The "New Woman"

Some scholars believe that these new laws reveal a recently deteriorating society with wives blatantly disregarding ancient customs of *pudicitia* or modesty. They allege that this "new woman" eschewed traditional morality as encapsulated in motherhood and wifely modesty in favor of riotous living, not unlike wealthy men's partying and cavorting. Augustus's laws were therefore an attempt to quell this immorality. Studying these prohibitions provides a window into what was really going on in Roman society, at least in its elite classes.[22] However, the theory that Augustus's laws were a response to the "new woman" falters at several points. Instead, the laws likely represent a weapon in his arsenal against attacks that he was changing Roman society and culture by instituting an imperial dynasty. At issue is whether Rome was infested with "new women" or whether this figure primarily emerged from the verses of Roman poets. Moreover, we must account for the "new man" who sought out this "new woman." Before presenting a critique of this theory, I offer a sketch of the evidence for the "new woman."

Defining the "new woman" is not easy, in part because this phrase is a modern construct designed to explain perceived changes within Roman culture. But historians note that in the beginning of the first century BC, the increased wealth flowing into Rome and the political instability resulting from the civil wars provided an unstable social environment in which women from elite families gained political influence. Social norms were fragile during the first century BC in Rome, with the result that traditional boundaries were tested or broken. Laws that had limited women's influence in the family were relaxed, giving them more say in handling estate matters. *Sine manu* marriages reduced a husband's direct control over his wife, and the many wars separated women from their soldiering fathers, husbands, and sons. The result was a

---

22. Bruce W. Winter, *Roman Wives, Roman Widows: The Appearance of New Women and the Pauline Communities* (Grand Rapids: Eerdmans, 2003).

more public presence of women, especially the wealthy, within the social and political arenas. (The new opportunities to use their wealth as patrons will be discussed in chap. 9.) But their involvement in what was previously understood by men as male turf led to stinging critiques and caricatures that offer little help in reconstructing real women.

The "new woman" is found as an idealized lover in the poems of Ovid, Catullus, and Tibullus, and in the arguments from the lawyer Cicero. Her characteristics include a measure of wealth and social clout, as well as a disregard for traditional social customs. The poets create scenes in which their lovers, most likely imaginary creatures, either share clandestine meetings or refuse to see them. For example, Ovid, in his pleadings with Corinna, never provides realistic settings for his muse, leading some to believe that Corinna is nothing more than his "ideal" lover existing only in his imagination.[23] The poet's unrequited love can lead to anger against the lover, or despair at her disdain. These poets expressed their enslavement to their lovers, a different posture than previously taken by men toward women. For example, Tibullus metaphorically describes himself as a slave to his Delia, but she and the other poets' lovers sound more like "imaginative creations than real flesh-and-blood lovers."[24]

All three poets lived at the end of the Republic, and all extol the extramarital affair. Historians have pondered why this posture appeared at this moment in Rome's history. One answer is that these men and perhaps others like them lost property in the civil wars and were disenchanted with politics and the social maneuvering that could be literally deadly. As it became harder to seek their fortunes through the regular channels of social networking and marriage because their families had lost much wealth, they enslaved themselves to women (or an ideal woman) whose passions they might arouse, but who stood poised to rebuff. They sought adventure not on the battlefield or in the senate, but in a personal tryst with a married woman. In swearing eternal love to her, they effectively absolved themselves of any need to be judged socially or materially successful. They remained perpetually youthful and as such dodged the responsibilities of adulthood—marriage and family—at least on the page, for we have no idea to what extent these poets acted on their words and whether high-status women participated in their lovemaking antics.[25]

The evidence from Cicero in his attack against Clodia is read by many as expressing historical reality. Cicero does speak of a real woman, Clodia, and he defames her character in an effort to deflect attention away from his

23. Ovid (43 BC–AD 17) was exiled from Rome in AD 8, perhaps for some indiscretion with Vipsania Julia, Augustus's granddaughter. She was exiled the same year for adultery, though not committed with Ovid.

24. Fantham et al., "The 'New Woman': Representation and Reality," in *Women in the Classical World: Image and Text* (New York: Oxford University Press, 1994), 282.

25. Fantham et al., "New Woman," in *Women in the Classical World*, 281–93.

client, Caelius Rufus, who was charged with (and likely guilty of) political violence (*Pro Caelio*). Cicero suggests that she seduced his client, but Clodia was the sister of Cicero's archenemy, Publius, which hardly gives confidence that Cicero is limiting himself to the "bare facts" of the case. Most scholars conflate Clodia with the poet Catullus's muse, Lesbia, and thus move the "new woman" from the pages of poetry to the real world.[26]

A careful reading of the evidence, however, suggests Clodia was not Lesbia. First, we must give full weight to the rhetorical strategy used by Cicero. Clodia Metelli's family owned property Cicero desired to possess, and Clodia was a widely influential patroness in her own right. Any opportunity for Cicero to take a swipe at this rival family would be welcomed. Destroying an opponent's reputation in court was standard procedure. Thus we should not expect calm, measured assessments in Cicero's portrayal of Clodia. Second, Cicero did not connect her with Catullus's Lesbia; that move was made by Apuleius in the second century AD. But scholars are ready to believe in this "hybrid" because they see in Catullus her betrayal and in Cicero her promiscuity, and they accept both as fact. Such willingness is probably based on the accepted wisdom (however misguided) of historians that Rome was a declining, debauched society—as evidenced by licentious women. But Cicero is hardly interested in fairly representing Clodia's character, and Catullus, writing poetry, is exploring the depths of human love and perfidy, not objectively painting a picture of a real woman. Third, equating Clodia with Lesbia stretches the evidence beyond what it can bear. For example, Catullus calls his muse a child, but Clodia is clearly an older woman. The details in Catullus are also distorted to fit with Clodia Metelli's husband's death in 59 BC, for the Lesbia poems are hard to place that early.[27]

The same acceptance as fact of personal invectives against women in high society has led some scholars to postulate an ever-widening influence of these "new women." Some point to Julia as the "new woman" who started it all because her father, Augustus, exiled her for adultery in AD 2.[28] In modern reconstructions of her life, late anecdotes about her frivolous nature often outweigh the more numerous examples of her noble behavior in bearing five children to her second husband, Agrippa, after her first husband died. Nor should we forget that the charge of adultery against her was often linked with treason, for a child from such a union might have a claim to the throne, to say nothing of the lover's aspirations. Pliny notes that she was accused not only of adultery but also of schemes to unseat her father.[29] Her alleged lover,

26. Catullus's lover was Clodia, but he refers to her as Lesbia in his writings.

27. For a detailed discussion, see Suzanne Dixon, *Reading Roman Women: Sources, Genres, and Real Life* (London: Duckworth, 2001), 134–45.

28. Augustus also exiled his granddaughter, Vipsania Julia, for charges of sexual immorality.

29. Pliny the Elder, *Nat.* 7.46.

who was executed, was Marc Antony's son, Iullus Antonius. Julia's exile, therefore, should be viewed not only through a moral lens, but also with an eye to political maneuvering within Rome. The standard charge against a male political opponent was treason, with the corollary of desiring supreme power himself. Technically a woman could not be charged with desiring supreme power, as the office was not open to her. Thus the charge of immorality was especially suited to casting aspersions on her character and rendering her politically impotent.[30]

In sum, the existence of the "new woman," who was sexually promiscuous and upset the balance of propriety in Rome and beyond, is more a poetic fiction and a political smear than a historical reality. There is no evidence of increased female immorality under Augustus, nor that prior to Augustus Roman women exhibited a high level of perfidy. Rather, male authors used the charge of female sexual misconduct as a weapon against political enemies. The charges of female immorality need not reflect actual misconduct in most cases, but rather reveal the increased presence of women in the political arena, where they became fair game for political opponents. Fictional characters, moreover, do not offer a direct window into the real world. Often they are a projection of the dreams, desires, and fantasies of their authors, and arguably the genre of love poetry offers little in the way of actual historical data. Nor can we assume that the alleged popularity of this poetry encouraged real women to emulate these fictional muses.

AUGUSTUS: THE "NEW RULER"

That said, we still would profit from exploring possible reasons for Augustus's marriage laws. First, the Roman landscape had been shifting drastically for about a hundred and fifty years before the empire was established. Augustus faced birth rates that had been declining for generations among Roman citizens. Though Stoics and Pythagoreans bemoaned the changes, Hellenism had both directed attention to the individual and lessened the hold of traditional local cults, which together served to weaken the old reason for marrying—producing children to carry on the ancestral worship. Second, Augustus's laws followed in a long line of ultimately futile attempts to prevent women from controlling some of Rome's newfound wealth. As the Roman Republic conquered much of the Mediterranean world, treasure poured into the capital, and Roman peasants were drawn off their land as the wealthy bought it or repossessed it for failure to pay taxes. The issue of women and wealth was on the front page at the end of the Second Punic War with the enactment of the Oppian law in 195 BC. This decree restricted the amount of gold owned by women and curtailed luxuries like expensive dress and transportation. Women

30. Richard A. Bauman, *Women and Politics in Ancient Rome* (New York: Routledge, 1992), 12.

gathered in protest of this law (perhaps the first women's demonstration in recorded history), and the law was overturned. It is possible that some men encouraged the repeal, as it provided them the opportunity to show off their wealth through their female family members. The Voconian law (169 BC) was another attempt at restricting wealth from women by making it illegal for a father to give his daughter an inheritance. This law sought to prevent women from owning large tracts of land, but it was easily circumvented through fathers offering daughters dowries of land, legacies, and gifts. The rise in *sine manu* marriages offered more independence to women, who with their newfound wealth had more power (albeit informal). Moreover, the civil wars, following hard on the lengthy and costly Punic wars, destabilized the wealthy Roman families and their interconnected power structure. Families with newly acquired wealth usurped status, and once-wealthy sons were left without the full value of their family estate.[31]

Shrinking family size, according to Polybius (a second-century BC rhetorician), was due to men's lack of a sense of duty to society.[32] Others chimed in that women lacked interest in motherhood. But ancient rhetoric cannot reveal a clear picture of motives, let alone a sketch of actual historical situations. While various sources reveal that family size was small, at least among the upper classes, that may be due to the dreadfully high infant and child death rate and childbirth mortality. Small families, therefore, might be merely the result of tragic historical exigencies. Augustus offered privileges to both men and women for marrying and having children (see chap. 3). In this he reinforced the 59 BC law of his adoptive father Julius Caesar that gave land to fathers of three or more children, suggesting that small families were not the result of "new woman" propaganda but were due to men deciding to have fewer children. The numerous loopholes and special exemptions from Augustus's laws signal that at least one important effect of the law was empowering the emperor in handing out favors. In wonderful historical irony, the two consuls who sponsored the *lex Papia Poppaea* were themselves unmarried.

In fact, a strong case can be made that Augustus, with these marriage laws, sought to propagandize his rule as tied closely with ancient tradition. Prior to his rule, the Roman Republic was governed by a senate, but it had endured a costly and bloody civil war. In establishing a dynasty, Augustus was beginning something very new—he was wresting power from the patrician leaders in the senate and claiming Rome as his own kingdom. How was he to legitimize this move? In part by claiming he represented all that was ancient in Roman culture. His marriage laws, therefore, might not reflect the need to change

---

31. Virgil, Horace, and Tibullus all claim to have lost estates.

32. Polybius declares that men resisted marriage because they were pretentious, greedy, and lazy (*Historiae* 36.17).

actual social situations as much as personal propaganda that he was faithful to Roman traditions. The following example illustrates this claim.

Augustus reestablished the ritual of *confarreatio*, an ancient marriage ceremony allegedly started by Romulus himself. The rite included a sacred loaf of bread offered to the god Jupiter Farreus (the latter designation refers to the grain, *far*, a type of wheat used in the bread).[33] Priests (*flamines*) performing the sacrifices and rituals must be of the highest level (serving Jupiter, Mars, and Quirinus) and must be married by *confarreatio* and have parents who were married by *confarreatio*. Once married, the wife was under the control (*manus*) of her husband, as in the Roman ancient past. These priests were scarce, and by Augustus's time, the office of *flamen Dialis* had been vacant for about fifty years. Obviously, during this time no marriage by *confarreatio* could be performed. Nor would it be easy to reinstate, as the priests must come from parents who were married by this ritual. Moreover, in Augustus's day, most marriages were *sine manu*, limiting the power of the husband (see chap. 1). Though Augustus restored the ancient ceremony, he added an important twist—the wife was not under the control of her husband except in ritual contexts. In all other ways, the wife had independence similar to that granted to her peers. In reviving this ancient marriage rite, Augustus could claim he followed traditional Roman practices, cloaking his own political innovations in the garb of archaic Roman custom.

We should be wary of using Augustus's laws to recreate the social setting across the empire, since his rulings addressed a limited target audience. Augustus was concerned with shoring up the Roman citizenry of his empire and sharply distinguishing social classes. Thus, his laws aimed at only a small slice of the population, those urban elite who made up a fraction of the empire's vast and diverse inhabitants. As Bruce Winter notes, "Social engineering by Augustus, the aim of which was to give the senatorial class a higher profile in society, depended upon their wives living up to expected standards."[34] We cannot draw a broader picture of what marriage was like from laws that focus on Roman elite citizens.

Finally, one should ask what Augustus hoped to gain by enacting the laws against adultery and fornication (by women). Some might argue that he felt a great burden to rid the empire, or at least upper-class Rome, of the plague of infidelity and adultery. Beryl Rawson suggests that Augustus was primarily concerned about pure lineage among the Roman upper class; he wanted to prevent illicit babies.[35] But that statement presupposes the rampant or at least common practice of adultery or fornication among Rome's elite. Is this an accurate picture of the Roman world or the city Rome in the

33. Gaius, *Institutiones* 1.112. See also Pliny the Elder, *Nat.* 18.10.

34. Winter, *Roman Wives*, 44. He argues that "new women" were behind Augustus's laws.

35. Beryl Rawson, "The Roman Family," in *The Family in Ancient Rome: New Perspectives*, ed. Beryl Rawson (Ithaca, NY: Cornell University Press, 1987), 34.

late first century BC? If we add up the rhetorical invectives against women leveled by jurists, satirists, and literary works from the first century BC, we might be tempted to suggest that the late Republic was in moral shambles due to rampant disregard of ancient moral codes. However, Susan Treggiari points out that "allegations of adultery were part of the republican orator's stock. . . . Such slurs, inspired by advocacy or politics, were easily invented."[36] Support for this contention is found in the frequency with which elite women accused of adultery were also accused of treason, as noted above in the case of Augustus's daughter, Julia. Moreover, even if the evidence could provide the number of allegations of adultery at this time, we could not assume that in each case the woman was guilty. Fathers or husbands or even outsiders might bring a charge against a wife for revenge. Outsiders might trump up the charge as an opportunity for profit by extorting money in return for their silence.

Two summary points should be made concerning both the "new woman" and Augustus as a new type of ruler. First, many of these "new" women were likely less a historical reality than an imaginary creation of the "new" men of Rome. Many of these male writers lost social prestige when they lost their estates (e.g., Virgil, Horace, Tibullus). And traditional values might have lost their appeal as irrelevant when the society imploded into civil war. Why invest in an unstable, unpredictable social order when we can control (and indulge) our private lives? "Subordination to a capricious woman was at least an individual choice, and these women may have been easier to satisfy than the military leaders with their incessant political realignments."[37] Second, when stability was restored by the emperors, and family and class hierarchies were reestablished, "the impetus to glamorize a different kind of partnership receded."[38] Thus, while adultery, primarily in rhetoric, imagination, and verse, seems to have increased during the turmoil of the civil wars, what Augustus arguably faced in his empire was the threat not of the "new woman" but of the "new man."

Marriage Ideals in Jewish Writings

Jewish writers of the same period reflect similar discussions on marriage as those found in their Greco-Roman counterparts. For example, Philo of Alexandria follows the ancient philosophers in connecting the well-being of the city with the stability of the household. In lauding Joseph, the ancient Hebrew statesman, Philo explains, "a house is a city compressed into small dimensions,

36. Susan Treggiari, *Roman Marriage: Iusti Coniuges from the Time of Cicero to the Time of Ulpian* (Oxford: Clarendon, 1991), 294.
37. Fantham et al., "New Woman," in *Women in the Classical World*, 289.
38. Fantham et al., "New Woman," in *Women in the Classical World*, 292.

and household management may be called a kind of state management."[39] His conclusions that women must remain within the house follow as expected. Just as men are made for the marketplace and courts, so women are made to care for the house, "organized communities are of two sorts, the greater which we call cities and the smaller which we call households. Both of these have their governors; the government of the greater is assigned to men, under the name of statesmanship, that of the lesser, known as household management, to women."[40] Josephus defends Jewish marriages as superior to non-Jewish traditions, though the characteristics he lists are quite similar to those of his gentile counterparts. He defends the Jewish law as teaching that "the woman, says the law, is in all things inferior to the man."[41] Richard Balch concludes that "Aristotle's outline of household submissiveness was adapted by Hellenistic rhetoric; and Josephus and Philo assimilated it to the extent that it was used to praise Moses' laws!"[42]

Authors such as Ben Sira present marriage as important to building up the community and as natural, praising the wife's beauty and her disciplined home; he admires a wife's lovely face, shapely legs, and steadfast feet (Sir. 26:16–18). He assumes that with such beauty comes a well-managed household. A wife must be modest and submissive, charming and silent (26:13–15). Ben Sira does not trust the bachelor because he is unsettled, a wanderer who does not fit in (36:26–31). A century later, Philo comments, "The harmonious coming together of man and woman and their consummation is figuratively a house. And everything which is without a woman is imperfect and homeless." Lest the reader think Philo has promoted a picture of equals, he adds, "For to man are entrusted the public affairs of state; while to a woman the affairs of the home are proper."[43]

In his polemical defense of Judaism, Josephus applauds Jewish marriage as solely for reproduction (though he does not say that sexual activity is solely for procreation).[44] Josephus may be overstating the case in his effort to defend Jewish marriages as superior to Roman ones in terms of embracing the ideals of procreation reflected in Augustus's laws. But his rhetoric matches the party line among Jewish writings—marriage should include procreation. Certainly this is based in part on the command in Genesis 1:28 to be fruitful and multiply that continued to inform Jewish thought. Philo speaks with evident sadness about infertile couples. He asks that they not be required to divorce, given their compatibility in all other things,[45] which implies that they

39. Philo, *De Iosepho* 38–39. Translation by F. H. Colson in Balch, *Let Wives Be Submissive*, 52. See also Philo, *Fug.* 36.
40. Philo, *Spec.* 3.169–71. Translation in Balch, *Let Wives Be Submissive*, 53.
41. Josephus, *C. Ap.* 2.201.
42. Balch, *Let Wives Be Submissive*, 55.
43. Philo, *Questiones et solutiones in Genesin* 1.26 (trans. R. Marcus, LCL).
44. Josephus, *C. Ap.* 2.199.
45. Philo, *Spec. Laws* 3.35.

might feel some pressure to divorce. The story of Zechariah and Elizabeth in Luke 1 expands the evidence of social pressure beyond Philo's description in Alexandria. In Elizabeth and Zechariah's case, they seemed prepared to stay married and childless, although Elizabeth laments her shame in infertility.[46] In both cases, the underlying presumption is that a married couple has the duty to bear children.

Making Sense of the Literature

The picture produced from these writers is not descriptive, but prescriptive. As such, we must be careful in interpreting its information as precisely replicating what was happening all around them. We must ask ourselves both what really took place in women's lives and why a particular source would present women's lives as it did. What criteria might be useful in determining a historical detail from its prescriptive surroundings? The reader's own perceptions of what could take place play a role in recreating history, but certain guidelines are also useful. First, a reader should note any statement that seems contrary to the flow of the argument. Such admissions might reveal the historical reality against which the author is writing. For example, Ben Sira speaks about watching over a daughter at all times and keeping her within the house. Philo does the same. Yet Ben Sira cautions his male readers not to look at a virgin (Sir. 9:5). This suggests that his admonition to fathers to keep their daughters under lock and key was not always followed, or else no man could gaze upon a virgin. Second, if the author's tone sounds defensive, perhaps that indicates he is losing a social battle. Looking again at Sirach, we read a rather lewd comment about an unwatched daughter offering herself to any passing man. His coarse remarks accuse the daughter of "opening her quiver to any arrow" (Sir. 26:12). Such a bawdy sexual innuendo seems misplaced in his otherwise staid discourse, which suggests heated passion (pun intended) on this issue. Perhaps in his context, daughters participated in the wider culture, including in venues where men were present, thus offending Ben Sira's sensibilities.

Moreover, we must consider that these authors spoke for and to the elite (or those who interacted with the elite) of the population. Their expectations for women's behaviors, therefore, might have applied primarily or even exclusively to those of the upper class, who made up a fraction of the population. Finally, these Jewish men, well educated and articulate, had their own agendas in writing. They present their own picture of how life should be, and might even offer hints of how life really was, but they do so within a larger enterprise. Discussions about women/wives are part of a larger drama instructing male readers on how to behave in elite society (Sirach) or how to understand

---

46. Even if Luke is placing these thoughts on Elizabeth's lips, it still provides evidence that an early Christian writer believed that at least some Jews (priestly families?) believed childlessness to be a social stigma.

Scripture (Philo), for example. Prescriptions about women are not an end in themselves but serve to advance a larger argument on male comportment. Like detectives, the modern reader must sift through the few clues within the prescriptive writings to discover bits and pieces of life as it was really lived by women at this time.

Endogamy and Polygyny

Jewish marriage arguably could be distinguished from non-Jewish marriages in two ways: Jewish concern with endogamy, as compared to the Roman focus on status and rank,[47] and the acceptance of polygyny. Endogamy is marriage within a specific social group, such as a clan or extended family. In general, the case is made by numerous Jewish authors that their group, *Ioudaioi*, should marry each other. It is important to note that the label "Jew" at this time does not denote merely religious sentiments but also cultural or ethnic identity. The book of Tobit stands as a prominent example of this concern. Tobit notes that he married within his family, and wants his son to do likewise (Tob. 4:12–13). Sarah prays that a kinsman would marry her (3:15), and the angel Raphael assures Tobias that as her only relative, he should take her hand (6:11). Sarah's father also supports the marriage of relatives (7:10, 12). Judith as well declares that she married her kin (Jdt. 8:2). The pseudepigraphic work *Jubilees*, likely written in the third or second century BC, in retelling the Genesis story identifies a wife as kin when her family history is not available. Several copies of the book were found at Qumran, indicating that at least parts of it were judged important to this group. A sectarian work from Qumran, 4QMMT, pushes endogamy even further by demanding that priests marry only women from priestly families.[48] This requirement was not universally held, as Philo indicated that priests can marry women from nonpriestly families, with the exception of the high priest.[49] Philo reveals his thoughts about endogamy in his remarks that a daughter should be married within her tribe. He reasons that this will keep her dowry portion within the larger tribal unit, reflecting perhaps either the ancient tribal land allotments assigned to each of Israel's twelve tribes or her family's ancestral lands.[50]

It is difficult to say whether the literary evidence reflects actual Jewish communities' decisions to marry only Jews. The discussion within the literature about endogamy often related to boundary issues between Jews and gentiles. Endogamy was a useful topos in distinguishing Jewish marriage from gentile.

47. Yet see Plutarch, *Mor.* 289d–e = *Quaest. rom.* 108, who wonders at the Romans' reluctance toward endogamy. Greeks practiced endogamy by encouraging marriage between uncle and niece, to preserve the family fortunes.
48. 4QMMT 75–82.
49. Philo, *Spec.* 1.110–11.
50. Philo, *Spec.* 2.125–36.

As such, it is difficult to say with any certainty how frequently Jews married non-Jews.[51] In the book of Acts, Timothy has a Jewish mother and a gentile father (Acts 16:1), perhaps an exception that proved the rule. And gentiles remarked, unfavorably at times, about Jews preferring to marry other Jews. For example, Tacitus acknowledges that Jews practiced endogamy, but discredits the tradition, declaring that "as a race, they [Jews] are prone to lust, they abstain from intercourse (*concubitu*) with foreign women; yet among themselves nothing is unlawful (*inlicitum*)."[52]

A second distinctive is the Jewish practice of polygyny, a practice wherein a husband is married to more than one wife simultaneously. If a husband has only two wives at one time the relationship can be called "bigamous." This custom was not recognized by Rome. We cannot say how widespread this practice was, but the Babatha archives[53] reveal that Babatha entered a bigamous relationship with a man named Judas who was already married to a woman named Miriam. This contract was written in Aramaic. Judas's daughter's marriage contract was in Greek, indicating that he could enact a Greek contract if he so chose. It seems probable that Judas and Babatha's contract was in Aramaic because they knew a Roman court would not entertain their marriage contract. Further support for the practice is found in Josephus, who admits that polygyny was part of Israel's past and lists contemporary examples such as Herod Archelaus and Herod Antipas.[54]

Some Jews, however, spoke out against polygyny. The Essenes at Qumran in their Damascus Document deride the "builders of the wall" (perhaps the Pharisees or maybe all other Jews) as practicing polygyny,[55] alluding to Leviticus 18:18 with the phrase "taking two wives in their lives" and interpreting it as forbidding polygyny.[56] They claim such a practice is contrary to Genesis 1:27, "male and female he created them," and to the example set by Noah in gathering animals two by two. The Temple Scroll from Qumran likewise supports a ban on polygyny.[57] The Septuagint seemed to critique polygyny

51. Satlow remarks, "Because these issues carried symbolic value, it is impossible to move from the quantity or quality of support for endogamy or condemnations of intermarriages to historical conclusions regarding the scope of the phenomenon" (*Jewish Marriage in Antiquity*, 146).

52. Tacitus, *Historiae* 5.5.2 (trans. C. H. Moore and J. Jackson, LCL).

53. For a full discussion see chapter 3. See Naphtali Lewis, Yigael Yadin, and Jonas C. Greenfield, eds., *The Documents from the Bar Kokhba Period in the Cave of Letters*, Judean Desert Studies 2 (Jerusalem: Israel Exploration Society, 1989). A translation and brief discussion is also found in Ross S. Kraemer, ed., *Women's Religions in the Greco-Roman World: A Sourcebook*, rev. ed. (Oxford: Oxford University Press, 2004), 143–52.

54. Josephus, *Ant.* 17.350.

55. CD IV, 20–V, 6.

56. CD IV, 20–21.

57. 11QT LVII, 15–19. For a discussion of Qumran texts, see David Instone-Brewer, *Divorce and Remarriage in the Bible: The Social and Literary Context* (Grand Rapids: Eerdmans, 2002), 61–65.

in its emendation of the Hebrew text of Genesis 2:24. Whereas the Hebrew reads "they shall become one flesh," the LXX adds, "they *two* shall become one flesh." This gloss is also attested in the Samaritan Pentateuch, the Syriac Peshitta, and the Vulgate, and is used in Matthew 19:5; Mark 10:8; and 1 Corinthians 6:16.[58]

Marriage Ideals in Christian Writings

Commitment, fidelity, and endogamy are perhaps the central marriage ideals found in New Testament writings. These differ little from their Jewish counterparts and are similar in many ways to the larger Roman culture, with the exception of endogamy (though Greek culture did lean in this direction). Unique to some Christian circles and a few Jewish sects such as Philo's Therapeutics and the Essenes at Qumran was a stress on celibate singleness as a laudable alternative to marriage. Yet even this tradition was not a Second Temple Jewish innovation but had its proponents among Greco-Roman philosophers. Nevertheless, the option of celibacy opened doors to Christian women, primarily in terms of autonomy. The ascetic movement flourished in the second century, but this development is beyond our project's focus. Hints of what was to come can be found in the mention of the apostle Philip's four daughters who were unmarried prophetesses (Acts 21:9) and in the order of widows noted in 1 Timothy 5:9.

Negative Portraits of Wives from Jewish and Non-Jewish Sources

Perhaps nothing captures the negative mind-set about marriage more than the oft-quoted barb from the censor Quintus Caecilius Metellus Macedonicus (late second century BC): "Since, however, nature has ordained that we cannot have a really harmonious life with our wives but that we cannot have any sort of life at all without them, we ought to consider our long-term welfare rather than brief pleasure."[59] As noted above, Josephus declares that "the woman, says the law, is in all things inferior to the man. Let her accordingly be submissive, not for her humiliation, but that she may be directed, for the authority has been given by God to the man."[60] His statement locates the woman's inferiority not in "nature" but in the Jewish law; however, this law is not identified by Josephus, nor can modern interpreters discover to what

58. Instone-Brewer, *Divorce and Remarriage*, 61. See also Pseudo-Phocylides 205, "Do not add marriage to marriage, calamity to calamity," as a possible reference against polygyny.

59. Translation in Rawson, "Roman Family," 11. The saying is quoted by Livy, *Periochae 59*, and Aulus Gellius, *Noct. att.* 1.6.1–6.

60. Josephus, *C. Ap.* 2.201 (trans. H. St. John Thackeray, LCL).

he was referring. Perhaps in fact there is no specific law per se, but rather this is his interpretation of the Jewish law as a whole. In that case, the lens he used to interpret the law was likely influenced heavily by the wider society's attitudes toward wives, expressed in Metellus's quotation above.

Using "Wife" as a Device to Critique Other Topics

Extensive critique of the wicked or lazy wife permeates both Jewish and gentile writings. But since we cannot assume that the ideal wife existed as other than society's social creation, so too should we hesitate to accept descriptions of wicked wives at face value. Male writers used the topos of marriage to speak about social order and exploited the wicked wife's stereotyped behaviors as a foil for discussing men's actions. Why should a man put up with a disruptive wife or take a chance that his bride will be a nagging bore? To this question both Jewish and gentile male writers would respond that duty to the *polis* outweighs any personal sufferings.

An example of how wives' misbehavior was used to argue an unrelated topic is found in Seneca's *De beneficiis* 3.15–16. He defends the status quo concerning how ungrateful clients are handled—they are not prosecuted by law, but judged by the community. Specifically, he was not in favor of criminalizing failure to repay debts owed by clients to their patron. Seneca argues that the bestower of a gift is like a god, and so should not require the legal system to make sure that the beneficiary of the gift is dutifully respectful and grateful. In fact, he argues that involving the legal system would only increase the number of disrespectful clients. To shore up his argument, he points to the newly implemented policy of listing divorces publicly. He howls that divorce became so well known as to be ubiquitous, and hence now all manner of women are divorcing. His point, however, is not to discuss divorce, but to convince the legal establishment that publicly punishing men who are ungrateful to their benefactors would dull the moral senses of the masses. The link between the two topics might be the issue of proper decorum—clients and wives should be subservient and grateful to their patrons and husbands, and should shun behavior that brings shame upon themselves and their social circle. The bottom line for Seneca is not divorce per se but social norms on debt repayment and gratitude to benefactors among men. He is arguing a case about men's behaviors and chooses rhetoric and hyperbole about wives' immorality to force home his point. Therefore, we cannot discern from his comments whether many or few women are divorcing, because he is using divorce and the "fact" of women's susceptibility to act foolishly or wickedly as a backdrop to discuss another subject entirely.

Using "Wife" to Control Family Stability

Failure of the wife to heed her husband greatly concerned the Jewish writer Ben Sira. For ten highly charged verses, he criticizes and condemns a wife's iniquities. Indictments include her garrulousness (when her husband is quiet) and her wealth (when her husband is poorer than she). Apparently Ben Sira is most upset over a woman who with a "boldness of speech" does not "go as you [the husband] direct" (Sir. 25:25–26). In this she is compared to Eve; "from a woman sin had its beginning, and because of her we all die" (25:24). The verb "to be" (rendered "had" in this verse) is not present in the Greek and must be supplied by translators. Scholars disagree about the tense of this verb, whether Ben Sira is reflecting on a specific woman from the past, namely Eve, or whether he is thinking about a wicked wife. The term for "wife" in Greek is the same as the term for "woman" (*gynē*), making the translation decision more difficult. The dominant interpretation, reflected in the translation above, suggests Ben Sira argues that the origin of sin and death rests with Eve. Another theory rejects the notion that Ben Sira is here alluding to Eve,[61] for in Sirach 25 and 26 *gynē* overwhelmingly refers to a wife. In this scenario, Ben Sira is speaking with hyperbolic intensity about the unsubmissive wife's danger to her husband's spiritual and mental health. Such a woman can drive a man to an early grave.

Perhaps we need not choose between the two theories but rather conclude that Ben Sira was deliberately ambiguous in phrasing his thoughts. He wanted to caution husbands against the perilous misdeeds and inclinations of their wives, as well as buttress his claims in the archetypal female sinner, Eve. This suggestion is strengthened by noting that the main concern expressed here is a woman's speech usurping the husband's authority. Throughout 25:15–26:18, Ben Sira reiterates the dangers of an impudent wife who speaks rather than holds her tongue. Such behavior directly challenges the status quo, which demands obedience and submission from the wife for the sake of the family's (husband's) honor. Ben Sira links bold speech with defiant sexual behavior, wherein "the haughty stare betrays an unchaste wife; her eyelids give her away" (Sir. 26:9). Bold speech and bold stare—both challenge the superiority of the husband and signal the promiscuity of the woman.

A wisdom poem from Qumran reflects a similar connection. This poem begins by condemning the words of the wicked woman and ends with a detailed description of her promiscuity. "She [. . .] utters futility and in [. . .]. She is always looking for depravities, [and] whets the word[s of her mouth, . . .] and implies insult, and is [bu]sy leading the community astray with non[sense]."[62] Toward the end of the short poem, it reads, "In the city squares she veils herself, and in the gates of the village she stations herself, and there is no-one who can ke[ep her] from (her) incessant [fornicat]ing."[63] The last line of the poem explicitly connects promiscuity and false speech, "to sidetrack man

61. Jack Levison, "Is Eve to Blame? A Contextual Analysis of Sirach 25:24," *Catholic Biblical Quarterly* 47 (1985): 617–23.

62. 4Q184 1 1–2.

63. 4Q184 1 12–13.

into the ways of the pit, and seduce the sons of men with smooth words."[64] The pattern is similar to the Seductress portrayed in Proverbs 7, though in the biblical text, the woman herself speaks, while in 4Q184 and Sirach, even the woman's voice is taken away.

Ben Sira adds a new element that threatens the delicate balance of honor/shame—a woman's wealth. He does not tie wealth and promiscuity together; instead, he suggests that even as a bold wife dishonors, so too a wife with more money than her husband shames him. Gender and wealth serve to establish the precarious social structure upon which the young scribe attempts to build his life. Any unbalance in the social order threatens to dislodge his social standing, and thus his livelihood. And yet Ben Sira walks a fine line between condemning wealth outright and encouraging enough wealth to weather financial setbacks that come with the scribe's lot as a retainer. Wealth offers social respectability, though too much of it casts doubt on the person's righteousness before God. In the same way, a good wife brings social respectability, while a wife with too much wealth (or too "head strong") puts the scribe's honor in jeopardy.

Thus both gender and wealth provide ways to talk about self-identity and insiders/outsiders. Within the honor/shame culture that was the Mediterranean world at this time, a man's honor was most vulnerable at its weakest points—the women in his family and the friends he chose. A discussion about women is also a discussion about the men who are honored or shamed by the former's behavior. Likewise, a man's friends brought him honor, and the judicial use of wealth increased his honor among his peers. Dishonorable women and disingenuous friends could with one stroke ruin a young, up-and-coming scribe's honor and plunge his livelihood into a tailspin.

Excursus: Roman Dining Habits and Baths

Sirach reflects the widespread concern for preserving women's modesty, usually by confining them (literally or figuratively) indoors or within the family fold. A literary picture is thus drawn of upper-class women living out their days and nights separate from all men except their immediate family (brothers, husbands, and fathers). Women who step outside this tightly drawn circle are condemned as immodest or worse. Two hotly contested arenas where women's presence was remarked upon and might cause a sensation are public dining and Roman baths. Modern historians, taking at face value ancient writers' invectives against women in these public places, have constructed an image of Hellenistic and Roman elite and upper-class matrons sequestered from these important social institutions, while at the same time stressing the presence of prostitutes and female slaves. A more measured and nuanced reading, however, suggests

64. 4Q184 1 17. See Florentino García Martínez and Eibert J. C. Tigchelaar, eds., *The Dead Sea Scrolls Study Edition* (Grand Rapids: Eerdmans, 1997), 1:377.

A dining scene from a funerary relief from Kyzikos in Mysia (Photo courtesy of Philip Harland)

that women from all classes and social statuses including wives participated at banquets and enjoyed the baths—in both cases with men present.

Dining in the Greco-Roman World

Dining in the Greco-Roman world was a key cultural channel for social engagement, status reinforcement, religious expression, and entertainment. In the second century AD, Plutarch records a Roman expression asserting that dining alone is not dining, but merely eating.[65] He remarks in his "table talks" that his worthy goal is to revive the recording of dinner conversations and to bury as a thing of the past the drinking party.[66] Then, as now, dinner invitations were extended for birthdays, weddings, and religious festivals, as well as gatherings with friends and clients. At any of these meals, even entertaining friends or celebrating an anniversary, the gods would be propitiated. Moreover, even family celebrations such as birthdays might be held in a temple, giving most gatherings some religious overtones. Though women were present in all these cases, there is less information about their presence in gatherings with

65. Plutarch, *Quaestionum convivialum* 697c.
66. Plutarch, *Quaestionum convivialum* 612d–e.

friends and clients.[67] This should not surprise us, as women patrons were fewer in number than male patrons.[68]

HISTORY OF DINING

Men and women participated in these meals, with men reclining and women usually reclining, though at times sitting upright. Such seating arrangements signaled a shift from the customs of ancient Greece, where, generally speaking, only men and *hetaerae* or prostitutes were present for the symposium that followed the meal (*deipnon*), though discussion continues on the extent of ancient Greek women's seclusion. The symposium or after-meal festivities might be either quite rowdy, with wine flowing in abundance, or sedate and dedicated to philosophical debate. The *hetaerae* would sing, dance, and play music, or would discuss the philosophical or ethical topic of the evening, depending on the mood of the event. In all cases, the women provided sexual sport as well; they reclined next to men, a position that indicated their status as prostitutes.

By the second century BC, however, men brought their wives to dinner parties. For example, Ben Sira urges the young scribe to be careful at banquets, including the admonition never to dine with another man's wife, "or revel with her at wine; or your heart may turn aside [or be inclined] to her" (Sir. 9:9). Later in the work he gives explicit directives on the proper manner of eating and participation in conversation (31:12–32:13), suggesting that his readers attend dinner parties with enough frequency to make their comportment a matter of concern. His mention of wine here implies that the women might stay through the symposium. Again, Cornelius Nepos, writing in the last quarter of the first century BC, distinguished Roman dining etiquette from the Greek: "For instance, what Roman would blush to take his wife to a dinner-party? What matron does not frequent the front rooms of her dwelling and show herself in public?"[69] This author's Roman pride notwithstanding, the scant information from the Hellenistic period, supported by the more extensive material from the imperial Roman period, indicates that more and more, married women joined their husbands at public meals and reclined while eating, though in some cases they sat upright next to their husbands.[70] The

67. Angela Standhartinger, "Women in Early Christian Meal Gatherings: Discourse and Reality," trans. Martin and Nancy Lukens-Rumscheidt (paper presented at the Society of Biblical Literature Annual Meeting, Philadelphia, PA, November 2005), http://www.philipharland.com/meals/AngelaStandhartingerWomeninMeals.pdf (accessed April 15, 2009). For additional photographs and papers on Greco-Roman meal settings, see http://www.philipharland.com/meals/GrecoRomanMealsSeminar.htm.
68. For a discussion of patronage, see chapter 9.
69. Cornelius Nepos, *Praefatio* 6–7 (trans. J. C. Rolfe, LCL). For a full discussion, see Kathleen E. Corley, *Private Women, Public Meals: Social Conflict in the Synoptic Tradition* (Peabody, MA: Hendrickson, 1993), 28–30.
70. Dennis E. Smith, *From Symposium to Eucharist* (Minneapolis: Fortress, 2003), 43. See also Treggiari, *Roman Marriage*, 422–24.

shift cannot be charted as a linear progression over time, nor can we assume that all locations practiced the same dining habits; but the cumulative evidence indicates that at given times and places, women participated with men in the important social ritual that was the Greco-Roman banquet.

Dining Posture and Seating Arrangements

A modern reading might miss the social status significance attached to the reclining position. It was initially seen as the hallmark of a free male. In such a position, one needed to be served, for only one arm was available for eating. This implied that the person reclining had servants, which was a status symbol. Moreover, where one sat also telegraphed status. The usual layout for a dinner was a U-shaped seating arrangement around a central table. Those of lowest status sat farthest from the seat of honor. The sitting position, over against reclining, was seen by many as a woman's posture. Thus reclining women were declaring a high social status.

Yet high social status was not the only value communicated by the woman's posture while dining. The ancient Greek practice that identified a reclining woman as a prostitute remained in the cultural memory, and so during the later years of the Roman Republic and into the imperial period, the seated position became a shorthand way of indicating a virtuous woman. Briefly put, the reclining position signaled that the man with whom the woman shared the dining couch was a sexual partner.[71] Thus, if a matron was reclining with her husband, her virtue was untarnished, for all expected that she and her husband were sexual partners. Again, if her husband reclined with a prostitute, no shame would attach to him or to his wife, for the husband was not censured for extramarital sex (except with another married woman). This connection between reclining and licit sexual relations helps explain why, well into the fourth century AD, chaste women and matrons were sometimes portrayed in art and literature as seated, when by this point in history, most matrons were reclining when eating.[72]

It is unclear how frequently women attended meals sponsored by various local clubs and associations, meals that female patrons would presumably have hosted. Patrons of clubs, trade guilds, and private funerary collegia could enjoy a meal with their clients. Female patrons were honored at meals, or served as hosts, reclining as did the men (and women) of the group. Wealthy patronesses might not partake in all the festivities of the evening, but again the individual situation likely determined the patroness's level of participation. Many of these clubs drew members from slaves or freedmen/women.

71. Matthew B. Roller, *Dining Posture in Ancient Rome: Bodies, Values and Status* (Princeton: Princeton University Press, 2006), 103–5.
72. Osiek and MacDonald (*A Woman's Place*, 160) note that the artistic depictions outlasted the actual practice, for probably by the first century AD married women reclined beside their husbands at formal banquets.

Unlike Roman matrons, women in these classes were (or had been at one time) sexually available, thus there were fewer social constraints prohibiting drinking and carousing. Three papyrus invitations sent by women for dinners celebrating religious holidays have been found.[73] At these particular events the guests would recline, so presumably the female hosts would as well.[74] The evidence points to active involvement in public meals by at least some women, including elite women who served as patrons.

Dining Habits and Social Protocols

Groups might define themselves over against another group based on their decorum at the dining table. Philo, in describing the Therapeutics, gives a detailed description of their dining habits. He explains that men and women reclined in the same room,[75] but the men were on the right side, the women on the left. After the meal, Philo explains that though the men and women sing hymns and celebrate together, they are "drunk" not with wine but with the lofty pleasures of sober worship.[76] Philo reveals that these Jewish women philosophers participated not only in the group's meal but also in the symposium or after-dinner activities. He was at pains to show that the women's behavior was chaste, sober, and edifying and thus promoted the dignity of the entire group. For our purposes, he offers an example of Jewish women participating freely with Jewish men in religious meals. The same dynamics operated for Jewish families at Sabbath meals and Passover celebrations.

An interesting question is whether women reclined while dining with Jesus. If one assumes that within the Jewish communities in Galilee and Judea reclining women were seen as morally suspect, a case could be made that in fact women dining with Jesus reclined. The Synoptic Gospels portray Jesus as eating with tax collectors and sinners (Mark 2:15–16).[77] Matthew goes one step further and explicitly defines "sinner" as "prostitute" (21:31–32). Earlier in the Gospel, Matthew notes that Jesus ate with or reclined while

73. P.Coll.Youtie 1.52 reads, "Herias asks you to dine in the (banquet) room of the Sarapeion at a kline of the Lord Sarapis tomorrow, which is 11th, at the 9th hour"; P.Fouad 76 reads, "Sarapous asks you to dine at the offering in honour of Kyria Isis in the house, tomorrow, namely the 29th, from the 9th hour"; see also P.Oxy. 4539. See G. H. R. Horsley, ed., *New Documents Illustrating Early Christianity: A Review of the Greek Inscriptions and Papyri Published in 1976* (North Ryde, Australia: Ancient History Documentary Research Centre, Macquarie University, 1981), 1:6–7.

74. John Fotopoulos, *Food Offered to Idols in Roman Corinth: A Social-Rhetorical Reconsideration* (Tübingen: Mohr Siebeck, 2003), 104.

75. This festive meal is not the Passover; however, in the latter case it was customary for Jews to recline as a mark of freedom from slavery in Egypt.

76. For an extensive discussion of the Therapeutics' dining practices, see Joan E. Taylor, *Jewish Women Philosophers of First-Century Alexandria: Philo's 'Therapeutae' Reconsidered* (Oxford: Oxford University Press, 2003).

77. For a useful discussion of this accusation against Jesus, see Joseph B. Modica, "Jesus as Glutton and Drunkard," in *Who Do My Opponents Say That I Am?* ed. Scot McKnight and Joseph B. Modica (London: T&T Clark, 2008), 50–75.

dining with tax collectors and sinners. If we assume that the sinners noted in Matthew 9:10 are to be understood as the same type of people in 21:31,[78] then it may be that at least on occasion he ate with women reclining. However, a few cautionary notes are in order. First, we must remember that the woman's dining posture spoke both of her social status and her moral virtue in a complex social matrix. Merely noting the reclining position does not necessarily suggest immorality. Perhaps this is why Matthew was at pains to establish the connection between "sinner" and reclining women. Again, we cannot presuppose that in Galilee and Judea, Jews would have assumed that any woman reclining at a meal was a prostitute; their experience at Sabbath and Passover celebrations would suggest otherwise. Again, some assume that a reclining position indicates a higher social status, since free wealthy men dine as a rule in a reclined position. Therefore, if the Jews followed Roman custom, they would not have been shocked if a woman of high status reclined with Jesus. We cannot assume, conversely, that a seated position necessarily indicated a lower social status or less influence within a group. Both the reclining and the seated position communicated the moral status of the woman, as noted above. Therefore, if it were shown that women did not recline at meals with Jesus, that fact would not be an indication that women were denied equality within the group. And if at some meals female disciples reclined, that posture in and of itself would not necessitate the label "sexually immoral."

Roman Baths

As with public dining, so too with the baths, people sought status and prestige by associating with those above them on the social ladder. Martial, in a clever take on a fellow desperate for a dinner invitation, describes the man pestering his targeted host at the baths. There is no escaping him, laments Martial, "when you pick up your towel which is dirtier than a child's bib, he will exclaim that it is whiter than snow. While you are combing your thick hair, he will say that you are styling Achilles' locks. . . . He will praise everything, he will marvel at everything, until finally, having endured his thousand tedious ploys, you say, 'Come and have dinner with me.'"[79]

HISTORY OF ROMAN BATHS

Roman baths were a ubiquitous part of the urban landscape.[80] While the ancient Greek gymnasium had only cold water to refresh the male athletes,

---

78. Corley, *Private Women, Public Meals*, 152. She contends that neither Mark nor Luke explicitly portrays women reclining with Jesus at meals.

79. Martial, *Epigrammata* 12.82. Translation in Shelton, *As the Romans Did*, 316.

80. For an excellent detailed history of Roman baths, see Inge Nielsen, *Thermae et Balnea: The Architecture and Cultural History of Roman Public Baths*, 2 vols. (Aarhus, Denmark: Aarhus University Press, 1990), esp. vol. 1, *Texts*.

by the first century BC, Romans had developed the hypocaust, a technology that allowed hot air to flow from a wood-burning furnace under a false floor held up by brick or cement pillars and between the double walls of the *caldarium* or hot bath space in the Roman bath.[81] This allowed for a hot bath and a warm bath (*tepidarium*). The old way of bathing, which involved individual hot water hip baths, took water from cisterns or wells. With the development of the aqueduct, towns had much more water available for bathing, and the bathing establishments grew in size and configuration. Instead of individual bathtubs, pools were built. And with the hypocaust system, the water could be maintained at the proper warmth more easily than heating individual bathtubs. With the changes of technology also came changes in practices, accompanied by debates on the morality of communal bathing. Sources throughout this period indicate either with condemnation or with acceptance that at least some public baths were establishments of mixed bathing.

Each day, usually in the afternoon, Roman women and men would make their way to the baths. Storing their clothes in the dressing room *(apodyterium)*, sometimes to be guarded by their slave, they might exercise in the large courtyard *(palaestra)*—running, wrestling,[82] lifting weights—or they might swim in the adjacent pool. After their exercise, they would get an oil massage and have the sweat scraped off before entering the baths, often beginning in the warm bath, moving to the hot bath, and finishing with the cold bath. People did not hurry the process; they enjoyed the lovely architecture and relaxing environment. Several authors note the luxurious materials used, such as marble and porphyry, and the beautiful appointments, such as marble statues and large windows.[83] Since entry fees were very inexpensive, people from all walks of life congregated at the baths, and hawkers sold food and drink. While the inner rooms of the bath might be more sedate, Seneca (first century AD), who lived above the baths for a time, bemoaned to a friend that he got no reading done due to the noise of athletes grunting, swimmers splashing, the masseur slapping his client—and perhaps the worst—a fellow who sings in the baths.[84] The pulse of the city ran through the baths.

MEN AND WOMEN BATHING TOGETHER

In the early part of the Roman Republic, baths had segregated facilities, as evidenced by the forum baths in both Pompeii and Herculaneum.[85] Within

81. For a description and photographs of Roman hypocausts, see http://www.ideal-heating .com/article.php?a=16 (accessed April 15, 2009).
82. Clement of Alexandria notes that women should not be encouraged to wrestle (*Paedagogus* 3.10).
83. Lucian, *Hippias* 508; Seneca, *Epistulae morales* 56.1, 2. See Shelton, *As the Romans Did*, 314–15, for translation.
84. Seneca, *Epistulae morales* 56.1, 2. See Shelton, *As the Romans Did*, 314.
85. See also Varro, *De lingua latina* 9.6.8; Vitruvius, *De architectura* 5.10.1.

The *caldarium* in Pompeii's forum bath; the basin was filled with cold water to refresh the hot bathers. (Photo courtesy of John Dalkin/flickr.com)

a single complex, there were men's cold, tepid, and hot bathing rooms and women's tepid and hot rooms. It seems that in some places women did not have a cold bathing room. The men's and women's hot bathing rooms shared a dividing wall to maximize the furnace's effectiveness. During the first century AD, however, an innovation in the bath's architecture modified the structure such that a single set of rooms was created around an axis. Numerous baths were built across the empire with axial symmetry, including the Capito baths in Melitus (ca. AD 47–52). The more rectangular configuration lent itself to a single set of hot, tepid, and cold rooms. The Suburban baths at Hercula-neum, completed before Vesuvius's lava flow covered the town, also had one set of rooms for both sexes. And this building was not unique: seventy-one baths from the first century had one set of rooms, while four to six had two sets of rooms.[86] These numbers suggest that men and women were bathing together. A ribald graffiti written by two men boasts sexual liaisons with two women at the Suburban baths—does this crowing carry any historical information?[87]

For help with that question, we turn to literary evidence. The material sup-ports the archaeological data: men and women bathed together, and women

86. Figures taken from Nielsen, *Thermae et Balnea*, 2:2–47. Discussed in Roy Bowen Ward, "Women in Roman Baths," *HTR* 85.2 (1992): 133–34.

87. Joseph Jay Deiss, *Herculaneum: Italy's Buried Treasure*, rev. ed. (Malibu, CA: J. Paul Getty Museum, 1989), 146–48.

from all social strata enjoyed the baths.[88] Romans bathed nude (*nudus*), but this term could imply the removal of regular clothes and the wearing of scanty or immodest attire. This type of dress (or lack of it) would have made sense since most people availed themselves of the baths after exercising; bathing complexes usually had a gymnasium area within their building. Some authors approve of mixed bathing. For example, Ovid, while happy that women are present, is frustrated that certain matrons pay him no attention; Martial laments the same.[89] While Ovid notes that women with slaves do not engage in sexual activity with them, he hints that perhaps some women have sexual encounters at the baths; he advises a young woman, occupied by holding her guardian's clothes, to slip away and lose herself in the many baths for an amorous tryst.[90] Martial's epigrams leave little to the imagination, with his rather explicit descriptions of sexual behavior at the baths. Neither author is writing a news story, however, so their bawdy observations might be intended primarily to titillate. From these accounts it is difficult to determine historical details. But in Martial's case, the effectiveness of his epigrams is based on the "shared cultural and social experiences of its audience."[91] Martial does not satirize the *presence* of women and men together at the baths; rather he lampoons certain behaviors and attitudes. From these examples, it seems clear that some women used the same baths that men used, and at the same time. Moreover, these women were not prostitutes, although clearly prostitutes would have been plying their trade here.

As with public dining, therefore, the evidence points to men and women, even matrons, participating in bathing together. Yet some Romans expressed deep reservations about the practices and customs. In the early first century AD, Pliny the Elder commented disapprovingly that women bathed with men and noted that they did so wearing no clothing.[92] But a well-bred matron saw what was prudent and honorable to see, and ignored the rest—just as the empress Livia once remarked, after inadvertently seeing naked men, that they

88. For a careful examination of the evidence, see Ward, "Women in Roman Baths," 125–47. See also Garrett G. Fagan, *Bathing in Public in the Roman World* (Ann Arbor: University of Michigan Press, 2002), 26–28; and Thomas A. McGinn, *The Economy of Prostitution in the Roman World: A Study of Social History and the Brothel* (Ann Arbor: University of Michigan Press, 2004), who writes, "the absence of a strict polarity of virtue and vice in the baths is precisely what generated both intense interest and criticism" (25).
89. Martial, *Epigrammata* 7.35.
90. Ovid, *Ars* 3.639–40. Juvenal mockingly describes a matron who leaves a dinner party to go exercise and enjoy the baths, including a sexual massage with oil, before returning to the banquet (*Sat.* 6.419–25). He castigates the woman's morals in pursuing sexual pleasure outside of marriage and her lack of attention to her banquet guests, making them wait while she enjoys the baths. But her presence at the baths is not at issue. Unfortunately, Juvenal does not make clear whether the bath is used by both men and women.
91. Fagan, *Bathing in Public*, 13–14.
92. Pliny the Elder, *Nat.* 29.26; 33.153.

were to her as no more than statues.[93] Quintilian too comments about women bathing with men, suggesting that men read no more into a woman bathing in mixed company than if she has a close friendship with a man—neither implies she is committing adultery.[94] Since only a freeborn woman or a citizen could commit adultery, Quintilian is not speaking about prostitutes. Also from the mid-first century AD, Seneca links bathing activities with the dangerous (contemporary) pursuit of pleasure, drawing a contrast with the days gone by when sturdy Roman virtues of hard physical work, valor in battle, and proper propitiation of the gods ruled society.[95] He is most upset at the ostentatious baths built by freedmen—their lack of status coupled with their vast wealth upsets the proper social hierarchy.[96] A generation later, Plutarch bewails the changes in Roman morals from that of times past when Cato the Elder refused to go to the baths with his son, since displaying one's nakedness before family members was viewed as indecent. Much to Plutarch's chagrin, in his day, men were unashamed of going naked at the baths, even when women were present.[97] Plutarch's complaint suggests that a range of possible behaviors was acceptable, with each person or family negotiating the tricky waters of social engagement carefully.

Cassius Dio remarks that the Emperor Hadrian, ruling early in the second century AD, commanded that men and women bathe separately.[98] Yet this statement derives from an eleventh-century paraphrase of the work, calling into question its usefulness in reconstructing earlier history.[99] If the account is reliable, it means that through the first century, men and women practiced mixed bathing. Also from Hadrian's time, an inscription from Lusitania (modern Portugal) lists the regulations of procurators of the imperial mines, which included that women use the baths early in the day, while men follow in the afternoon. Many scholars have generalized this inscription to represent Roman practice throughout the empire, ignoring the numerous indications that at other places and times, men and women bathed together.[100] While the New Testament does not mention baths, early Christian writers talk about how gentile converts should negotiate the public, mixed-bathing establishments. The earliest to write on this was Clement of Alexandria, who recognizes that

93. Cassius Dio (*Hist. Rom.* 58.2.4) does not mention the incident happening at the baths; the men were probably captured enemy soldiers.
94. Quintilian, *Inst.* 5.9.14.
95. Seneca, *De vita beata* 7.3.
96. Seneca, *Epistulae morales* 86.6–7. For a discussion of Seneca, see Catherine Edwards, *Politics of Immorality in Ancient Rome* (Cambridge: Cambridge University Press, 1993).
97. Plutarch, *Cato Maior* 20.5.
98. Cassius Dio, *Hist. Rom.* 69.8.2.
99. Ward, "Women in Roman Baths," 139. The paraphrase is by Xiphilinus, a monk in Constantinople (see *Dio's Roman History*, trans. E. Cary, LCL [Cambridge, MA: Harvard University Press, 1914], 1:xxii–xxiii).
100. Ward, "Women in Roman Baths," 140–41.

men and women (rich and poor) bathed together. He cautioned new gentile converts to avoid bathing for lustful pleasure.[101] Instead he permits bathing for health and cleanliness only.[102] Tertullian, far from condemning the baths, writes that Christians participate in most of the social and economic institutions of the city, including attending the baths.[103]

Summary of Women's Dining and Bathing Habits

As we reflect on the practices of public dining and bathing, a rather clear picture emerges of women from all social spheres present and participating in these common and widespread cultural institutions. The rhetorical diatribes against matrons reclining at meals and attending the baths are, on close examination revealed to be thin and brittle. Literature, poems, and satire lambaste women's public presence (at least those with a high social status) in these two key areas, and charge them with immodesty, but the evidence overwhelmingly supports women, including matrons, engaged with men both while dining and at the baths. Women from every walk of life attended public meals, though a matron's experience would differ from a prostitute's. Women enjoyed the festivities of dinner parties, and if they were so inclined, participated in the discussions during the symposium. Female patrons received the honor due them by their clients and built social, economic, and political networks at dinner parties and at the baths.

Increasingly throughout the Greco-Roman age and extensively in the imperial period, women from all classes and social strata ventured out to the baths, where they participated in all the baths had to offer. Women took advantage of the pleasures associated with bathing, exercising, and massage, even as did their fathers, brothers, husbands, and male clients. Partaking of the baths was a key part of an elite Roman man's day, and we should not assume that wealthy patronesses, matrons, and widows, did not also congregate to enjoy the gossip, talk of politics, and hatch new business deals. At the risk of overstating the case, as we picture the Roman baths and dining practices, we might draw upon modern images of beaches populated by men and women, some with picnic lunches. The presence of women was taken for granted (although critiqued at times), then as now. As we will see in upcoming chapters, the forum and temples of every city[104] in the Greco-Roman world were filled with statues of women—goddesses, benefactors, imperial family members. Public inscriptions lauded the beloved wife. In short, women were present to the public eye in positive ways throughout the ancient city, and real women participated publicly in the city's daily activities.

101. Clement of Alexandria, *Paedagogus* 3.5.
102. Clement of Alexandria, *Paedagogus* 3.9.
103. Tertullian, *Apologeticus* 42.2.
104. Jerusalem and surrounding Judea are exempted.

Conclusion

"Man's best possession is a sympathetic wife," said Euripides.[105] But he also lamented, "Never say that marriage has more of joy than pain."[106] Such views reveal the paradoxical assessments that marriage as an institution is often an unpleasant necessity, but happiness can be found in a good wife. A virtuous wife offered great value to her family, husband, and children, and gained public commendation for her chastity, modesty, thriftiness, and handiwork. Augustus praised those senators who married and begot children with this word of encouragement: "For is there anything better than a wife who is chaste, domestic, a good housekeeper, a rearer of children; one to gladden you in health, to tend you in sickness; to be your partner in good fortune, to console you in misfortune; to restrain the mad passion of youth and to temper the unseasonable harshness of old age?"[107] The perfect wife obeyed her husband in everything, remained in his shadow, and preserved the family's honor. Yet wives could be blamed for husbands' personal calamities and social unrest. Not only was she often the butt of jokes and the center of malicious slander, but political maneuvering gone wrong could result in charges of adultery, leading to divorce, exile, or even death. Literary caricatures of a "new woman" titillated Roman readers and fueled the royal dynastic pursuit, but they offer little in the way of a realistic picture of Greco-Roman women. Jewish authors shared their non-Jewish counterparts' perspective for the most part, differing mainly in their promotion of endogamy and acceptance (in some quarters) of polygyny.

All of this leaves us wondering, what were real marriages and real wives like? How did real marriages work? What did real wives do? Those questions are the focus of the next chapter, as we examine evidence on the reality of married life for women in the Greco-Roman world.

105. Euripides, *Antigone*, fr. 164.
106. Euripides, *Alcestis*, stasimon 1.
107. Cassius Dio, *Hist. Rom.* 56.3 (trans. E. Cary, LCL).

3

Wives and the Realities of Marriage

For most women in the ancient world marriage was a passage from childhood to adulthood. Girls usually married in their teens,[1] and for many, marriage introduced motherhood. Marriage brought families together, cemented political alliances, advanced family honor and wealth—in other words, marriage in the Greco-Roman world involved much more than the husband and wife. The literary and epigraphic sources do not always present a consistent picture, and the situation among Jews might differ at points from Greco-Roman arrangements. In general, however, the image that emerges from the vantage point of the daughter is that she moves from her childhood home, based on an alliance arranged or approved of by her father (or guardian), to a marriage in which the husband has varying degrees of control over her property and wealth. Widowhood, divorce, and second marriages loomed large in a context where life expectancy was short (on average, twenty-five years) and where marriage alliances preserved and increased family wealth.

A survey of the evidence suggests that marriage in Early Judaism and first-century Christianity followed in large measure Greco-Roman custom. This included the father having significant control of both the (first) marriage and possible divorce of his daughter, as well as the custom of dowry payment from the bride's family to the groom. If a husband divorced his wife, or the father

1. The sources offer a range of ages. Ross Kraemer, "Typical and Atypical Jewish Family Dynamics: The Cases of Babatha and Berenice" in *Early Christian Families in Context: An Interdisciplinary Dialogue*, ed. David L. Balch and Carolyn Osiek (Grand Rapids: Eerdmans, 2003), 140–41. See also Susan Treggiari, "Divorce Roman Style: How Easy and How Frequent Was It?" in *Marriage, Divorce, and Children in Acient Rome*, ed. Beryl Rawson (Oxford: Clarendon, 1991), 32.

ended the marriage in favor of another (often more prestigious) match, the wife left with her dowry. Although gaining a handle on the numbers is difficult, it seems that divorce was relatively common in the Greco-Roman period and did not necessarily carry social stigma, although much of our information comes from elite families who jostled for political position using marriage to shore up their standing. Jewish and Christian sources suggest that divorce was also present within their communities. Rabbinic claims concerning marriage are difficult to assess, but a shift apparently occurred from a dowry system to one that required the groom to pay a fee if he divorced his wife. When this change occurred is a matter of debate, but my own sense is that the dowry custom predominated during the Greco-Roman period.

In general, women had some freedom to choose spouses or initiate divorce, but exceptions reveal a complex situation. On the one hand, if the father was still living, he usually arranged the marriage of his daughter, and either he or other male guardians oversaw her divorce proceedings or made sure her widow's assets were allotted to her. On the other hand, papyri evidence may indicate the possibility of women suing for divorce directly, while Roman practice seemed to permit a woman's male guardian or relative to sue for divorce on her behalf. Thus a wife was not entirely without recourse, but she was not afforded easy access to courts and the legal system.

Roman Marriage in the Greco-Roman Period

During the late Roman Republic when a daughter married, her father (or male relatives) retained control or authority (*manus*) over her. This arrangement was known as a *sine manu* marriage, that is, one that did not transfer authority over the daughter from the father to the husband.[2] A bride brought a dowry or sum of money/valuables with her into the marriage, and upon her husband's death or divorce, her dowry was returned to her. The practice of *sine manu* marriage was especially prevalent among elite Roman families. This system could protect a daughter from the whims of her husband and allow her to retain close ties with her blood family. She was capable of bringing wealth and honor to her family through the marriage alliance. Perhaps some women embraced their power to affect their family's social status and enjoyed their influence among their relations.

The husband was placed in a potentially vulnerable position, as his wife might be divorced from him if she or her father believed a better marriage could be arranged. To limit this possibility, the husband had every incentive to please his wife, and even more, please his father-in-law. This took on a special urgency since divorce meant the loss of her dowry, including the potential

2. See the previous discussions in chapters 1 and 2.

earnings it generated. From this angle, the *sine manu* marriage seems to favor the wife; however, it could also benefit the groom's family, as the wife would not inherit any of her husband's property upon his death. Theoretically, the wife was at risk to the possibly capricious whims of her father, who might end her happy marriage and send her to another man. In that case, her husband kept the children, which certainly would have caused her pain. Her value as a commodity to increase the wealth of the family might supersede any consideration of her personal joy. Much depended on her father, the head of the family. This unpleasant scenario, however, likely did not occur with any frequency, as Romans valued a close relationship between spouses. Only in extreme cases motivated by politically extenuating circumstances would a father decide to break up a happy couple to forge a new marriage alliance.

Before the marriage, a couple might be engaged, although how widespread the practice was is hard to pin down. Elite parents were anxious to make auspicious matches and would check a potential spouse's family reputation and wealth. Once a partner was found, the families or other mediators declared the engagement with a party. Under the *lex Julia* of 18 BC, men were penalized if they did not marry; however, an engaged man was considered married for purposes of this law. Thus men who wished to remain engaged and not marry took advantage of this loophole. The *lex Papia Poppaea* of AD 9 closed this escape hatch by specifying an engagement period of no more than two years. This law also prevented men from becoming engaged to very young girls. Perhaps a ring was sent to the soon-to-be bride, but other gifts were also given. Romans did not share the modern custom of wedding/engagement rings carrying intentions of loyalty and love. Thus a ring could be an acceptable gift as a pledge of love in an extramarital affair or as a token of commitment in commercial transactions. If the couple broke their engagement they would usually return the gifts if they had been given on the condition that the marriage take place.[3]

To understand the legal dimensions of Roman marriage, it is necessary to appreciate the role that citizenship played. Specifically, only Roman citizens had the right of *conubium*—the right to enter a licit marriage. *Conubium* means that the children follow the status of their father and thus are Roman citizens with all the attending privileges. Moreover the children are under the authority of their father (*patria potestas*). All other marriages were illicit, and the children follow the status of their mother—but this does not imply that the relationship is immoral.[4] Thus for our purposes, I will distinguish between licit marriages, those contracted between two Roman citizens, and illicit marriages, those entered into by everyone else. Thus, licit marriage usu-

3. Susan Treggiari, *Roman Marriage: Iusti Coniuges from the Time of Cicero to the Time of Ulpian* (Oxford: Clarendon, 1991), 125–60.
4. For a detailed discussion, see Treggiari, *Roman Marriage*, 43–49.

ally involved the upper class or those freedmen and women with considerable wealth. Today we do not associate wealth with the ability to contract a licit marriage, because any person regardless of their social standing can enter into a legal marriage.[5] The ramifications of the Roman arrangement concerning licit and illicit marriage and social status impact Jewish and Christian communities; the latter group is generally understood to be located on the lower rungs of the social ladder, and both groups tend to be non-citizens of Rome. However, much of the expectations surrounding marriage and the wife's behavior vis-à-vis her husband and her family honor was consistent regardless of whether the marriage was licit or not. Therefore, only when the distinction is crucial will I note if the marriage is licit.

Unlike modern governments, which grant marriage certificates directly or empower religious bodies to do so, in the Roman Republic and imperial periods, no such certificate was necessary or available. Instead, the legal document that signaled a marriage (either licit or illicit) was the dowry agreement. To be married, a man and a woman needed only to agree that they wished to be husband and wife. Intention was crucial—did these two people consider themselves to be married to each other? If they both answered "yes," then the culture accepted it. They were not required to exchange special religious rites or make specific vows. The government only got involved when the dowry contract was written up, for it was a legal document that had the weight of the law behind it. Thus if no dowry was exchanged, then no legal certificate was produced to indicate a couple's marriage.

By focusing so heavily on legal documents, we run the risk of misrepresenting marriage as it was lived out by most families in the ancient world. The documents preserved do not validate the marriage in the eyes of the community per se. That is, if these documents were destroyed, the couple would not cease to be married. Nor does the absence of documents nullify a marriage. These documents served to protect economic assets and secure the future of those most vulnerable in the relationship: the wife and children. Thus dowry contracts were useful to those families who had enough wealth to worry that a dowry not be frittered away by a lazy husband and to the wife who was concerned that her children not be cheated out of their inheritance from her. Many average couples without financial means had no formal dowry contract but simply celebrated their good fortune with the village and settled quickly into the daily grind of getting food and raising children.

If either spouse wanted to end the marriage, he or she simply expressed the intention to do so. The husband dismissed or repudiated his wife, and the wife was described as going in a different direction from her husband. Usually no public reason was given. As soon as their intentions changed from

5. In the United States, state governments place age requirements and certain other minimal restrictions on spouse selection.

wishing to be married to wanting to be out of that relationship, the marriage was over. In sum, just as no written certificate declared a marriage, so too no specific document confirmed a divorce unless a dowry was involved. Cicero recounts an interesting dilemma: A man was married to a woman; they lived in Spain and had a son. He left to go to Rome, and there he married another woman and also had a son. He did not tell his wife in Spain about this new "arrangement." When the man died intestate, each wife claimed her son deserved inheritance as the eldest heir. Cicero argued that the man's second marriage nullifies the first marriage, because the second marriage signals the husband's intentions that his first marriage was over (since Roman law did not allow for bigamy).[6]

Divorce

Divorce was familiar within Roman elite society, though it is unclear how frequent it was. Susan Treggiari rightly cautions that legal recourse to divorce does not necessarily mean that most Romans took advantage of it. While no religious sanctions were present, she suggests that social pressures kept divorce rates down. "The line between divorce which social peers would accept as unfortunate but justified and divorce which would be seen as irresponsible and self-seeking was hard to draw."[7] Moreover, she examines the two types of evidence for divorce and finds they present quite different pictures. Actual divorces known from historical records number about thirty-two over the span of 100 to 38 BC, and many of these were made for political gains. Remarkably, the most notorious women who flaunted their unconventional attitudes did not divorce.[8] This contrasts sharply with the literary evidence from Juvenal, Martial, and Seneca, whose rhetoric caustically attacks women as divorce-mongers. Treggiari notes only one instance where a woman clearly acted alone to file for divorce: Valeria Paulla divorced to marry Demicus Brutus (the lead conspirator in the assassination of Julius Caesar). Treggiari concludes, "the sparsity of actual instances where divorce was decided by the wife is (even in relation to our scanty data on women) in striking contrast with the stereotypes presented in imperial literature."[9]

Less is known about the divorce customs of poorer Romans. If divorce was done primarily to increase the family's wealth, then one might suspect the divorce rate was lower among the poor. It is unlikely that the poor, as

6. Cicero, *Orationes philippicae* 2.69.
7. Treggiari, "Divorce Roman Style," 41.
8. Treggiari, "Divorce Roman Style," 43, lists Servilia (Cato's half sister), Clodia Metelli, Fulvia, and Sempronia who in the literature are accused of flagrant disregard for conventions, though the male authors usually had axes to grind, and their accounts are more bluster than fact.
9. Treggiari, "Divorce Roman Style," 44.

well as freedmen and freedwomen, had the social net worth to make divorce and remarriage a common practice. Yet because it was relatively easy to obtain a divorce, there was little financial penalty for the poor in deciding to divorce, unless a dowry was involved. Treggiari holds that in the lower class, a craftsman might have used all the dowry monies to develop his trade, and could not pay it back in divorce. And a woman might have invested heavily with her own labor in making the family business work such that she would be reluctant to end the marriage. "Only if the dowry was a mere token and the couple were supported by independent manual labour . . . would divorce perhaps be feasible."[10]

Remarriage

Remarriage was a common occurrence, especially given the high infant mortality and death rate among women dying in childbirth and men in accidents and war. The *lex Julia* and *lex Papia Poppaea* passed by Augustus had provisions that benefited large families. Bachelors were forbidden to receive inheritances or legacies, and widows were required to remarry within two years, or a divorcee within eighteen months. Tacitus recounts that Augustus enacted these laws to combat the practice of (male) celibacy,[11] but in reality, they had little effect. Marriages and births did not increase substantially, for childlessness, according to Tacitus, offered too many advantages.

Scholars are not in agreement over what those advantages might have been. Some suggest that bachelors enjoyed unencumbered sex.[12] Others note the expense involved in raising children. For example, the senatorial class would need to provide their daughters with a dowry suitable to their wealth and social status. Their sons needed to be financed through the *cursus honorum* (a series of public political and military posts on an ascending ladder of political power). Moreover, childlessness freed a man from the social risks inherent in having a daughter who shamed the family or a son who underperformed. Instead, a man could adopt an adult son, one of whom he approved. Adoption was not shameful, and it served to align families much as marriage did. Caesar Augustus was probably the most famous example, adopted as a son by his great-uncle Julius Caesar. In the second century AD, four of the five emperors adopted their heirs from outside the family;[13] adoption served to smooth succession.

Alongside the legal system, which regulated aspects of adoption, divorce, and remarriage, an ideal existed that celebrated a wife's faithfulness to her

---

10. Treggiari, "Divorce Roman Style," 39.

11. Tacitus, *Ann.* 3.25.

12. Bruce W. Winter, *Roman Wives, Roman Widows: The Appearance of New Women and the Pauline Communities* (Grand Rapids: Eerdmans, 2003), 54. He draws on Cassius Dio's comments in *Hist. Rom.* 56.7.6–8.1.

13. The four emperors included Nerva, Trajan, Hadrian, and Antonius Pius.

husband. The term used to describe this first-century AD ideal, *univira* (a woman who only married once), had a more expansive meaning and exclusive application during the Roman Republic period. In the first century BC the term was applied mainly to upper-class women who married directly from their father's house and who remained chaste, staying with their first husband for the length of the marriage. By the first century AD, however, *univira* implied a woman who did not divorce her husband but remained married until her death, or a widow who remained unmarried to honor perpetually her husband's memory.[14] Valerius Maximus wrote in the first century AD that "the mind of a married woman was particularly loyal and uncorrupted if it knew not how to leave the bed on which she had surrendered her virginity."[15] It is unclear how frequently the *univira* ideal was exercised by women who were divorced or widowed, most of whom would likely need the support of their family in this situation. Probably a wealthy woman would have a greater opportunity to refuse to divorce or to remarry a second husband.

Even with the popularity of the "once-married" ideal, Augustus's laws gave financial and status incentives to marriages that produced children, thereby encouraging widows and widowers to remarry and have children. Cassius Dio records that Augustus "allowed all upper-class men who wished, except senators, to marry freedwomen, and he ordered their children to be considered legitimate."[16] Generally speaking, freeborn women of the senatorial class were not to marry freedmen, but it seems to have occurred repeatedly.

Concubines

Given the importance of status in choosing suitable marriage partners, a brief word should be said about concubines. A concubine is a woman in a relationship with a man of higher status, who thus is unable to enter a licit marriage with her.[17] A concubine was often a freedwoman who could not engage in a legal marriage or who did not possess a dowry. She might have been formerly convicted of prostitution or adultery, or she might have been an actress. She might have once been a slave whose owner had chosen to free her and then take her as a concubine. Beryl Rawson finds that poorer men

14. An inscription from 38 BC praises Cornelia as a *uni nupta* or a "one-married" woman. The term *univera* is not used, perhaps because at this point its definition was broader, referring to a chaste woman who devoted herself to one man, her husband, as long as she remained married to him. See Majorie Lightman and William Zeisel, "Univira: An Example of Continuity and Change in Roman Society," *Church History* 46.1 (1977): 19–32.

15. Valerius Maximus, *Fact. dict. mem.* 2.1 (trans. D. R. Shackleton Bailey, LCL).

16. Cassius Dio, *Hist. Rom.* 54.16.1–2. Translation in Jo-Ann Shelton, *As the Romans Did: A Sourcebook in Roman Social History* (New York: Oxford University Press, 1988), 29. Legitimacy included the status of Roman citizenship.

17. Carolyn Osiek and David L. Balch, *Families in the New Testament World: Households and House Churches* (Louisville: Westminster John Knox, 1997), 67.

often had concubines, perhaps because a good number of these relationships began when the woman was a slave. Rawson finds no incontrovertible evidence that two free persons would choose concubinage over marriage.[18] An older widower might choose a concubine instead of a second wife so that his estate would not be diluted if children were born to his second wife. A young man might prefer a concubine until he is ready to make a socially appropriate marriage. A female slave owner was restricted from marrying her freed male slave, but this taboo was ignored not infrequently. Perhaps in many of these cases, the woman was a former slave herself. Any children born to a concubine remained hers, for they were illegitimate. The concubine herself had no protection under the law.

Roman Marriage Documents

Whether or not a marriage was licit in the eyes of Rome, many non-Roman citizens married and had families. Documents certifying the arrangement generally outlined the financial obligations of each party. We will compare two Greek marriage contracts from Egypt. The first was written in 311 BC between two free Greeks,[19] and the second was written in 13 BC.[20] In each case, both the wife and husband pledge to uphold certain behaviors with respect to the marriage. Both contracts delineate the dowry amount and repayment conditions. And in both cases, the bride is represented by a male.

Husband and Wife Responsibilities

In the first document, the bride's father *and mother* are listed: "Heraclides takes as his lawful wife Demetria of Cos from her father Leptines of Cos and her mother Philotis."[21] Philotis's participation in the marriage of her daughter is not exceptional; Cicero's wife planned the marriage of their daughter, for example. It is remarkable that the bride has both parents living, which may signify her youth and that this is her first marriage. While the mother appears to be involved with the marriage contract, only the father is listed as responsible in part for where the couple will live: "We shall live together in whatever place seems best to Leptines and Heraclides, deciding together." The bride, Demetria, apparently has no say in where they might live, but she is given recourse against Heraclides if he reneges on any aspect of the marriage arrangement, including bringing home another woman or having a child with

18. Beryl Rawson, "The Roman Family," in *The Family in Ancient Rome: New Perspectives*, ed. Beryl Rawson (Ithaca, NY: Cornell University Press, 1987), 15.
19. P.Eleph. 1.
20. *BGU* IV.1052.
21. P.Eleph. 1. Translation in Sarah B. Pomeroy, *Goddesses, Whores, Wives, and Slaves: Women in Classical Antiquity* (1975; repr., New York: Schocken, 1995), 127–28.

First-century AD
funerary relief
showing the mar-
ried couple Popil-
lius and Calpurnia,
a freedman and
freedwoman (Photo
courtesy of Mary
Harrsch/flickr.com)

another woman. Any alleged breach of this contract must be determined by
a "jury" of "three men whom they both approve." Demetria will receive back
her one-thousand-drachmae dowry, as well as another one thousand silver
coins taken if necessary from his estate. While Demetria can act as a free
agent in bringing a charge against her husband, the contract acknowledges
she will be represented by men who take up her case ("those helping Demetria
to exact payment").

The second marriage document, from Egypt in 13 BC, reads:

> To Protarchus [a government official], from Thermion daughter of Apion, ac-
> companied by her guardian Apollonius son of Chaereas, and from Apollonius
> son of Ptolemaeus—Thermion and Apollonius son of Ptolemaeus agree that
> they have come together for the purpose of sharing their lives with one another.
> The above-mentioned Apollonius son of Ptolemaeus agrees that he has received
> from Thermion, handed over from her household as a dowry, a pair of gold
> earrings . . . [fragmented text]. From now on he will furnish Thermion, as his
> wedded wife, with all necessities and clothing according to his means, and
> he will not mistreat her or cast her out or insult her or bring in another wife;
> otherwise he must at once return the dowry and in addition half again as much
> . . . [fragmented text]. And Thermion will fulfill her duties toward her husband
> and her marriage, and will not sleep away from the house or be absent one day
> without the consent of Apollonius son of Ptolemaeus and will not damage or
> injure their common home and will not consort with another man; otherwise
> she, if judged guilty of these actions, will be deprived of her dowry, and in ad-
> dition the transgressor will be liable to the prescribed fine. Dated the 17th year
> of Caesar [Augustus].[22]

22. *BGU* IV.1052. For a translation, see Shelton, *As the Romans Did*, 44.

Several observations should be made about this contract. Not surprisingly, the woman is represented by a legal guardian, in this case not her father but Apollonius son of Chaereas. Furthermore, wording indicates both the bride and groom chose to enter into this relationship, for Greco-Roman marriages were defined by the intentions of the two parties. Moreover, the dowry is carefully established, and reasons for its return are succinctly detailed. For example, the husband is responsible to take care of his wife, including making sure she is properly attired ("necessities and clothing"). If he neglects to do so, or if he actively abuses her or brings home another woman as his wife, he has forfeited her dowry and must pay a fine to her amounting to fifty percent of the total dowry worth.

The wife's responsibilities are also carefully laid out, and if she fails to meet them, she loses her dowry. She is not responsible to provide for her husband's daily needs; rather she is to maintain their house and "fulfill her duties" to her husband and marriage. The language is vague here, which probably in-dicates a common understanding of what a wife's duties would entail. Most likely they would include caring for any children, getting food and prepar-ing meals—in general, running the household. She might be responsible to oversee household slaves, make clothing, or work in the family business. The contract calls for her to remain at home each night, unless her husband allows her to travel. She must not consort with another man. While the husband is charged not to marry another, the wife is warned against having an affair. The comment about the transgressor has generated several theories. Some argue that the transgressor is the wife, and claim she is penalized for rejecting the restrictions on her sexual behavior outside their union, much as her husband would be for failing to follow the guidelines laid for his sexual conduct. But the transgressor in this case could be the hypothetical "other man." In this reading, he would be taking or abusing what belongs to another man and so should be fined.

Marriage and Children

Interestingly, the latter contract does not discuss children. No provisions are made for barrenness; no specifics are established on whether the dowry will go to the children of this union. Perhaps the silence is due to high infant mortality rates.[23] Small families were the rule, not necessarily out of preference, but due to the deadly dangers of disease, starvation, and accidents. Again, why base a marriage on the need for children, especially when adoption was a perfectly acceptable option? Although within the *lex Julia* special incentives

---

23. Romans celebrated the day their child was given a name, which was nine days after a boy's birth and eight days after a girl's. Infant mortality was high, thus not all families enjoyed the naming celebration. This celebration was called the *lustratio* and was the occasion of a large party.

were instituted for families of three or more children,[24] exceptions were awarded with enough regularity that one suspects the emperors used this law to grant favors through exemptions.[25] Finally, perhaps the Egyptian marriage contract highlights the general lack of concern about bearing children in marriage, the very attitude Augustus's laws targeted.

One final note: many modern historians have observed that Romans spoke about marriage as being a close bond between husband and wife. Roman society was deeply patriarchal and hierarchical, with men above women and free men/women above freedmen/women and slaves. The marriage was to be a harmonious relationship with each partner committed to the well-being of the other. This ideal was likely not realized in many situations, much like in our own world today, but I raise this issue to make the point that many in the ancient world did not marry in the first place to have children. Most expected that children would come with the marriage, but they did not see the marriage relationship as having failed if it produced no living children.

Two citations illustrate my point. In the Laudatio Turiae, a funerary inscription offered by a husband to his beloved wife of forty years is often held up as a classic example of a happy marriage. The husband praises his wife, Turia, for her wool-making skills and her generous spirit, which extended to avenging the murders of her parents and caring for her in-laws. He laments bitterly that Fate took her before him, and fears that his mourning will be long and painful. In this lengthy tribute, he remarks that during their marriage, she declared she would gladly divorce him because they had no children. He claims he completely repudiated her suggestion because of his deep love for her. He writes:

> (31) When you despaired of your ability to bear children and grieved over my childlessness, you became anxious lest by retaining you in marriage I might lose all hope of having children. . . . So you proposed a divorce outright and offered to yield our house free to another woman's fertility. . . . You declared that you would regard future children as joint and as though your own, and that you would not effect a separation of our property. . . . (40) I must admit that I flared up so that I almost lost control of myself; so horrified was I by what you tried to do. . . . To think that you had been able to conceive in your mind the idea that you might cease to be my wife while I was still alive. . . . (44) What desire, what need to have children could I have had that was so great that I should have broken faith for that reason and changed certainty for uncertainty? . . .

24. An infant surviving to the naming day fulfilled the requirement of a live birth under the *lex Julia*.

25. In ca. AD 97, Trajan offered Pliny the Younger the same status as a man who had three children even though he was childless. His second wife had recently died (perhaps in childbirth) and this may have been Trajan's way of benefiting Pliny for his political support.

Fragment of the Laudatio Turiae (Photo courtesy of Marie-Lan Nguyen/Wikimedia Commons)

You remained with me as my wife, for I could not have given in to you without disgrace for me and unhappiness for both of us.[26]

In another instance, the general and later dictator Sulla (first century BC) divorced his wife Cloelia allegedly for infertility. Yet because he remarried so soon after the divorce, some are skeptical about his given reasons.[27] Even if he did divorce her in part because of infertility, she was not humiliated or dishonored in this, but was given high praise and gifts. No shame attached itself to infertility in the Greco-Roman context.

Roman Divorce Documents

To this marriage contract from Egypt in 13 BC we will compare a divorce document from the same period. It reads in part:

To Protarchus [a government official] from Zois daughter of Heraclides, accompanied by her brother and guardian Irenaeus son of Heraclides, and from Antipater son of Zeno: Zois and Antipater agree that they have separated from

26. *ILS* 8393. Translated by E. Wistrand in Mary R. Lefkowitz and Maureen B. Fant, *Women's Life in Greece and Rome: A Source Book in Translation*, 3rd ed. (Baltimore: Johns Hopkins University Press, 2005), 135–39 (quotation, 138).
27. Rawson, "Roman Family," 8–9.

one another and severed their arrangement to live together. . . . And Zois agrees that Antipater has returned to her, handed over from his household, the items he received as her dowry, namely clothing valued at 120 silver drachma (similar to the Roman denarius) and a pair of gold earrings. Both parties agree that henceforth the marriage contract will be null and void . . . and from this day it will be lawful for Zois to marry another man and for Antipater to marry another woman, with neither party being liable to prosecution.[28]

Husband and Wife Responsibilities

Not surprisingly, the wife is represented in the contract by a guardian, in this case her brother. Both husband and wife have agreed to separate, and both are now allowed to remarry. In fact, it seems expected that one or both will remarry. No stigma appears to be attached to a divorced woman or man. Explicit mention is made of the dowry returned in full. As in the marriage document above, children are not discussed. Perhaps the couple had no children. In some cases, a divorced mother might continue to help her children through her own money or part of the dowry. This appears to be the case with Cicero and his wife Terentia concerning their adult son, Marcus. Cicero and Terentia had a licit marriage, then divorced by the time their son, as a young adult, began his senatorial climb (as did all male youths of his status). Part of Terentia's dowry was retained by Cicero, as agreed upon by her, for Marcus's allowance. Specifically, Terentia's dowry included properties whose rents would provide ample income for Marcus. Terentia did not have a tutor or guardian; she was *sui iuris* and could manage her own business affairs without the approval of any man. She negotiated with Cicero and his liaison, Atticus, on the amount to be taken from her dowry for her son's care.[29]

Reasons for Divorce

Like most divorces at this time, the text above offers no reason for the separation. It might be as simple as the couple being disinclined to live together or as serious as one of the pair committing adultery. Because no reason need be given to justify a divorce, we can only surmise what might have occurred by looking at why people married in the first place. Some married for love, in which case "falling out of love" or falling in love with another person might have contributed to a divorce. Because bigamy, polygyny, and adultery were outlawed in Roman law (though polygyny was present in the Jewish commu-

---

28. *CPJ* 144. Translated in Ross S. Kraemer, ed., *Maenads, Martyrs, Matrons, Monastics: A Sourcebook on Women's Religions in the Greco-Roman World* (Philadelphia: Fortress, 1988), 88.

29. Suzanne Dixon, "Family Finances: Terentia and Tullia," in *The Family in Ancient Rome: New Perspectives*, ed. Beryl Rawson (Ithaca, NY: Cornell University Press, 1987), 107–9. Dixon draws on Cicero's letters, including *Epistulae ad Atticum* 12.23.2 and 12.28.24.

nity at least through the second century AD), this might have played a role in the couple's decision. It is possible that the husband or wife wanted children and determined to remarry another to further this goal. If this is the case, the document clearly attaches no shame to the other partner; the wife's dowry was simply returned to her, and she was free to marry another. From a legal standpoint, the document shows the relative ease with which people in the Greco-Roman world entered and exited a marriage. That it was "easy" to get married or divorced, however, does not mean that men and women took the relationship lightly. It signals, rather, that at this point, marriage and divorce were primarily a family matter, not a government concern. The law stepped in when dowries and inheritances were at stake. Beyond that, people were free within their families to make marriage arrangements. Social pressure to live up to marital ideals structured these relationships and filled them with meaning.

Jewish Marriage in the Greco-Roman World

Bride Price and Dowry

Much of the Jewish evidence turns on vocabulary definitions, so a brief summary of terms is useful as we enter the discussion. The Hebrew Bible discusses the "bride price" or *mohar*. For example, Exodus 22:16–17 speaks about a fine levied against a man who rapes a virgin. This amount was paid to the father at the wedding (though the father might refuse to give his daughter to the rapist). We also find Saul asking a bride price of a hundred Philistine foreskins for his daughter Michal (1 Sam. 18:23–26). In the rabbinic writings, the bride price was listed by the house of Shammai as one denarius, and as one perutah (less than a denarius) by the house of Hillel.[30]

A second important term is "dowry," an amount of money and perhaps property and physical items such as jewelry, which belongs to the bride but was available for use by the groom. The daughter takes this money or property into the marriage, and she is owed this money if her husband divorces her. Usually the dowry is given to her children should she die before her husband. With this change from bride price to dowry, the financial burden was shifted from the groom to the bride's family.

A final term comes from rabbinic writings. A *ketubbah* refers to a marriage contract, as well as to the amount of money guaranteed by the husband to the wife if he should predecease or divorce her. Unlike the bride price, this money is not paid until the marriage is dissolved through divorce or death. Moreover, this money is given to the wife, not to her father. The situation becomes complicated because within the rabbinic corpus the term can carry

30. *m. Qidd.* 1:1.

also the sense of either dowry or a modified bride price. This confusion will hopefully be sorted out in the course of the following discussion.[31]

In Early Jewish literature, one of the first mentions of a marriage contract occurs in the deuterocanonical book of Tobit. In Tobit 7:13, the bride's father, Raguel, asks his wife to "bring writing material; and he wrote out a copy of a marriage contract." It is a pity that the novelist does not provide wording for the contract. But from the conversation between the characters, we discover that Raguel expects Tobias to care for his daughter as he would his own sister. He expects Tobias to consider Raguel and his wife as his own parents. Thus the prevailing note sounded is the integration of two families, both from the same tribe.[32] Raguel provides his new son-in-law, Tobias, with half of his wealth, and promises that on the death of Raguel and his wife, the rest of his property will be turned over to Tobias (Tob. 8:21; see also 10:10). The custom described here is ambiguous. Is it that Sarah, Raguel's daughter, brings to the wedding a large dowry, which will increase at her father's death? Or is Raguel treating Tobias as his son and providing an inheritance for him? However one wishes to label the money Raguel transfers to Tobias, it is clear that Tobias does not offer any financial contribution to his new father-in-law. He is not offering a bride price, nor is he promising any monies (*ketubbah*) should he divorce Sarah.

From the second century BC, the book of Sirach seems to presuppose the dowry system. Ben Sira cautions against becoming ensnared by a woman's beauty and wealth (Sir. 25:21). The context of his remarks laments the wicked woman who practices iniquity, for example, by talking too much. Following his warning against becoming entrapped by a wife's money is the conviction that a wife supporting her husband is disgraceful. In other words, Ben Sira is warning his (male) readers against the temptation to marry a wealthy woman and live off her earnings. He implies that women with money/wealth are likely troublesome and that men are susceptible to putting up with an unruly wife for the sake of her fortune. He does not have high opinions of either wealthy women or eager young men. Similar disdain is shared by Pseudo-Phocylides, who warns, "do not bring as a wife into your home a bad and wealthy woman, for you will be a slave of (your) wife because of the ruinous dowry" (199–200). Perhaps in this author's mind, one might discover a good wealthy woman, though evil and wealth seem tied tightly together. A few lines further, he remarks that a woman will not "reject a bad man when he is rich" (204).[33] This implies that the lure of riches draws both men and women into its ruinous clutches.

31. A brief reminder to the reader: most Jews at this time would have entered into illicit marriages, as they were not Roman citizens.

32. Note that Tobit stresses endogamy, in line with Ezra's reforms; see chapter 2.

33. Translations in James H. Charlesworth, ed., *Old Testament Pseudepigrapha* (Garden City, NY: Doubleday, 1985), 2:581.

Philo of Alexandria, during the early decades of the first century AD, comments on the dowry. Like Pseudo-Phocylides, he warns against the seduction of large dowries. But in his work *De fuga et invention* (*On Flight and Finding*), he commends the man who generously provides a large dowry for daughters in poor families.[34] In this context, the wealth is seen as being poured into the larger community: "throwing all your own property into the common stock, you will invite to a participation in it all who are worthy of favour."[35] In his work *De specialibus legibus* (*On the Special Laws*), Philo comments on the dowry's importance for those virgins who are unmarried at the time of their father's death.[36] In the same century, Josephus writes that Jewish law of marriage "commands us also, when we marry, not to have regard to portion."[37]

The practice of dowry as described in the literary evidence is supported by the Septuagint (LXX). In this Greek translation by Jews in third-century BC Egypt, the Hebrew term "bride price" (*mohar*) is translated as "dowry" (*phernē*). This is somewhat surprising, as there is a Greek word for "bride price" used by Homer. In the *Iliad*, Agamemnon promises Achilles that he might have a bride without paying the bride price. "He may lead away whichever one he likes / with no bride-price asked, home to Peleus' house. / And I will add a dowry, yes, a magnificent treasure. . . ."[38] By choosing the Greek term for dowry, the translation reflects cultural shifts within the society; it seems likely that the audience of the LXX (or at least the translators) no longer used the bride price system, but had incorporated the dowry custom.[39]

What might have caused a shift among Jews from bride price to dowry? At least two factors may account for the change. First, Hellenization likely played a role, as the Greek culture was vastly influential in those cultures that fell within its grasp. For the Greeks, a dowry established the legitimacy of the marriage. Elias Bickerman writes, "we may suppose that dowry entered the

34. Philo, *Fug.* 29.
35. Philo, *Fug.* 29 (trans. F. H. Colson and G. H. Whitaker, LCL). Michael L. Satlow ("Reconsidering the Rabbinic *ketubah* Payment," in *The Jewish Family in Antiquity*, ed. Shaye J. D. Cohen [Atlanta: Scholars Press, 1993], 136–37) rightly cites Philo's discussion of the firstborn son's double inheritance in *Spec.* 2.135–37 as a place where Philo, had he known of the rabbinic *ketubbah* practice, would certainly have drawn upon it to support his argument. See also Satlow, *Jewish Marriage in Antiquity* (Princeton: Princeton University Press, 2001).
36. Philo, *Spec.* 1.125–27 (trans. F. H. Colson, LCL).
37. Josephus, *C. Ap.* 2.200 (trans. H. St. John Thackeray, LCL).
38. Homer, *The Iliad* 9.75–77; see also 16.190. Translation by R. Fagles, Penguin Classics (New York: Penguin, 1998), 256.
39. Satlow, *Jewish Marriage in Antiquity*, 69–73, discusses the equally interesting translation of the Hebrew term for betrothal. He concludes that inchoate marriage was uncommon to the point of almost nonexistence among most Jews of the Early Jewish period. The only reference to such practice is found in Matt. 1:18–19, which speaks of Mary's betrothal to Joseph as carrying legal weight and only ending in either death or divorce. For a discussion of Mary, see chapter 4.

Jewish marriage contract in the Greek age as a borrowing from the Greek law."[40]

Second, the dowry allowed the family flexibility in passing down its wealth. Certain advantages came with a dowry system coupled with a tradition of giving gifts directly to the daughter.[41] The dowry allowed the family to express its wealth and therefore boost its status in the community. But the dowry amount could also be limited if the father determined that the husband might mismanage the money. The husband had full use of the dowry money and could use its income to further his own estate. In the event of a divorce, he was only required to return the dowry, not the income it generated. Thus the father might gift his daughter with property apart from the dowry agreement. This guaranteed that the money or property stayed within his family and was given to his grandchildren. The husband had no claims on this gift during the marriage, and it remained in the wife's possession if the couple divorced or the husband died. This maneuver of giving gifts to the daughter also accomplished another goal—that of keeping a family's estate together if the sole surviving heir is a daughter. The father could wait until the couple had a child before giving a gift to his daughter, thereby insuring that his property would be kept in the family as his grandchild's inheritance through his mother.

Jewish Marriage Documents

The language shift from bride price to dowry found in Jewish documents is evident also in some Jewish marriage contracts written in Greek. The non-financial parts of these documents include a discussion on providing food, clothing, and marital relations to one's wife. David Instone-Brewer notes that in non-Jewish Greek marriage contracts there is a reference to *deonta* or "necessities," rather than food. This is reflected also in the LXX translation of Exodus 21:10–11, which reads *deonta*, along with "clothing." But the Jewish marriage contracts include the promise of "feeding and clothing" the wife. Instone-Brewer suggests that these Jewish contracts are drawing on a tradition that might predate the LXX or that uses another translation of Exodus. Perhaps this "variant" reflects a well-established tradition within a Hebrew contract that was directly translated into its Greek form.[42]

DIVORCE

Some also argue that the Jewish marriage contracts (and rabbinic texts) reveal a presumption, absent from their non-Jewish counterparts, that the

---

40. Elias Bickerman, "Two Legal Interpretations of the Septuagint," in *Studies in Jewish and Christian History, Part 1* (Leiden: Brill, 1976), 213.

41. Satlow, *Jewish Marriage in Antiquity*, 204–5.

42. David Instone-Brewer, "1 Corinthians 7 in the Light of the Jewish Greek and Aramaic Marriage and Divorce Papyri," *Tyndale Bulletin* 52.2 (2001): 228–29.

Jewish marriage will continue until the death of the spouse. Jewish contracts did not expect the couple to file for divorce, unlike the non-Jewish contracts that read as though divorce is a possible outcome.[43] For example, the language in Jewish contracts discusses who will get the dowry money if the wife predeceases her husband and who will care for the wife if the husband predeceases her. No mention is made of divorce. In non-Jewish contracts, however, divorce provisions are discussed but stipulations regarding the death of a spouse are not. The implication is that at least some Jewish families assumed marriage was for life, while non-Jewish families assumed marriage was not a lifelong commitment. For those Jews who permitted polygyny, a man's fear that a wife would not be suitable is mitigated by the knowledge that he could marry another without divorcing the first.

However, the above observation about Jewish marriage contracts not mentioning divorce may be overreaching the evidence and may be open to other interpretations. For example, one Jewish marriage contract that refers to the groom's faithfulness (*pistis*) also mentions the wife's option to demand her dowry be returned to her. This contract makes provision for divorce, if the wife (or her representative) desires it.[44] Again, the assertion that Jews viewed marriage as a lasting commitment might not take full account of the numerous discussions about divorce in rabbinic and New Testament writings. The disagreement between the houses of Hillel and Shammai, as well as the discussions between Jesus and the Pharisees, suggest a climate where divorce was encountered with enough frequency to warrant debate. Moreover, Josephus divorced twice, with no apparent social reprisals.[45] In the Salome Komaïse archives (see below), Salome divorced and remarried.[46] Evidence from a broad spectrum suggests that at least some Jews followed the dominant culture in allowing divorce. Distinctive practices probably fell along social or class ranks as well as along religious lines.

Finally, even if we grant that Jewish contracts did not mention divorce, we cannot assume that because non-Jewish contracts did not mention the groom's faithfulness, they were indifferent to or had no expectation of a lifelong marriage. The argument falters under the assumption that the Greek and Roman

43. Instone-Brewer, "1 Corinthians 7," 229–30. He notes that "there was almost an expectation that the [Greek] marriage would end in divorce rather than death" (230).
44. P. Yadin 18. Translation in Naphtali Lewis, Yigael Yadin, and Jonas C. Greenfield, eds., *The Documents from the Bar Kokhba Period in the Cave of Letters*, Judean Desert Studies 2 (Jerusalem: Israel Exploration Society, 1989), 80. See also the discussion by Instone-Brewer, "1 Corinthians 7," 226–30.
45. Josephus was first married at about thirty years of age to a woman (virgin) chosen for him by Vespasian. Both were captives of Rome at this point. He had three children with her, two of whom died. With his third wife, whom he married when he was about forty years old, he had two children (both lived).
46. Salome Komaïse was previously married to a man named Sammouos, probably before AD 127, and was divorced by AD 129.

contracts would express the duty and loyalty of the husband in the same way as a Jewish document might. Reference or allusion to the Mosaic law is not surprising in a Jewish context, but we should not assume that the absence of a parallel comment in a non-Jewish contract implies that the non-Jew expected the marriage to end in divorce. The social constraints against arbitrary divorce might have seemed sufficient guard against a husband's willy-nilly dismissal of his wife. Moreover, the *sine manu* marriage system allowed for her family's continued close involvement in the wife's well-being, perhaps making a statement about the groom's behavior seem unnecessary.

BABATHA AND SALOME KOMAÏSE

Further exploring the papyri evidence, in a valuable cache of second-century AD documents concerning the Jewish woman Babatha, there are two marriage contracts.[47] In neither case is the groom said to have paid a bride price, nor is he beholden to pay a *ketubbah* if he divorces his wife. This is consistent with other evidence, for neither *mohar* nor an equivalent term is used in any papyri from the Judean desert.[48] Less clear from these documents is the specific financial arrangement agreed upon, because money is contributed by both the bride and the groom. Examining the details from the archives, we can recreate the story of Babatha's marriages and gain a better handle on her financial situation. She grew up on the southern shore of the Dead Sea in Mahoza, Arabia, which became a Roman province in AD 106. Her family was wealthy. For example, in AD 99 her father bought four date groves, and in 120, he gave them to Babatha when she married. A short time before her marriage, he willed to his wife, Miriam, all his other possessions upon his death.

In AD 124, Babatha's husband, Jesus, died. If her husband was in his early twenties when he married, he died before he turned thirty years old. She was left a widow with one son, also named Jesus. Babatha remarried a man named Judah probably between the years of AD 125 and 128. Judah was at that time also married to a woman named Miriam, thus Babatha was part of a polygynous relationship. Judah and Miriam had a daughter named Shelamzion. Babatha's marriage contract (written in Aramaic) stipulates that Judah received four hundred denarii cash as her dowry (the term here is *ketubbah*). The contract does not require him to care for her son Jesus, but Judah does promise to bequeath her monies (dowry) to their male heirs and to care for their daughters until the daughters marry.

47. See Lewis, Yadin, and Greenfield, *Documents from the Bar Kokhba Period* for a discussion of the marriage document of Shelamzion and Judah (76–82) and the marriage document of Salome Komaïse and Jesus (130–33). A translation and brief discussion are also found in Ross S. Kraemer, ed., *Women's Religions in the Greco-Roman World: A Sourcebook*, rev. ed. (Oxford: Oxford University Press, 2004), 143–55.
48. Satlow, *Jewish Marriage in Antiquity*, 201.

In AD 128, Judah borrowed three hundred denarii from Babatha, and six weeks later his daughter Shelamzion was married with a dowry of two hundred denarii, which included jewelry and clothing, to which her husband, Cimber, added three hundred denarii.[49] The Greek document is signed by Cimber, "I acknowledge the debt of silver denarii five hundred, the dowry of Shelamzion my wife. . . ."[50] Judah also gave his daughter one-half of a courtyard in En-Gedi, with the other half to follow at his death. Judah died two years later without leaving money to repay the dowry or the loan, and so Babatha seized his date groves as payment on his debts. Her actions were contested by his first wife, Miriam, who took possession of his house and personal belongings.

In Babatha's archives, six marriages are mentioned, including those of Babatha's parents and her husband Jesus's parents, as well as her two marriages, Judah's marriage to Miriam, and the daughter Shelamzion's marriage. Also mentioned are the death of her two husbands, a remarriage, and polygyny. It does not appear that marriages between relatives took place, but evidently all the couples were from the same town or area. As in the fifth-century BC Elephantine papyri, so too here marriage included a gift to the bride by her father.[51]

A second important collection of documents provides a window into the life of Salome Komaïse.[52] Her mother's name was Salome Grapte, who likely knew Babatha, a younger contemporary. Their lands shared the same neighbors and their contracts were signed by the same witnesses. Salome Grapte married her first husband, Levi, probably before AD 113, and they had at least one son and one daughter together. In AD 127 the son died, predeceased by his father. At this point the daughter, Salome Komaïse, wrote her mother a deed of renunciation against any claims of her deceased father's or brother's property.

Why did she write this deed? Salome Komaïse was married to Sammouos, son of Simon, probably in or before AD 127. For some reason, her father did not offer her a dowry. When both her father and brother died, her mother worried that Salome might sue for a stake in the property as her "dowry." Salome

49. P. Yadin 18.

50. Kraemer, *Women's Religions*, 150. Michael Satlow notes that in the Aramaic subscription, the amounts contributed by the bride and groom are combined and identified as *phernē*, which is the usual term for dowry, but can refer to other forms of payment as well. He suggests that because the amounts are combined, it lessens the likelihood that a *ketubbah* payment, as understood by later rabbis, is intended ("Reconsidering the Rabbinic *ketubah* Payment," 139).

51. The Elephantine papyri are too early for the period under discussion here but are consistent with what emerges in the Hellenistic period. For information on these papyri, see *TAD* B2.3; Cowley 8; *EPE* B25 and *TAD* B2.4; Cowley 9; *EPE* B26.

52. Hannah M. Cotton and Ada Yardeni, *Aramaic, Hebrew and Greek Documentary Texts from Naḥal Ḥever and Other Sites, with an Appendix Containing Alleged Qumran Texts*, Discoveries in the Judean Desert 27 (Oxford: Clarendon, 1997). A translation and brief discussion are also found in Kraemer, *Women's Religions*, 153–54.

therefore granted her mother a deed of renunciation. By AD 129, Salome and Sammouos divorced, and she was living in an "unwritten" marriage to Jesus son of Menahem. Her mother gave her a gift of a date grove and one-half of a courtyard. In AD 131, Jesus and Salome drew up a marriage contract. Perhaps at this point, they had a child and wanted to secure his or her future.[53]

In both these archives, the specter of death stands just off stage, stepping in frequently to snatch a key player. Babatha lost both husbands, Salome Grapte her husband and son. This raises the question of life expectancy and average age at marriage. Based on a survey of inscriptional evidence, men married for the first time in their mid to late twenties. Women entered marriage for the first time by their late teens or early twenties. Using statistics from modern, preindustrial communities to estimate demographics in the ancient world, we find that the average life expectancy was twenty-five years. If a woman married at age twenty, and her husband was thirty years old, then the likelihood that her father was alive at her wedding was approximately fifty percent. If we lower the male marrying age to twenty-five, then more fathers would likely be alive to see their daughter's wedding.[54] Rabbinic writings encourage a father to marry his daughter before she reached the age of twelve and a half, but did this prescription reflect reality? Michael Satlow suggests that the rabbis might have encouraged a young age for marriage so the father had control, thus resulting in greater honor for himself.[55]

Marriage in Rabbinic Writings

The evidence overall strongly suggests that during our period, Jews followed the Greco-Roman practice of dowry in marriage. Ross Kraemer notes that "the dynamics of Jewish families do not appear appreciably different from those of non-Jews (of similar class and status conditions) in the early imperial Roman period."[56] However, within the rabbinic material appears another marriage custom, known as the *ketubbah*. While the codification of rabbinic writings occurred after the Greco-Roman period, the rabbinic texts are referred to so frequently in discussions of marriage practices among the Jewish people in the first century AD that we will examine this evidence here. For the most part, rabbinic information cannot be relied upon to reflect historical reality for the

53. Satlow, *Jewish Marriage in Antiquity*, 99–100.
54. See Satlow, *Jewish Marriage in Antiquity*, 311n79 for a chart listing the different probabilities based on the father's age at his daughter's birth.
55. Satlow, *Jewish Marriage in Antiquity*, 109–10. He cites with approval Jonathan Z. Smith, "The Bare Facts of Ritual," in *Imagining Religion: From Babylon to Jonestown* (Chicago: University of Chicago Press, 1982), 53–65.
56. Ross S. Kraemer, "Typical and Atypical Jewish Family Dynamics," 155.

majority of Jews in the Julio-Claudian period; each claim must be carefully examined for historical usefulness.

With that caveat, we proceed to the rabbinic writings. The rabbinic materials include provisions that the husband will feed and clothe his wife and that she will perform her wifely duties. The husband did not pay a bride price, nor was he given a dowry. Instead, he owed the wife a pre–agreed upon amount of money should he divorce or predecease her. This money was guaranteed by the husband's estate and was paid directly to the wife (not her father). These changes moved the marriage configuration away from the Roman system of *sine manu* and gave the husband more control over his wife's assets. Rabbinic discussion suggests that this shift was put in place to allow a man the opportunity to marry young, and also to penalize him for divorcing his wife.

Rabbinic literature is written primarily in Hebrew, but the discussion and documentation of the *ketubbah* is done in Aramaic.[57] While other Jewish legal documents as well as other (nonmarital) early traditions in the Mishnah are also in Aramaic, it may be significant that the *ketubbah* is preserved in Aramaic, since the marriage contract of Babatha is also in Aramaic. On the one hand, this might suggest a long-standing tradition of using Aramaic in the marriage contract, which was carried over into the later rabbinic writings. The rabbis then embraced and also modified this traditional form. On the other hand, Babatha's marriage contract may have been written in Aramaic because the marriage was polygynous, and thus illegitimate in the eyes of Rome. Perhaps a Greek contract of marriage with dowry stipulations would have been unenforceable in court. The marriage contract drawn up by Babatha's husband Judah for his daughter is in Greek, indicating that he was not reluctant to use Greek contracts per se.

Crucial questions for historians center on when and how the rabbinic *ketubbah* custom—wherein two hundred denarii was paid to a virgin divorced or widowed, while one hundred was paid to a woman previously married—was put into practice. As noted above, all non-Rabbinic evidence points to the use of dowry during the Greco-Roman period; however, rabbinic sources claim that the *ketubbah* was developed in the first century BC by the founder of the rabbinic tradition, the Pharisee Simeon ben Shetah. The Tosefta refers to ben Shetah's saying in *t. Ket.* 12:1: "At first, when her *ketubah* was kept at her father's house it was easy in [her husband's] eyes to divorce her. Shimon ben Shetah established that her *ketubah* should be with her husband, and he should write for her, 'All of my property will be surety for your *ketubah*.'"[58] The passage's interpretation hinges on how the term *ketubbah* is understood. One theory argues that if we acknowledge the fluidity of the term *ketubbah*,

___

57. Prior to AD 70, Aramaic was the dominant Semitic language used in legal documents; after AD 70 Hebrew grew to become predominant, although Aramaic was used again in legal documents ca. AD 200.

58. Translation in Satlow, *Jewish Marriage in Antiquity*, 213.

ben Shetah's use likely denotes dowry. The term's fluctuating meaning allowed the rabbis to preserve a Pharisaic tradition while at the same time modifying the intent of that saying as their own (later) position on marriage contracts shifted. Thus ben Shetah's statement to his contemporaries would have instructed the husband to return to his wife all that she brought to the marriage as dowry if he divorced her. This decree would fit with the standards established in the wider Greco-Roman culture and from Jewish literary writings. But after the Mishnah was codified, ben Shetah's saying was understood to speak to a recent shift within rabbinic marriage practices, specifically that the husband paid a fee to the wife when he divorced her. What would have brought about this change? Perhaps it arose when these rabbis restricted the right to file for divorce to the husband alone. The wife was compensated for her lack of legal power by the promise of a payment should her husband divorce her.[59] This Tosefta saying of ben Shetah probably reflects the pre-70 rabbi's instructions that the husband's property must be surety for the *ketubbah*, with the important caveat that the term *ketubbah* means dowry. In the event of divorce, ben Shetah's rules guarantee that the wife would receive back her dowry.[60]

Shimon ben Shetah's statement is expanded and commented upon in later rabbinic texts, and interpreted in the Babylonian Talmud to mean that a *ketubbah* payment of two hundred denarii is owed by the husband or his estate to his widow or divorced wife.[61] If this interpretation is presumed to reflect ben Shetah's intentions, then it becomes harder to understand the argument about divorce between the Pharisaic sects known as the houses of Hillel and Shammai. From *Sifre Deuteronomy* 269, the houses of Hillel and Shammai discuss Deuteronomy 24:1, in which Moses addresses grounds for divorce. In this passage, those aligned with Shammai claim that divorce is only possible in the case of sexual infidelity, while those on the side of Hillel suggest that divorce is allowed for any reason—even burning the supper. The text reads: "From this Beth [the house of] Shammai say: A man may not divorce his wife except if he finds unchastity in her, for it is said: [Deut. 24.1] *Because he found in her a matter of unchastity*. And Beth [the house of] Hillel say: Even if she spoils his broth, for it is said: [Any] *matter*."[62] Rabbi Akiba, from the early second century, is recorded here in support of Hillel's position. He says that finding a prettier woman is adequate grounds to divorce one's wife.[63] Would

59. Satlow, *Jewish Marriage in Antiquity*, 214.

60. *y. Ket.* 8:11, 32b–c.

61. *b. Ket.* 82b.

62. Translation in David Instone-Brewer, *Techniques and Assumptions in Jewish Exegesis before 70 CE* (Tübingen: Mohr Siebeck, 1992), 136.

63. Instone-Brewer (*Techniques and Assumptions*, 137) suggests that the house of Shammai understood Deut. 24:1 as speaking about one thing only—unchastity—while the house of Hillel saw two things mentioned—unchastity and "any other matter apart from unchastity." The latter interpret the biblical text as lacking redundancy (based on the exegetical principle that Scripture contains no superfluous or redundant phrases [on redundancy, see p. 21 of Instone-Brewer]).

Jewish men be willing to divorce for such a seemingly insignificant offense as burning supper? They would end up paying for a very expensive meal! They would have to disburse the wife's *ketubbah*, perhaps liquidating their estates to pay the agreed upon price. Was the house of Hillel simply speaking hyperbolically, knowing that few men would ever follow their position?

Perhaps a story from the New Testament can help sort through this confusion. In the Synoptic Gospels, Jesus is asked on what grounds a man might divorce his wife. He states that only for unfaithfulness can a man divorce his wife, similar to the house of Shammai (Matt. 19:9; Mark 10:2–12; and Luke 16:18, which does not mention unchastity as grounds for divorce). In Matthew, the disciples are astonished at this news and exclaim that perhaps it is better not to marry at all. Does Matthew's text expose a prevailing attitude that divorce should be relatively easy to accomplish? If so, it may be that the process was not financially devastating to "average" Jewish men (from which group Jesus pulled many of his disciples). Most people did not have two hundred denarii in their bank accounts, lessening the possibility that *ketubbah* here carries its later rabbinic meaning. In our period of study, grounds for divorce varied, and different answers to the perceived problem were given. Yet all answers, I suggest, used the dowry system as the foundation for the marriage relationship. From there, different sects debated the relative merits of divorce, usually in light of a biblical text.

Marriage in Christian Writings

Within the New Testament, there are few discussions of or references to historical marriages. Within the Gospels, the Samaritan woman's husbands are noted (John 4) and there are also some women identified as wives, such as Joanna the wife of Chuza (Luke 8:3). A few couples, like Ananias and Sapphira and Aquila and Priscilla, are mentioned in Acts. The preceding discussion on marriage contracts should help us explore the specific situations described in the New Testament.

Samaritan Woman

The Samaritan woman's story (John 4) has captured my attention for many years, not in small part because I believe her story has been misunderstood by many readers, in particular that she is immoral. John narrates that Jesus meets this woman at noon by a well and asks her for water. Jesus tells her that he is living water, and that she has had five husbands but her current companion is not her husband. From these slim details, most commentators suggest that she is a dissolute woman. Given the social norms of the day, however, I suggest a different reading.

Many expositors focus on the woman's presence at the well at noon as a signal that she is a social outcast. But this conclusion is not based on any parallel description or implication within the Greco-Roman world that moral women went to the village well at certain times and degenerate women visited at other times. Nor is there evidence that the absence of other women indicates she is immoral. While company certainly makes chores seem lighter, and so villagers might choose to work together, a lone person working the fields, tending animals, or grinding grain should not immediately suggest suspect morality. The accusation of immorality comes not so much from her presence at the well at noon as from the description of her past marriages and current situation. From the story's standpoint, it makes sense that Jesus is thirsty at noon, as opposed to, for example, 7:30 in the morning.

WAS THE SAMARITAN WOMAN DIVORCED OR WIDOWED?

The point that the Samaritan woman was married five times should not necessarily strike the reader as indicating promiscuity—perhaps she was just very unlucky. Other biblical characters had suffered similar loss, such as Naomi. The data from our period does not yield another example of someone having five spouses, but some people were married three times. While a few elite might divorce even twice to better climb the social ladder, there is no record of someone divorcing five times. There is also no testimony of someone being widowed five times, but unfortunately it was common to lose two spouses during one's lifetime. If the Samaritan woman fits this pattern, we might expect that she was widowed a few times and perhaps divorced, or was divorced, a few times.

First-century BC funerary relief of a husband and wife (Photo courtesy of Zingaro/flickr.com)

Because neither situation necessarily casts a shadow over one's character, we cannot assume that her marriage history made her a social pariah. We might ask here why she experienced divorce. If the Samaritan woman was barren, perhaps she was divorced these five times; however, we do not have clear and compelling evidence for barrenness creating a social stigma. And if she lived within this village all her life, a common experience with most people, then why would the fourth or fifth man take a chance on marrying a woman who was barren? It is, however, possible that a particular husband would choose to divorce her on grounds of barrenness. Perhaps another husband divorced her to marry another woman—this decision would not be frowned upon necessarily, depending on the local circumstances. Jewish law in general reserved the right of divorce to the husband, although there is at least one divorce certificate that indicates the wife initiated the proceedings (discussed below).

Many commentators, however, assume that the woman was in her current situation because she filed for divorce five times. Despite Juvenal's satire that impugns all women as fornicators preying on innocent men and merrily running off to divorce court with great frequency, the satire's rhetoric hardly gives great confidence in its historical reliability. We do better to examine the legal records and contracts. It is unclear whether the Samaritans followed the Roman practice allowing either spouse to initiate divorce. There is no record from this time of any woman filing for divorce more than one time; such behavior was a rare occurrence and happened at the social level of the Roman elite.[64] Among the handful of Greek and Aramaic Jewish divorce documents, only one appears to have been initiated by the wife. This text reads, "This is from me to you a bill of divorce and release."[65] The woman, Shelamzion daughter of Joseph Qebshan, is represented by a man named Mattat son of Simon who writes the document at her request. In this Aramaic document, a Jewish woman is following the Greco-Roman custom in initiating a "no fault" divorce. Does this one "exception" prove the rule that women did not or could not initiate divorce? Or does this divorce contract suggest that divorce proceedings were more complex than the rabbinic sources might imply? From this single example we should not draw any general conclusions beyond the recognition that at least one Jewish woman in the Greco-Roman period initiated her own divorce.

Nor should we forget that women did not have direct legal recourse to the courts. They had to go through their guardian or a male representative.[66]

64. Valeria Paulla divorced her first husband to marry Demicus Brutus, the lead conspirator behind the assassination of Julius Caesar. A discussion is found in Treggiari, "Divorce Roman Style," 42–44.
    65. P.Se'elim 13.8. Translation in Kraemer, *Women's Religions*, 156.
    66. An important exemption from male guardianship was made for female Roman citizens who had three live births and a freedwoman who had four live births. These conditions were

For example, the Babatha archive includes several legal documents detailing disputes Babatha had with her son's guardians (her first husband, Jesus, died while their son was young) and outlining a loan of three hundred denarii she offered to her second husband, Judah. In the first case, Babatha is represented by Yehudah (Judah) son of Khthousion, who is described as her "lord."[67] In the second situation, her "lord" is Jacob son of Jesus. This man might be her former brother-in-law. While Babatha is free to distribute her wealth as she wishes, she is formally represented by a male relative in the transactions.

If it seems highly unlikely that the Samaritan woman was divorced five times, it is entirely credible that she was a widow several times, given the high death rate in that era. According to Josephus, the Herodian princess Berenice had been widowed twice and had borne two children by age twenty-two.[68] We do not know the age of the Samaritan woman, but we cannot rule out that she was a widow at a young age. We also cannot say whether she had any children. Moreover, we do not know if her former husbands had children in previous marriages.

WAS THE SAMARITAN WOMAN A CONCUBINE?

It is Jesus's statement that the man she is with now is not her husband that causes most commentators to conclude the Samaritan woman is immoral. Jesus's words and her reaction indicate that both agreed her current situation was in some way different from her previous arrangements. Her current relationship, with a man Jesus identified as not her husband, might be classified as concubinage, not an unusual situation within the larger Greco-Roman world. Perhaps she was in this relationship because the man was a Roman citizen and could not legally marry beneath his social rank. Or perhaps this arrangement was made precisely to prevent any children she might bear in the relationship from inheriting his wealth. If he was an older man with children in their teens or twenties, he might feel family pressure to keep their inheritance from becoming diluted with other children born in his relationship to the Samaritan woman.

A second-century AD marriage document from the Judean desert (P.Yadin 37; P.XHev/Se gr 65) is relevant to our discussion.[69] Salome Komaïse and Jesus son of Menahem agree to marry, but the wording raises important questions. Specifically, the Greek text reads "[that they continue] life together . . . as also before this time." The pertinent verb is *symbioō*, which generally means "living

established from the *lex Julia* and *lex Papia Poppaea* enacted under Augustus (Gaius, *Institutiones* 1.145, 171).
67. P.Yadin 15.
68. Josephus, *Ant.* 19.277.
69. Tal Ilan, "Premarital Cohabitation in Ancient Judea: The Evidence of the Babatha Archive and the Mishnah (Ketubbot 1.4)," HTR 86 (1993): 247–64; reprinted in her book, Integrating Women into Second Temple History (Peabody, MA: Hendrickson, 2001), 235–51.

together." The noun form *symbios* is usually translated "spouse." Normally, a marriage contract includes the verb *gameō*, which denotes the specific act of a man taking a wife. The Salome Komaïse document does not use *gameō*, lending support to the conclusion that in this case the couple cohabitated before marrying.

Though details are missing, this cache of documents related to Salome Komaïse is enormously helpful in recreating historical circumstances and reinforcing the picture created by other material. Salome was divorced and remarried, with her father and brother dead at the time of her second marriage. Her mother remarried and gave a gift to Salome to preserve the family estate and inheritance. All of these situations appear also in other documentation. What is new is the "unofficial" relationship presumably shared by Salome and Jesus for some stretch of time prior to a formal document. Yet this should not be surprising as I noted earlier that Greco-Roman marriages were not certified by the state. Instead, a couple set up a home together, and they were therefore seen as married by their families and neighbors. It was discussed above how, in most cases, a marriage contract basically certified a dowry and detailed how that money would be used or, in the case of divorce, returned. If Salome had no dowry, perhaps there was no need to make a formal contract. When her mother gave her a dowry, then a formal contract was prudent.

When Jesus meets her, does the Samaritan woman's situation parallel that of Salome Komaïse? Are the woman and her partner waiting for a gift or dowry before writing a contract? If this was the case, Jesus's comments reveal that he expected a formal arrangement irrespective of a dowry contract. As John describes it, the woman does not contest Jesus's assessment that her previous and current living situations differ. To match her previous state of affairs, would a wedding ceremony be necessary? Would a formal document from a town elder or religious figure be essential? The preserved records do not give enough information to conclude that Jesus or anyone in his day would have expected all marriages to have an official written component (although later rabbinic evidence suggests that all marriages should have this).

Was the Samaritan Woman a Second Wife?

At the risk of complicating matters all the more, the Samaritan woman might have been a second wife in a polygynous relationship; that is, perhaps the man she was currently living with was already married. From the Babatha archives, we know that Babatha herself was a second wife, for her husband Judah was also married to a woman named Miriam. Why did she marry Judah? Exploring the intentions of a historical figure is highly problematic, but perhaps we can rule out some common reasons why a woman might marry. Babatha was well off, as she had significant date groves and thus a decent income. In fact, records indicate that she loaned Judah three hundred denarii, which he then probably used as a dowry for his daughter from his wife Miriam. We also know that with her first husband, Jesus (now deceased), Babatha had a son. It seems likely, therefore, that she did not marry for financial security or to have a child.

Could she have married for that sentimental, eternal reason—love? Suzanne Dixon presents a cogent argument that at least some Roman men married because they were romantically drawn to their wives. "So strong indeed was the cultural presumption that Roman men did expect sexual pleasure in marriage, particularly in the early years, that husbands were conventionally cautioned against sexual infatuation with their wives."[70] The literature does not give direct insight into why women might marry because the sources speak from a male's point of view. But material evidence of magic potions and amulets meant to secure a husband's fidelity and to increase a wife's appeal suggest that women were also interested in romance as part of their married life.

Plutarch (early second century AD) accepts that wives might use spells and charms to make themselves more alluring, though he suggests that such magic lulls the husband into a stupor.[71] Love magic was illegal, but it was thought to be used widely, such that women were in danger of being accused of using love magic to vent their jealousy. Tacitus, also from the second century AD, tells a riveting tale of a woman charged with inciting her former husband to kill his new wife.[72] The husband, Plautius Silvanus, was convicted of throwing his wife Apronia out a window. When her father discovered his daughter's death, he brought the case to Emperor Tiberius. Silvanus pleaded he was asleep at the time, and that his wife committed suicide. But when the house was inspected, clear signs of struggle were discovered. At this point, Silvanus received a gift from his grandmother—a dagger. Silvanus's attempt at suicide was unsuccessful, and so the authorities finished the work. Tacitus adds that Silvanus's former wife, Numantina, was subsequently charged with using magical incantations that caused him to become insane. She was later acquitted.

We cannot know whether Babatha married Judah and entered into a polygynous relationship because she loved him, but she seemed under no readily apparent constraints to marry, especially a man currently married. Her actions of financial support for him and his daughter suggest emotional ties. Could the same be said of the Samaritan woman? Was she in love with the man with whom she was currently abiding? Was that love so strong that she was willing to "share" her man with his wife? It may be that in her community the Samaritan woman was "married" as the second wife, but in Jesus's eyes, her marriage is null and void because he rejected bigamy.

70. Suzanne Dixon, "Sex and the Married Woman in Ancient Rome," in *Early Christian Families in Context: An Interdisciplinary Dialogue*, ed. David L. Balch and Carolyn Osiek (Grand Rapids: Eerdmans, 2003), 127–28.
71. Plutarch, *Mor.* 139a (= *Conj. praec.* 5).
72. Tacitus, *Ann.* 4.22.

In sum, we can devise any number of scenarios to explain why the Samaritan woman had five husbands and is currently not married to the man she lives with. As the narrative unfolds in John, Jesus does not explicitly condemn her situation.[73] Moreover, the villagers accept her testimony that a prophet is among them—hardly a reaction one would imagine if she was without any moral scruples. Finally, within John's Gospel, her dialogue with Jesus bears interesting similarities to his exchange with Nathanael (1:43–51). The latter approaches Jesus, who identifies him as an Israelite in whom there is no deceit. Nathanael is dumbfounded—how could Jesus know who he is? Jesus replies that he saw him sitting under a fig tree just a few minutes earlier. This statement, indicating that he could see into Nathanael's past, evokes from Nathanael the declaration that Jesus is the Son of God and the King of Israel. The Samaritan woman's assertion is similar: Jesus is a prophet because he told her everything she had ever done (4:29).

In the final analysis, the Samaritan woman has been harshly treated by centuries of commentators who have labeled her a promiscuous vixen bent on seducing unsuspecting men, and who therefore becomes the village pariah. Our careful examination of marriage and divorce documents and traditions sharply critiques such assessments. From the surviving evidence, no one from any social class divorced five times; moreover, women could not represent themselves in court. While the possibility existed for a woman unilaterally to initiate divorce from her husband (through a male representative in court), as seen in the marriage contract from Egypt dated 13 BC, there is only one specific documented case of a woman divorcing her husband. Usually a woman filed for divorce with the encouragement or aid of her father, brother, or other male relative. Thus it seems unlikely that the Samaritan woman was involved in a series of divorces that she initiated. It remains an open question whether her husbands chose to divorce her.

Because of the high death rate, many women were left widows and usually went on to remarry. We do not know whether the Samaritan woman had economic needs or was financially stable. Her history of several husbands does fit the pattern we find of women marrying in their early to late teens and becoming widows very young. The Samaritan is a woman of her times, living with fairly simple marriage traditions, relatively easy divorce laws, and haunted by the threat that death might at any time steal away a husband or child.[74]

73. Elsewhere in the Gospels, Jesus's teachings present legitimate marriage as between one man and one woman (Matt. 19:4–6) and speak against adultery (Matt. 5:27–29). My point is not that her particular situation was viewed by Jesus as entirely acceptable, only that the narrative itself does not implicitly or explicitly condemn her.

74. It is beyond the scope of this work to explore the moral uprightness of the Samaritan woman's choices or Jesus's theological teachings within this story in John's Gospel. Were it to be shown that John's story does not rest on an actual encounter in Jesus's life, the points made

Ananias and Sapphira

The scenarios that could explain the Samaritan woman's marital history allowed us to dig into the cultural expectations and possibilities surrounding marriage. Records of married couples within the church, such as Ananias and Sapphira, help elucidate other aspects of married life in the ancient world. In this pericope from Acts 5:1–11, the couple agrees to deceive the church, and both are held equally responsible for the deception. The details of the story match what we know about the economic arrangements in marriages. Ananias owns land that he sells. The property belonged to Ananias rather than Sapphira. According to Roman law a wife's property was not owned or deeded to her husband when they married; it remained hers to dispose of as she saw fit (in line with her family's consent, usually). So Ananias sells his land and receives the money, of which he keeps a portion and brings the rest to the disciples. Sapphira is fully aware of her husband's business dealing, just as Cicero's letters to his wife indicate frequent communication about financial matters in the home.

Ananias and Sapphira are buried side by side: "they [the young men] carried her out and buried her beside her husband" (Acts 5:10). Lack of clear evidence from epitaphs prohibits us from saying with confidence that most husbands and wives were buried together. Nor can we detect any clear pattern specific to Jewish families in this regard. But the evidence does suggest that husbands generally buried their wives and were responsible for their epitaphs. Widows were often buried by their children. Divorced women might be buried by their children or their parents or other relatives. In Acts 5, "young men" from the church bury both Ananias and Sapphira. This corresponds with the service offered by many ancient associations and trade guilds.[75] It may be that the early church provided burial service, especially to its poorer members, but clearly Ananias and Sapphira had money. We do not read of any children responsible for their burial.

Priscilla and Aquila

Another church couple, described in Acts 18, meets with a happier fate. Priscilla and Aquila are a peripatetic couple who were driven from their home in Rome and settled for a time in Corinth and then Ephesus (see Acts 18:1–4, 18, 26). A Jewish couple, they were tentmakers as was Paul. Luke describes them as working together, but did he mean that Priscilla worked with Paul and

---

above would still stand—widowhood, remarriage, and cohabitation appeared to be options open to women in the first century AD.

75. Philip A. Harland writes, "Christian congregations, too, could serve a similar purpose, providing burial and related funerary honors for their members, especially the less fortunate (cf. Tertullian, *Apology* 39.5–6)" (*Associations, Synagogues, and Congregations: Claiming a Place in Ancient Mediterranean Society* [Minneapolis: Fortress, 2003], 84).

her husband? We will explore the topic of work and daily activity in chapter 7; my concern here is how closely the couple appears to work together. Not only are they described as doing tentmaking jointly, but they also teach together. "He [Apollos] began to speak boldly in the synagogue; but when Priscilla and Aquila heard him, they took him aside and explained the Way of God to him more accurately" (18:26).

Does this pattern of shared activities reflect a larger Roman custom or milieu? Does it match what we know about Jewish couples? The evidence is ambiguous. In the Jewish sources, Aseneth's parents visit their fields together to survey their harvest. Yet in both Sirach and Tobit, wives work in domestic services, clearly not jobs their husbands would do. Interestingly, it is precisely these activities of working in another man's house that cause friction between Anna and Tobit. Overall, I suggest that when Priscilla and Aquila participated together as a couple in work-related or religious activities, they were following established norms. The society around them would not have considered it odd that a couple might work together in the family business or in the association to which they belonged (in this case, a church). Moreover, the early church apparently accepted missionary couples traveling and working together (1 Cor. 9:5).

One final point should be made concerning Priscilla and Aquila: Priscilla's name is mentioned first in two of the three cases in Acts. When Paul sends greetings to the Corinthian church from the couple, he writes Aquila's name first (1 Cor. 16:19), but in Romans 16:3 he lists Prisca[76] first and then Aquila (see also 2 Tim. 4:19). Because the culture was highly stratified, the order in which someone was named in a group could have status implications. Some scholars suggest that Prisca had a higher social status than her husband. Perhaps like Terentia (Cicero's former wife) she was *sui iuris* and could make business decisions with her own resources without the approval of any kin or tutor.[77] Others suggest that Prisca had more wealth and so was treated with proper honor in noting her name before her husband's. The couple seemed to have enough money that they were able to have a house that could accommodate a modest-sized church gathering. They led a house church both in Ephesus and in Rome. Perhaps Prisca's money financed this lifestyle. Additionally, Paul commends them to the Roman church as risking their necks for his sake. In this enigmatic phrase, Paul may be suggesting that the couple acted as benefactors or patrons who used their social status or wealth to help him out of tight spots.

Paul indicates in 1 Corinthians 9:5 that apostles are often accompanied on their journeys by their wives. Unfortunately, Paul does not elaborate on his comment, and Prisca and Aquila offer perhaps the best window into this practice. In Romans 16:7 another missionary couple is mentioned, Androni-

76. "Prisca" is the formal name, and "Priscilla" is the diminutive form.
77. We do not know the marital status of Lydia (Acts 16), but she too could be *sui iuris*.

cus and Junia. Paul describes them as his "relatives," which probably means they were Jewish. Paul met them after the couple had joined the Christian movement. He compliments their courage and faithfulness, even to the point of being imprisoned with him for the sake of the gospel. Junia's name is a Latin family name (*nomen*), which might mean that she was a freedwoman or the descendant of a slave who was freed by a member of the Junian family.[78] Junia offers us another example, along with Priscilla and Aquila, of Jews with Latin names who preached or taught the gospel at great personal risk. Like Priscilla and Aquila, they are described as a team doing the same work for the church community.

Conclusion

A poignant epitaph from the imperial period expresses much of what we discovered in this chapter: "To Scribonia Hedone, with whom I lived 18 years without a quarrel. At her wish, I swore that after her I would not have another wife."[79] Romans valued love and harmony within marriage, at times demonstrating their devotion by not remarrying. Yet the reality was that most did remarry, for life was short and marriages often brief. Alongside the affection felt by many in marriage was the option taken by some to divorce. Many times divorce was done to move up the social ladder or create new political alliances. Women brought to marriage a dowry that they retained if divorced or widowed. As such, women remained closely tied with their kin, not their husband's family. They could use their money to support their children, even though in a licit marriage the children were the responsibility of the father and remained with his family in a divorce. Jewish marriages for the most part followed the Greco-Roman pattern, although at least among some there appears a special emphasis on marrying other Jews (endogamy) as well as an acceptance of polygynous households. The Jewish and gentile women who joined the early church would have brought their respective expectations about marriage with them.

Perhaps somewhat surprisingly for modern readers, we do not find a tight link between the successful marriage and raising children. Neither Jew nor gentile felt obligated to break up a marriage over issues of barrenness. Yet given the unreliable birth control methods of the time, sexual intercourse often led to pregnancy. In other words, most couples could assume that marriage would bring children, or at least pregnancy. For wives, that meant a new role—motherhood—to which we turn in the next chapter.

78. Another possibility, that Junia represents the Latin name of Joanna (Luke 8:1–3), will be discussed in chapter 9 (see also chap. 6).
79. *CIL* XI.1491; *ILS* 8461. Translation in Lefkowitz and Fant, *Women's Life in Greece and Rome*, 206.

4

Motherhood

The sorrow of so many mothers, both in the ancient world and now, is to die before they see their children settled as adults. From North Africa, we read of a young mother's last request on her epitaph: "Here lies Pompeia Chia, who lived 25 years. I hope that my daughter will live chastely and learn by my example to love her husband."[1] Her wishes for her daughter reflect the attitudes and behaviors of the general Roman population—a wife should be modest and feel affection for her husband. Fortunate were those mothers whose children lived into adulthood to fulfill such wishes. Valerius Maximus preserves a saying associated with Cornelia, the mother of the Gracchi, who bore twelve children, only three of whom survived to adulthood. In response to a visiting matron's question about her jewelry, Cornelia pointed to her children and said, "These are my jewels."[2]

Motherhood was tightly connected to marriage in the literary writings and exalted in epitaphs. But the previous chapters have revealed that historical realities can be far more complex than an initial reading of the literary evidence might suggest. Unlike today in the West, where divorced women are usually given custody of their children, in the ancient world in most cases the husband's family was legally accountable to raise the child. The husband in a licit marriage had the duty to accept or reject the infant at birth; a rejection meant the child was exposed. But if a woman was carrying an illegitimate

1. *CIL* VIII.8123; *CLE* 1287. Translation in Mary R. Lefkowitz and Maureen B. Fant, *Women's Life in Greece and Rome: A Source Book in Translation*, 3rd ed. (Baltimore: Johns Hopkins University Press, 2005), 190.

2. Valerius Maximus, *Fact. dict. mem.* 4.4. Translation from Lefkowitz and Fant, *Women's Life in Greece and Rome*, 191.

The Great Cameo of France, a large sardonyx cameo from around AD 20, includes many imperial family members in the middle level. Seated in the center is the emperor Tiberias, and to his left, also seated, is his mother Livia. (Photo courtesy of Marie-Lan Nguyen/Wikimedia Commons)

child, it was her decision whether or not to raise the baby. If the mother was a slave, the child belonged to her master, regardless of whether the child was biologically his offspring.

Illegitimacy was not a serious social obstacle, for licit marriages between two Roman citizens was not the only socially condoned marriage arrangement. In most cases, the illegitimate child inherited the social status of the mother,[3] although a law from ca. 90 BC dictated that the child of a foreign man and a Roman woman would take the lesser social status. Perhaps this was enacted to prevent foreigners from producing children with citizen status.[4] The complexity of such a situation can be gleaned from the example of the slave Aelius Aelianus, who had a child with his freed wife, Claudia Zosime. Their daughter was illegitimate (because the parents were not in a licit marriage) but freeborn, taking the status of the mother. If the husband gained his freedom, and with that his citizenship, they could form a licit marriage and any subsequent children would be legitimate and under his control. In fact, one could imagine a scenario in which a slave woman had her first child, who was property of her master. She was later freed and gained citizenship

3. An exception is the child of a Roman senator and a freedwoman—the child would be a Roman citizen and illegitimate. For a careful description of the legal system, see Suzanne Dixon, *The Roman Family* (Baltimore: Johns Hopkins University Press, 1992), 123–26.

4. Dixon, *Roman Family*, 124.

as part of her manumission, and had a second child with a slave. This child would be illegitimate, but would be a Roman citizen. Later, this freedwoman married a Roman citizen. Since this would be a licit marriage between two citizens, the child would be under the authority of her husband, who would have all legal rights. Thus in one woman's story, there could be three different experiences of motherhood.

During Augustus's rule, he established laws that gave mothers freedom from a guardian. Specifically, the *lex Julia* and *lex Papia Poppaea* allowed free women who had three live births and freedwomen with four live births to be *ius liberorum* or independent of their guardian and patron (former master), respectively. This status allowed women to conduct business and legal affairs without a tutor. A child must live eight or nine days to be counted as a live birth, and the freedwoman's children must all have been born after she gained her freedom. The more children a couple had, the greater the inheritance possibilities of the wife or husband. If a couple had no children, the surviving spouse could inherit only ten percent of the other's estate. But with each child born, the wife (or husband) could claim a further tenth of the other's estate, so long as the child lived long enough to be named (about eight days). And if the husband or wife had children from a previous marriage, they also counted toward the final percentage. The rules of inheritance were complex, and the individual's circumstances could shift quickly with a spouse's death and subsequent remarriage (to someone with children perhaps). Thus writing and executing wills was complicated and intricate.

Childbirth in the Greco-Roman World

Many women died in childbirth, and many children died in infancy or early childhood. In a tender testimony to his wife, Titus Julius Fortunatus, a Roman centurion,[5] speaks of her incomparable nature and exceptional devotion (*pietas*) to him. They married when she was eleven years old and their marriage lasted sixteen years, until her death at age twenty-seven. During that time, she had six pregnancies, but only one child lived to adulthood.[6] This harsh statistic unfortunately reflects the norm. Even in the upper echelons of society, infant mortality and the mother's death in childbirth were frighteningly high. Death was no respecter of wealth or status; Julius Caesar's daughter, Julia, died while giving birth (54 BC). Rich and poor suffered alike, as evidenced by Cornelia, the mother of Tiberius and Gaius Graccus—of her twelve live births, only three, including the two infamous brothers, survived into adulthood.

5. Dixon (*Roman Family*, 92, 126) notes that soldiers beneath the rank of centurion could not enter into marriage while in service.

6. *CIL* III.3572. For a translation, see Jane F. Gardner and Thomas Wiedemann, *The Roman Household: A Sourcebook* (New York: Routledge, 1991), 99.

A brief medical excursus might help explain the high death toll surrounding childbirth in the ancient world. We are fortunate to have several diverse pieces of evidence upon which to build our picture. These include the observations of Pliny the Elder (first century AD) and the medical works of physician Soranus (second century AD), corroborated by reliefs representing the birthing process. Such evidence suggests that poor women, who made up the vast majority, relied on suspect folklore and even dangerous superstitions, while wealthier women benefited somewhat from the more expensive and healthier procedures.

Childbirth Folklore and Customs

Pliny the Elder draws on ancient folklore and offers a head-spinning array of bizarre treatments for lessening pain in childbirth. Pliny, a highly educated man, presents this information as acceptable practice, not as silly superstition. He describes placing the right paw of a hyena on the woman to guarantee a safe delivery, cautioning that the left foot causes death.[7] Other amulets such as a vulture feather or a snake's slough were thought to be efficacious.[8] He writes of potions containing sow's dung or sow's milk mixed with honey wine,[9] even goose semen mixed with water.[10] Valerie French notes that some of these practices might introduce unwanted germs, but drinking fluids could help prevent dehydration, provided the contents are relatively innocuous. Moreover, French notes that all these remedies include direct focus by others on the welfare of the mother. What is lacking in "scientific" or "medical" knowledge is therefore perhaps made up by the treatment's placebo effect and the emotional care given to the mother by the midwife and other women attending her.[11]

Medical Guide to Childbirth

Contrasted with Pliny's information is Soranus's medical guide to delivery. He instructs the midwife on best practices, which include using a hard bed for the initial stages of labor, and then a birthing chair at the time of delivery. He suggests gentle massage with warm olive oil (that has not been used previously for cooking) and placing bladders filled with warm oil (similar to modern hot water bottles) next to the laboring woman. Once the delivery of

7. Pliny the Elder, *Nat.* 28.27.102.
8. Pliny the Elder, *Nat.* 30.44.129–30.
9. Pliny the Elder, *Nat.* 28.77.250.
10. Pliny the Elder, *Nat.* 30.143.124. Celsus, *De medicina* 5.25.14, notes that some suggest drinking hedge (or wild) mustard in lukewarm wine to ease a difficult delivery.
11. Valerie French, "Midwives and Maternity Care in the Roman World," in *Midwifery and the Medicalization of Childbirth: Comparative Perspectives*, ed. E. R. van Teijlingen et al. (New York: Nova Science, 2004), 54.

the baby is imminent, the mother is shifted from the bed to the birthing chair, and the midwife is joined by three aides who stand on either side and at the back of the chair. All four women offer calming words of encouragement to the anxious parturient.

Soranus's instructions appear to correspond to actual practice in at least some cases, though perhaps they are more representative of wealthy women's experiences. A fresco at Pompeii portrays a delivery scene that includes the mother, the midwife, a helper at the back of the birthing chair, and a fourth woman who may be ready to offer a blessing at the birth of the baby. From the second century AD, the tomb of Scribionia Attice from Ostia preserves a terra-cotta relief of a delivery, with the parturient seated on the birthing stool, the midwife seated on a low stool in front of the chair, and an attendant supporting the mother at the back of the chair. Perhaps this relief indicates Scribionia worked as a midwife.[12]

Men had little role in the birthing process. Soranus describes a male physician offering instructions at a difficult birth, but it is the midwife who provides the care directly. A remarkable marble relief from a private collection offers interesting variations from the reliefs noted above.[13] First, the mother, who has just delivered the baby, is seated on a regular chair with pillows around her, not on a birthing chair. The room is well appointed, suggesting wealth. Second, the scene includes not only the midwife and an attendant slave, but also two men, perhaps physicians, as one is holding what resembles modern obstetric forceps. Both men have a hand on the parturient's arm.

In sum, most people in the Greco-Roman world viewed childbirth as a risky undertaking. Women were surrounded by other women, usually including a midwife, to offer at least emotional support throughout the arduous ordeal. Many had only superstitions and amulets on which to rely for protection and health. Unfortunately, more than a few women did not survive the event, nor did their babies. As a woman from Mauretania, North Africa, in the first or second century AD was memorialized: "Rusticeia Matrona lived 25 years. The cause of my death was childbirth and malignant fate. But stop crying, beloved spouse, and take care of our son with love. For my spirit is now with the stars in the heavens."[14]

12. For a picture of the terra-cotta relief, see Lefkowitz and Fant, *Women's Life in Greece and Rome*, photo no. 13 in the insert between pp. 164 and 165; and chapter 7 below.

13. Professor Silvestro Baglioni owns the relief and dates it to the second or third century BC. For a photo, see Harvey Graham, *Eternal Eve* (Garden City, NY: Doubleday, 1951), 68–69. See also French, "Midwives and Maternity Care in the Roman World," 57.

14. *CIL* VIII, supp. 20288; *CLE* 1834. For a translation, see Lefkowitz and Fant, *Women's Life in Greece and Rome*, 263.

Childbirth and 1 Timothy 2:15

While the metaphor of childbirth is found throughout the Bible, perhaps no single mention of it is as contested as 1 Timothy 2:15, "but women will be saved through childbearing—if they continue in faith, love and holiness with propriety" (NIV). The preceding four verses speak of women learning, keeping silent, and not teaching. Adam and Eve are brought in as an example, though of what is hotly debated. The summation of the argument falls in verse 15. We will sidestep the questions generated by the previous verses and focus on how verse 15 might have been understood, given the nature of childbirth in the ancient world. We will focus on three terms: "saved," "by" or "through," and "childbearing."[15]

One possible explanation of the text is that it promises a woman will successfully endure the birthing process. This interpretation focuses on the verb "saved." Although the term for "saved" is generally used by New Testament authors in a theological sense with a view to a future time (the same root term is used elsewhere to speak of eternal salvation; e.g., 1 Tim. 2:4), it can also indicate being delivered or kept from death—in this case, death during delivery. Such a promise would be welcome news and give great comfort to Christian women (and their families), who were well aware of the dangers to themselves and their unborn. This seems to be the interpretation of the Moffatt translation, which reads, "women will get safely through childbirth." On the other hand, most exegetes do not think this verse is promising physical safety in childbirth, mainly because in fact many Christian women died during delivery. Moreover, they point out, the preposition (*dia*) in the phrase "saved *through* childbirth" generally does not mean "during," calling into question the translation "saved during childbirth."

Another interpretation centers on the term "childbearing." This Greek term (*teknogonia*) is rather elastic and can indicate pregnancy, delivery, or raising the child. The article "the" appears before "childbearing," which suggests a specific event is in mind. Often pointed to is Mary's birthing Jesus. In Genesis, Eve is told that through her seed redemption would come (Gen. 3:15). In this interpretation, 1 Timothy 2:15 would suggest that Mary, the counterpart to Eve, through her obedience to God reversed the damage done in the Fall with the birth of the Messiah. In this sense, women are delivered from the effects of Eve's sin with the Messiah's birth. Some argue that the women are delivered from Satan, the implied villain in the previous verses. Alternatively, the verse might promote pregnancy and childbirth as a means of being delivered, not from death, but from a restriction mentioned in the preceding verses— the restriction against teaching and the use of abusive authority (2:12). The

15. For a useful summary of the arguments, see A. Köstenberger, "Ascertaining Women's God-Ordained Roles: An Interpretation of 1 Timothy 2:15," *BBR* 7 (1997): 107–44; reprinted in *Studies on John and Gender: A Decade of Scholarship* (New York: Peter Lang, 2001), chap. 14.

Christian woman's embracing of parenthood and godly virtues releases her or "saves" her from the above listed constraints.[16]

Many ancient commentators suggest that the woman is called not only to bear children but to raise them in the Christian faith. And with the rise of asceticism, the text was interpreted metaphorically as well to include those women who took vows of celibacy or who were widows. The emphasis was on "birthing" virtues of holiness, not raising a family. The childless woman's good works substituted for children. Interestingly, Clement of Alexandria, writing at the turn of the third century against the Gnostic heresy, applies this text to the Christian husband. He begins with 1 Timothy 5:14–15, and then notes the encouragement given for a man to have a wife (1 Tim. 3:2), adding that if that man's marriage is above reproach he will be preserved by fathering children.[17] With the Reformation came a shift to seeing the term in a more literal sense. For example, John Calvin suggested in his commentary on 1 Timothy that the verse encouraged women to accept their God-given vocation, that of child rearing, as a daily act of obedience that is highly valued by God. Calvin understood the term "childbirth" to be shorthand for all things domestic, including bearing children, and the term "saved" to speak of the future rewards granted those women who persevere in a faithful life.

Some believe this text was written in response to a false teaching that denigrated having children. In this Christian community, so the argument goes, some were promoting abstinence and childlessness as a more "spiritual" life. They eschewed the material world, including the messiness of family, for a higher, otherworldly, "divine" existence.[18] First Timothy 2:15 challenges that view by encouraging women to become pregnant and bear children, for in that they are spiritually blessed and "saved." By procreating, they demonstrate sacred virtues of faith, love, holiness, and propriety.

Another scenario recreated the backdrop of this passage by suggesting that the immorality in Rome, evidenced by Augustus's laws demanding repercussions for adultery and promoting a higher birthrate among Roman citizens, had traveled to Ephesus.[19] In this interpretation, verse 15 endorses Roman modesty codes to counter Christian women's sexually inappropriate behavior, upholding the goal of raising children. The passage implicitly discourages abortions and elevates pregnancy and childbirth as supreme virtues. Noted above in chapter 3, however, was the faulty assumption that laws (especially

16. I wish to thank John H. Walton for this helpful interpretation.
17. Clement of Alexandria, *Stromata* 3.12.89–90.
18. Richard Clark Kroeger and Catherine Clark Kroeger, *I Suffer Not a Woman: Rethinking 1 Timothy 2:11–15 in Light of Ancient Evidence* (Grand Rapids: Baker Books, 1992), chap. 16.
19. In this theory, Paul is the author of 1 Timothy and has sent the letter to Ephesus. See Bruce W. Winter, *Roman Wives, Roman Widows: The Appearance of New Women and the Pauline Communities* (Grand Rapids: Eerdmans, 2003), 97–122.

those that seek to change moral culture) accurately reflect that society was behaving in the opposite manner. Specifically, Augustus's laws on marriage and childbirth might have been imperial propaganda rather than reflecting actual social malaise. And there is little evidence that the excesses of Rome extended widely around the empire or sunk deeply into the soil of the entire populace.

In the end, the numerous options for interpreting 1 Timothy 2:15 reveal its complexity. The fluidity of the term "saved," whose meaning ranges from preservation from physical harm to one's eternal salvation, allows for either an interpretation that locates the verse's impact in the here and now or one that situates it in the hereafter. The preposition can be understood as "by" or "through," though some have argued "during," which muddies the waters further. Finally, the Greek noun translated "childbirth" reflects a breadth that encompasses pregnancy, delivery, child rearing, and (metaphorically) general domestic duties. It is impossible to know with any certainty how the initial recipients of the letter understood the verse, but women of childbearing years and their families would have been concerned about the dangers inherent in pregnancy and delivery, and about the viability of the infant. Any promise that such dangers could be averted would have been welcomed.

Motherhood and Grief

Pliny the Younger, in the early second century AD, put a human face on the tragedy of infant mortality and maternal death in childbirth. He wrote of the tragic case of sisters dying in childbirth, leaving their bereaved husbands to raise the newborn daughters on their own (with help from a wet nurse). "I am overwhelmed with grief . . . for it seems to me so tragic that two very virtuous young women, in the prime of their youth, were snatched away from us even as they were giving life to a new generation."[20] In another letter, Pliny praises Arria, the wife of Caecina Paetus, on her steadfastness at the death of her son. Her husband was also sick at the time, and fearing that news of his son's death would hinder his own battle against illness, she hid her grief from him. She would answer her husband's questions about the boy's welfare by saying that he was recovering his appetite and sleeping well. Pliny praises her selflessness in choosing to grieve alone, without the aid of her husband's comfort. Arria's courage is all the more remarkable to Pliny because such actions do not lead to public honor. He contrasts this with her better known deed of committing suicide with her husband when Emperor Claudius demanded his execution. Pliny explains:

20. Pliny the Younger, *Ep*. 4.21.1–2. Translation in Jo-Ann Shelton, *As the Romans Did: A Sourcebook in Roman Social History* (New York: Oxford University Press, 1988), 292–93.

Her best known deed was, of course, heroic, when she unsheathed the sword, stabbed herself in the breast, pulled out the sword, and handed it to her husband, saying these immortal, almost divine words: "Paetus, it does not hurt." But still she had before her eyes, as she was acting and speaking thus, the hope of fame and immortality. How much more heroic was it to conceal her tears when she had little chance of gaining immortality, to hide her grief, with little chance of fame, and to continue acting like a mother after she had lost her son.[21]

Her public suicide, including her "almost divine" words of encouragement, increased her, and her family's, public status. Her private grieving revealed, at least to Pliny, the depth of her devotion to her husband. And it revealed the true character of a mother, which apparently included strength of will under duress with no hope of public recognition.

A similar strength of character grounded a mother's courage in the face of her own death, and that of her sons, as told in 2 Maccabees. The well-known story of a Jewish family facing persecution by the Seleucid ruler, Antiochus IV Epiphanes, highlights the ideals stressed in Pliny's letter: steadfast courage and dedication to her sons. "The mother was especially admirable and worthy of honorable memory. Although she saw her seven sons perish within a single day, she bore it with good courage because of her hope in the Lord. . . . Filled with a noble spirit, she reinforced her woman's reasoning with a man's courage" (2 Macc. 7:20–21). Robin Darling Young is likely right when she asserts that "there is no good reason to doubt that an actual mother of seven sons existed and was put to death publicly along with them."[22] She adds that the author likely hoped the mother would serve as a model for other women to emulate. This is possible, but perhaps she also served as a declaration to male readers that Jewish women were steadfast and "manly" in their courage, and thus were superior to Greek women (and even Greek men).

In 2 Maccabees 7, the mother watches as all seven of her sons undergo torture and death. Gruesome details confirm the agony she witnesses. Yet her dialogue with several of her sons makes clear that her hope of resurrection trumped all fears of physical pain. She speaks "in the language of their ancestors" (7:21), which probably means Aramaic, while the king understands only Greek. She shows no grief, sheds no tears, at her sons' deaths. She is as in control of her emotions as was Arria. Her behavior raises the ire of the Seleucid king, who believes she is treating him with contempt as she speaks

21. See Pliny the Younger, *Ep.* 3.16.3–6, for the entire story. Translation in Shelton, *As the Romans Did*, 296.

22. Robin Darling Young, "The 'Woman with the Soul of Abraham': Traditions about the Mother of the Maccabean Martyrs," in *"Women Like This": New Perspectives on Jewish Women in the Greco-Roman World*, ed. Amy-Jill Levine (Atlanta: Scholars Press, 1991), 68. While in 2 Maccabees the mother remains nameless, Young recounts that later Jewish tradition refers to her as Hannah or Miriam bat Tanhum; Greek Christian texts, as Solomone; and Syriac Christian tradition, as Mart Simouni (67).

in a language he cannot understand and behaves with "manly" courage. He was hoping to win over her sons by breaking down their mother. He has greatly miscalculated, for she encourages her sons to remain steadfast: "Accept death, so that in God's mercy I may get you back again along with your brothers" (7:29).

For both of these women, emotional control was part of a larger conviction that public grief brought dishonor. In Arria's case, she would dishonor her husband if she wept in his presence, for that might hinder his healing, while for the mother in 2 Maccabees 7 grief would signal a questioning or even rejection of the belief in resurrection. In both cases, open exhibition of heartache would have negated higher values and convictions. However, Arria did grieve, though privately. Moreover, Pliny does not condemn her for shedding tears for her departed son. Similarly, Seneca (a first-century AD Stoic) speaks about a widow's and a mother's grief as acceptable, but only for a short period of mourning. He condemns those mothers who, at the death of their child, put on mourning clothes and never remove them. His words are especially poignant because he is writing from exile to his own mother, Helvia. Somewhat harshly, he writes, "Do not use the excuse that you are a woman, who has the right to weep immoderately. . . . The best compromise between devotion and reason is to feel the grief and to suppress it." Later in the same letter, he points to another mother, Rutilia, who endured the exile and then death of her son, Cotta. When he was exiled, she followed him and remained with him. At their return, she watched his career soar only to be cut short by his death. Seneca praises her motherly devotion exhibited both in her exile and in her careful grief. "No one saw her crying after the funeral. She showed strength of spirit towards her son in exile, and wisdom when she lost him." Seneca asks that his own mother might show similar strength of character by suppressing her grief, given that she "who never had women's defects cannot now plead womanhood as an excuse" to grieve.[23]

The mother in 2 Maccabees 7 and Arria also faced their own deaths heroically, after their sons' deaths, and in Arria's case, alongside her husband. In the latter case, Pliny suggests she knew that she would gain immortality and honor in her suicide. But in the former case, this mother expressed confidence in God's resurrection promises. In one of the earliest known declarations of the doctrine of creation *ex nihilo* ("out of nothing"), she declares, "I beg you, my child, to look at the heaven and the earth and see everything that is in them, and recognize that God did not make them out of things that existed. And in the same way the human race came into being. Do not fear this butcher, but prove worthy of your brothers" (2 Macc. 7:28–29). She speaks eloquently of

---

23. Seneca, *Ad Helviam* 16. Translation in Lefkowitz and Fant, *Women's Life in Greece and Rome*, 192–93.

theologically complex ideas as she concludes that God will raise up her sons; he will "in his mercy give life and breath back to you again, since you now forget yourselves for the sake of his laws" (7:23).

Motherhood and Children's Education

What can we make of such religious sophistication by this mother in 2 Maccabees? Can we assume that many women shared her degree of knowledge of Jewish traditions and teachings? There is some evidence highlighting a mother's influence on educating her sons and daughters, to which we will turn in a moment. But it is also possible that the author of 2 Maccabees placed on the lips of this woman profound theological truths to further shame Antiochus IV. There is a hint of this in Antiochus's reaction to her speech (which he cannot understand because she speaks in her mother tongue), as the author says that Antiochus felt he was treated with contempt. A common literary motif among authors in the ancient world was to shame their opponents by having them bested by a woman. Clearly this mother shows more courage than most men, including the Seleucid king. To base a conclusion about women's or mothers' knowledge of religious tradition solely on this text might overstate the case.

Fortunately, other evidence combines to secure a more definite picture of Jewish mothers having an important role in the education of their children. Tobit offers praise to his grandmother, Deborah, who taught him the law of Moses. After detailing his tithing habits, he tells how he ate with the widows, orphans, and converts to Judaism "according to the ordinance decreed concerning it in the law of Moses and according to the instructions of Deborah, the mother of my father Tobiel" (Tob. 1:8). Susanna's parents are credited with training their daughter "according to the law of Moses" (Sus. 1:3). In 4 Maccabees (written in the first century AD), the mother of the martyred sons grows in stature until she can fill the shoes of Abraham: this work applauds her willingness to sacrifice her sons and says she demonstrates the character of Abraham and has his soul (4 Macc. 14:11–20). But the text states that her task was harder than Abraham's, for two reasons. First, as a woman she was weaker, less rational, and prone to excessive emotion. Second, her maternal love, of a lower order than a father's love, grew even weaker the more children she had. Having seven sons created the very real threat that she would succumb to Antiochus's pressures. Interestingly, at the end of the book, the final speech attributes the sons' education not to their mother but to their father, including teachings on the resurrection. The father figures not at all in the rest of the book, so his appearance at the end of the text might signal "damage control" by the author: to preserve the honor of his heroine, he must keep her in a "pious, domestic setting."[24]

It is not, however, her learning to which the martyrs' mother refers in 2 Maccabees 7 when she encourages her sons to be steadfast in the face of torture. Instead, she claims authority based on her experience in pregnancy and breast-feeding as well as her constant vigilance over their education throughout their youth (2 Macc. 7:27). Her authority to speak was therefore rooted in her biological role as mother, as well as in her social role in caring for them as infants up through their formative years.

Both claims to authority by the mother reflect ideals in the larger Greco-Roman culture. Concerning the latter, Roman sons praised their mothers for their careful instructions and encouraged mothers to be well educated. The rhetorician Quintilian (first century AD) advocated the education of mothers because he believed that contributed to the eloquence of their sons. He cites Cornelia, the mother of the Gracchi, as one example of a well-educated woman: "the erudition of her speech has been handed down even to the present day in her letters."[25] Philip of Macedon's mother and Alexander the Great's grandmother, Eurydice, was set up as a model mother to follow, for she pursued education so that she could better educate her sons.[26] These disparate pieces of information do not add up to a full picture of a mother's role in educating her children, but a few summary remarks are possible. First, a high value was placed on a mother's education because it was assumed that in one way or another, such learning would benefit the child. Second, mothers might be directly involved with the child's training or in overseeing the child's tutor. Third, the content of the training seemed not to be vocational in the sense of teaching a daughter to weave, for example. Instead, the education consisted of important religious matters or philosophical virtues. Finally, this emphasis on a mother's education suggests a commitment by her parents and her husband that she learn. The extent to which she could devote her leisure time to learning was probably highly dependent on her wealth and social status.

A Mother's Care for Her Infant Child

Nursing Mothers and Wet Nurses

Another notable appeal by the mother in 2 Maccabees is to the fact that she breast-fed her sons. The idyllic scene of a mother nursing her child was idealized on inscriptions, in literature, and by philosophers. A Latin inscrip-

24. Young, "Woman with the Soul of Abraham," 79.
25. Quintilian, *Inst.* 1.1.6. Translation in Lefkowitz and Fant, *Women's Life in Greece and Rome*, 166.
26. Pseudo-Plutarch, *Moralia* 14b–c. For a translation, see Lefkowitz and Fant, *Women's Life in Greece and Rome*, 166.

A well-preserved relief from the sarcophagus of M. Cornelius Statius (second century AD) high-lights events in a young boy's life; the first carved image is of his mother nursing him while his father gazes fondly at the pair. (Photo courtesy of Sebastia Giralt/flickr.com)

tion found on a second- or third-century AD marble sarcophagus reads, "Of Graxia Alexandria, distinguished for her virtue and fidelity. She nursed her children with her own breasts. Her husband Pudens the emperor's freedman [dedicated this monument] as a reward to her. She lived 24 years, 3 months, 16 days."[27] Pudens enjoyed high status as a freed imperial slave, and his praise for his wife's breast-feeding fits the pattern of using that as a synecdoche for being a loving mother.

In the few literary sources that speak on the matter, breast-feeding symbol-izes the mother's concern for the child over against the siren calls of society and its emphasis on physical beauty. Philosophers endorsed breast-feeding as a way to promote bonding between mother and child, and its absence was thought to reduce the emotional attachment between the pair. Rhetorical arguments denounced as selfish and shallow the matron who would pursue glamour and parties but forgo nursing. Also included are xenophobic fears against the non-Roman nurse who offers substandard milk and poor Latin skills to her charge. And breast-feeding (or not) provided a platform for some to censure abortion and other degenerate social practices, casting their eye wistfully back to the imagined glory days of ancient, moral Roman society.

Reflecting commonly held sentiments, Favorinus (ca. AD 85–165) attacks matrons who refuse to nurse their own infants as consumed by concerns for beauty. He accuses them of rejecting breast-feeding because they do not want to change the shape of their breasts. From here, he launches into a tirade against matrons who abort their babies to keep their stomachs flat.[28] He indicts them on charges of laziness, wanting neither the discomforts of pregnancy nor the hard work of childbirth. Breast-feeding serves as a convenient topos for disparaging the wealthy Roman matron as it introduces a series of "conven-

27. *CIL* VI.19128. Translation in Lefkowitz and Fant, *Women's Life in Greece and Rome*, 188.
28. Ovid, *Amores* 2.13–14, suggests that his love, Corinna, aborted her fetus to avoid a wrinkled belly.

tional platitudes."[29] But his attack does not stop with Roman elite women; he also scorns foreign women who serve as wet nurses. These alien women degraded the pure Roman heritage. The infant swallowed bad morals with the substandard milk of a "barbarian" wet nurse. The baby was corrupted by the ugliness, wantonness, drunkenness, or dishonesty of a wet nurse chosen only because she had milk.[30] Wet-nursing provided a platform to express the rampant racism permeating Roman writers. Favorinus offers his tour de force by declaring that in rejecting breast-feeding, the mother fails to offer milk that has been infused with the father's semen. Thus she prevents the father from contributing to his infant's welfare. With this comment, Favorinus reveals that breast-feeding is not entirely (or perhaps even primarily) about the mother, but rather about the father's control over his children.

Plutarch,[31] writing from the early second century AD, laments the emotional distance between mother and infant resulting from employing a wet nurse. He suggests that nursing mothers show more care and develop greater affection for their infant than a wet nurse, who performs her duty insincerely. He holds up as a standard Cato the Elder's (born ca. 234 BC) wife, Licinia, who nursed her own son and would occasionally nurse their slave children as well. She is unique in the literature as a matron nursing slaves, but Plutarch's explanation for her behavior is consistent with other ancient opinions: Lucinia believed her slave children would grow fond of her own child because they drank the same milk. In this, she shared the belief that milk carried with it morals (good or bad) and influenced behaviors and attitudes.

Underneath these comments flows a more disturbing critique, that of men's control over women's activities. A nursing woman is closely tied to her nursling, bathing and swaddling it as well as breast-feeding it. She is therefore restricted in where she can go and when. In short, she is closely bound to the house. It may be, then, that what interested the pundits was not breast-feeding in and of itself but the fact that it restricted women from social interactions and limited their exposure with those outside the household. It functioned similarly to the topos of women's spinning, which permeated Roman ideals of marriage but probably reflected very little on the actual daily activities of well-born women.

Some scholars have argued that behind the trend to use wet nurses was an attempt by the wealthy to create distance from the pain that would result if the child died. To shield themselves from excessive mourning and to lessen their emotional attachment to the child, mothers handed off nursing

29. Keith R. Bradley, "Wet-Nursing at Rome: A Study in Social Relations," in *The Family in Ancient Rome: New Perspectives,* ed. Beryl Rawson (Ithaca, NY: Cornell University Press, 1986), 215.

30. Aulus Gellius, *Noct. att.* 12.1.

31. Plutarch, *De liberis educandis* 1.1.5. Most scholars believe that this work is spuriously attributed to Plutarch, but many believe it is consistent with his other writings.

responsibilities, as well as the daily care of the infant, to a slave or hired wet nurse. These women subsequently grew quite close to their charges and were often devastated at their premature death. Bradley takes this argument a step further and charges the wealthy with exploiting the emotional well-being of wet nurses.[32]

But did the orators and philosophers accurately diagnose the reasons behind the apparently widespread practice, at least among the elites, of employing wet nurses for their infants? Were upper-class women overtaken by social pressures to abandon breast-feeding? And did their husbands protest their decision? While accusations against morality might apply in some cases, in other circumstances the family's social status, concerns about the mother's health, and the expectations about motherhood all served to de-emphasize maternal breast-feeding as essential.

In most cases, those who employed wet nurses were the wealthy who had the means to hire them or had the slaves available for the task. Moreover, the wealthy defined their high social status in terms of leisure time. Clearly the efforts of breast-feeding, and the jobs of cleaning up after and watching over the baby, were quite time-intensive. Just as the matron did not spend her days spinning wool or making clothes, even though these duties were praised in the literature, so too she would not "demean" herself by toiling in labor-intensive tasks.[33] Wet-nursing, therefore, was a status symbol in two ways—it signaled money to employ a wet nurse, and it represented the attitude that manual labor was for lower classes or slaves.

Beyond concerns about social status, however, interest in the mother's health was also an underlying impetus for using a wet nurse. Favorinus mocks one mother's concern for her adult daughter's health as her reason for employing nurses (plural). But the mother's response, as told by Favorinus, is instructive. "The girl's mother said that her daughter should be spared this [breast-feeding] and nurses provided—so as not to add the burdensome and difficult task of nursing to the pains of childbirth."[34] Fearing that her daughter could not endure the added physical strain of breast-feeding, the mother sought wet nurses.

The use of wet-nursing is quite foreign in most places in the world today, probably due in large part to the widespread availability of the bottle and baby formula. The practice's unfamiliarity has given rise to several generalizations about Roman attitudes toward mothers and mothering, often negative. Usually the charge is leveled that women did not care (enough) for their babies. Two

32. Bradley, "Wet-Nursing at Rome," 221.

33. Augustus bragged that his clothes were made by his wife, but it seems unlikely that Livia toiled day and night to produce clothing. Augustus's comments served his political purposes of legitimating his rule as consistent with ancient Roman values and virtues. Suetonius, "Lives of the 12 Caesars," *Augustus*, 73.

34. Aulus Gellius, *Noct. att.* 12.1. Translation in Lefkowitz and Fant, *Women's Life in Greece and Rome*, 189.

responses come to mind. First, in the Roman system, often a father (not the mother) made the ultimate decision about whether a baby would live, and he took his parental decision very seriously. Plutarch notes that Cato the Elder apparently would visit his infant after his wife had fed and swaddled him. To imagine that a majority of mothers (at least in the elite class) could revolt against their husbands' demands to breast-feed, given the active responsibility placed on fathers for the children they chose to raise, seems out of step with the evidence. In other words, if most men really insisted that wet-nursing was wrong, immoral, or downright evil, they had the social power to insist that their wives breast-feed their children. The fact that only a few philosophers promote maternal breast-feeding suggests that it was not an overriding concern among Roman husbands and fathers.

Second, and equally important, historians are in danger of imputing into the evidence their own modern evaluations about what makes a healthy child and a good mother. In large measure, a mother today is judged based on the emotional ties she exhibits toward her infant. But in Roman culture, men and women were rewarded for guarding their public display of joy or sorrow. A woman was judged strong and wise if she controlled her grief; the same was true of a man. This is not to say that a mother did not care deeply about her child, but only that she cared as much as did the child's father. Roman social norms did not elevate a mother's affection for her young children above that of a nurse or father.

A Mother's Bond with Her Child

Rather than emphasize the earliest stages of a child's life as being the most influential time for mothers, as we often do today, Roman culture focused more heavily on the bonds between a mother and her adult children, especially sons.[35] In fact, the mother's influence over her adult children might be seen as oppressive by today's standards of individualism and emphasis on adults forming their own nuclear families.

Moreover, Roman sentiment did not romanticize babies as we do in the West today. Seneca rather severely reproves a friend, Marullus, who is grieving over his young son's death. He declares that such emotional outbursts might be better suited to the death of a friend: "You are like a woman in the way you take your son's death; what would you do if you had lost an intimate friend? A son, a little child of unknown promise, is dead; a fragment of time has been lost. . . . Had you lost a friend (which is the greatest blow of all), you would have had to endeavor rather to rejoice because you had possessed him than

35. Suzanne Dixon remarks, "Where we [in the West] refer to typically maternal characteristics in relation to small children, Roman literary stereotypes tend to focus on mothers and adolescent or adult children, particularly male ones" (*The Roman Mother* [Norman: University of Oklahoma Press, 1988], 134).

to mourn because you had lost him."[36] Seneca admits that he is being harsh, but he believes, consistent with his Stoic perspective, that uncontrolled grief does more harm than good.

Seneca never had children, and one wonders whether that contributed to his cold admonition, or whether his reproach represented the majority view. Such emotional austerity might, in fact, reflect more than merely Seneca's personality. Pliny the Younger, about a generation later, cautioned a friend about being too severe toward a mutual friend whose daughter had died suddenly, saying, "remember not to use conventional expressions of consolation that he [our friend] might construe as reproof but to be soft and sympathetic. He will accept consolation more easily with time. Just as a fresh wound recoils from the healing hand but later receives it, so a mind when its grief is fresh rejects consolation, soon desires it and calmly accepts what is offered." Pliny perhaps suspects that his friend, Aefulanus Marcellinus, will be harsh with the father, Fundanus, who has "lost a daughter who was like him in manner as in physical appearance and who copied her father in everything with a marvelous similarity."[37]

Preventing and Terminating Pregnancy

Even though dead infants were not to be mourned excessively, terminating pregnancies outraged several Roman authors. Seneca praises his mother that she "was never ashamed of her fertility. . . . You never tried to hide your pregnancy as though it were indecent. . . . Nor did you ever extinguish the hope of children already conceived whom you were carrying."[38] Ovid fears that an abortion might end his lover's life. He complains that Corinna is planning an abortion to keep her stomach smooth from wrinkles and beseeches her not to attempt an abortion, noting that no mammal tries to kill her offspring, with the exception of young girls. "They don't however, escape punishment, for she who destroys the children in her womb often dies herself . . . and is carried to the funeral pyre, and everyone who sees her pyre shouts, 'She deserved it.'"[39] It is difficult to determine whether this rhetoric reflects historical reality, but medical texts outline ways for women to prevent conception. As Keith Hopkins points out, however, because little was known about the mechanics of conception and the length of gestation (described as anywhere from seven to ten months), prevention and abortion

36. Seneca, *Epistulae morales* 99 (trans. R. M. Gummere, LCL).
37. Pliny the Younger, *Ep.* 5.16. Translation in Lefkowitz and Fant, *Women's Life in Greece and Rome*, 194.
38. Seneca, *Ad Helviam* 16. Translation in Lefkowitz and Fant, *Women's Life in Greece and Rome*, 192.
39. Ovid, *Amores* 2.14.5–40. Translation in Shelton, *As the Romans Did*, 27.

were often not distinguished.[40] This might explain the lack of discussion in literature about contraception.

Soranus provides some clarity, offering numerous means of preventing pregnancy. For example, he advocates smearing olive oil, cedar resin, or honey on the opening of the uterus, or plugging the opening with fine wool. While these might work as contraceptives, he also suggests that directly after coitus the woman squat and sneeze to push out any semen.[41] By mixing superstitions with medically viable practices, the user was not likely to achieve any repeatable positive results. Moreover, given that most believed conception was likeliest to occur directly after the menstrual period, any contraceptive methods would be used when the woman was unlikely to be ovulating, rather than when they were most needed.

If contraception failed and pregnancy was suspected, Soranus offers several methods of aborting the fetus.[42] These range from energetic walking, carrying heavy items, and leaping about, to vaginal suppositories and being bled. He insists that a great deal of blood should be taken, citing Hippocrates that a healthy woman, if bled, will miscarry. The theory is that because the uterus contains much blood, draining blood from the woman will cause the uterus to lose its blood, dilate, and drop the fetus. Soranus prefers the use of ointments and poultices to the use of anything sharp, for the risk is that other parts of her body will be injured.

Of course, not all miscarriages were intentional; it is possible that many pregnancies ended before the woman realized she was pregnant. Such is the case in a letter from Pliny the Younger to the grandfather of his third wife (Calpurnia) concerning her miscarriage. Pliny concurs with his grandfather-in-law that it would be beneficial for the elderly man to see a great-grandchild produced by his granddaughter. But he adds the dismal news that she miscarried. Pliny remarks that she was young (they married when she was fourteen and he was forty years old) and inexperienced and did not know she was pregnant. In her ignorance, she did things (we do not know what) that brought about the miscarriage. He puts a positive spin on the news, remarking that at least the miscarriage confirms that Calpurnia can conceive. And Pliny is grateful that she did not perish in the miscarriage. Such concern matches the sincere and earnest love expressed in his letters to her.[43] We know nothing about his first wife, and his second wife died, perhaps in childbirth. Pliny closes by saying, "you cannot want great grandchildren more than I want children.

40. Keith Hopkins, "Contraception in the Roman Empire," *Comparative Studies in Society and History* 8.1 (1965): 124.
41. Soranus, *Gyn.* 1.61. Translation by O. Temkin in Lefkowitz and Fant, *Women's Life in Greece and Rome*, 253.
42. Soranus, *Gyn.* 1.64. Translation by O. Temkin in Lefkowitz and Fant, *Women's Life in Greece and Rome*, 254.
43. E.g., Pliny the Younger, *Ep.* 6.4.7; 7.5.

Descent from your side and mine will give them an easy path to office and a well-known name and an established family tree. Let them now be born and turn our sorrow into joy."[44]

As it turns out, neither Seneca nor Pliny the Younger had children. In Seneca's praise of his mother, Helvia, for not attempting to reduce her fertility, he contrasts her noble behavior with women who apparently limit their pregnancies because of their vanity.[45] Pliny praises a friend, Rufus, who brought up his numerous children as a good citizen should and now enjoys the role of grandfather.[46] Comments like this imply that at least at the upper levels of society, the assumption was that men could limit the size of their family; the husband could control the number of legitimate heirs he had. Does this mean that couples used contraceptives? Did husbands turn a blind eye to abortive techniques? It is true that at the highest levels of society, children were a tremendous financial drain. The social expectations for dowries and money needed for political careers could bankrupt a family. Suetonius speaks of Hortensius Hortalus, a senator whose four children nearly ruined him financially.[47] The evidence overall suggests ambivalence toward family size— it was important to produce heirs (although adoption of adult children was an option for the elite) but not to bankrupt the family in the process. In the rhetoric, large families symbolized patriotism and loyalty to Rome, but they also, practically speaking, presented serious financial constraints. Because of the latter concerns, if a couple did not have children (or had only one or two) the assumption by others was that measures were being taken to keep the number low. Whether such assumptions are grounded in fact is unknowable. But the chatter about men and women taking measures to control their number of pregnancies and births, as well as the reality of infanticide and infant exposure, suggests that the Greco-Roman world was preoccupied with issues of birth and family size.

Motherhood in the Christian Story

The events of pregnancy, childbearing, and nursing are central to the Christian story in important ways and on several levels. They serve as metaphors for hope as well as impending disaster. They contribute to the miraculous background of key characters in the narrative. And they offer hints about the daily lives of real women.

44. Pliny the Younger, *Ep.* 8.10. Translated in Lefkowitz and Fant, *Women's Life in Greece and Rome*, 186.
45. Seneca, *Ad Helviam* 16.3. For a translation, see Lefkowitz and Fant, *Women's Life in Greece and Rome*, 192–93.
46. Pliny the Younger, *Ep.* 4.15.3.
47. Suetonius, *Tiberius* 47.

Elizabeth

Two new mothers take center stage at the beginning of Luke's Gospel. Elizabeth has been married to her husband for many years, but they are childless. Later rabbinic material suggests that a husband must divorce his wife after ten years if they do not have children. But Elizabeth and Zechariah, both from the priestly line, represent the general Greco-Roman sentiment that supports long-lasting relationships regardless of producing children. Such sentiment was also found among ancient Israelites such as Hannah's husband, Elkanah, who attempts to console her in her barrenness, saying that he loves her and asking whether he is not better than ten sons to her (1 Sam. 1:1–8). Apparently the answer from Hannah is no, but she refrains from telling Elkanah directly. Instead, she prays for a son, and the Lord hears her and opens her womb (1:20). The examples of Elkanah and Zechariah are in keeping with the evidence from the Greco-Roman period, which generally does not show husbands divorcing their wives due to infertility.

An option apparently available to Zechariah was polygyny, a situation common in ancient Israel (as with Elkanah, who had another wife, Peninnah). It also appears that later, polygyny was still acceptable in some Jewish circles, as attested by Babatha's marriage to an already married man (see chap. 2). But among Romans, this custom was against the law and apparently not practiced. For both Zechariah and Elizabeth, it seems the pull for a devoted marriage was stronger than the desire for children. A similar attitude is reflected by the Laudatio Turiae. In this lengthy eulogy, the husband discusses in detail his abhorrence of his (now deceased) wife's suggestion that they divorce so that he might marry a woman who could produce an heir for him. She even agreed to continue their financial arrangement so he would not suffer any loss. The devoted husband was shocked at her suggestion. How could she even think to separate their marriage?[48]

Elizabeth's response to her pregnancy is revealing in this regard, for she sees her new situation as taking away shame she has endured for many years among her people. Luke writes that she felt the Lord looked favorably upon her, as evidenced by her pregnancy. The sentiment resembles that found in Hannah's prayer. Given that in the following chapter of Luke, Mary's song is practically a recital of Hannah's song in 1 Samuel 2:1–10, Luke likely wanted to draw parallels between their situations. Elizabeth's reference to shame in childlessness stands out against the overall attitudes of the Greco-Roman world. There is little evidence of individual women tormented by society for their failure to produce children.

Mary, Mother of Jesus

Perhaps the best known mother in the New Testament is Mary, the mother of Jesus. And yet while she plays a distinguished role in the history and theology

48. See the previous discussion of this funerary inscription on pp. 109–10.

of the church as the Theotokos or Mother of God, the biblical text provides surprisingly little concrete historical data. What information we do have has been variously understood with respect to the claims of how she became a mother and charges that her son was illegitimate. She also is presented as having a complex relationship with her adult son, as historical features are teased from the thick theological points made by the Gospel writers. I do not propose to draw a heavy line between theology and history; rather, I want to alert the reader that in the discussion below, we will not consider the (necessary and arguably important) theological thrust of the Gospels from a literary perspective. My hope is more modest: to sketch a picture of the historical Mary, mother of Jesus, as she illustrates the complexity of motherhood in the ancient world.

Most authors today assume that Mary faced great social shame and ostracism due to her pregnancy. They base this on the assumption that she was an "unwed mother" and on the argument that Jesus was accused of being illegitimate. Looking first at the contention that she was an unwed mother, such a conclusion does not take into account the betrothal customs of the day. Mary and Joseph had a binding contract of marriage; all that awaited them was the wedding. If they engaged in sexual intercourse with each other, that was not seen as a violation of any norm.[49] What is shocking is that Mary is pregnant and Joseph knows he is not the father. The problem is not that a betrothed couple had sex but that presumably Mary had sex with another man—she committed adultery.

This explains Joseph's impulse to divorce her, for that is the legal remedy when faced with infidelity during the betrothal period. As Matthew tells us, Joseph wanted a quiet, "no fault" divorce. In the end, however, Joseph decided against divorce. In the narrative, his decision to divorce and his change of heart are not common knowledge; no one in the village would suspect that he was not the child's father. He stays with Mary, and thus the child, Jesus, would be considered his son unless the couple chose to speak about the mysterious work of God in their lives, as portrayed in the infancy narratives of Matthew and Luke.[50]

Mary's alleged shame is adduced from another angle, namely the claim that Jesus was accused of being illegitimate.[51] Concerning the alleged accusations

49. Even later rabbinic writings allow that a future groom who has sexual relations with his bride-to-be at her father's house is not guilty of immoral behavior. If pregnancy occurs before the wedding, this is not a problem because the parentage is secure. See *b. Yevam.* 69b–70a.

50. While some might conclude that the birth narratives were written to counter the supposed illegitimacy of Jesus, a better suggestion is that Matthew and Luke determined that his status as from the lineage of David was insufficient in describing Jesus's honor as God's son.

51. The discussion of Jesus's illegitimacy extends as well to whether he was considered a *mamzer*, a term that suggests illegitimacy or one born of a prohibited marriage. This term appears to be a legal category for later rabbis; our immediate concern is the community's social judgment of Jesus's parentage, and by extension, the social status of Mary. For a discussion about Jesus as

of Jesus's illegitimacy, the evidence is weak. Many point to Mark 6:1–6, where Jesus is described by his fellow townspeople as the carpenter and the son of Mary. Some argue that by not mentioning Joseph, they are slighting Jesus's parentage. As further proof, they claim that Matthew changes this slur to read "carpenter's son" so as to portray Jesus in a better light. But in Mark, the crowd is upset because Jesus's heritage is too average to warrant his teaching claims in their synagogue. By identifying Jesus as a carpenter they implicitly testify to Joseph having raised him, for what man would train an illegitimate child in the family business? Instead Jesus fits the adage "he followed in his father's footsteps." Again, the context in Mark identifies Jesus in relation to his siblings. It is possible that Mary is Joseph's second wife, and thus these are half- (or step-) siblings of Jesus from Joseph's wife of a former marriage. Or it is possible that all the children mentioned are Mary's; since the other children's legitimacy is not questioned, and Jesus is grouped with them, we could assume that the townsfolk are not commenting on Jesus's illegitimacy. Moreover, one of the oldest manuscripts of Mark (P[45]) reads "son of the carpenter and of Mary." If this represents the more original reading, then the scribal change that removed the reference to carpenter's son might be an attempt by the later scribes to hint at the virgin birth, since Mark does not include a nativity narrative. Finally, it seems that in certain situations, identifying a son by his mother's name was an indication, not that his father was unknown, but that his mother's family had more prestige. Whether this was Mark's opinion is difficult to say, but Matthew and Luke connect Joseph with David's line.[52]

A second text pointed to in support of Jesus's alleged illegitimacy is John 8:41, in which Jesus's antagonists declare that they are not illegitimate. The argument is that implicitly they are declaring that Jesus is in fact illegitimate. But the exchange does not necessitate such a conclusion. In fact, another interpretation seems more natural to the overall story line. Jesus throws the first rhetorical punch by calling into question whether his conversation partners are truly children of Abraham. Their response, that indeed they are true children and not illegitimate, fits the overarching theological interchange. There is no need to suggest that they intended an insult toward Jesus's birth. Additionally, in John 6:42 some who are disgruntled with Jesus's teachings that he came down from heaven declare that they know his father and mother, and that he is Joseph's son. Thus, for the reader of John, Jesus is clearly identified as Joseph and Mary's son (see also John 1:45).

---

mamzer, see Scot McKnight, "Jesus as *Mamzer* (Illegitimate Son)," in *Who Do My Opponents Say That I Am?* ed. Scot McKnight and Joseph B. Modica (London: T&T Clark, 2008), 133–63. Another perspective is offered by James F. McGrath, "Was Jesus Illegitimate? The Evidence of His Social Interactions," *Journal for the Study of the Historical Jesus* 5 (2007): 81–100.

52. For a discussion of Jewish examples of sons identified by their mothers, see Tal Ilan, "'Man Born of Woman . . .' (Job 14:1): The Phenomenon of Men Bearing Metronymes at the Time of Jesus," *Novum Testamentum* 34 (1992): 23–45.

Finally, the accusation that Jesus befriended tax collectors and sinners is generally agreed to be historically accurate. But this claim actually calls into question the notion that he is illegitimate, for this reason: if he was illegitimate, no one would comment on the fact that he was mixing with what would be seen as his own crowd. That he is with those "beneath" him on the social ladder is what generates the comments and the shock. If he was the illegitimate outcast that some describe, no one in any leadership capacity would give him two minutes of their time. If he truly was a bastard, then he challenged no Jewish leader's honor, and could be ignored as a demented fool. But instead, it seems that Jesus spoke in synagogues, dined with Pharisees, and did the sorts of things that no outcast or illegitimate son would have the opportunity to do.[53] Evidence from Paul's epistles could be brought to bear in the discussion. Paul, writing before the Gospels, notes in Romans 1:3–4 that Jesus is a descendant of David. Because the association with David's lineage brings the individual honor, it would make no sense to have applied it to someone who was known to be illegitimate.

If the reader is still unconvinced that Jesus was not understood as illegitimate by his contemporaries, perhaps the descriptions of Mary will shed light on the issue. How would we expect people to treat a woman who had an illegitimate son? Presumably in some way as an outcast, however that might be understood. Sirach 23:22–25 speaks of the long shadow of dishonor and disregard that illegitimacy casts.[54] But Mary participates in social events such as a local wedding in John 2. Servants listen to her, which might imply that she is family and/or that she has clout in the group. Either way, it does not seem likely that they would pay attention to someone whom every wedding guest presumably would ignore. Mary is also described as traveling regularly to the temple and with large groups (Luke 2:41–52). In the narrative, Joseph and Mary are traveling in a group large enough that Jesus's absence went undetected for an entire day. This picture does not suggest that Mary was a social pariah. Instead, in these sketches she participates fully in the social and cultural network of Jewish villages in Galilee and Judea.

Finally, some argue that Matthew is emphasizing Mary's marginality by highlighting four immoral women in Jesus's genealogy: Tamar, Rahab, Ruth, and Bathsheba, referred to as the wife of Uriah (Matt. 1:3, 5–6). However, it is debatable whether all four have tainted histories. Tamar is credited with doing the right thing in holding her father-in-law to account for failing to look after her. Ruth is repeatedly praised for her obedience to her mother-in-law and to Boaz. Bathsheba was taken from her home by King David, and the text places no blame on her for his misdeed. Only Rahab is identified as a prostitute, but in saving the Hebrew spies and siding with Israel, she redeemed herself and

53. McGrath, "Was Jesus Illegitimate?" 87.
54. See also Wis. 3:16–19.

her family—she is a heroine of the story. It remains unclear to me exactly what motivated Matthew to compose his genealogy as he did, but we can rule out the suggestion that the list reinforced Mary's suspected sexual impropriety, and by extension, Jesus's later call for sinners to repent.[55]

Conclusion

In the modern era, motherhood is largely connected with young children, but in the Greco-Roman world, mothers had more influence with their adult children, and grew closer to their children as they aged. Mothers with significant dowries and family funds could finance their children's future, as did Terentia, Cicero's wife (later divorced) and mother of two. But if they lacked funds and found themselves widowed, they were at the mercy of their children. A second-century AD letter between two brothers highlights this: "I have been told that you are not looking after our dear mother very well. Please, sweetest brother, don't cause her any grief. . . . We ought to revere as a goddess the mother who has given us birth, especially a mother as good and virtuous as ours."[56] The concerned son reminds his brother that their mother gave birth to them, and we have seen that this was no small thing.

The letter also exalts their mother as good and virtuous. As portrayed by the literary evidence, a good and virtuous mother is one who carries the pregnancy to term, breast-feeds her infant, educates her child (or oversees the education), supports her husband, and lives chastely. Plutarch reports that Gaius Gracchus, the son of Cornelia and brother of Tiberius Gracchus, upon hearing his mother insulted, declared, "Do you dare to speak ill of Cornelia, who gave birth to Tiberius?"[57] In his quotation, Plutarch hints that this first-century BC mother has been elevated almost to a concept or model because Gaius identified her with her name, not as "my mother."[58] A statue was later erected to memorialize her, and the inscription read: "Cornelia, daughter of Africanus, Mother of the Gracchi." Cornelia achieved a higher status than any other woman of her time, and her position was tightly connected to her reputation as mother.

The reality of motherhood is less exalted. Childbirth was treacherous; medical knowledge of both pregnancy and delivery could be harmlessly inexact or

55. Contra Kathleen E. Corley, *Private Women, Public Meals: Social Conflict in the Synoptic Tradition* (Peabody, MA: Hendrickson, 1993), 147–52.

56. *SB* 6263. Translation in Shelton, *As the Romans Did*, 23.

57. Plutarch, *Tiberius et Caius Gracchus* 4.4. Translation and discussion in Richard A. Bauman, *Women and Politics in Ancient Rome* (New York: Routledge, 1992), 44.

58. Caesar Augustus's wife, Livia, would continue this trend with her title Augusta, given after her husband's death. Her son Tiberius resisted formal declarations of her deification and other honors, but within Rome she had a strong following who wanted her recognized as a "constitutional entity," and as "an institution" (Bauman, *Women and Politics*, 131–32).

dangerously wrong. Given the risks, legal incentives were enacted, including freedom from tutors to those mothers who qualified by having three or four live births. The infant mortality rate was very high, thus even a successful pregnancy could not promise a healthy baby. Grief was an unwelcome but frequent guest in many homes. If the mother and child beat the odds and both lived through the delivery, either the mother or a wet nurse took over the care of the infant, assuming the father agreed to raise it. Infanticide and infant exposure were practiced to varying degrees across the centuries and among various social groups, except among Jews (see chap. 1). Roman families were generally small, due to a number of factors, including the relative health of the mother and child, as well as the family's financial situation. Poor families might not be able to feed another mouth; wealthy families might want to keep the estate together or might feel unable to sponsor several children through their political careers or to offer enough dowry in keeping with their family's prestige. If the children grew to adulthood, the mother could exercise some influence, such as finding suitable spouses or using her dowry to further her children's careers. Overall, motherhood was idealized as a woman's civic, patriotic duty to state and family. And mothers' concerns have been immortalized in inscriptions and votive offerings that beseech the gods to care for their children. A fitting example is Numisia Aphrodite, who offered a gift to "Hercules on behalf of the health of my son and my family."[59] Because women's devout acts included more than pleading with the gods on behalf of their children, in the next chapter we explore in depth gentile women's religious activities.

59. *CIL* VI.286. Translation in Celia E. Schultz, *Women's Religious Activity in the Roman Republic* (Chapel Hill: University of North Carolina Press, 2006), 104.

5

Religious Activities of Gentile Women and God-Fearers

The title of this and the next chapter could be misleading: in the ancient world, religion was not separated from "secular" society. Religious activities were infused with political and economic values. We need think no further than the imperial cult to recognize the symbiotic relationship between religion and the larger culture. The sacred/secular split was a child of the Enlightenment; such views were virtually incomprehensible in the ancient world. Yet we are stuck with the faulty terminology. The reader should be alert, however, to the tight connections the ancients made between what we today separate as religious behaviors and thoughts, and political, economic, and cultural ideas and actions.

As we have seen in earlier chapters, mining the data for information on historical women is fraught with difficulties. The same concerns apply to women's religious activities; the sources present interpretive challenges. For example, an often used source, *Paulus ex Festo*, is quoted indiscriminately and without consideration for the fact that it represents the compiled works of three different men. In its current form, the book is a list of definitions. It began in the first century AD with Verrius Flaccus, who drew on ancient sources for women's religious rituals, wedding customs, mourning rites, and other social habits. His dictionary was epitomized late in the following century by Pompeius Festus, and then further edited in the eighth century by Paulus Diaconus. Though Flaccus included much on women's history, Festus removed some of this material, and Paulus erased even more. Some fragments of Festus's original remain and can be compared with Paulus's redaction.[1] A comparison shows clearly how women were expunged from history. Even more, at times Paulus transforms women into men! For example, Festus describes a characteristic of the *flaminicae* (priestesses), which in Paulus becomes a detail of the *flaminibus* (priest).[2] This means that there is far less material about women from which to draw a complete picture. But a careful, critical reading of the remaining evidence suggests that Roman women were active at every level in the cults of ancient Rome.

A word about terms is necessary. I will speak of "cult" when talking about the total sum of activities devoted to a deity—festivals, sacrifices, prayers, etc. "Rite," "ritual," "observance," and "celebration" are all terms indicating specific acts of religious devotion, which may or may not be repeated regularly.

Women's Religion in the Home

For most women in the ancient world, and in the majority of cultures today, the home is the primary workplace. Tending to children, preparing meals, making clothing, soap, and so many other necessities of life bound women's lives tightly to the home. Of course, slave women would have a different domestic rhythm, as would the wealthy elite. But the vast majority of peasants lived in villages and worked in agriculture, or sought employment in the cities. For women (and also men), raising children was important. So too was personal and familial health and happiness. Women sought the protection and blessings of the gods and goddesses and in turn offered donations and other forms of honor in thanksgiving for requests granted. In the past, scholars have assumed that women were mainly concerned with childbirth and raising children and so would gravitate toward goddesses who promised safety in childbirth. While it is true that childbirth took as many women's lives as the battlefields took soldiers, it is not the case that women only prayed about childbirth or the health of their children.

Historical sources in general do not comment on average, daily tasks. Therefore, reconstructing religious life in the home as it concerns women is quite difficult. The limited sources suggest that women were responsible to see that

---

1. Amy Richlin, "Carrying Water in a Sieve: Class and the Body in Roman Women's Religion," in *Women and Goddess Traditions in Antiquity and Today*, ed. Karen L. King (Minneapolis: Fortress, 1997), 330–76. For a critical edition of *Paulus ex Festo*, see W. M. Lindsay, ed., *Sexti Pompei Festi De verborum significatu quae supersunt cum Pauli epitome*, Inscriptiones Latinae Liberae Rei Publicae II.803 (1913; repr., Hildesheim: Georg Olms, 1965). This edition includes the fragments of Festus with the excerpts from Paulus, which allows comparisons.

2. Richlin, "Carrying Water in a Sieve," 333–34. For the *Paulus ex Festo* text, see Lindsay, *Sexti Pompei Festi*, 152–53.

This first-century AD lararium shrine from the house of Vettii in Pompeii shows the paterfamilias's *genius* (spirit) between two lares. (Photo courtesy of Patricio Lorente/Wikimedia Commons)

preparations for special feast days were done properly. Two primary areas of the house come into play in this regard—the hearth (*focus*) and the storage room (*penus*). Cato the Elder offers directions to the overseers of the house when the master is away. These injunctions presumably would be followed by the mistress of the house if she were present. The matron was obligated to keep the hearth clean and to decorate it for festivals. She propitiated the family's guardian spirit (*Lar familiaris*) on special days and offered prayers to the household *genius* or ancestor. Because of her responsibility over the storeroom, she honored the *Penates*, the deities who watched over it. Ovid presents a delightful story about a family religious celebration.[3] The wife carried a bit of the hearth fire on a broken potsherd to the place where the husband had prepared wood for a fire. When the fire got going, the son tossed some grain into the flames, while the daughter threw in honeycombs. Notice the importance of the hearth fire and the food, presumably taken from the storeroom. The woman's role in preparing and performing the family ritual is evident.

Women in Religious Cults

There is much more information about women in specific cults—but this is not to say that we can be any more certain about women's religious activities in these rituals. Continued caution is our byword as we read the literary evidence against the grain.

3. Ovid, *Fasti* 2.645–54.

Vestal Virgins

Perhaps no figure is as well known in popular imagination of Roman religion as the Vestal Virgin. And perhaps no figure has been studied as extensively or has as many theories attached to her. A basic outline of the Vestal Virgins can be sketched from the sources, but much still lies in mystery.[4] The religious order was thought to have been established by the second king of Rome, Numa Pompilius (715–673 BC). The job of the Vestals was to keep the sacred hearth fire of Rome burning continually. They had charge of the sacred Palladium, a religious object that secured the safety of Rome itself. They were also charged with preparing the *mola salsa*, the sacred "salt" that was sprinkled on every sacrifice offered in Rome. The Vestals participated in religious festivals such as the rite of Bona Dea, held in the home of the city's leading matron. The sacred temple area also served as a repository of state treaties, important documents, even (later) the emperor Augustus's will. Exactly six women were to serve at the sacred fire at all times. Each woman served for a minimum of thirty years, after which she was free to leave the order and begin a conventional life, even to marry. If one died while in service, a search for her replacement began immediately.

BECOMING AND LIVING AS A VESTAL VIRGIN

Very strict criteria were used to choose a Vestal. She had to be between the ages of six and ten, her parents wealthy elite Roman citizens, both of them still living. The young girl could have no physical disabilities, abnormalities, or disfigurements. The selection process varied across time. In the group's early period, several girls, perhaps twenty, were nominated, and from those one was chosen by lot. With her appointment she was given a large sum of money. Later, it was acceptable for a father to offer his daughter to the priesthood by speaking with the Pontifex Maximus, the head priest of the Roman state religion (beginning with Augustus, each emperor took this title). Interestingly, by the imperial period, many families were reluctant to offer their daughters as a Vestal. This prompted Augustus to declare that if he had any eligible granddaughters, he would gladly put them forward.[5]

Perhaps some of the families' reluctance was due to the fact that if their daughter became a Vestal, they had no legal claims to her property. Once a girl was chosen, she was removed from her home by the Pontifex Maximus, and all ties with her family were officially severed.[6] She was no longer in any

---

4. For example, see Ross S. Kraemer, *Her Share of the Blessings: Women's Religions among Pagans, Jews, and Christians in the Greco-Roman World* (Oxford: Oxford University Press, 1992), 81–84.

5. Suetonius, *Divus Augustus* 31.4.

6. Certainly the Romans recognized that the Vestals had real parents and kin. Cicero defends Fonteius in part by pleading with the senate to remember his sister is a Vestal and to consider her sadness should they convict her brother (*Pro Fonteio* 21).

legal sense her father's daughter. She was outside of any legal male control; more specifically, she was outside the *patria potestas* system. This familial structure placed the eldest male as head of the extended family. Grown sons were under their father's legal control until the latter's death, at which point they became the leaders of their families. Daughters remained under their father's control, and at his death, such power was transferred to his male kin, such as his brother, son, or nephew, as guardian. As we saw in previous chapters, Augustus ruled that a Roman mother of three children was exempt from having a tutor, under the *lex Papia Poppaea*. The Vestal's autonomy was more far-reaching, as she did not need to pursue any legal arrangements to free herself from the *patria potestas*, as would her brothers (until their father died). And unlike most other women, she could make her own will.

The young girl was taught by the older priestesses. The women lived in a large villa very close to their sacred temple in the Roman forum. The Vestal was not a prisoner of her home, however. She was free to move about the city, enjoy dinner parties, go to the theater, and visit the circus. Her only requirement was that she behave with the decorum fitting her status. The Vestals had their own stable and horses, so they did not need to hire transport. If while out in the city they met a prisoner heading to his execution, the criminal was spared.[7] The Vestal traveled around the city in the company of a lictor, a freedman who was a Roman citizen and acted as her bodyguard. This exalted privilege was granted when a Vestal once complained that she was not honored appropriately in public. She was returning from a dinner party, and someone acted disrespectfully to her (we are not told what happened).[8] Prior to this ruling, only the magistrates and the *flamen Dialis* (priest of Jupiter) were allowed a lictor. In fact, Tiberius limited his mother, Livia, to using a lictor only when she was functioning as *flaminica Divi Augusti*, priestess to the imperial cult. Tiberius was jealous of his mother's potential power and sought to limit it.[9] Providing Livia a lictor when she officiated at the imperial cult created more prestige for the cult.

The Vestals' costume has been much debated. What we know for certain is that they wore their hair in a distinctive manner used only by Roman brides on their wedding day—a style that is identified as *sex crines*. On their heads they wore a bride's veil (*flammeum*), a covering the color of flame, perhaps a bright red, yellow, or saffron. Another order of priestess also wore this veil, the *flaminica Dialis* (the wife of the *flamen Dialis*; see discussion below). Whether the Vestal wore a stola, the dress of the Roman matron, or an extra long tunic is debated.

7. Plutarch, *Numa* 10.5.
8. Cassius Dio, *Hist. Rom.* 47.19.4. Dio remarks that this new privilege was granted shortly after the death of Julius Caesar in 44 BC.
9. Tacitus, *Ann.* 1.14.3; Cassius Dio, *Hist. Rom.* 56.46.2.

The remains (rebuilt in the second century AD) of the circular temple of Vesta in the Roman forum (Photo courtesy of Neil Scott/Wikimedia Commons)

DYING A VESTAL VIRGIN

The life of a Vestal was unequaled, and so was her death if she was convicted of unchastity—she was buried alive. Such inhumane, savage punishment takes one's breath away now, and it did so in the Roman world as well. Scholars have noted that it is precisely this punishment that catches the interest of most ancient authors, not a Vestal's legal or social status, important as those are.[10] Following their lead, we will explore how and why such a punishment was meted out, for these answers fill out the picture of what a Vestal Virgin symbolized and signified in Rome.

Plutarch offers a poignant description of the convicted Vestal's ordeal.[11] He notes that along the city wall near the Colline gate, a small room was dug into the ground, entered by means of a ladder. In the room, a bed, a lamp, and a bit of bread, water, milk, and oil were provided because it was deemed "impious to allow a body that was consecrated to the most holy rites to die of starvation."[12] When the room/tomb was ready, the offending Vestal

10. Mary Beard, "Re-reading (Vestal) Virginity," in *Women in Antiquity: New Assessments,* ed. Richard Hawley and Barbara Levick (New York: Routledge, 1995), 172.

11. Plutarch, *Numa* 9.5–10.7. Her accused lover was beaten, perhaps to death, or exiled.

12. Plutarch, *Numa* 10.5. Translation in Mary R. Lefkowitz and Maureen B. Fant, *Women's Life in Greece and Rome: A Source Book in Translation,* 3rd ed. (Baltimore: Johns Hopkins University Press, 2005), 289.

was taken from her home and placed on a litter that was encased in curtains shielding her from view and preventing any of her cries from being heard by the crowd. Plutarch remarks that as the Vestal passed through the Forum, the people stood in utter dejection, dismayed at the tragedy. Arriving at the execution site, the chief priest offered prayers before guiding the veiled Vestal to the ladder. She descended alone, and then the ladder was drawn up. The entrance hole was refilled with dirt, but the site was not forgotten; it became a place to offer prayers.

Pliny the Younger speaks of a specific case in which the chief Vestal Cornelia is condemned (falsely, he believes) by Domitian. Refused the lawful right to defend herself of the charges, she nonetheless declares, "How can the Emperor imagine I could have broken my vows when it was I who performed the sacred rites to bring him victories and triumphs?"[13] Cornelia reveals in her rhetorical question the close connection between the success of the state and the purity of the Vestals. She maintains not only her innocence, but also her decorum, behaving in a chaste manner. Pliny notes that as she is descending into the pit, her dress gets caught. She stops to adjust it, and the executioner offers his hand in aid. Pliny describes her disgust at the idea of having her pure body violated by his loathsome touch. Thus she maintains her sanctity in spite of Domitian's unjust verdict.

It is noteworthy that in most cases the execution of a Vestal occurred during times of great political and social stress in Rome. Because their chastity represented safety for Rome, when Rome was endangered, their sexual self-restraint was presumed to be compromised and they served as scapegoats. As with any scapegoat, the ritual surrounding their death was very important and potent in deflecting any further harm. The status of scapegoat might explain why ancient authors never question the method of killing the Vestal but only mourn her falling. In other words, while the virginity of the Vestal was crucial for the state, her status as unchaste was equally important, albeit vastly more dangerous, for the state. Her crime was infused with ritual significance, and so must be dealt with using strict ritual procedures. In this way, the continuity of the state was secured.

Two major outbursts of execution during the republican period occurred when Rome faced potential extinction.[14] In 216 BC, Hannibal destroyed the Roman army at Cannae, and in 114 BC, the Roman troops were annihilated at Thrace. In the first case, two Vestals were accused: one committed suicide and the other was buried alive. In the second case, three Vestals were tried, and

---

13. Pliny the Younger, *Ep.* 4.11 (trans. Betty Radice, LCL).

14. Interestingly, Livy (*Hist.* 22.57.2) notes that human sacrifices were also made at these two critical points in Roman history. In both cases a Greek man and woman and a Gaulish man and woman were buried alive in the Forum Boarium. But significantly, he draws no analogy between the death of the Vestals and these human sacrifices. Instead, he declares these acts strange and repugnant to Roman sensibilities.

one was acquitted by the pontifical court. Not satisfied with their verdict, the tribune established another court to judge her guilt. Significantly, at other times Vestals were accused (singly) and acquitted perhaps in part because Rome was more politically secure. For example, Crassus was accused of an affair with a Vestal, but further inquiry revealed that he merely discussed buying some of her property.[15] Again, Livy notes that a Vestal was tried because she seemed too free and easy in her public appearance, but she too was acquitted of indecency.[16]

The Vestal is killed (more accurately, left to die) only for breaking her vow of chastity, that is, by losing her virginity.[17] Since the Romans as a rule would not treat their daughters with such severity, it must mean that the Vestal's virginity carried tremendous ideological weight. Since a Vestal served for thirty years, she was eligible for "retirement" at about thirty-six to forty years old. At this point, she is likely beyond childbearing age. This suggests that the Vestal was repressing or controlling her reproductive potential, redirecting that power for the good and stability of Rome.[18] Such power was symbolic of the hearth fire the Vestals tended. Even as the Vestal was not executed in a technical sense, but left to die, so too fire is never fully extinguished but can "go out" naturally. Just as one cannot really destroy fire, so too one cannot destroy the Vestal; she remains sacred, even when unchaste, and so must be handled in ritually appropriate ways.

Her symbolic power was tied inextricably to her femaleness and its ideal posture of chastity. Although we have no direct analogies today to draw upon, I suggest that Lady Liberty, who greets all who venture into New York City's harbor, could not symbolically represent the welcoming of all the tired and poor if the statue was that of a man. Our Western culture's understanding of womanly virtues includes compassion and giving aid—and so the Statue of Liberty must be a woman. Again, we often picture justice as a woman blindfolded, perhaps because the female image suggests to us mercy (the blindfold suggests impartiality). In a similar way, the Vestal Virgins represented to the Roman imagination a female ideal that was woven into the daily expectations of women's behaviors as aspiring to a virtuous and chaste life.

The Bona Dea Cult

Not only did the Vestal Virgins tend the sacred hearth of Rome, they also presided over religious festivals, including the December rites honoring the Bona

15. Plutarch, *Crassus* 1.2.
16. Livy, *Hist.* 4.44.1.
17. If a Vestal allowed the sacred fire to go out accidently, her punishment was to be beaten by the Pontifex Maximus. The extinguished fire, however, could be interpreted as indicating her unchastity.
18. Ariadne Staples, *From Good Goddess to Vestal Virgins: Sex and Category in Roman Religion* (New York: Routledge, 1998), 148.

Dea. Cicero is a leading source for information on the Bona Dea (although, as we have seen with other literary evidence, his information should be viewed alongside epigraphic and archaeological evidence). Twice this goddess acted in his favor, he believed. In one incident, he claims she directed his political goals, and in another, she defeated his archenemy. His stories hold the promise of revealing bits of information about this goddess, but the reader must beware that Cicero's primary agenda is to exonerate himself and condemn his enemies, not to describe the festivals of the Bona Dea.[19]

THE BONA DEA CULT RITUALS

The Bona Dea was worshiped in two festivals each year, one on May 1, about which there is little information.[20] The other took place in early December at the leading Roman politician's home. The cult was associated with Roman nobility and the prominent matrons of the city. The home was prepared by removing all myrtle, perhaps because this plant was closely associated with Venus, while the Bona Dea was a chaste deity.[21] Sources agree it was a women-only event; all males, including slaves and animals, were removed from the premises. Busts and statues of men were draped, so that no male eyes could observe the function. Blindness was the punishment for any man who ventured uninvited by the goddess into her temple. Cicero spoke what appears to be a general sentiment within the literature: "Bona Dea is that goddess whose name must not even be known by men."[22] Ironically, the place for the festival was chosen based not on the status of the matron of the home but on that of her husband. It was in the home of the ranking political figure in Rome, always a man, that the festival was held. For example, Cicero was the consul the year the festival was held in his home, and Caesar was the praetor when in the following year he hosted the event in his home. In this way, the official celebration was done under the control of the leading men of Rome. The question of whether men were present at the December festival factors significantly in Cicero's defamation of his rival Clodius, a problem I will tease out below.

The Vestal Virgins presided at the December festival, offering a sacrifice (perhaps a pregnant sow) on behalf of Rome. The altar probably included a statue of the goddess and also a serpent. The snake harks back to the mythic beginnings of the cult. The Vestals' presence suggests a high degree of decorum for the rite, further emphasizing the modesty characteristic of this goddess. Her rites were done in secret, during the night, away from

---

19. Plutarch, *Life of Cicero*, 9–10 and 19–20. Translation in Lefkowitz and Fant, *Women's Life in Greece and Rome*, 291–93.

20. Ovid, *Fasti* 5.147–58. See H. H. J. Brouwer, *Bona Dea: The Sources and a Description of the Cult* (Leiden: Brill, 1989), 185–86, 370–72.

21. Plutarch, *Quaest. rom.* 20, suggests that the absence of myrtle may be related to the founding myth of Bona Dea. In one telling, the goddess's husband beat her with myrtle because she was drunk.

22. Cicero, *De haruspicum responso* 17.37.

Coin with Gaius Caligula's profile (left) and a seated Vestal (right) holding a *patera* (shallow libation bowl) and a scepter (Photo courtesy of Joe Geranio, Julio Claudian Iconographic Association)

men's eyes. The Vestals' presence also signaled the cult's particular Roman heritage. The Bona Dea was viewed as exclusively and primarily Roman. Her history goes back to the time of Hercules and before. In Hercules' journeys, he chanced upon a celebration of the goddess. He asked for a drink, but was denied because men cannot drink of her sacred water. The exclusiveness of the cult as "for women only" was ancient. She stood for Roman tradition and piety.

Juvenal, however, presents this festival as nothing short of a Bacchic orgy, with women drunk with wine and behaving in a sexually promiscuous manner.[23] Then again, Juvenal's satirical depiction reveals his extreme dislike for women's religion and so is probably not the best place to find an impartial, dispassionate description of the Bona Dea. Juvenal was convinced that current standards of decorum had dropped precipitously. He longed for the mythical Roman past when women were chaste, proper, and demur. Juvenal can be useful as a resource, nonetheless, because we can fill in the gaps and focus on what he reveals unwittingly. Though the genre of satire presents problems when reading it for historical information, "satire is only effective if it has some correspondence to reality."[24] We can study Juvenal (and other male writers) against his agenda and his negative construction of women. Such a reading is possible because texts presume the historical agency of marginalized persons, certainly including women and slaves.

Corroborating information hints that the festival was joyous and celebratory. Both Cicero[25] and Plutarch[26] claim that the festival involved music and revelry that went on all night. Other sources speak euphemistically of wine as "milk" carried in honey jars, which was the key libation of the festival. This reference might reflect the ancient beginnings of the cult when perhaps milk was used instead of wine. In the republican period, by referring to wine as "milk," the Bona Dea's respectability was increased. A constant refrain throughout Roman literature is that a drunken woman is an adulteress. The

23. Juvenal, *Sat.* 6.314–45. For a translation, see Brouwer, *Bona Dea*, 203–5.
24. Shelly Matthews, *First Converts: Rich Pagan Women and the Rhetoric of Mission in Early Judaism and Christianity* (Stanford, CA: Stanford University Press, 2001), 25.
25. Cicero, *De haruspicum responso* 44.
26. Plutarch, *Mor.* 268e.

devotees, the elite matrons of Rome, could not be associated with wine when performing a sacred duty for the state.

Most information centers on the December rite at the home of the leading statesman. These rites were not official in the sense that they offered sacrifices on behalf of Rome; that job was given to the Vestals. Instead, these devotees represented the religious piety of those who were less wealthy and of freedwomen (and likely slaves).[27] Most of the goddess's cult officials were women. Interestingly, freedwomen make up the largest group of those who offered dedicatory inscriptions to the Bona Dea. Ovid speaks of courtesans (which would have included freedwomen and slaves) at the goddess's temple, which could imply that they also partook of the December festivities in private homes.[28] Propertius identifies the devotees as *puellae*, a Latin term that carries a range of meanings, including daughter (young, unmarried woman), matron, concubine, and prostitute. The only connotation it does not carry is that of old woman. Propertius's word choice reinforces the inscriptional evidence that women of all ages and statuses participated in the worship of Bona Dea.

Cicero's Stories of the Bona Dea

The most famous descriptions of the Bona Dea come from Cicero. In one story, he explains that the festival was held in his home.[29] The political scene was tense with threats of assassinations, insurrections, and senate takeovers. Plutarch describes Cicero's frustration at his main political rival, Cataline, a man he would like to see exiled or executed. On the night of the December festival for Bona Dea, Cicero is at a friend's house discussing what to do with Cataline and other rivals. Concurrently, at his home, the sacred fire, now only embers, suddenly emits a brilliant flame. The Vestals declare it a portent and convey to him through his wife Terentia that he should do what he was planning, for the goddess ordained it and will protect him.

Key points from this story are worth highlighting. First, the festival ended at a decent hour. The fire was all but extinguished, while Cicero was awake pondering the fate of Rome with his allies. No all-night revelry is portrayed here. Second, the Vestals and Terentia are of sound mind, able to interpret the goddess's message. No hint of debauchery or drunkenness pervades the story. Of course, it would not suit Cicero's purpose to mention any such details (if they did exist, which is uncertain). He was intent on shoring up his own actions with approval of the goddess who cares for Rome. What better ally than the Bona Dea to support one's rule? A strong case can be made from the various references throughout his writings that Cicero viewed the

27. Plutarch, *Quaest. rom.* 20; *Caesar* 9.
28. Ovid, *Ars* 3.243–44.
29. Cicero's own account remains only in fragments, but Plutarch presents the story in *Cicero* 19–20.

Bona Dea as his special patroness.[30] Yet his claims of support would only carry weight if others shared his perception of the goddess's character and capabilities on behalf of Rome. Evidence suggests that Livia, Augustus's wife, also understood the Bona Dea to be her personal patroness.[31] This suggests that the Bona Dea was an important Roman deity whose favor was sought by men and women alike. The evidence shows her appeal for personal and state matters.

The most notorious story of the Bona Dea revolves around the escapades of another of Cicero's rivals, Clodius. The basic shell of the tale as Cicero tells it is that Clodius desired Julius Caesar's wife, Pompeia. He seized an opportunity to visit her during the all-female December festival of the Bona Dea. In several places, Cicero mentions Clodius's behavior that night, including comments about him wearing women's clothes, women's sandals, and purple stockings.[32] Numerous authors pick up this story and embellish it. Plutarch describes this story twice, and his details are interesting.[33] He declares that Clodius disguised himself as a female flute player to enter the home and meet with Pompeia. He is young and beardless (although at this point, Clodius must be about thirty!).[34] His plan came apart when a slave girl discovered after speaking with him that he was a man. She screamed; he ran but was subsequently found, and a scandal developed. Seneca elaborated the story even more, claiming that Clodius and Pompeia committed adultery that night and that the subsequent trial against Clodius was rigged, with the jury bribed to find him innocent.[35]

Several details of the story do not add up, including that Clodius would be so rash as to venture into a home during which a women-only religious rite, done on behalf of the state, is in progress. In fact, the description of Clodius's transsexual disguise is a common folklore motif.[36] Clodius's character as discerned from other contemporary data does not suggest a foolhardy risk-taker. Moreover, how would any man in his thirties still be beardless? How could he reasonably imagine that he would escape detection, especially when flute players wore transparent gowns and his face was well known in elite circles? If Clodius did not dress to deceive, did he nonetheless attend the festival dressed as a woman? Ancient sources indicate that it was acceptable for men in some

---

30. Brouwer, *Bona Dea*, 263–66, 397–98.

31. See Ovid, *Fasti* 5.147–58. Also, women of the *vicus ad Bonam Deam* celebrated Livia's birthday, presumably because that day was to be honored by the Bona Dea. See Brouwer, *Bona Dea*, 266n56 and 185–86, for a translation of Ovid.

32. Cicero, *De haruspicum responso* 3.4; 21.44.

33. Plutarch, *Cicero* 28; *Caesar* 9–10. See Brouwer, *Bona Dea*, 198–201, 367–68.

34. Clodius had been elected quaestor, which meant he was at least thirty years old.

35. Seneca, *Ad Lucilium* 16.97.2. See Brouwer, *Bona Dea*, 192, 367n341.

36. David Mulroy, "The Early Career of P. Clodius Pulcher: A Re-examination of the Charges of Mutiny and Sacrilege," *Transactions of the American Philological Association* 118 (1988): 167–69.

contexts to don transsexual attire for religious purposes.[37] Perhaps Clodius
went to the festival believing that it was acceptable for him to be present and
that he should dress as a woman.

Supporting the possibility that Clodius was within the boundaries of propriety at least for some elite men is the fact that when his deed was discovered,
no immediate verdict was rendered. The matter was given to the Pontifex
Maximus and the Vestals to decide whether he should be punished, indicating that Clodius's fate was not a foregone conclusion, that there was room
for debate about his deed. Moreover, why would the population of Rome
support his side if he desecrated the Bona Dea?[38] Probably the confusion
surrounding his punishment reflects the ambiguity of the festival itself. It
included both public and private aspects—the public sacrifice of the Vestals
on behalf of the Roman people and the private celebrations in homes. These
curious inconsistencies suggest that his attendance at Caesar's house was not
entirely out of line but was at least very poorly timed. Had he attended after
the public sacrifice, would there have been an outcry of sacrilege? Finally,
how was Pompeia implicated? In the stories, she never comes near Clodius,
nor do they exchange any words. Yet shortly after this event, Caesar divorces
her. Instead of assuming stealth on their part, a simpler solution is to imagine
that Pompeia opened the door to Clodius or greeted him as a guest. Most
likely, suspicions about their relationship were circulating, and this event
ignited the scandal.[39]

Based on the literary evidence, stemming mainly from Cicero, Clodius's
attendance at the Bona Dea is a bizarre act indicating either total rejection of
tradition or an unstable mind. Yet no other evidence supports this portrait.
Assuming that Clodius did not have a breakdown and that the other data of
his life correctly characterizes him, we are left to ask why he would seek the
Bona Dea celebration. Our answer lies in part in the epigraphic and archaeological witness. While the literary evidence stresses the exclusiveness of the
Bona Dea, the epigraphic and archaeological evidence gives a diametrically
opposite view. Inscriptions show that men offered prayers and votives to the
Bona Dea, sought healing from her, and perhaps served as priests. Ovid notes

37. Mulroy, "Early Career of P. Clodius Pulcher," 175, cites Cicero, *In Pisonem* 22, 25, who
describes Gabinius as dancing naked and wearing rouge, perfume, and braided hair. Also Plutarch, *Quaest. rom.* 55, describes flute players who worked alongside priests in the sacrifices.
The flute players attended an all-night party dressed in women's raiment and from that time on
strutted through Rome in fancy women's dress.

38. A reference in Plutarch (*Caesar* 9–10) notes that though several prominent senators
brought charges against Clodius of committing incest with his sister, as well as the claims of
sacrilege, the people took Clodius's side, which disheartened the jury, who then refused to act
against the people's wishes. Caesar repudiates his wife, Pompeia, but does not accuse Clodius;
Caesar defended this action by saying his wife must be above any suspicion, but many believed
he wanted to save Clodius. See also Suetonius, *Divus Julius* 74.4.

39. Mulroy, "Early Career of P. Clodius Pulcher," 176.

that men entered the Bona Dea's temple on the Palatine, but only those men whom the goddess called.[40]

The evidence so far suggests both a public and private aspect to the worship of the Bona Dea. Cicero especially emphasizes the goddess's public role as protector and defender of the state, her ancient status, and accompanying traditions. But he also represents the cult's private side, for he views the Bona Dea as his personal patroness. Said another way, the Bona Dea cult had both official and unofficial rites and practices associated with it. In its official capacity, the goddess was propitiated at her December and May festivals; at the former the Vestal Virgins offered a sacrifice on behalf of the people. Yet throughout the year and in various places throughout Italy, her shrines and temples, in towns and in homes, were places of devotion.

BONA DEA INSCRIPTIONS

In general, the inscriptions develop a picture of an openly accessible religious group, not one shrouded in mystery (as in the literature). Inscriptions reveal the organizational structure of the cult, its special cult objects, and rituals that accompanied the worship of Bona Dea. Both men and women worshiped the Bona Dea, though women outnumbered men. Contrary to the picture developed in the literature that stressed the aristocratic element, more slaves and freedmen/women participated in this cult. Interestingly, the oldest inscriptions, all from the first century BC, come from the same time as Cicero, who is our earliest literary source. A brief comparison of the two types of data offers an intriguing window into the problems of interpreting sources. The three Roman inscriptions include one from a male slave who recovered from an eye disease, one freedman who was fulfilling his vow, and one freedwoman who was giving on behalf of a man.[41] With a bit of reflection, a few continuities emerge that help pull together a more coherent picture of the goddess and her worship. The reference to healing an eye disease should be read in light of the injunctions against men violating her temple. Perhaps the goddess was known for both healing and rendering blindness; her powers over sight could work both ways. The numerous surviving inscriptions as a whole reveal a personal goddess who cared for her devotees. In like manner, Cicero presumes that the Bona Dea is his personal ally.

The inscriptions reveal several types of women leaders in the cult. Brouwer notes that the title *magistra* refers to a woman who led the religious *collegium*, which probably included characteristics of a social club or burial society. Members paid dues to facilitate burial of their deceased members and maintenance of their property (burial grounds and perhaps a building). The

---

40. Ovid's evidence is enigmatic, but could be translated as suggesting male cult officials within the Bona Dea (*Ars* 3.637–38).

41. Brouwer, *Bona Dea*, 260–61.

collegia were approved by the government, even serving at times as honorary members. During times of unrest a *collegium* could be threatened, as we will see below with the Bacchanalia scandal of 186 BC. Throughout the imperial period, religious *collegia* were carefully watched, while military and political *collegia* were strictly forbidden. The Bona Dea *magistra* oversaw the sacrifices and offerings and the cultic meal, and probably handled the financial matters and internal running of the cult. Numerous freedwomen were identified as *magistrae* of her cult throughout Italy.[42] In other inscriptions, women are identified as *sacerdotes* or priestesses attached to a sanctuary in town. Probably the smaller chapels excavated in the countryside did not have their own priestesses but rather were sites for individual worship or were monuments set up in honor of the goddess's blessings. An inscription by Calpurnia in the early first century AD from near the Dalmatian coast highlights the special qualities of this goddess that endeared her to so many men and women. Calpurnia dedicates an altar to the goddess, "Bona Dea Domina Heia Augusta Triumphalis, the Mistress of Land and Sea, the Protectress, Mistress of wisdom and medicine, the Goddess of right judgement."[43] Both the public (reference to Augusta) and private (reference to medicine) shine forth. She protected the house, the fields, the livestock; she watched over those at sea (Calpurnia lived on an island). She conformed to the needs of the worshipers, even as she remained the protector of the Roman state.

The epigraphic and inscriptional evidence, coupled with the literary evidence, suggests that the Bona Dea was a complex deity who was worshiped by men and women in various levels of society and with a range of needs and requests.[44] The cult had both public and private aspects to it, a state constituent and a local cult organization component.

The Bacchanalia and the Maenads

The recurring mention of wine as part of the official ceremony, as well as music and dancing, suggests that the Bona Dea had much in common with the Bacchanalia, the worship of Dionysos.[45]

RITUALS OF DIONYSOS WORSHIP

From Euripides' play *Bacchae* (presented in 405 BC), well known in the Hellenistic period, basic assumptions about the Dionysos cult included that the god was worshiped by both young women and matrons called "maenads." They would travel at night into the forests or wilderness outside of town and

42. Brouwer, *Bona Dea*, 297; Kraemer, *Her Share of the Blessings*, 88.
43. Translation and description in Brouwer, *Bona Dea*, 127–29, 386–96.
44. Brouwer concludes, "Even though her nature conveys a different meaning to different people she remains recognizable as Bona Dea" (*Bona Dea*, 299–300).
45. Mulroy, "Early Career of P. Clodius Pulcher," 170–73.

celebrate the god with ecstatic worship and sacrificing. The initiates were sworn never to reveal the secrets of their mystery. Euripides presented the women as chaste and modest, though also mad and violent, critiquing King Pentheus's views of women as lustful and immoral. Euripides used poetic license to describe the cult, but whether his romantic and explicit story shaped the cult's future activities is unclear.[46] Whatever the case, the *Bacchae*'s portrayal of the cult was central in the imagination of the populace, including that the cult was the domain of women only.

More contemporary information is found in Plutarch, who describes acts similar to those outlined in the *Bacchae*. For example, he speaks about women in an ecstatic state handling snakes, using thyrsus wands, wearing garlands, which were all part of Euripides' description. Interestingly, Plutarch notes that men were terrified to see the women handling snakes, implying that men did witness these "secret" rites. He speaks highly of his friend Clea who was a priestess of the Delphic maenads (she was also the priestess of Osiris at Delphi). He also recounts a story of maenads lost during their night revelry who end up in the nearby enemy town of Amphissa. The women of this town guarded the exhausted, sleeping maenads until sunrise, at which point they escorted the "enemy" home safely.[47] In another story, maenads are trapped by a sudden snowstorm, and a search party finally rescues them unharmed.[48] In both these stories, the maenads are accepted and even valorized. No men seem threatened by their activities; indeed, they are happy to assist.

The opposite picture is drawn by Livy, who offers a lively, elaborate description of the cult in his assessment of the Bacchanalia scandal in 186 BC.[49] His position is summed up through the words of the Roman praetor: "nothing is more deceptive in appearance than false religion."[50] Livy argues that conspirators used the veil of (foreign) religion to cover their clandestine plans to overthrow the ruling status quo. Thus he speaks at length about the corruption found at these nocturnal orgies—young noble boys not yet twenty years old were taken by the priests and debauched.[51] Livy puts forward that the cult was exclusively female until a scandalous priestess broke with custom and initiated a foreign practice that also corrupted her son and other men, who used the cult as an avenue to indulge their most heinous deeds, including sexual debauchery, as well as forgery, murder, and treasonous plans. His scorching denunciation of the main antagonists cautions the reader against assuming that his description of their nocturnal antics is entirely accurate.

46. Kraemer, *Her Share of the Blessings*, 38.
47. Plutarch, *Mulierum virtutes* 13.
48. Plutarch, *De primo frigido* 18.
49. Livy, *Hist.* 39.8–19.
50. Livy, *Hist.* 39.16 (trans. Evan T. Sage, LCL).
51. It is no accident that Livy mentions the social status of these vulnerable youths—the future of Rome's leadership is threatened.

This marble relief of maenads dancing is a first-century AD Roman copy of an earlier Greek model. (Photo courtesy of Marie-Lan Nguyen/Wikimedia Commons)

In his contradictions and assumptions lies a more accurate historical picture of this ancient rite and the women who participated. For example, he claims that the cult was unknown to the Romans and introduced by a lowborn Greek man. Later he claims the rites were brought by the priestess Paculla Annia, who revised the cult to allow men to participate and shifted the celebration to the night.[52] Her son is implicated as one of the chief coconspirators of the scheme to disrupt the state. Though these two accounts vary, in each case a male was directly connected with the beginnings of the cult in Rome. Furthermore, Livy declares that the cult was relatively new to Italy, arriving in the second century BC, but inscriptional evidence confirms the worship of Dionysos in Italy in the fourth century BC. Further support comes from Plautus's comedies, most of which were written before 186 BC and mention the Bacchic cult as rather humorous, not as dangerous to the state.

Perhaps most intriguing for our purpose is Livy's insistence that men were present as devotees of the cult and that both men and women served as priests for the cult. His colorful story is substantiated on this account by the senate's ruling following the scandal. In the *Senatus consultum de bacchanalibus* they

52. Other sources speak of Dionysos rituals being done at night, only every other year (Kraemer, *Her Share of the Blessings*, 45).

forbid Roman men from serving as priests; this assumes that prior to this time, men did in fact hold official posts or that such was possible. Further, Livy claims that the cult, in allowing men and women to worship together, introduced a custom unfamiliar and foreign to Romans. This claim is patently false, as we have already seen in exploring Roman religion. Men and women worshiped at the same festivals and offered votives to the same gods/Goddesses; very few cults were exclusively male or female.

In sum, Livy probably wants to degrade and defame his male antagonists as effeminate, and so he suggests that this cult was exclusively women-only until the shocking innovations cited above were implemented. In fact, Livy was probably not worried about the religious sensibilities of these Bacchic revelers as much as their political aspirations and social rank. The leaders of the group and many of those arrested were from the second tier of the upper class. These were not from the most powerful families, but from those who could threaten them.[53] Moreover, the cult drew from all levels of society, which offended the upper crust's sensibilities—the social classes were to keep separate and a strict hierarchy was to be maintained.

Another account of the rite, by Tacitus, also betrays a strong political agenda. He describes Silius (a political enemy of emperor Claudius) and Claudius's wife, Messalina, celebrating a Bacchic rite—she with flowing hair and carrying a thyrsus (staff), and he wearing an ivy crown and buskin, while the wine flowed and the music played.[54] Both were condemned as traitors, not specifically due to this religious action, but because of their plots against Claudius. Tacitus, however, presents their revelry as indicative of debased morals.

EVIDENCE FROM INSCRIPTIONS AND ART

Inscriptional evidence can help adjudicate the literary evidence. The ban executed by the senate was not as severe as Livy portrays, and the cult continued to flourish, as indicated in the lovely frescoes celebrating Dionysos found in the Villa dei Misteri in Pompeii. An inscription from Miletus (western Turkey) describes the priestess's duties:[55] she performs the holy rites on behalf of the city, not merely for initiates of the cult. Apparently these rites include throwing raw meat, for the inscription notes that no one is permitted to throw meat until the priestess has thrown pieces on behalf of the city.

---

53. Celia E. Schultz suggests that local wealthy families from Etruria and Campania used the Dionysos cult as a cover for their political schemes (*Women's Religious Activity in the Roman Republic* [Chapel Hill: University of North Carolina Press, 2006], 91).

54. Tacitus uses this incident to explain or justify why Claudius divorced Messalina, who married (illegally) Silius while still married to Claudius, a deliberate attempt to overthrow Claudius which failed.

55. Tacitus, *Ann.* 11.31.2; *LSAM* 48. See translation by A. Henrichs in Ross S. Kraemer, ed., *Women's Religions in the Greco-Roman World: A Sourcebook*, rev. ed. (Oxford: Oxford University Press, 2004), 21; also in Lefkowitz and Fant, *Women's Life in Greece and Rome*, 273–74.

Also, no one can assemble a *thiasos* (club) until the public *thiasos* has been convened. Finally, any woman who wishes to perform a biennial initiation (whether in the city, the countryside, or on nearby islands) must pay a gold piece to the priestess.

Another later inscription from AD 150 praises Pompeia Agrippinilla, priestess of the *thiasos*.[56] In this inscription, men make up about two-thirds of the group. Men were initiated into the cult, but probably did not participate in all rites. Literary evidence corroborates men's participation in the cult. Euripides' *Bacchae* includes two male protagonists, Cadmus (the former king of Thebes) and Teiresias (the blind seer), readying themselves to worship Dionysos. They put on a fawnskin cloak and prepare to dance. Unlike the women, however, they do not sacrifice, nor are they driven insane.[57] Later in the play, the chorus describes a male celebrant leading the group of women into the mountains. Dressed in fawnskin, he dances much as does Dionysos himself. In this case, a man is presented as leading women, which conforms to Livy's description of male leaders within the cult. Plato uses the masculine plural to refer to the devotees, *bakchoi*.[58] This is significant because in Greek, an all-female group would not be given a masculine plural ending. Diodorus speaks of men and women participating in the festivals and sacrifices.[59]

The Dionysos cult was popular in many places during the Hellenistic and Roman periods. Generally speaking, with due allowance to cultural and geographic variations, the public face of the cult encouraged a biennial celebration of young women and matrons who would sing, dance, and offer sacrifices to the god. This ecstatic celebration took place at night, away from town, and was only for initiates of the mystery. There is no conclusive evidence that men participated with women in the ecstatic rites performed on the mountains outside of town. Other rites included public sacrifices with men and women feasting and drinking wine, but unlike the mysteries at Eleusis, which were institutionalized by the Athenians, Dionysiac rites never came under the control of a city. It seems that men were initiated into the rites dealing with the afterlife. The frescoes in the Villa dei Misteri at Pompeii suggest that the devotee's fear of death was transformed into blissful assurance with initiation into the cult.[60] Plutarch consoles his wife on the death of their daughter with the promise that their own Bacchic initiation taught them to not fear death.[61]

---

56. The inscription, known as the Great Bacchic Inscription, is in the Metropolitan Museum. Pompeia Agrippinilla was the wife of Gavius Squilla Gallicanus.

57. Euripides, *Bacchae* 195–96; see also *Ion*, 550–66, where he notes that Xuthus participated in the Dionysos rites at Delphi.

58. Plato, *Phaedo* 69d.

59. Diodorus, *Bibliotheca historica* 4.3.2–5. See also Herodotus of Halicarnassus, *Historiae* 4.79, which details King Skyles' initiation into the Dionysiac mystery.

60. This fresco shows a woman initiate.

61. Plutarch, *Mor.* 611d–e.

A close reading of the evidence suggests a multidimensional cult that had two foci, one related to the afterlife and one concerned with issues in the here and now. Not only was Dionysos honored by a biennial festival, but he was also credited with the power to safely carry the deceased to their blessed place of rest.[62] The men were primarily involved in the cult's focus on the afterlife and public sacrifices, while the women, sharing those concerns, also participated in the private, ecstatic biennial rites.

Female Priestesses

Both the literary and epigraphic evidence show that women served at the highest levels in pagan religious cults. Vestals and *flaminicae* occupied the most prominent positions, but women served as *sacerdotes*, *magistrae*, and *ministrae*. The *sacerdotes* likely officiated at services, while the *magistrae* and *ministrae* looked after the daily maintenance of the cult sites and activities.[63] In certain cases, the sexual status of the woman was critical—the Vestal must be a virgin and the *flaminica* must be married (not a widow). In many cases, the social status was also important, as both the Vestal and the *flaminica* were chosen from wealthy families. Finally, even age factored into the choice at times, for the Vestals were chosen between ages six and ten, while the *flaminicae* must be old enough to be married. An inscription from rural Italy memorializes Petilia Secundina, the daughter of Quintus Petilius. This girl, honored as a priestess of Minerva, died when she was a few months shy of her tenth birthday. Her mother, who established this inscription, remembers her "tireless sense of duty" (*infatigabilem pietat[em]*).[64] Given the young age of induction to the Vestals, we should not assume that Petilia's title was honorary, though most inscriptions indicate priestesses were inducted as adults (or when married, in a girl's teen years).

Each cult had its own requirements for its priests and priestesses. We noted the extensive list of prerequisites and entailments of the Vestal Virgins above. Another influential priestess was the wife of the *flamen Dialis*, known as the *flaminica*. This priestly couple served Jupiter in Rome. They could only occupy their position if married through a specific, elaborate marriage ceremony. Both had explicit dietary restrictions as well. If either spouse died, the other was relieved of their duties and title. Like other priestesses, the *flaminica* wore

62. A gold tablet found in a woman's tomb in the late fifth or early fourth century BC in Italy describes instructions for the deceased. See Susan Guettel Cole, "New Evidence for the Mysteries of Dionysos," *GRBS* 21 (1980): 223–38: "The gold tablet itself is a reminder to the dead person to make the right choice on reaching the underworld, the waters of Mnemosyne rather than the waters of death" (237).
63. See Schultz, *Women's Religious Activity*, 70–71, for a list of inscriptions.
64. *CIL* IX.307. See also Richlin, "Carrying Water in a Sieve," 337–38.

special attire, including the *rica*, a special square-shaped purple head covering or scarf trimmed with fringe. Exclusive to the *flaminica* was a tall headdress called a *tutulus* that was tied in place with a purple ribbon.

Though each cult had its own symbolic clothing and ritual implements, most included animal sacrifices and festivals involving a meal of some sort. Priestesses presided over the sacrifice; there is no overarching prohibition against women wielding the knife in sacrifice. Indeed, they handled the same type of knife that their priest counterparts used. For example, in an inscription honoring the priestess of the goddess Ceres, she is praised for "the ceremonies most respectably provided."[65] On a tombstone relief of a *sacerdos* of Ceres and Venus, a woman (presumably the deceased) is offering the sacrifice.

Not only did priestesses offer sacrifices, but they also contributed financially to the cult. In fact, holding religious office provided an avenue for public display of wealth, which added to the woman's prestige and honor.[66] Numerous inscriptions testify to the devotee's use of her own money. For example, a representative inscription from Cisalpine Gaul reads, "To Bona Dea Pagana, Rufria Festa daughter of Gaius [Rufrius], Caesilia Scylace freedwoman of Quintus [Caesilius] *magistrae* with their own money; Decidia Pauli(na) daughter of Lucius [Decidius] and Pupia Peregrin(a) a freedwoman of Lucius [Pupius] *ministrae* of Bona Dea built this temple with their own money."[67] This inscription highlights not only that women used their own resources for religious purposes but also the priestly hierarchy evident in the Greco-Roman world. Interestingly, freedwomen are in both categories, highlighting a social reality that upward mobility for freed slaves was often gained through religious offices. As indicated by the inscription's location, priestesses were active not only in Rome (or other major cities) but also in small towns and villages. Other inscriptions show priestesses working alongside brothers or husbands, or even men to whom they were not related.[68] Such evidence further reinforces the fact that men and women were free to participate in most cults, even if certain rituals within a given cult were limited to one sex.

Though technically "matron" was not a religious title, leading matrons in Rome served as officials in certain rites, such as the festival of the Bona Dea. As a group, matrons were seen as religiously important to the well-being of Rome, for they were asked to offer prayers and propitiations for the state. For example, the matron Valeria was chosen by the leading matrons of Rome to represent them in making the first sacrifice at the newly built temple of Fortuna Muliebris. The matrons had initially asked the senate for

65. *CIL* XI.3933. See also Richlin, "Carrying Water in a Sieve," 330–76 (quotation, 342).

66. Richlin writes, "It has become almost a commonplace to say that the municipal aristocracy defined itself through officeholding" ("Carrying Water in a Sieve," 341).

67. *CIL* V.762; see also Richlin, "Carrying Water in a Sieve," 339–40.

68. For example, see *CIL* IX.1538–42 and the discussion in Richlin, "Carrying Water in a Sieve," 341.

permission to build the temple, but were denied. The same Valeria led an all-women embassy representing Rome on a mission of peace to the Volscians and negotiated the hostilities to cease.[69] Note that Valeria was both politically and religiously influential. About this same time (207 BC), when lightning struck the Juno Regina temple in Rome, the matrons chose twenty-five of the most esteemed from among their ranks to spearhead a collection to repair it. In another example, Sulpicia represented the reinforcement of social and religious standards. In 112 BC, she was chosen by Roman matrons as most chaste among them to dedicate a statue to Venus Verticordia, a goddess who the senate hoped would concentrate women's attention on their chastity and turn them away from lust.[70]

Religion, Class, and Gender

Before turning in detail to Jewish and Christian women's experiences, several key points about pagan women's religious activities should be emphasized. First, women were active at all levels of religious cult life—from mere devotees, to simple ministers of cult sites, to high priestesses offering sacrifices on behalf of the empire. Second, pagan women were involved in religion, but not so much in the ways generally described by male writers, who suggested that women were gullible, hysterical, and given to excesses in religious devotion (as in all areas of life). The literary evidence, written overwhelmingly by men, often employs women and religious cults as vehicles to discuss politics, class, or philosophy. Cicero, for example, used (or viewed) the Bona Dea cult in terms of his political career, and therefore described it to best fit his wider concerns. Juvenal's convictions that women and promiscuity are inseparable create a wildly distorted picture of pagan (and Jewish) women. Epigraphic and archaeological evidence mediates the excesses somewhat, but even inscriptions are often stock phrases produced for public consumption and committed to standard social morals.

Third, a careful reading of the data suggests that women, like men, offered prayers for health and votives of thanksgiving, made pilgrimages to sacred sites, worshiped at home, took care to appease ancestors and Fate, and saw around them the activities of the gods/goddesses. In so many ways, women's religion looked a lot like men's religion, that is, pagan activities such as sacrifices, prayers, singing and dancing at festivals, drinking wine and feasting (or fasting). Even an apparently female-only cult, like the Bona Dea, included male priests and worshipers.[71] Some cults, however, might have certain rites

---

69. Plutarch, *Marcius Coriolanus* 33.1; Dionysius of Halicarnassus, *Antiquitates romanae* 8.39.2.
70. Valerius Maximus, *Fact. dict. mem.* 8.15.12.
71. Richlin, "Carrying Water in a Sieve," 344–45.

limited to only men or women. For example, previous scholarship on the cult of Hercules confused rite and cult and therefore determined that women did not participate in this cult. But while women were restricted from a particular rite, they were not restricted from the cult as a whole. Women could not participate in worship at the Ara Maxima, which was the center of the public cult in Rome, but could worship at other cult sites.[72]

A careful look at the epigraphic evidence reveals that women and men had many similar requests as they sought the favor of the deities. The votives and dedications at the deities' shrines show that men and women worshiped deities and participated together in festivals. Women often expressed religious convictions through donations, as well as pilgrimages from their town to the country or to a far off land. For example, in the town Pisaurum on the Adriatic coast, dedications at a central shrine site were made to at least ten different goddesses. One of the goddesses, Minerva Memor, received eleven dedications by men and seven by women, although two of the men's inscriptions were dedicated to female relatives. Thus there are an equal number of dedications from (or on behalf of) women and men, and most of them deal with answered requests for healing. One woman traveled all the way from Cisalpine Gaul to fulfill her vow.[73]

Celia Schultz discovered that early in the Hellenistic period, terra-cotta anatomical votives were quite popular, but inscriptions soon became more popular. By the Augustan period, we find few anatomical votives. In the republican period, however, anatomical votives were offered to any god or goddess, not simply to the traditional healing gods. A good number of these votives were gender inclusive: "the evidence of votive deposits appears to indicate that men and women worshiped the same gods in the same sanctuaries at least as often as they worshiped different gods in different sanctuaries."[74] While there are exclusively female deposits (and exclusively male deposits), the evidence overall suggest that gender-exclusive cults were no more prevalent than gender-inclusive ones. Interestingly, about 60 to 70 percent of votives lacked any gender specificity. These findings confirm that "it is likely that women often worshiped the same gods in the same sanctuaries as did men: temples and sanctuaries open to worshipers of both genders were at least as common as those restricted to one group or the other."[75]

The distinction between women's and men's religious activities lay not so much with what was done or said but with how it was done. For women, everything had to be done with decorum and modesty to be accepted by the patriarchal Roman culture. So even when participating in the Dionysiac ecstatic rites, women could maintain their chastity by segregating from "nor-

72. Schultz, *Women's Religious Activity*, 61–67.
73. *CIL* XI.1306.
74. Schultz, *Women's Religious Activity*, 117.
75. Schultz, *Women's Religious Activity*, 119.

mal" society. In this they may have enjoyed autonomy, though only within the confines offered by the larger, male-dominated society. Also, as these rites were understood to be ancient, they were endowed with the weight of tradition. In sum, unlike the classical age in Greece, which promoted strong gender segregation, the Hellenistic period softened and blurred those lines, "creating more congruence in the social experiences of women and men, and hence in the kinds of religious activities in which they were likely to participate."[76]

Fourth, women's religious experience was impacted not only by gender but also by class and ethnicity. Perhaps not surprisingly, the voice of the slave woman's worship is all but silent in our evidence. Only a handful of inscriptions identify a slave woman as a *magistra* and *ministra*. We assume that they participated in the family religion. If they were from the eastern parts of the empire, transported to Rome, perhaps they would follow their native traditions, but that would depend on their owners. We must keep this in mind as we explore in the next chapter the spread of Christianity. Acts describes how the master of the house and the *household* converted—this would include slaves. And we find the slave girl Rhoda answering the knock of Peter; she was aware of and perhaps participating in the prayers of the household (Acts 12:12–16). Her evidence that Peter was himself at the door is roundly dismissed, a typical response by free/freed people to slaves. A slave woman's celebrations often differed greatly from that of the wealthy Roman matron. The exception (for example, the Bona Dea festival where, from Cicero's descriptions, slave women mingled with matrons) proved the rule—strict separation between classes. In the Matralia festival, held in the temple of Mater Matuta, a slave girl was brought into the center of the group of matrons and ritually slapped and driven from their midst.[77] Conversely, in the Matronalia, a festival celebrating Juno Lucina, matrons served their slaves food.[78] The exceptional nature of the event served to solidify social status structure.

In a related case, a matron named Verginia married beneath her class and was thereby expelled from worshiping Pudicitia Patricia (Patrician Chastity). Stung by what she saw as unwarranted banishment, she started her own cult, Pudicitia Plebeia and built a shrine in her home. She limited participants to plebeian *univirae* (women married only once). The cult appears not to have survived any appreciable time.[79] There is very little evidence for slave women serving as officials of a cult.[80] The emphasis on

76. Kraemer, *Her Share of the Blessings*, 48.
77. Plutarch, *Quaest. rom.* 267d.
78. Richlin, "Carrying Water in a Sieve," 354.
79. Livy, *Hist.* 10.23.3–10.
80. Richlin, "Carrying Water in a Sieve," 345–46. On p. 355, Richlin cites the Nonae Caprotinae festival in which slave women feast and perform a mock battle outside the city walls. Both slave women and matrons worshiped Juno Caprotina.

class and ethnic distinctions mirrored the larger social context where social status was all-important.[81]

Fifth, women's religious activity and chastity were tightly connected. A religious cult was judged good if it reinforced the traditional morals of Rome, which promoted a wife's fidelity to her husband. The Vestal Virgins represented the idea of chastity and modeled chaste behavior. The Bona Dea encouraged chastity and strongly limited men's access to the women's rites, even though the goddess was propitiated by both men and women. Any deviation from the standard of chastity was punished, at times horribly, as in the case of the unchaste Vestals buried alive.

Ironically, however, by linking chastity and the well-being of the state, women, especially matrons, enjoyed important, informal power. Their behavior was important to the security and prosperity of Rome.[82] For example, Caecilia Metella, daughter of Q. Caecilius Metellus Balearicus, received a vision from the goddess Juno Sospita, who declared she was fleeing Rome because her temple was not cared for properly. The senate responded quickly, indicating that her vision was taken seriously in the political realm.[83] In another example, the official prayers of matrons were enjoined in an effort to turn the tide in the war against Hannibal.[84] The senate gave orders to follow a prophecy mandating that games for Apollo be held and sacrifices be made following the Greek custom, including having one's head uncovered and wearing a garland. The senate added to the prophecy that the matrons should hold a supplication, possibly because the Greek custom of sacrifice excluded women, while Roman practice allowed both men and women to be part of the citywide festival. Moreover, the matrons' supplications were not spontaneous but were an official part of the festival. Thus both men and women participated in the expiatory rituals geared to strengthening the military and political health of Rome.

Female Conversion

Two areas that served as a lightning rod for male writers were female conversion and the influence of foreign cults on women. Though of course not all

81. Richlin remarks, "six of the seventeen festivals involving special women's rituals include a marked element in which women are divided into classes" ("Carrying Water in a Sieve," 356).

82. We cannot say whether the standards of chastity were embraced as deeply by Roman matrons as by their husbands, only that their close following of such standards (or not) could tip the balance for or against Rome. It is not perhaps accidental that during the Second Punic War, there was a significant uptick in women priestesses and matrons propitiating on behalf of the state.

83. Perhaps not surprisingly, this vision occurred during the "social wars" (about 90 BC) when various Italic peoples were integrating into Rome. Juno Sospita was the chief deity of the Lanuvium people, conquered by Rome in 338 BC and granted limited citizenship.

84. Livy, *Hist*. 25.12.2–15. See also Macrobius, *Saturnalia* 1.17.27–28.

writers were as extreme in their distaste for foreign cults as Juvenal, many in Rome during the late Republic and early Empire were highly suspicious of eastern cults, including Judaism. In discussing conversion to foreign cults, the male writers draw on stock assumptions about females, including their inherent gullibility and promiscuity. Moreover, Roman male writers were highly suspicious of and deeply opposed to the mixing of social classes, especially wealthy free women mingling with lower classes. We also find Jewish and Christian authors who are at pains to distance their "cult" and women from the negative stereotype. A brief look at women converts and devotees of foreign cults reveals how the literature uses the theme of conversion not only to discuss religion but also to construct feminine characteristics.

Josephus on Roman Women and Foreign Religions

Turning first to a Jewish author, Josephus presents an interesting case study on views of female conversion and the influence of foreign cults on Roman society, particularly as they affected the upper class.[85] In two adjacent stories, Josephus describes a Roman matron's encounter with Isis's consort, and then speaks of a matron's gift to the Jerusalem temple. The uproar caused by these events, Josephus maintains, led to the expulsion of Jews from Rome.[86] The stories play off of gender stereotypes in surprising ways.

PAULINA, DEVOTEE OF ISIS

First, a brief sketch of the Paulina and Isis story: The matron Paulina was a well-placed, influential social elite, chaste and devoted to her senatorial-ranked husband. She rebuffed the advances of Mundus, a man from the Equestrian class, who in despair decided to starve himself. His freedwoman, Ida, encouraged him with a plot that would gain him access to his love. Paulina was a devotee of Isis, whose consort was named Anubis. The freedwoman bribed the Isis priests to allow Mundus to be alone in the temple with Paulina. The priests were told to send a message to Paulina that the god Anubis was eager to meet with her. Paulina took herself to the temple, dined, and then slept. She was awakened by the "god" who had sex with her. She returned home in the morning convinced that she had met with the god. Mundus could not contain himself, however, and bragged about the escapade. She informed her husband of the deceit and was exonerated. Mundus was punished, and his freedwoman executed.

Josephus's version of the story relies on several motifs prevalent in characterizations of women's religious activities. The heroine is a model of decorum and chastity, the classic Roman matron. But she is also female, and so is gullible. Similarly, Juvenal lumps Judaism and the worship of Cybele together as

---

85. Josephus, *Ant.* 18.3.4–5.
86. Neither Suetonius (*Tiberius* 13–14; 23–24) nor Tacitus (*Ann.* 2.85.5) mention Paulina's story specifically, but they do speak of Tiberius exiling Jews and Egyptians in 19 AD.

foreign cults that prey on women because they are naturally more susceptible to such "nonsense."[87] The female villain in the story, Mundus's freedwoman, is also drawn in classic lines—from the lower class, deceptive, conniving. The foreign cult priests are disreputable, willing to work against the chaste ideals of a Roman matron and against the upper class. And throughout, the tension of sex: the would-be lover pines for his chaste prize, and the sexual encounter occurs in the temple of Isis. Foreign cults and sexual immorality are seen as two sides of the same coin, and are the currency used most often by women, according to male critics.[88]

FULVIA'S DONATION TO THE JEWISH TEMPLE

When Josephus turns next to describe Fulvia's gift to the Jerusalem temple, he is at pains to disassociate her experience from that of Paulina. In Fulvia's case, a group of four Jewish men (Josephus paints them as renegade Jews) convince Fulvia to donate to the Jerusalem temple, after which they abscond with her donation. What is not said is as important as what is. First and foremost, these men do not desire sex with Fulvia—the encounters are well within the bounds of protocol. She never leaves her house, and she does not mingle with "foreigners" (in this case, Jews). Second, Fulvia's desire to support the temple is admirable, and only the evilness of the swindlers prevents her laudable goal from being realized. Third, Josephus does not mention the class of these Jewish thieves, but Tacitus describes the four thousand exiled as descendants of enfranchised slaves.[89] Josephus presumably would rather not emphasize the social status of his fellow Jews, even though he decries their behavior. He does not want all Jews smeared with the label "lower class," however accurate that assessment might be.

We might also determine from these stories that wives were able to follow their own religious sentiments. Paulina was drawn to the Isis cult, while her husband was not. Fulvia was master of her own money in choosing to give to a religious cause she deemed worthy. Both women experienced some autonomy in this regard, in keeping with the conventions of the day. Both confide in their husbands, following accepted matronly behavior.

Sympathizers and God-Fearers

Fulvia's attention to the Jewish temple is representative of a group known as God-fearers. This is a difficult category to classify because the term seemed

---

87. Juvenal, *Sat.* 6.542–47.

88. Augustus attacked both foreign cults and adultery. Horace (*Carmina* 3.6.17–24) supports Augustus's reforms and writes that crumbling temples and sullied marriage beds are responsible for Rome's troubles. Likewise, Tacitus (*Historiae* 1.2) blames the Vesuvius eruption on sacred rites defiled and the numerous adulteries.

89. Tacitus, *Ann.* 2.85.5.

to cover a range of behaviors and attitudes.[90] God-fearers were gentile women and men who stood on the boundary between Judaism and paganism (and often Christianity as well). They were attracted to Judaism but had not become proselytes. As Levinskaya writes, "so long as they [gentiles] showed some kind of sympathy with the Jewish religion they were considered God-fearers."[91]

ROMAN EVIDENCE

Without doubt, some pagans in the Greco-Roman world showed an interest in Judaism. The ancient Roman historian, Cassius Dio, recounts the deaths of the consul Flavius Clemens and his wife Flavia Domitilla (a relative of Emperor Domitian) under Domitian for suspicion of atheism and following Jewish ways.[92] Interestingly, Suetonius, a contemporary of the events, does not mention the charge of atheism. Instead he suggests that Flavius Clemens's sudden death was the result of Domitian's fears (which Suetonius believes were unfounded) that he was plotting an overthrow of the government. Flavius's sons were officially recognized as Domitian's heirs, perhaps encouraging paranoid feelings against the boys' father. Taking both historians' information into account, we might suggest a religious reading of the evidence: that Flavius Clemens and his wife were truly intrigued with tenets of Judaism. Support for the possibility that members of the Roman elite would be attracted to Judaism comes from Josephus; he lauds Poppaea Sabina, the wife of Emperor Nero, for her sympathies toward Judaism and identifies her as a God-fearer.[93] Or we might offer a political reading: Flavius Clemens resisted Domitian's insistence on his own divinity. If so, it was an easy step for Domitian to conclude that Flavius Clemens was rejecting all state gods, and thus was acting as a Jew. Finances might also factor in, for Domitian pursued with great vigor the payment of the *fiscus Ioudaios*, a tax on all Jews.[94] With Domitian's relentless pursuit of this tax, it was suddenly imperative to establish strict delineations on who was Jewish, and the blurry category of God-fearer became a tool by which to eliminate political enemies.

90. The most important source of inscriptional information on God-fearers is the Aphrodisias inscription from Asia Minor. See Joyce Reynolds and Robert Tannenbaum, *Jews and God-Fearers at Aphrodisias: Greek Inscriptions with Commentary*, Proceedings of the Cambridge Philological Society, supplement 12 (Cambridge: Cambridge Philological Society, 1987).
    91. Irina A. Levinskaya, *The Book of Acts in Its First Century Setting*, vol. 5, *Diaspora Setting* (Grand Rapids: Eerdmans, 1996), 78.
    92. Cassius Dio, *Hist. Rom.* 67.14.1–3.
    93. Josephus, *Ant.* 20.189–98.
    94. At the fall of the Jerusalem temple under Vespasian, he established a two-drachmae annual tax on all Jews who previously paid the temple tax. Suetonius remarks that during Domitian's rule, he persecuted both those who followed the Jewish lifestyle without publicly acknowledging themselves as Jews and those who were from the Jewish community but concealed their origin and did not pay the tribute (*Domitianus* 12.2).

Some analyses of the epigraphic evidence suggest that up to 80 percent of God-fearers were women.[95] Even if this number reflects an overconfidence in the term "God-fearer" as representing a specific group, given that women are generally underrepresented in our sources, we can safely assume a large number of women were included in this group. For instance, Euphrosyna is praised as a God-fearer on her tombstone.[96] Often these women were wealthy benefactors to Jewish communities. For example, Capitolina, a God-fearer, donated to the synagogue at Tralles, Asia Minor, the entire dais and added facing to the staircase in fulfillment of her vow.[97] A critical inscription comes from Aphrodisias, Asia Minor. This stele includes two inscriptions, probably written a century or so apart. The front of the stele includes a list of fifty-five Jews and fifty-two God-fearers, separated into distinct groups. This inscription was likely done in the fourth century. It is unclear why these people are listed, but probably they donated to the Jewish synagogue. We cannot say for certain whether the God-fearers were connected religiously to the synagogue, or only socially. The left side of the stele includes a later inscription, which lists about thirteen men of a specific group dedicated to learning and worshiping the Jewish God. In this group are two God-fearers and two proselytes. Clearly the God-fearers are part of the religious community of Jews but are not proselytes.

EVIDENCE FROM THE ACTS OF THE APOSTLES

God-fearers represent an important Christian category, especially for Luke in the Acts of the Apostles.[98] In several places, Luke identifies two groups, the *Ioudaioi* (Jews) and the *Hellēnes* (gentiles), explaining that the women in the latter group are prominent in the community (Acts 14:1; 17:4, 12; 18:4). Cornelius is an example of a God-fearer because he prays and gives alms to the Jewish God (10:2, 22), representing a group from the nations who fear God and do what is right (10:35). Titius Justus, identified from the context as a God-fearer, is clearly a gentile (18:7). Luke reveals a pattern of usage indicating that Jews and gentile God-fearers were part of the synagogue landscape. As Luke tells the story, the God-fearers were especially receptive to the gospel message, for they had already taken steps away from their ancestral paganism and, at least at some level, were part of the local Jewish community.

95. Matthews, *First Converts*, 67. She rightly cautions that not every case of the term *theosebēs* or its Latin equivalent, *metuens*, indicates a distinct group or a technical usage.
96. *CIJ* 731e; for a translation, see Kraemer, *Women's Religions*, 328. This inscription, from Rhodes, is undated.
97. *CIG* 2924; for a translation, see Kraemer, *Women's Religions*, 163. This inscription is from the third century AD.
98. Luke uses two different expressions in Greek to convey this category, "God-fearer" (Acts 13:16, 26) and "God-worshiper" (Acts 17:4, 17, 18; 18:7). (I assume the traditional authorship for the Gospel of Luke, however, my argument does not rely on this position.)

Lydia

Lydia, who meets Paul when he travels to Philippi, is a prominent example of a God-fearer. As Luke tells the story (Acts 16), Paul arrives at Philippi and, on the Sabbath, walks outside the city walls to the river, where he expects to find a place of (Jewish) prayer. A group of women have gathered, and he preaches the gospel to them. One of their number, a God-fearer named Lydia from Thyatira, is convinced of the message, and she and her household are baptized. She successfully implores Paul and Silas to stay at her home. Though the story seems simple enough, almost every detail about Lydia is contested by scholars. Before I develop a picture of Lydia, I should lay out some of my basic assumptions. First, Lydia reflects an actual person; she was not invented by Luke to serve his theological agenda. Second, Lydia, though a historical person, functions as much more than that for Luke as he elaborates on the gospel's reception in the Roman Empire. We must hold these two—historical detail and theological emphasis—in creative tension.

Luke calls their meeting place a *proseuchē* (place of prayer, Acts 16:13, 16), not a synagogue, his usual term. The use of this special term, coupled with the mention of only women as part of the group, often lead to the conclusion that not enough Jewish men lived in Philippi to make a synagogue. We need not accept that argument from silence. Luke uses particular, even unique, terms specific to a location. For example, the city council leaders in Thessalonica are called *politarchai*, a term not used for other city councils, but confirmed by local inscriptions to be the preferred term in Thessalonica. Perhaps a similar situation occurred in Philippi where this community referred to itself, or was referred to, as a *proseuchē*. The comment about women is not necessarily connected with the term, although given the possibilities of women gathering for religious rites, it is not impossible that certain women from the synagogue, including interested gentiles, met on the Sabbath without men. Nothing in Judaism precludes this possibility. We should also note that *proseuchē* is used elsewhere to describe the Jewish community. Luke is not creating a new term but merely using a familiar one in a singular way in Acts.

Several characteristics of Lydia invite investigation, including her social status in Philippi, her identification as a God-fearer, and her function as Paul's benefactor. Personal characteristics include that she deals in purple cloth. Does this mean she is wealthy? Most commentators believe so, as purple dye was a very expensive commodity. Rome held an imperial monopoly over one type of purple dye (Tyrian murex), but another type (from the madder plant) was less expensive. If Lydia dealt with the former type of dye, she might have been a freedwoman from the imperial household. A minority voice cautions that most dealers were also the dyers—a smelly, messy job.[99] In fact, the Greek

---

99. Luise Schottroff (*Let the Oppressed Go Free: Feminist Perspectives on the New Testament* [Louisville: Westminster/John Knox, 1993], 131–32) notes that to make the dye one used urine

term for purple dealer was the same as that for purple dyer. But perhaps Lydia employed people to do the dyeing and selling. She does have a household, which could include slaves and freed men and women. Probably we can safely assume that she was a woman of some means, if not wealthy. This group was likely the target audience for Acts: people with some means, some education, and some social status, but hardly elite.[100]

Another curious detail is that no husband is mentioned. Most conclude that she is a widow, as were many women were at this time. If she was married, perhaps her husband was away for extended periods of time on business or government assignment. It is possible, however, that she is a slave or a freed-woman who made and sold purple cloth for her owners. A slave could have a household of sorts, but this suggestion stretches the data. It is more feasible to consider her a freeborn or freed woman who owned slaves. It would not be out of the ordinary for freedwomen to be wealthy. Luke presents her as master in the home, for she leads her household in baptism, much as the jailer does later in the story (Acts 16:33–34). Moreover, she invites Paul and Silas into her home, again presenting a picture of one in charge of the household. Her position was common for widows, especially if her guardian (or father) lived in Thyatira, where she moved from when she settled in Philippi.[101]

The name Lydia has raised numerous questions. It may be an ethnic nick-name ("from Lydia") or even an ethnic slave name. Some argue it supports her slave status (or that she was once a slave) because this class was often named for the place they came from. In this case, Lydia would reflect the area near Thyatira in Asia Minor. If she was an imperial freedwoman, her social status would be linked to the imperial *domus*, and so her standing in Philippi would be high. If Lydia is merely a nickname, perhaps she is represented by her formal name in Paul's letter to the Philippians, namely as either Euodia or Syntyche.[102] This is pure conjecture, but Lydia's status as Paul's benefactor would make a leadership role in the church likely. We need not assume, however, that her name indicates a former situation of slavery or represents a nickname. From the first or second century AD, two inscriptions (one from Sardis and one from Ephesus) bear witness to a Julia Lydia. The latter held the titles of high priestess and daughter of Asia.[103] Because the name can symbolize the wealth of both the region of Thyatira and its purple-dye industry, Shelly Matthews

---

as well as the dye from the muricid mollusk, which flourished in the waters near Thyatira; dyeing clothes was hard work, which we have failed to appreciate in Lydia's case.

100. In the Gospel of Luke, the marginalized are the poor Jews; in Acts, the marginalized are the gentiles, even if they are wealthy or powerful, such as the centurion Cornelius (Acts 10:1–2) and the proconsul Sergius Paulus (13:6–12).

101. She might also have gained her freedom from tutelage.

102. For a brief discussion of this possibility, see Davorin Peterlin, *Paul's Letter to the Philip-pians in the Light of Disunity in the Church* (Leiden: Brill, 1995), 128–30.

103. Sardis: *SEG* XXVIII.928; Ephesus: *SEG* XXVIII.869.

and others conclude that Luke created Lydia from whole cloth. Yet Matthews cautions that Lydia reflects real women whom Luke knew in the early church.[104] Rich symbolism, however, need not negate the historical reality of a figure. The Lydia who greeted Paul in Philippi, then, might be a well-born and prosperous commercial trader; the fact that she had a home large enough to accommodate Paul and his group, as well as the finances to care for their needs, suggests that she was wealthy.

More serious is the argument from silence—Paul does not mention Lydia in his letter to the Philippians. Assuming Paul did write Philippians (which most do), he composed this about a decade after first visiting Philippi. We do not know how old Lydia was when he arrived the first time, but it is entirely possible that she had since died. Or perhaps the message did not "stick" and she returned to the synagogue. This argument from silence is not strong enough to erase a real person from history—we can be reasonably confident Lydia was an actual person described by Luke, who molded her story to reinforce theological points recurrent in Luke-Acts.

Lydia is a home owner, and she invites Paul and Silas to stay with her. Some complain that Luke has demoted her involvement in the Christian movement by denying her any leadership role. Two points must be argued against this conclusion. First, Lydia is portrayed as a benefactor, a very privileged position in the Hellenistic world (including Judaism). We must not downplay her role in terms of our twenty-first-century culture and imagine she cooked and cleaned for them. By giving them a place to stay, she revealed her generosity, and thus was honored by the group. Another female benefactor, Phoebe, was also a deacon (Rom. 16:1–3) in the church at Cenchreae, a port of Corinth.[105] Leadership and benefaction went hand in hand in the Greco-Roman world. Second, Lydia was probably the leader of the group that continued to meet in her home. Note that when Paul and Silas prepared to depart Philippi, they went to her house (not the jailer's home) and met with the believers there. Presumably Lydia followed the pattern found throughout the New Testament that the owner of the house in which the church met was also a church leader. Luke therefore does not diminish Lydia's leadership role—rather, he presents it in Greco-Roman terms of benefaction, which do not sound "religious" to our ears, but which carried great social prestige in the first century.

Philippian Slave Girl and Jailer

Lydia's character is filled out by contrasting it with two other important individuals in Philippi: the slave girl possessed by a spirit and the jailer. The slave girl, representing a foreign cult that preys on the average person, pro-

---

104. Matthews, *First Converts*, 93.
105. See chapter 9 for a discussion of Lydia and Phoebe as benefactors.

vides an important contrast to Lydia in several ways.[106] First, she is described as having a "python spirit" (*pneuma pythōna*), which probably reflects the Apollo cult—Apollo slew the serpent named Python at Delphi, and the Pythia (priestesses) from Delphi claimed to receive inspiration from that serpent. While the slave girl is possessed and mantic, Lydia presents a decorum matching the proper role of Roman matrons. Luke steers clear of any hint of spirit possession by Christian women, noting only briefly Philip's virgin daughters who were prophetesses (Acts 21:9).[107] Second, the slave girl annoys Paul, even though what she says is technically true. The reason for Paul's reaction is that everyone knows she is from a competing foreign cult and so is mocking Paul's message. Paul's exorcism shows that his God is more powerful than her Apollo. The owners' response to Paul's actions is to maintain their cult's status as authentically Roman and well within acceptable social limits. They highlight Paul and Silas's Jewishness in contrast to "us Romans," trying to assert their cult's conventional status. Third, Luke notes that her owners made money from her. This is a classic denunciation of foreign cults, that they are greedy and prey on unsuspecting simple people. Josephus recognizes this in his depiction of the Jews who trick Fulvia. And Paul defends himself against such charges in 1 Thessalonians 2:5.[108]

The jailer also offers an interesting contrast to Lydia. Though Paul and Silas stay with Lydia, they eat only with the jailer. This is curious because in so many ways Lydia mirrors Cornelius, who offers hospitality to Peter and is baptized (with his household; Acts 10). Luke characteristically, however, does not describe women in public meals in his gospel, and so his silence about meals with Lydia should not surprise.

Resistance by God-Fearing Women

Luke also notes a strong resistance to the Christian gospel by some God-fearing women. He writes that while Paul and Barnabas were in Pisidian Antioch, leading Jews in the city agitated these women and also leading men (not labeled as God-fearers) against Paul and Barnabas (Acts 13:50). Clearly these women's sympathies were with the Jewish community, and their high social

---

106. Robert M. Price puts forward a creative, but ultimately unsatisfactory, theory. He suggests that Luke morphs the "real" Lydia into two figures: the upstanding Lydia and this unnamed slave girl in order to condemn all female preachers and prophets. "My guess is that the text before him [Luke] depicted the Pythoness as a Philippian convert having joined Paul in his evangelistic activity there—and that her name was Lydia" (*The Widow Traditions in Luke-Acts: A Feminist-Critical Scrutiny* [Atlanta: Scholars Press, 1997], 228).

107. He also records the quotation from Joel 2:28–32 in Acts 2:17–21, which states that God will pour out his Spirit on his male and female servants and they will prophesy. Other than the brief mention of female prophetesses in Acts 21, however, there is no unambiguous record of this occurring among women in the Christian communities in Acts.

108. It may also be that Paul is not so much defending himself as presenting a good role model for the Thessalonians. My point still stands that preachers of foreign religions were open to attacks that they were greedy.

standing gave them political leverage to force the Christian missionaries to leave the region. Not surprisingly, the Jewish synagogue worked to retain support of their affluent, socially well-connected, God-fearing gentile women even as the Christian missionaries tried to persuade them. Irina Levinskaya probably overstates the case only a bit when she concludes, "They [God-fearers] could be (and actually were) either the backbone of the Gentile Christian communities or the greatest impediment to the spread of the Christian mission."[109]

Both Josephus and Luke tackle head-on the biases against foreign cults' attraction to (gullible) women. They also take advantage of prejudices that favor wealth and status, a prejudice that often trumps gender. Both writers laud wealthy women who benefit, or even convert to, their religion. They take care to present these women as chaste and acting well within the proper spheres of the status quo. We need not doubt that such women existed, but should acknowledge that Josephus and Luke shape the story so as to give maximum benefit to their cult, recognizing the sensibilities and predispositions of their larger gentile audience. Indeed, women converts can actually speak well of the group, if those women are from high society and follow proper decorum.

WHY GOD-FEARERS?

One final but important point should be made about God-fearers. Regrettably, some scholars, in attempting to discern *why* some gentile women were attracted to Christianity from Judaism, resort to anti-Jewish arguments. Claims disparaging Jewish law or ritual or even "legalism"—evaluative statements all—are presented as historical analysis.[110] Such potshots at Early Judaism do little to extend the critical exploration of women in the ancient world and may blind us to real historical causes. For example, if it is true that following the Jewish legal code was a burden to gentiles, how does one explain the draw of circumcision to Paul's churches in Galatia? Luke makes the *theological* point that Christianity is superior in part by describing how some socially influential, God-fearing women left the synagogue and joined the church, thereby diminishing the social standing of the Jewish community. Historians interested in real women at this time should not make the same theological claims under the guise of historical rigor. We cannot conclude, as historians, that Christianity had more to offer these women God-fearers than Judaism. We can no longer allow Judaism to serve as a straw man or foil against which a particular aspect of Christianity is projected.

109. Levinskaya, *Book of Acts*, 126.

110. For example, Ben Witherington III, *Women in the Earliest Churches* (Cambridge: Cambridge University Press, 1991), 148, writes, "that women could constitute the embryonic church, but not the embryonic synagogue, reveals the difference in the status of women in the two faiths at that time." He describes Lydia's change from being marginal—on the outskirts of the Jewish community—where "she could never receive the covenantal sign to being a central figure in the local Christian church, and the first baptized convert in Europe" (149).

Conclusion

When we think about gentile women and religion, several key characteristics emerge: the centrality of religious practices and rites in the daily lives of all women, the opportunities for informal social influence and power, and the numerous possibilities for religious expression. Religious rights partially shaped a woman's routine, with frequent offerings to the family gods and guardian spirit, as well as communal gatherings with other women or with men and women in celebration or in propitiation. Women's participation in religious rites was encouraged, and failure to act in a proper, modest manner was thought to bring out the gods' wrath. Some women took on high level roles within the religious cult, with the Vestal Virgin and the *flaminica Dialis* being uppermost on the status scale. But even slaves (though not many, if the evidence is accurate) could hold office in certain cults. Priestesses performed rites similar to their male counterparts, and female worshipers petitioned the deities for needs comparable to their male family members. Within paganism, women had specific responsibilities to their ancestral traditions, but also could devote themselves to a particular god or goddess. They might travel to a temple or holy site, or entertain fellow devotees in their homes. The opportunities allowed for exploring foreign cults such as Isis or Judaism, or becoming a God-fearer. In the next chapter we will explore the religious acts of Jewish women, including those who followed Jesus.

6

Religious Activities and Informal Power
of Jewish and Christian Women

About ten years into the second century AD, Pliny the Younger, governor of Bithynia, wrote to Emperor Trajan that he had arrested two female deaconesses or *ministrae*, beaten them, and questioned them about their cult, Christianity.[1] As noted in the previous chapter, the title *ministrae* can refer to those who look after the daily maintenance of the cult sites. Since churches were likely meeting in private homes at this point, this sense of the term does not apply directly. The title was also used in an inscription noting freedwomen who donated their own money to build a temple to the Bona Dea.[2] In the present case, these Christian women were slaves, not freedwomen, and would not have had the wherewithal to make major financial contributions. It is thus unclear what was intended with the use of *ministrae*, except that they were questioned as though they could give an accurate testimony of this prohibited group.

Pliny the Younger was writing to Trajan to ask what should be done with those who followed this new, and thus illegal, religious cult. It was not lost on later commentators that the "leaders" of this new group were women—some even slave women. From another second-century figure, Celsus's infamous condemnation has sounded through the centuries—Christianity is a religion of women and slaves.[3] In this chapter, I set out to explore how Christian women lived out their religious convictions in the first century AD. Since most of these

1. Pliny, *Ep.* 10.96–97.
2. Celia E. Schultz, *Women's Religious Activity in the Roman Republic* (Chapel Hill: University of North Carolina Press, 2006), 71.
3. Origen, *Contra Celsum* 3.44.

women were not raised as Christians but were instructed in the traditions of their Jewish or gentile parents, the last chapter explored the pagan woman's religious activities; this chapter will examine Jewish women's religious life and some aspects of Christian women's religious concerns.

Depictions of Jewish Women

The world of Jewish women both in Roman Palestine (Judea and the Galilee) and in the Diaspora lies in deep shadow. Gentile authors' comments are typically caustic but could reveal some historical data if analyzed carefully. Jewish writings similar in genre to the Greco-Roman novel, such as Tobit or *Joseph and Aseneth*, require careful reading to glean an accurate descriptive picture of women. Historians like Josephus focus on the politically important women in Palestine, which makes his information difficult to generalize. Inscriptions throw a bit of light onto the scene, highlighting women's financial contributions to synagogues and their leadership status. Rabbinic writings, however, present a picture often at odds with the inscriptional evidence. Specifically, rabbinic material focuses on three key areas of women's piety—the dough offering, the lighting of Sabbath candles, and menstrual purity laws (*Niddah*).[4] Yet no extant inscriptional evidence references these acts, although comments within the Dead Sea Scrolls suggest that at least menstrual purity laws were viewed as ritual markers for godly women. Careful scrutiny of the literary evidence, probing beneath the rhetoric and reaching behind modern scholars' biases, will be rewarded with a clearer (though not entirely clear) picture of Jewish women's religious lives in the Greco-Roman world.

Often studies divide the Jewish world into Diaspora and homeland Jews. The assumptions undergirding this decision include the claims that Diaspora Jews were closer to their pagan neighbors in much of their outlook, while Roman Palestinian Jews were closer to "true" Judaism. As attractive as such a slick demarcation is for modern scholars, this dichotomy gets harder and harder to maintain as more evidence is unearthed. The variety of Jewish religious expression is due not to a simplistic judgment about how close (or far) one slides toward Hellenism (mistakenly assumed to be static and well defined) but to a complex combination of class, setting (rural or urban), wealth, and historical exigencies. The relative size of the Jewish community, and its relationship to gentile neighbors, plays an important role in its boundary markings. These classifiers—the group's size and solidarity relative to outsiders—are

---

4. One of the earliest references to these areas of piety is *m. Shab.* 2:6, which declares that women who neglect these acts of piety are doomed to die in childbirth (cf. 1 Tim. 2:15 and the discussion above in chap. 4). On the rabbinic literature, see Ross S. Kraemer, *Her Share of the Blessings: Women's Religions among Pagans, Jews, and Christians in the Greco-Roman World* (Oxford: Oxford University Press, 1992), 93–95.

fluid. For example, interaction between poor Jews and pagans might swing between tolerance and hostility, while social relations between wealthy Jews and (wealthy) God-fearers and pagans in the same location might follow a different path. From one city to the next, exchanges between these various groups might look different, and within the same city, relations vary. For example, in Syrian Antioch there were sporadic outbursts of violence against Jews amidst a general calm. The same can be said for Alexandria, Egypt. The relative majority status of Jews in Judea and Galilee impacted their relationship with resident gentiles in terms of nationalistic sentiments, although class and social status played a significant role in exhibited religious practices and beliefs. Purity issues obtained tremendous importance for men and women in connection with Jerusalem and the temple and were, generally speaking, less significant outside of that sacred space.

A starkly unflattering portrait of a first-century Jewess is sketched by Juvenal, whose malice against Jews (and all foreigners) is well documented. He paints a haunting portrait of an old women, gnarled, grasping, promising to reveal the will of heaven for a few cents.[5] Juvenal characterizes her as interpreting Jewish laws, acting as a "high priestess with a tree as temple."[6] Indeed, under Juvenal's biting sarcasm, this Jewish beggar, with her basket and truss of hay, fares no better than the Isis devotee or the follower of Cybele. Martial, a contemporary of Juvenal, declared that Jewish boys were taught by their mothers to beg.[7] While Juvenal, if read charitably, leaves some possibility open that the Jewish beggars have fallen on hard times, Martial eliminates any sense of extenuating circumstances. For him, begging was a learned behavior, taught at the mother's knee. Why the mother and not the father? Perhaps because Martial believed (or represented a belief) that a Jew was determined to be such through his mother's line, not his father's. Or it might be another dig at women in general, that as a group they lack strong moral fiber and social virtue, further compounded in foreign women (in this case, Jewish mothers).

But can any historical data be siphoned from such accounts? Specifically, Juvenal makes several intriguing allusions worthy of exploration. First, he notes that the woman interprets the Jewish law. Second, she does so in public, perhaps speaking to other women primarily. Third, she takes money for her pronouncements and dream divinations. Finally, unlike so many other women characterized by Juvenal, the Jewess is not presented as sexually immoral. That he does not seize the opportunity to accuse her of this goes a long way

5. Juvenal, *Sat.* 6.342–47.
6. As described by Kraemer, *Her Share of the Blessings*, 109. See also Ross S. Kraemer, ed., *Maenads, Martyrs, Matrons, Monastics: A Sourcebook on Women's Religions in the Greco-Roman World* (Philadelphia: Fortress, 1988), 25.
7. Martial, *Epigrammata* 12.57.

in suggesting that Jewish women did not have a reputation of promiscuity.[8] To determine whether Juvenal has (unwittingly?) preserved historical evidence of real Jewish women's religious activities, we must examine other writers and epigraphic evidence.

Jewish Women Interpreting the Law

Therapeutrides (Female Therapeutics)

Did Jewish women interpret the law? Perhaps the best example of women engaged in serious study of the law is Philo's Therapeutrides, female members of a group known as the Therapeutics. These women analyzed scriptures allegorically and composed hymns that were presumably in concert with their theological perspective. We will examine this group in chapter 7, where I note that their philosophical analysis of the Scriptures placed the Therapeutrides in a rarefied group of highly educated people in the ancient world. Their ascetic practices won them lofty praise from Philo of Alexandria, a writer whose misogynistic views are widely acknowledged. These women hardly represented the majority at the time, even as their male counterparts could scarcely be said to reflect widespread Jewish male perspective and behavior. A similar group to the Therapeutics lived in Judea—the Essenes. We will shortly turn our attention to this group, mentioned by Philo, Josephus, and Pliny the Elder,[9] and represented by the Dead Sea Scrolls,[10] to explore their description of women.

Philo applauds the Therapeutrides for their steadfast commitment to allegorical interpretation of the biblical text, which makes the silence about female Essene ascetics all the more interesting. Most scholars assume that his silence, and that of Josephus and Pliny, proves in fact there were no such creatures. But in light of the antagonism these Jewish authors had toward women, we should not be surprised if they "neglected" to note what women were doing. In the case of the Therapeutrides, Philo has several compelling reasons why he

8. In an interesting anti-Jewish reference, Tacitus speaks of male Jews who abstain from intercourse with foreign women (gentiles) but who act lustfully with Jewish women (*Historiae* 5.5.2). One could draw from this that Jewish women were not known to have gentile sexual partners.

9. Philo, *Hypothetica* 11.14; Josephus, *B.J.* 2.119–61; *Ant.* 18.18–22; Pliny the Elder, *Nat.* 5.17.4.

10. The relationship between the Scrolls and the archaeological site at Khirbet Qumran is controversial, with the majority position stating that the Scrolls are connected to a group that resided at the site near the caves. A vocal minority suggests the Scrolls were a deposit placed in the caves by Jews fleeing Jerusalem, and several suggestions for the site, besides being a community of celibate men, have been floated. For the sake of argument, I will proceed with the majority position that the Scrolls and the site are a product of (a group of) Essenes who preserved and also created the texts and lived nearby.

The Habakkuk commentary scroll reflects a deep commitment among Jews to the biblical text. (Photo courtesy of Todd Bolen/bibleplaces.com)

must speak about them, however reluctantly. First, they are but a short distance from his local audience, who could check on the group and who might already be aware of them. Second, the group celebrates with periodic banquets that include both men and women. Philo is at pains to distance this event from the debauched Roman banquet and the sexual immorality associated with it. Thus, he must treat their practices so as to show their moral superiority. Third, Philo genuinely embraces the Therapeutics' exegetical approach to Scripture, so he feels compelled to portray them as positively as possible. However, the same constraints do not appear to be present in relation to the Essenes in Judea and Galilee, specifically concerning banquets and Scripture interpretation. We should not, then, assume that the silence in the secondary sources reflects the absence of Essene women—it might only indicate the sources' lack of interest in women. We must examine the Scrolls themselves to see if and how women were involved in the community, and secondarily whether (and if so, how) they examined the law.

Essenes

Until the mid-twentieth century, we knew of the Essenes primarily through Philo, Josephus, and Pliny the Elder. The discovery of the Dead Sea Scrolls in the 1940s revolutionized the study of the Essenes, to say nothing of Early Judaism and the New Testament and first-century Christianity. The biblical, apocryphal, pseudepigraphical, and sectarian documents found in several caves near Khirbet Qumran exposed the modern world to a community and its texts that had been frozen in time for two thousand years. Extensively analyzed and hotly contested, surprisingly the Scrolls have only recently been examined in terms of their view of women or evidence for women's participation in the Essene sect. The reasons for this failure are several, including the androcentric bias of much scholarship and the description of the group as primarily made up of celibate men. Both these factors currently are being challenged, and interesting theories about the role of women in the Essenes and at Qumran have attracted attention. We will look at several areas where women are central to the identity of the Essenes, as well as historical possibilities for women within the group. Specifically, we will look at the presumption of male celibacy, as well as injunctions concerning oaths, women's titles and testimonies, marriage, and certain purity codes that are suggestive of women's active participation within the Essene movement.

CELIBACY

Perhaps for our purposes the most important assumption about the Essenes and the community at Qumran is its emphasis on male celibacy. Josephus makes a big deal about this group's adherence to self-control in all areas of life, especially sexual abstinence. For his Roman audience, these Jewish men (in Josephus's hands) become paragons of the grand ideals of self-control and virtue. In contrast, he gives only a paragraph to those Essenes living in families,[11] yielding another unfortunate assumption, that the Essenes were separated between "superior" celibate men and the families who lived in towns (discussed further below). But in drawing the group this way, does Josephus perhaps obscure the historical contours of the community?

The Dead Sea Scrolls themselves offer a markedly different picture.[12] The sectarian scrolls[13] do not exhibit Josephus's highly negative attitude toward women, though often scholars presume this attitude based on the imported assumption that the male celibates chose their life path because of a suspicion or outright hatred of women. Yet celibacy in itself is not necessarily negative toward women; in fact, women often flourish in ascetic communities. In the Scrolls, purity matters are connected with both female and male.

As a mere historical accident, one of the earliest Scrolls to be published was the Rule of the Community (1QS), which makes no mention of women beyond

11. Josephus, *B.J.* 2.160–61.

12. Abel Isaksson (*Marriage and Ministry in the New Temple: A Study with Special Reference to Mt. 19.13–12 and 1 Cor. 11.3–16* [Lund: C. W. K. Gleerup, 1965], 38–65) argues, based primarily on the War Scroll, that Essenes (he uses the term only for men) between the ages of twenty and twenty-five years were to marry and procreate, and at twenty-five, they were to cease having marital relations with their wives and join the "war" against the forces of darkness. At this point, he suggests, they may have divorced their wives, although they were not required to do so. Until they reached twenty-five years and began their celibate lifestyle, they were not full members of the sect. Women, children, and the young married men did participate nominally in congregation life, but women never became full members. Isaksson's argument is weakened by the fact that the Deut. 24:5 passage (see also Deut. 20:7) that allows Israel's newly married men to refrain from fighting for a year is not cited, nor is there any discussion about what is to be done with the family once the husband reaches twenty-five years of age.

13. It is quite difficult to determine the dates of the sectarian scrolls and whether they were composed by the Essenes or copied by them. If they were written outside the group, the questions become how they reflect the ideals of the Essenes, how they functioned within the group, and what their relative level of authority was for the group. For example, if the Damascus Document was written outside the group, then the text could reflect a wider swath of Jewish life in the second century BC, even though it was preserved only by the Essenes.

the phrase "born of a woman"; thus, early on in Scrolls research, this cemented in many scholars' minds that the Essenes were predominantly celibate males living away from regular contact with the broader society. Only recently has this assessment been challenged. Closer examination has revealed that 1QS is an anomaly in its silence about women—many of the other texts refer to women in both practical and abstract ways. No longer should we imagine that a group of celibate men represented all that is essential to the Essenes; instead, we must explore more deeply the numerous injunctions, discussions, and even asides that together draw a picture of women's participation in the Essenes.

Membership and Oath Taking

The Essene community was built upon its members' oath taking—their first and most important pledge was to follow the group above all else in the service of God. Some scholars suggest that the pledge of celibacy was the second most important decision an Essene would make, and that the larger community was thus divided into the highly dedicated celibate members who resided at Qumran and the average members who lived in towns with their families.[14] Most go on to assume that only men were in the elite celibate group, and this bias informs translators who assume the masculine language entails only male presence in the Qumran group. Eileen Schuller, however, cautions that nothing in the Scrolls would prohibit a woman from being part of that celibate group. Since no specific legislation would be necessary for women to live celibately, the Scrolls rendered the women "virtually invisible" by passing over their existence.[15] Although such an argument from silence is by its very nature weak, women are vastly underrepresented in ancient literature. More-over, the Scrolls' masculine language is ambivalent and ambiguous. Maxine Grossman perceptively notes that "the language of the text constructs the covenanter [group member] as normatively male but also permits for specifi-cally gendered references should they become necessary."[16] She recognizes that the masculine plural can refer to men and women, and suggests that at the level of Qumran community participation, women should be envisioned as legitimate actors alongside men.[17]

Though most scholars suggest a two-tiered Essene community configura-tion, with the celibate members at Qumran more highly esteemed, Cecilia

14. One important dissenter is Lawrence H. Schiffman, *Reclaiming the Dead Sea Scrolls* (Philadelphia: Jewish Publication Society, 1994), 52–53, 135. For a summary of the literature, see Cecilia Wassen, *Women in the Damascus Document*, Academia Biblica 21 (Atlanta: Society of Biblical Literature, 2005), 6–9.

15. Eileen M. Schuller, "Women in the Dead Sea Scrolls," in *The Dead Sea Scrolls after Fifty Years: A Comprehensive Assessment*, ed. Peter W. Flint and James C. VanderKam (Leiden: Brill, 1999), 2:131.

16. Maxine L. Grossman, *Reading for History in the Damascus Document: A Methodological Study*, Studies on the Texts of the Desert of Judah 45 (Leiden: Brill, 2002), 48.

17. Grossman, *Reading for History*, 53.

Wassen challenges this configuration by reexamining a key passage in the Scrolls:[18] "All those who walk in these in holy perfection according to all his teaching, God's covenant is an assurance for them. . . . And if they live in camps according to the rule of the land, and take wives and beget children, then they shall walk according to the Torah and according to the precept established according to the rule of the Torah."[19] Wassen claims that rather than describing two groups in different locations and with different lifestyles, the lines offer parallel portrayals of the same group. The label "those who walk in perfect holiness" is not descriptive of celibate members but is used to describe all members.[20] The contrast being made in the larger passage is between the holy group members and those outside the group, who are seen as despising the truth. Thus she undercuts the argument that women could only be part of one group (family) and not the other (celibate) by declaring that the entire group (including women) is identified as walking in holy perfection.

So far we have explored the possibility that women were active members of both the Qumran community and the Essenes who resided in towns, based on the suggestion that the Scrolls themselves can be read to support this. But a further question is whether women could join the Essenes independently or whether they were members only through their family or spouse. That is, could a woman take the oath of obedience to the community, or was her membership of a secondary status, mediated through a male family member? To answer this question, we must examine oath taking in the community. The Scrolls discuss the application of the biblical injunctions about oath taking found in Deuteronomy 23:23 and Numbers 30:1–16, with an interesting twist. The Numbers text allows a husband or father to annul a vow made by his wife or daughter. The Damascus Document, however, stipulates that the father or husband does not have discretion to decide whether the woman's oath may be kept; instead the vow must be evaluated based on the group's interpretation of the covenant.[21] Only if the vow clearly transgresses the community's standards and teachings is the man permitted to cancel the vow. This places an external criterion of authority above the male head of the house and increases the community's authority over all its members. It also suggests that women had a relative measure of freedom to pledge and fulfill religious vows if they were in concert with the group's mandates; in this they were similar to their male counterparts. "One significant consequence of this reinterpretation of Numbers 30 is that women are empowered to be responsible for their own pledges by oath and are allowed to express their religiosity by taking pledges

---

18. Translation in Wassen, *Women in the Damascus Document*, 123; see also the discussion on pp. 122–28.

19. CD VII, 4b–8a.

20. See CD VII, 4b–6a; XIV, 1b–2a.

21. CD XVI, 6–12.

as they themselves see fit."[22] Yet two other scrolls suggest that such individual authority might not have been the norm, revealing a frustrating characteristic of the Scrolls in general: they can present a variety of perspectives and pictures of the community.[23] In the Temple Scroll, the biblical injunction is followed closely with no interpretive changes,[24] while 4QInstruction, though fragmentary, suggests that a husband should restrict the number of vows his wife makes because he has been set over her in authority.[25] It is not certain, therefore, that married women or daughters were free to make and fulfill their own vows, but at least one important Essene document permitted it so long as the oath was within the limits of the covenant as the Essenes saw it.

This fact opens the door to women on their own joining the Essenes.[26] To explore this possibility, we will look at discussions about group membership. An important passage is CD XV, 5–17, which outlines the initiation process. Interpreters differ on whether the text refers to those who take the oath of the covenant as "boys" or as "children." The translation "children" fits with the overall tenor of the text.[27] Moreover, the scene is reminiscent of the biblical oath-taking scenes found in Nehemiah 9–10 and Deuteronomy 27–30, where men, women, and children pledged their commitment to the covenant. Finally, the Rule of the Congregation (1Q28a or 1QSa) states clearly that men, women,

22. Wassen, *Women in the Damascus Document*, 93.

23. Establishing the date of each scroll would be helpful in this regard, but sadly, like so much of Scrolls scholarship, this too is contested. As consensus is achieved, we might find that the community shifted its views over time. Moreover, the Scrolls and the secondary material do not always match, as in the case of slavery. Secondary sources insist that the Essenes did not have slaves, but the Scrolls discuss treatment of slaves, giving the impression that they owned them. It could be, however, that the Scrolls are describing their community based on scriptural texts that assume Israel had slaves. Since the Essenes saw themselves as the true Israel, they commented upon those texts and created a picture of their community in line with those texts even though it did not reflect the current reality of their community. For a similar argument, see Grossman, *Reading for History*, 53–54.

24. 11QT LIII, 11– LIV, 7.

25. 4Q416 2 IV, 7b–10. See Daryl F. Jefferies, *Wisdom at Qumran: A Form-Critical Analysis of the Admonitions in 4QInstruction* (Piscataway, NJ: Gorgias, 2004), 259–62.

26. The War Scroll (1QM VII, 3–6) does exclude women from the group, in terms of entering the camp and going to war. This scroll also excludes impure people. The War Scroll speaks to a different situation than that imagined by the Damascus Document. In the latter text (as well as 1QSa), those with physical and mental disabilities, both male and female, are excluded from the "midst of the congregation . . . [and] of the men of renown." The War Scroll likely draws its perspective from Deut. 23:9–14, which lists rules for a war camp, like relieving oneself outside the camp. And Num. 1:2–3 states explicitly that only men age twenty and older can be in the war camp. It makes sense, therefore, that women are excluded from the community in the War Scroll and why, for example, there is concern in the scroll about nocturnal emissions (1QM VII, 4–5).

27. Grossman writes, "And to the extent that the text imagines the community as a microcosm of the people of Israel, it may make *better* sense to see this covenant community, like the people of Israel more generally, as a group including both male and female actors" (*Reading for History*, 53).

and children should be present to hear and be instructed in the covenant.[28] This same group is then addressed when describing the education they receive in their youth, and their enrollment into the community after their training. Though many translators at this point use the masculine singular to describe the person instructed, nothing in the Hebrew demands this shift. Instead, we should follow the plural inclusive subject (men and women) from line 1 through line 8 of column I, because the subject matter is the same.[29] This means that young women and men were equally enrolled in the community.

TESTIMONY

Certain entailments follow from community membership, including loyalty to the group beyond any familial ties. This becomes evident in the injunctions for wives to testify against their husbands. The text from 1QSa I, 11 reads, "at that time she shall be received to bear witness of him (concerning) the judgments of the law and to take her place at the hearing of the judgments."[30] This passage suggests that a wife's testimony about her husband's sexual behavior was sought in the effort to maintain a pure community. Lawrence Schiffman's careful reading of the text fails at this point when he exclaims, "Imagine what marriages this would have made!"[31] He amends the text by removing all traces of the female; but if we allow the text to stand and examine it in relation to other texts within the corpus, we find that women were encouraged to promote holiness and purity in the community, especially by maintaining purity in their sexual behavior with their husbands.

For example, this injunction should be read alongside another that states a man who has illicit sex with his wife will be excommunicated.[32] What does this passage mean? Probably it refers to men having intercourse with their pregnant wives—the act is not for procreation and so was understood as fornication.[33] If this is the correct understanding, then it means that the community was very concerned about male sexual behavior and needed the cooperation of wives to ensure the community as a whole stayed pure. A further entailment was that wives must be instructed in the ways and laws

28. Schiffman, *Reclaiming the Dead Sea Scrolls*, 133, states that this document describes the eschatological blessed messianic community, which enjoys holiness at the End of Days.

29. 1QSa I, 1–3 discusses the end-time community faithful to the covenant, lines 4–5 describe the renewal of the covenant by its members, and lines 6–11 outline the various responsibilities of members according to their life stages, such as education when they are youths. See Wassen, *Women in the Damascus Document*, 141–42.

30. Translation in Wassen, *Women in the Damascus Document*, 141.

31. Schiffman, *Reclaiming the Dead Sea Scrolls*, 135. He continues, "Those familiar with how limited women's roles were in ancient Jewish and general legal proceedings would understand why this emendation [changing the feminine pronouns to masculine] makes more sense."

32. 4Q270 7 I, 12–13; see parallel text 4Q267 9 VI, 4–5.

33. For a detailed discussion of this and other interpretations, see Wassen, *Women in the Damascus Document*, 173–82.

of the community and be present at meetings to affirm (or deny) that their marriages were in line with the covenant. The penalty for illicit sex was severe and was meted out to the husband only. This suggests at least three important points. First, the husband was the initiator of intercourse and was therefore the only one judged. Second, it reveals that community bonds were stronger than marriage ties. The wife was expected to place the community above her marriage, and they would support her by excommunicating the husband who was making the community impure through his behavior. Finally, it shows that the community was ready to believe a woman above a man, a wife above her husband. Her testimony as a truthful witness to events was expected and supported.

In a related situation, fragments 4Q270 4 and 4Q266 12 speak about the rite of the *Sotah*—the woman accused of adultery by her husband. Numbers 5:11–31 outlines the process: the husband takes his accusation to the priest, who brings the woman to stand before the Lord at the tabernacle. The priest puts the woman under an oath to reveal whether she was unfaithful, and she must reply "amen" to accept the curses should she lie. Then from the priest's hands she drinks a mixture of holy water, the ink used to write the curses, and dust from the tabernacle's floor. If she is guilty of adultery, her abdomen will swell or she will miscarry. If innocent, she will be able to have children. Both the Damascus Document and Philo reveal significant innovations to the biblical text in declaring that the accused woman is allowed to give her testimony.[34] The Damascus Document states that the woman can declare, "I was raped." Furthermore, this text requires a witness who saw the woman doing something suspicious.[35] The text breaks at this point, but perhaps it went on to describe a compromising place or inappropriate encounter. It is noteworthy that evidence from two different geographic and conceptual places within Early Judaism (Essenes and Philo in Alexandria) affirm a woman's testimony being heard concerning key issues that affect her sexuality. Perhaps this indicates a general trend in interpretation within Judaism as later rabbinic writings also assume that the woman makes a statement.[36]

Women's testimony was sought for other situations as well. In 4Q271 3 14, special examiners were called to examine a bride-to-be to ascertain whether she was a virgin. Later rabbis took that responsibility on themselves, and biblical texts demand that the parents display the bloody linens to prove their daughter's virginity. But in the Scrolls, the bride was examined beforehand so that no charges could be brought after the wedding night. Astonishingly, women determined the crucial status of the bride. Given the general fear expressed by ancient authors about women gathering together, and the overall assessment

---

34. Philo, *Spec.* 3.52–63.
35. Rabbinic writings also insist that witnesses be brought forward (*m. Sot.* 1:1–2).
36. *m. Sot.* 1:5.

of female fickleness, it is remarkable that the Scrolls hand over this extremely important determination to them, rather than wait until the wedding night to allow the parents or husband to make the determination. For the Essenes, it seems they permitted women to join as members and sought their participation in the community through careful observance of purity laws within marriage and examination of brides.

EDUCATION

The reconstruction of women's experiences within the Essene community has stressed that women were educated in the particular ways of the community. A remarkable text within the Wisdom literature of the Scrolls highlights how important the group believed women's education to be. Although 4QInstruction was likely not written by the Qumran community, the fact that eight copies have been found suggests the work was revered within the sect. This strongly eschatological text focuses on the "mystery that is to come" and probably resonated strongly with the community. Unique to all Early Jewish Wisdom literature, in 4QInstruction a woman is addressed directly.[37] Though the text is fragmentary, most likely the woman is asked to honor her father-in-law and her marriage with his son. Both "your soul" and "your covenant" are found, but the text, sadly, breaks off. Perhaps a young wife is the addressee, or perhaps the focus is every young woman and the desire for her to grow in wisdom. In any case, the shocking thing about this wisdom text is that it explicitly addresses women, breaking with the genre's tradition of only addressing the male.

Interestingly, 4QInstruction has no references to Folly as a woman, nor does it include the "bad woman" trope. Since the text is fragmentary, perhaps these references are simply no longer extant. But in other Scrolls texts, including nonsectarian ones like Sirach and Proverbs and possible sectarian writings such as 4Q184 (named the "Wiles of the Wicked Woman" by John Allegro in 1964), Folly is personified as a woman, the antitype of Woman Wisdom. Though it is uncertain whether 4Q184 is sectarian, this text amplifies the character of Dame Folly even as it neglects any practical advice. Thus, those texts that promote wisdom and folly as female personifications lack practical instructions, while 4QInstruction lacks a personification of wisdom and folly, but includes plenty of practical advice. We have no way of knowing whether 4QInstruction set the tone for the community's views on women, but I suggest that we are on fairly solid ground when imagining the Essenes as including both men and women members.

The Scrolls also contain an example of what has been called gender-inclusive exegesis. In the Damascus Document there is a discussion of the passage from Leviticus 18:6–18 addressing appropriate marriage partners: a man should not

37. 4Q415 2 II.

At Qumran, there are numerous ritual bathing sites, called *mikvaot* (singular *mikvat*). Jews would descend unclean into the pool of "living" or running water and step out ritually clean or pure. *Mikvaot* are found throughout Judea and Galilee. (Photo courtesy of Todd Bolen/bibleplaces.com)

marry his mother's sister.[38] The Damascus Document explains that the law against incest pertains not only to males but also to females; thus a daughter who uncovers the nakedness of her uncle is guilty of sinning.[39] This interpretation of the biblical text is remarkable in at least two ways. First, the Leviticus passage is generalized to include women. This interpretive principle also lies behind the expansion of oath taking to include married women and daughters having the power to make vows. "Therefore it is quite possible that reading biblical laws gender-inclusively was not an uncommon perspective in the community behind D [the Damascus Document]."[40] Second, the biblical text is made more stringent by equating men's and women's potential for transgressing in areas of purity.

38. CD V, 7b–11a.
39. We cannot know if any political condemnation was intended here, but it is interesting that a large number of marriages within the Herodian family were uncle/niece pairs.
40. Wassen, *Women in the Damascus Document*, 121.

As a similar example of exegesis, fragments 4Q266 and 4Q272 parallel men and women in their potential to transmit impurity through bodily emissions. This expands on the biblical text, Leviticus 15:4–12, which says that a man with a bodily discharge transmits impurity whether he touches another person or is touched by them. Further, in Leviticus 15:19, 25 and the Damascus Document, anyone who touches a menstruant or a *zavah* (a woman with a bodily emission) or anything she sat or lay upon will be unclean. However, the biblical text is silent about whether the touch of the menstruant or *zavah* conveys impurity, but the reconstructed argument from fragments 4Q266 and 4Q272 seems to suggest that they do, probably drawing a parallel with the *zav* from Leviticus 15:11.

How might such interpretations of the law have played out among the Essenes, especially those in towns, and in the broader Jewish community? At one level, the expanded command gives women more power to affect their surroundings, for by their touch they can render another unclean. Yet we do not know whether this expanded interpretation was followed by any Jews other than Essenes. There is an example of a *zavah* in the New Testament—the bleeding woman (Matt. 9:20–22; Mark 5:25–34; Luke 8:43–48). She is not a menstruant but a sick woman who has spent all she had on doctors, to no avail. The story says that she touched Jesus's cloak. According to Leviticus 15:25–27, she is unclean during her discharge, anything she sits or lies upon is unclean, and anyone who touches her is unclean. But the text does not say that if she touches someone, she will transmit uncleanness. If there were Essenes in the crowd, they likely would have viewed Jesus as unclean at this point. Would other Jews have followed suit? Or did they understand her actions in line with the Leviticus 15 injunctions? Did she surreptitiously touch Jesus's cloak because she did not want him to reach out and touch her? According to Leviticus 15, Jesus was not defiled by the woman. As a further speculation, the woman was not necessarily an outcast for she did not transmit uncleanness except where she sat. As long as the crowds knew about her history, they could avoid initiating contact and maintain their cleanness. As the story unfolds, no one seems worried that she is jostling in their midst.

Evidence suggests that women could take oaths and could therefore join the community. And, not surprisingly, it seems that the group raised children to become members when they came of age. But could a woman join the group without her husband? The penalties against a married couple having sex under certain conditions address only the husband, but if only the woman was joining, the husband would be an outsider and presumably condemned anyway. If a woman took the oath apart from her husband, her allegiance to the group over her family might have caused alarm, but perhaps family members would have seen her as deeply dedicated to the law. Placing her finances under the authority of the examiner might have created concern from her family and her husband, but if the man was well liked in the community, perhaps not much was made of the situation. Nothing in the Scrolls rules out a woman joining the group separate from her husband, but such an arrangement was likely complicated to live out. In all, the Scrolls suggest that women were active learners of the groups laws, participating with men in studying and applying the group's teaching.

Rabbinic Evidence

In rabbinic writings from the late second century AD, there is conflicting evidence concerning women's participation in studying the law. In one Mishnah passage, a father may teach Scripture to his sons and to his daughters.[41] In a second example, the context involves rabbis arguing about the effectiveness of the *Sotah* ritual in determining a woman's guilt of adultery. One rabbi suggests that a father should teach his daughter the law, while a second sharply disagrees—he declares that to teach a woman the law (Torah) is to teach her immodesty or adultery.[42] Why such a negative reaction against a woman knowing the law? The case hinges on the point that studying the law provides her with merit toward a righteous standing in the community and before God. The more she studies, the better she knows the law and the higher her status. At some point, so the argument goes, she would have saved up enough merit that her punishment would be suspended for a time.

The Babylonian Talmud (fifth to seventh century AD) would later take issue with the contention that the *Sotah* rite would be rendered ineffective by a woman's high merit.[43] A third case is noted from this same section in the Talmud. The story takes place at the time of the Talmud and involves an unnamed widow who travels past her local synagogue to pray daily at the study house of R. Yochanan.[44] She recognizes the merit in studying the law, and is pointed to as an example of a model widow. It is hard to know how far these hypothetical arguments reflect actual women's experiences, but coupled with other evidence outside the rabbinic corpus, it seems plausible that (some) women studied, and even interpreted, the law.

Jewish Women's Titles of Authority and Honor

Mother

In the Dead Sea Scrolls, some women are described as Elders and as Mothers (of the congregation?). Some scholars suggest these are honorary titles, and

41. *m. Ned.* 4:3.
42. *b. Sot.* 20a. The first opinion is that of R. ben Azzai, student of R. Joshua. The second is from R. Eliezer (the speaker of the passage), who is often presented as in conflict with R. Joshua. Both men are second-generation Tannaim (ca. AD 90–120).
43. *b. Sot.* 22b.
44. *b. Sot.* 22b. For a discussion, see Kraemer, *Her Share of the Blessings*, 106.

we will discuss this position below. We will assume for the sake of argument, however, that these titles represent some formal responsibility in the community, much as does the title for male Elder and Father of the congregation. Though the texts that include these titles are fragmentary, we can reconstruct some of the context. In 4Q502, a liturgical text of praise, different groups defined by gender and age are mentioned. The groupings, often in pairs of male and female, most likely represent formal groups within the community, and not merely the age of its members. For example, 4Q502 19 3 lists "male and female Elders" and 4Q502 24 4 mentions a "council of Elders." This suggests that women and men served together on the council of Elders, perhaps coordinating this particular liturgy or having responsibilities beyond it.[45]

Another text sharpens our understanding of women's authority. In 4Q270 7 I, 13–14 (4QD[e]), the punishment for murmuring against the Fathers is permanent expulsion from the community, while murmuring against the Mothers results in a ten-day punishment. The reason for this great disparity is that Mothers lack "authority" in the congregation. The term translated as authority (*rwqmh*), however, is quite unusual and hard to translate. The noun generally refers to embroidery and is used with that definition elsewhere in the Scrolls. Perhaps a special cloth was worn by the Fathers and signified their authority. Because the Mothers did not wear this special item of clothing, they were understood to be without the same authority as the men who wore this cloth. We should note, however, that less authority does not mean *no* authority; those who disrespected the Mother of the congregation were punished.

Archisynagōgissa

Leadership titles within the Qumran texts are "extremely valuable for reconstructing the social history of women in second temple Judaism."[46] So too are Jewish women's titles in the larger Greco-Roman world. Several inscriptions (though overall a small minority of extant inscriptions) note that women were leaders of synagogues, elders, and priestesses.[47] Most scholars assume that Jewish men holding similar titles interacted in an authoritative manner within

45. For an extended discussion, see Sidnie White Crawford, "Mothers, Sisters, and Elders: Titles for Women in Second Temple Jewish and Early Christian Communities," in *The Dead Sea Scrolls as Background to Postbiblical Judaism and Early Christianity*, ed. James R. Davila (Leiden: Brill, 2003), 177–91.

46. Crawford, "Mothers, Sisters, and Elders," 184.

47. The evidence for this latter category is puzzling. Bernadette J. Brooten (*Women Leaders in the Ancient Synagogue*, BJS 36 [Atlanta: Scholars Press, 1982], 99) concludes that the function of Jewish male priests in inscriptions unrelated to temple service is complex; thus the three inscriptions that identify Jewish women as priests are even more problematic. However, she also rightly notes that if a man's name was found instead of a woman's in these inscriptions, scholars would have accepted the designation "priest" without a second thought.

the community. Yet precisely what these titles reveal has yet to be determined definitively. We will examine in detail the most common title, *archisynagōgos* (leader of the synagogue; fem., *archisynagōgissa*), for several reasons. First, it is found in many literary works, including pagan and Christian, as well as Jewish.[48] This suggests that it was well known in the Greco-Roman world. Second, it applies almost exclusively to Jews, and so allows a distinctive glimpse into synagogue life. Third, the title is found throughout the Mediterranean world and across several centuries.

Unfortunately, the most agreed upon characteristic of this title is its fluidity. The term *archisynagōgos* defies tight definition, even as it suggests influence and authority or status within the community. The breadth of meaning includes benefaction, political influence, and authority to plan and execute synagogue liturgy and other religious duties. It designates men, women, and children; in the latter case, the title is likely honorary or hereditary. The lack of uniformity in use and definition means a relative lack of clarity in terms of function and authority within a given Jewish community. Yet we should not conclude from this that synagogues were unorganized gatherings. Instead, the evidence seems to point to creative, dynamic, and relatively independent synagogues throughout the Mediterranean world that structured their organizations in a variety of ways, using various terms to demarcate the different ways authority could be exercised within a group.

In the past, scholars commenting on *archisynagōgissa*, the title used for women, would assume it carried only an honorific sense or that it referred to the wife of an *archisynagōgos*. They denied it implied any authority, especially religious, within the community. Bernadette Brooten argues persuasively, however, that we should assume the women possessing these titles enjoyed the same responsibilities as their male counterparts.[49] She points out that in paganism, while some wives of priests were given a title of priestess, those women had specific religious functions and requirements to fulfill. It would be inaccurate, therefore, to suggest that the title was functional for the husband and honorary for the wife. In the case of honorary titles, such as *vir clarissimus*, given to men of senatorial rank, the title in and of itself did not imply any specific function or responsibilities; it was purely honorific. His wife was known as *clarissima femina* and could retain that title even if she was no longer married to the senator. Brooten concludes that no evidence within the paganism or Judaism of the day would suggest a double standard of interpretation; instead, both women and men held functional titles, or both held honorary titles, but the same title did not operate as functional for men and honorary for women.

---

48. See Lee Levine, "Synagogue Leadership: The Case of the Archisynagogue," in *Jews in a Graeco-Roman World*, ed. Martin Goodman (Oxford: Clarendon, 1998), 195–213.
49. Brooten, *Women Leaders in the Ancient Synagogue*, 30–33.

Tessa Rajak and David Noy remind us, however, that honor and authority were tightly connected in the Greco-Roman world, and titles such as *archisynagōgos* might express a community's wish to honor those it held in high regard, without implying that the honoree functioned as a leader in the community.[50] They argue that inscriptional evidence points to understanding *archisynagōgos* as a title of tribute to a financial contributor. In a similar way today, a university might extend an honorary degree to a commencement speaker, thereby adding to the institution's prestige in acknowledging its illustrious guest and elevating the speaker with a valuable gift (a degree). The speaker did not complete the specific graduation requirements, and so the degree is distinguished as "honorary," and they remain an "outsider" with no influence within the governance of the university community. This analogy, however, devalues the extensive literary evidence that ascribes religious functions to the *archisynagōgos*. Therefore, we should not assume at the outset that this title has no religious implications. Further issues related to honorary titles and the underlying patronage system are addressed in chapter 9.

Pairing inscriptional evidence with literary evidence reveals a more complex, overlapping picture.[51] In the New Testament, the evidence indicates at least some religious responsibilities for the *archisynagōgos*, in addition to general leadership and organizational duties. Though the New Testament's polemic against Jews cautions against a naïve and simplistic reading, the particular places where *archisynagōgos* is used seem to reflect historical knowledge about the general patterns of synagogue activities rather than tendentious denunciation of Jewish leaders. The *archisynagōgoi* in Luke-Acts and Mark apparently have some responsibilities for the religious activities of the synagogue. For example, in Luke 13:10–17, the *archisynagōgos* criticizes Jesus's healing of a woman on the Sabbath. He therefore makes a religious pronouncement within his community about proper behavior on the Sabbath in relation to Jewish law. In Mark 5:22, Jairus is introduced as the *archisynagōgos*; however, in the Lukan parallel (8:41), the title is "*archōn* [ruler/leader] of the synagogue," implying leadership within the community.[52] Acts 13:15 mentions *archisynagōgoi* requesting Paul and Barnabas offer a word to the congregation, an explicitly religious context. The male plural of the term does not rule out the possibility that women were among their members, but we have no way of knowing whether they were. What is fairly certain is the prestige and

50. Tessa Rajak and David Noy, "Archisynagogoi: Office, Title and Social Status in the Greco-Roman Synagogue," *JRS* 83 (1993): 75–93.

51. Rabbinic writings rarely mention the *archisynagōgos*, who is called *rosh knesset*, but when used, the context is usually religious and liturgical. See Levine, "Synagogue Leadership," 204–7.

52. Matt. 9:18, 23, have only *archōn*.

leadership represented in the title, especially as it reflects the religious aspects of the synagogue community.[53]

In sum, the specific context of each usage should guide our analysis, rather than the presumption that underneath the diversity lies a singular definition that can or should be imposed. For women *archisynagōgoi*, we cannot assume the title implies religious authority—but we can explore how the woman's social and political status was enhanced or established by this title. For example, a second-century AD inscription records the wishes of Rufina of Smyrna, who built a tomb for her slaves (exposed infants taken in by her) and freedpersons. She is identified as a Jewess and head of the synagogue.[54] Brooten rejects the interpretation that Rufina is merely the wife of the synagogue leader, for there is no mention of a husband in the inscription.[55] Rather, Rufina represents a wealthy Jewess who enjoyed independence and assisted those in her care, as fitting a benevolent patron. An interesting feature of this inscription is its designation of fines for any unauthorized person using the burial site. The instructions mandate that about half the fine be paid to the Jewish synagogue, but the other half to the "sacred treasury," perhaps the local temple. Does this imply that she was a Jewish convert?[56] Or is it merely further evidence that ancient temples acted as banks?

In another case, Veturia Paulla's epitaph indicates that she lived eighty-six years, and at age seventy, she converted to Judaism.[57] She was called the "mother" of two synagogues, that of Campus and of Volumnius, both near Rome. Two other inscriptions from the synagogue of Campus identify fathers of the synagogue, which suggests that in this community the title "father" or "mother" indicated a functioning authority figure. Similar to Rufina's inscription, no husband is mentioned. Perhaps he died before she converted? If this was the case, it means that her title was not based on her husband's place in the community. Another similarity between these Jewish leaders is their presumed wealth. Rufina had a large group of dependents (the tomb was not for her family—presumably they were buried elsewhere), which suggests money. Veturia's sarcophagus was finely decorated with traditional Jewish symbols (shofar, lulav, menorah), indicating at least some wealth. The titles of both women suggest their roles as patrons of the synagogue, expected by the congregation to provide for it out of their plentiful resources.

53. Lee Levine writes, "the New Testament evidence attests to an office which was prestigious on the one hand, and on the other, functioned in a leadership role within the synagogue in the political and especially the religious realms" ("Synagogue Leadership," 203).

54. *CIJ* 741. See also *CIJ* 731c, the fourth- or fifth-century AD epitaph of Sophia of Gortyn, elder and head of the synagogue of Kisamos (Crete); and *CIJ* 756, from the same period in Myndos, Caria, which honors Theopempte, head of the synagogue, and her son Eusebios.

55. Brooten, *Women Leaders in the Ancient Synagogue*, 10–11.

56. Kraemer suggests this possibility (*Her Share of the Blessings*, 121–22).

57. *CIJ* 523.

In another inscription from Asia Minor, dated to the second century, a husband eulogizes his wife Regina for her observance of the law and her love for her people.[58] Sadly, he does not elaborate how, specifically, she observed the law. Yet such a description suggests that she was actively involved in the Jewish community and its practices.

Christian Women's Titles and Authority

Unfortunately, the New Testament exhibits similar ambiguity with respect to titles given to women. As with Jewish women above, the approach must be to assume, unless warranted otherwise, that a title carries the same meaning and responsibilities whether attached to a man or a woman. This means that a female apostle or deacon would share the same responsibilities and authority as her male counterparts. This reasonable assumption has led some in the church's history to insist that no woman held titles of significant authority. Perhaps the most famous example of such a case is Junia/Junias, apostle and friend of Paul (Rom. 16:7).

Junia

At the end of Paul's letter to the Romans, listed among women and men to whom Paul sends his greetings are a pair named Andronicus and Junia/ Junias (Rom. 16:7). Like many of the names in the list, English readers cannot tell by looking at them if they signify a man's or a woman's name. In American culture, some names can refer to either a man or a woman—like my own name, Lynn—with the same spelling and sound for either gender. If I attached an "e" to the end of the name in print, people would assume I am female. Also in English, a name does not change spelling based on its place in a sentence. I always write "Lynn" whether it is the subject or object. It stays the same whether I say "Lynn went to the bank" or "Jim went with Lynn to the bank."

In other languages such as Greek and Latin, however, names have different endings depending on their place in the sentence. In the present case, the singular name is in the accusative form and is written *Iounian*. The question is whether this name represents the female name *Iounia* or the postulated masculine name *Iounias* ('Ιουνίας or 'Ιουνιᾶς, both masculine nouns of the first declension). The name Junia is a very common Roman name from the gens Junia;[59] it occurs over 250 times in Roman inscriptions alone. However, the masculine name Junias is unattested in any evidence. Instead, the attested Latin form is *Iunianus*

---

58. *CIJ* 476.

59. Five Greek manuscripts of Romans have the name Julia, which is clearly feminine. See Eldon Jay Epp, *Junia: The First Woman Apostle* (Minneapolis: Fortress, 2005), 31.

(*Iounianos* in Greek). Recently it has been suggested that *Iounian* represents a Hellenized version of the Hebrew name *yhwny*. The Hebrew name has been found twice in inscriptions, but the postulated Greek form is not represented in any literary or epigraphic source, making the hypothesis theoretically possible, but at this point, a weak argument from silence.[60]

The church fathers, not known for feminist leanings, consistently understand Paul to be referring to Junia, a woman. Echoing John Chrysostom, John of Damascus writes, "And to be called 'apostles' is a great thing . . . but to be even amongst these of note, just consider what a great encomium this is."[61] However, in the late thirteenth century, Aegidius (or Giles) of Rome performed a miracle—he changed a woman into a man.[62] Aegidius was reading his Latin Vulgate, and when he saw the name *Iuniam* and its variant *Iuliam*, he chose the latter and concluded it was a male name, even though a natural reading in Latin identifies the name as a woman's. How could he do this? To answer this question we must understand how Latin transcribes a name from Greek. In general a Greek masculine name with more than two syllables, written in the accusative and ending in ᾶν, reads in Latin as *an*. A two-syllable name would be transcribed as *am*. Thus the Latin should read *Iunian* to be understood as a man's name, but the Vulgate has *Iuniam*, clearly a woman's name. All this was brushed aside, however, and her fate was sealed in no small part by Martin Luther, whose influential translation of the Bible into German included the reference to two men, Andronicus and Junias.

Some argued, without evidence and against general practice, that Junias was a diminutive form of Junianus.[63] This effort probably took shape in the early eighteenth century and gathered steam in the late nineteenth century. The argument states that the accusative form *Iounian* is the masculine name *Iounias* (Ἰουνιᾶς), which is a shortened form (or hypocorism) of the Latin name *Iunianus* (Junianus). Junianus is indeed a common name, but the diminutive form Junias never occurs—in fact, there is no record of a shortened form of Junianus. Moreover, Latin masculine names ending with *us* are written in Greek with *os*, while names ending in *ius* become *ios*. In this case, for the name to be masculine, it would need to be written *Iunium* (accusative of *Iunius*). Instead appears *Iuniam*, clearly a woman's name. Again, if the

---

60. Al Wolters, "IOYNIAN (Romans 16:7) and the Hebrew Name *Yĕḥunnī*," *JBL* 127 (2008): 397–408. However, he does not take a position on whether the name in Rom. 16:7 reflects a masculine Hebrew name or a feminine Latin name.

61. John of Damascus, *Commentarii in epistulas Pauli* (PG 95:565). Translation by Linda Belleville, "Ἰουνιαν . . . ἐπίσημοι ἐν τοῖς ἀποστόλοις: A Re-examination of Romans 16.7 in Light of Primary Source Materials," *New Testament Studies* 51 (2005): 235. Cf. Epiphanius, *Index discipulorum* (attributed to Epiphanius by a ninth-century monk, but its authorial ascription is suspect), which names Junias as a bishop of Apamea, Syria, using a masculine pronoun, but also identifies Prisca as Priscas, male bishop of Colopho.

62. Epp, *Junia*, 32–35.

63. See Epp, *Junia*, 25 for a complete discussion.

Greek name *Iounias* were to be shortened, it would be *Iounas*, dropping the second *i*. What about the name Ἰουνίας, with the accent on the penultimate syllable?[64] It seems that only two of the twenty-six masculine names in the New Testament that end in unaccented *as* come from the Latin—*Agrippas* (Agrippa) and *Akylas* (Aquila). Both of these names are common cognomen of the first declension. But *Iunius* was a common nomen, not cognomen (the nomen indicates the gens, which is a loose group of families).

After analyzing the necessary literary and epigraphic evidence, it becomes clear that the male name Junias is unattested in the Greco-Roman world, while the female name Junia is widely witnessed. The pressing question becomes, why have so many of the Greek critical editions, and translations relying upon them, insisted on Junias? The answer lies in the committees' convictions that a female apostle was unlikely, and so this name Junias—unknown throughout the Greco-Roman world—was created ex nihilo to match their presuppositions. Recognizing the weakness of the argument for the name Junias, some have suggested that Paul did not in fact address Andronicus and Junia as holding the office of apostle, but rather acknowledged that apostles were very impressed with the pair. Said another way, Andronicus and Junia were highly regarded by the group of apostles. The key issue is how to interpret the phrase *"episēmoi en tois apostolois"*; is the dative inclusive or exclusive? That is, is Paul suggesting that Junia is included in the group of apostles, or is she an outsider who is well known to the apostles? In the first case, a comparison is implied—the two are more famous than other apostles. Such a reading makes perfect sense of the Greek, and a parallel might be drawn from Matthew 2:6 (quoting Mic. 5:2): "And you, Bethlehem, in the land of Judah, are by no means least *among the rulers* of Judah."[65] This was the understanding of the Greek church fathers, including Origen and Theodoret. The latter wrote, "Then to be called 'of note' not only among the disciples but also among the teachers, and not just among the teachers but even among the apostles . . ."[66]

So, if the text says that Junia was an apostle, what does that mean? Paul identifies himself as an apostle and describes as apostles Timothy, Silvanus, Epaphroditus, and Barnabas (1 Thess. 2:6–7; 1 Cor. 9:5–6; Phil. 2:25). In the latter instance, Paul is likely using the term in the nontechnical sense of a messenger sent by the Philippians to aid Paul in his imprisonment (see also 2 Cor. 8:23). The term might also carry the sense of a traveling missionary and might be implied in the title for Timothy and Silas/Silvanus and perhaps others who spread the gospel message. But if that were the case, it seems less likely that Paul, in Romans 16:7, would use

64. Accents began to be used in the seventh century and were common by the ninth; all New Testament authors wrote in unaccented Greek.
65. See Richard Bauckham, *Gospel Women: Studies of the Named Women in the Gospels* (Grand Rapids: Eerdmans, 2002), 178.
66. Theodoret, *Interpretatio in quatuordecim epistolas S. Pauli* (PG 82:200). Translation by Belleville, "Ἰουνιαν," 234–35 (on Origen, see 235–36).

the definite article "the" in referring to this group to which Junia and Andronicus belonged. Why not instead simply say that they were outstanding among
apostles? Luke identifies Barnabas as an apostle alongside Paul in Acts 14:4, 14.
Paul stresses that he was called as an apostle to the Gentiles (Gal. 1:13–17) and
suggests that this calling is rooted in part in having seen the (risen) Lord (1 Cor.
9:1; 15:5–9). This matches Luke's statements of Peter in Acts 1. Here Peter calls
for a vote to replace Judas as one of the twelve apostles. The criterion for the post
is that one walked with Jesus from his ministry in Galilee until his resurrection.
While the title carried a range of meanings, all but one New Testament reference
(Phil. 2:25) suggest an authoritative figure in the community.

Women Teachers

One aspect of apostolic authority is teaching, a function attributed to women
in the New Testament. With approval Luke notes the instruction given by Priscilla
to Apollos (Acts 18:26). However, the seer John, author of Revelation, disapproves
strongly of the teachings of the prophet "Jezebel," for they lead astray the faithful (Rev. 2:20). It is not entirely clear whether the person responsible for the false
teachings is female, as one method of denigrating a male opponent is to liken
him to a woman. Nonetheless, given the other examples of women instructing
the church, this "Jezebel" could be a historical woman. If this is the case, we
can be reasonably certain that she did not self-identify as Jezebel; rather, John
indicted her character and teachings by connecting her with the infamous Jezebel
of Israel's past who tormented and killed God's prophets (1 Kings 18:13; 19:1–2;
21:1–16). Another example of a prophetess is more positive. Luke describes the
prophetess Anna, a widow for some time, who prays and fasts in the temple
daily. Luke characterizes her as virtuous, honoring the memory of her husband
by remaining a widow (a Greco-Roman virtue as well). She announces the infant
Jesus's identity to those awaiting "the redemption of Jerusalem" (Luke 2:36–38).
Could it be that those who heard her were not random visitors to the temple,
but a group, perhaps led by Anna, that had specific expectations about Jerusalem's redemption? Nothing in the story necessitates this reading nor precludes
it; however, her title of prophetess suggests that she had around her those who
viewed her teachings as authoritative.[67]

Religious Activities: Synagogue, Sabbath, and Menstrual Rites

Synagogue and Sabbath

In the opening caricature of the Jewish "prophetess" painted by Juvenal,
this woman is portrayed as speaking publicly about Judaism. We should not

---

67. The only other place where the New Testament mentions prophetesses is Acts 21:9, which
notes that the four daughters of Philip prophesied.

imagine Juvenal's "soap box on the street corner" image is historically accurate, but it is suggestive. Juvenal places the Jewish diviner under a tree, which could hint at a women's gathering outside city walls as in the story of Lydia at Philippi, where Luke notes that a group of women met down by the river for their time of prayer, their synagogue meeting. Juvenal might be parodying this sort of meeting.

The preponderance of evidence indicates that women participated alongside men in synagogue worship. Unlike the Jerusalem temple, synagogue space was not sacred. Gentiles were welcomed as Jews prayed, read Scripture, and discussed the law. Evidence for specific synagogue liturgy is scarce, and hotly contested, thereby making any reconstruction of synagogue practices tentative. The limited archaeological evidence does not support a women's balcony or women's quarter.[68] We cannot say definitely whether women read Scripture or prayed publicly, because this answer depends in great part on whether the titles given to women include functional responsibilities within the religious life of the Jewish community. I have suggested that evidence points to at least some of these women performing religious duties.

Juvenal's Jewish "priestess" takes money for her divinations, but not a lot. In one swing, Juvenal is able to condemn her for profiting from religion and mock her for not getting enough. These claims about begging and greed are stock accusations flung at those disliked by the author. Juvenal repeats his condemnation of the woman in his more general snarl against the Jews of Rome who hang about the Porta Capena with their baskets and a truss of hay—all their earthly belongings.[69] The "basket and hay" reference has been explained by an ancient commentator of Juvenal as an allusion to the Sabbath meal, kept warm in a basket covered with hay.[70] This passing comment probably indicates that many Jews took Sabbath laws about not working (preparing a meal) seriously—at least enough Jews did to make an impression on cynical Juvenal.

Menstrual Purity Rites

At first glance, Jewish women's activities might not differ much from their gentile counterparts in certain religious devotion activities. For example, they both paid homage to the god of their home. Jewish women participated in Sabbath meals, while gentile women were enjoined to offer a libation to the hearth god. In the rituals and beliefs surrounding menstruation, however, the two groups differed widely, and later Christians created a third possible

---

68. Lee I. Levine, *The Ancient Synagogue: The First Thousand Years* (New Haven: Yale University Press, 2005), 431; James F. Strange, "Ancient Texts, Archaeology as Text, and the Problem of the First Century Synagogue," in *Evolution of the Synagogue: Problems and Progress*, ed. Howard Clark Kee and Lynn H. Cohick (Harrisburg, PA: Trinity Press International, 1999), 34.

69. Juvenal, *Sat.* 3.10–16; see also 3.290–96.

70. See Louis H. Feldman and Meyer Reinhold, *Jewish Life and Thought among Greeks and Romans: Primary Readings* (Minneapolis: Fortress, 1996), 394n99.

v

A first-century synagogue in Gamla, Galilee (Photo courtesy of Todd Bolen/bibleplaces.com)

response. The Greco-Roman society did not censure menstruating gentile women, nor were they judged impure. Menstruating women held power, potentially dangerous power, but they were not considered unclean.

THE LEVITICUS CODE

In contrast to Greco-Roman society, Judaism considered women unclean during their menstrual period, according to the Leviticus code. Leviticus contains four passages that regulate menstruation in the Israelite community.[71] In chapter 15, discharges from both men and women are discussed, and 15:19–30 explicates how the woman cleanses herself from either her period or another type of discharge. A menstruant is called a *niddah* and a woman with a discharge is called a *zavah*. A woman during her period is unclean, and anyone who touches her is unclean—they must wash and will be unclean until evening. Unclean persons cannot approach the tabernacle because they will defile God's dwelling place. But it must be emphasized—unclean is not the same as sinful. A menstruant is no more impure than a husband who has sex with his wife and emits semen (15:18), and neither is judged sinful.[72]

71. Lev. 12:1–7; 15:19–30; 18:19; 20:18; see also Num. 5:1–4.
72. This does not rule out the possibility that at times "unclean" was used metaphorically to indicate sin; a parallel might be the connections made metaphorically between darkness and sin, even though darkness is not intrinsically related to sin.

Numbers 5:1–4 expands the boundaries of holiness to encircle the entire camp, not just the tabernacle proper. As a result, any man or woman suffering from a skin disease or discharge of any kind was sequestered outside the camp so as not to defile it. The Temple Scroll found at Qumran carries forward this sentiment in its charge to keep all impure men outside the city wall and to forbid all impure women (not just those who are menstruating) from entering the city. It designates a special place outside the town's walls where impure men can reside until their purity is restored. Clearly this vision is utopian, not descriptive. There is no evidence that any Jewish group in the first century AD isolated menstruating women or women with discharges from the community.[73] Josephus may hint that menstruants were dissuaded from touching sacred objects, but his statement is ambiguous. In his retelling of Rachel stealing her father's idols, he duly notes that she claimed her period prevented her from rising from her seat under which were the stolen idols. He adds, "Laban thought that his daughter would not approach the images while having such an affliction."[74] Laban may be speaking for contemporary Jews who believed a menstruant would defile sacred objects; however, Josephus makes clear earlier in the story that neither Rachel nor Jacob saw the objects as sacred. Josephus remarks that Rachel took them as a bargaining chip to use later if her father became unreasonable.

Josephus, in responding to gentile polemics that Moses was a leper, recounts the restrictions against lepers in Numbers 5:1–4 and Leviticus. He asks rhetorically whether Moses would place such severe restrictions on lepers—they must remain outside the camp until healed—if he was himself a sufferer. Of course not, Josephus declares. In his explanation, Josephus distinguishes between the fate of a leper (or someone who has a skin ailment) and that of a person with a bodily emission, a person who touched a dead body, or a menstruant. The latter are unclean for seven days, while the leper is perpetually unclean. Josephus puts it starkly—the leper is dead to the community and lives outside the town. Continuing to discuss Leviticus, in this same section Josephus details the menstruant and the parturient. Those who recently gave birth are prevented from entering the temple (i.e., the tabernacle) or from touching a sacrifice until their time of uncleanness has passed. If they had a boy, they must wait forty days, if a girl, eighty days. When describing the temple of his own day, he reiterates the restriction that menstruating women or women with a flow of blood are forbidden to enter the temple, while lepers are restricted from Jerusalem itself.[75] Interestingly, no restriction to enter the outer court of

73. Shaye J. D. Cohen, "Menstruants and the Sacred in Judaism and Christianity," in *Women's History and Ancient History*, ed. Sarah B. Pomeroy (Chapel Hill: University of North Carolina Press, 1991), 278.

74. Josephus, *Ant.* 1.19.10 (232). Translation in Cohen, "Menstruants and the Sacred," 282.

75. Josephus, *B.J.* 5.5.6.

the gentiles is laid upon Jewish males who suffered impurity through emission of bodily fluids.

If we assume for the sake of argument that Josephus accurately reflects current practice, why were Jewish women with a flow of blood singled out as pollutants when even gentile males (and nonmenstruating females) entered the outer courts? The answer may lie in Leviticus's repeated use of the term "purify" to describe both the woman's blood and the blood of the sacrifice. In Leviticus 12, the parturient remains in the purifying of her blood, while in chapter 16 Aaron uses sacrificial blood to purify Israel. Joan Branham states, "according to these and other biblical passages, the role of the two bloods seems to be inseparable. Reproductive blood purifies, sacrificial blood purifies."[76] A conceptual and linguistic link joins sacrificial blood and the life-giving menses, for the former gives atonement or life to the soul, while the latter brings forth human life. Branham muses that the eighty-day purification period for birthing a girl reflects her potential as a future life-giver and implicitly recognizes her latent power. She concludes, "what appears to be an absolute antipathy between the two fluids may arise from their *kindred or similar powers* of purification, life, and rebirth."[77]

THE DEAD SEA SCROLLS

While no extant documents from antiquity articulate a theory like Branham's, the Dead Sea Scrolls do testify to the importance (whether conceptually or actually, or both) of purity codes. The Essenes used purity codes to self-identify and to distinguish themselves from other Jews. Wassen notes that for Essenes, "the impurity prescriptions constitute an elaborate, coherent system with parallel laws for men and women affected by similar kinds of impurity."[78] The principles of interpretation are similar in this case to those noted above: the text's implications are expanded such that men's stipulations are placed on women as well.[79] As interesting as the interpretive principles are, one could argue that they do not reveal directly the community's habits. That is, even though the sect developed interpretations of the biblical text concerning women's purity, we cannot determine from that evidence whether women followed these practices. Such caution is appropriate when looking at legal codes because one cannot be sure whether they reflect reality or simply describe an ideal setting. Yet there seems to be historical veracity reflected in some of the sectarian documents, which suggests real women were active within the group. If that is the case, they would likely be governed by the purity laws that were apparently influential for the male members of the group. If this

76. Joan Branham, "Bloody Women and Bloody Spaces: Menses and the Eucharist in Late Antiquity and the Early Middle Ages," *Harvard Divinity Bulletin* 30.4 (2002): 15–22.

77. Branham, "Bloody Women and Bloody Spaces," 15.

78. Wassen, *Women in the Damascus Document*, 47.

79. Wassen, *Women in the Damascus Document*, 50.

reasoning is correct, then we have Second Temple evidence for some women following the prescriptions for menstrual (and discharge) purity. We must reiterate here an important reminder: uncleanness did not equal sinfulness. Thus restriction from the temple for impurity reasons did not cast a moral shadow over the person, including the menstruating woman. Nor did it prevent the person from continuing daily activities, apart from participating in sacred functions within sacred space, namely the temple. The evidence allows that menstruating women would be at the markets, in the fields, in the synagogues (perhaps standing or bringing their own stools)—in general, acting alongside men in all capacities.

The New Testament

The New Testament does not refer at all to menstrual purity codes; its silence can be read a number of ways. It might be that the Jews who gravitated toward Jesus's teachings came from backgrounds that did not emphasize the menstrual purity codes. Or it may be that the practices of menstrual purification were ubiquitous and did not warrant any comment. The question is further complicated because issues of purity related to food laws and association with gentiles played a significant role in the earliest church. Since the woman's menstrual purity affected her husband, it was not just a "woman's issue" but impacted men, making the New Testament's silence all the more intriguing. Later, some church practices introduced restrictions on women participating in church and partaking of the eucharist if they were menstruating.[80]

Although the discussion of menstrual purity is not shared by New Testament authors and Jewish writings, the examples of the Therapeutrides and women among the Essenes open the door to speculation about women following Jesus or the message of the apostles without their husband's involvement in the sect. While we often assume that a woman named without a husband is a widow, divorced, or unmarried (Mary Magdalene comes to mind), it is possible that they were married but their husbands did not follow Jesus's teachings. Another assumption is that women had to remain at home, and thus it was not possible for them to follow Jesus around. Yet Jesus taught in the predominately Jewish areas of Galilee. The towns were as close as a day's walk, and villages were governed by customs of hospitality so that even distantly related folk would open their homes for relatives. Female disciples would have found appropriate shelter.

Furthermore, it would not have been suspect for men and women to participate together in a religious movement. Josephus speaks of families living at Masada at the end of the First Revolt. Also, the Babatha archives (discussed in chap. 2) were discovered in the same cave that included letters written by

---

80. For example, see the third-century Dionysius of Alexandria, *Epistula ad Basilides*. Translation in Kraemer, *Maenads, Martyrs, Matrons, Monastics*, 43.

supporters of Simon bar Kochba, the rebel leader/messianic figure who led the failed Second Revolt against Rome in AD 132–35. We cannot say whether Babatha was a follower, but a nearby cave revealed skeletons of men, women, and children who apparently starved to death rather than surrender to the Romans. Perhaps some women chose to align themselves with bar Kochba independent of their male family members. Overall, the evidence points to the possibility of Judean and Galilean women actively pursuing religious activities with various sects and with the several teachers traveling about the countryside. They could enjoy community life, travel, hold responsible positions within their group, and investigate Scriptures in pursuit of a more holy and pure life.

Conclusion

Judaism and Christianity were not exclusively or even predominately male domains. Though he meant his comment disparagingly, Celsus might be closer to the mark than previously appreciated when he accented the role of women (and slaves) in the church. Such activity was present as well in Judaism. Jewish women were active in the synagogue—present with men in the congregation, not segregated to a woman's balcony. Some were "mothers" of their congregations; others assumed the title and responsibilities of an *archisynagōgissa*. These women likely had both honor and leadership roles within the governing structure of their local synagogue, much as did men who held similar titles.

Some women chose a celibate, cloistered life, the life of a Therapeutic. With scrolls as their companions most days, they focused on the allegorical understanding of the biblical text and composed hymns to God. At weekly celebrations, they joined the male members of the sect for sacred meals and celebrations. Other women chose to join the Essenes, with its focus on purity and apocalypticism. They vowed to support the group's ideals, even if that meant testifying against their husbands in areas of sexual conduct. In the Essene community, women were sincerely devoted to the religious life. They were also educated in the practices and beliefs of the group. This indicates a commitment to education and learning by women and by the community. Both the Essene women and the Therapeutrides witness to the ability of women to identify themselves as members of a religious community first, and as wives or mothers second.

These characteristics of devotion, learning, and autonomy were exhibited in different ways by other Jewish and Christian women. Some joined resistance movements fighting for Jewish freedom from Roman imperial domination. Others followed after prophets and teachers, including those women who followed Jesus of Nazareth. Jewish women could travel in the company of an itinerant preacher without assuming a label of immodesty. And like Jewish women in synagogues, some women in the earliest Christian groups held positions of authority, such as Junia the apostle and Prisca the teacher.

Overall, women had freedom of movement to pursue religious interests and convictions. They had opportunities to choose expressions of faith that differed from those of their families or husbands. For women inclined toward the religious, Judaism and Christianity offered opportunities for expressing their convictions. But for most women, pursuing religious convictions did not take up the bulk of their day. Like men, the vast majority of women worked hard to earn daily bread and a roof over their head. In the next chapter we discover the myriad of jobs, tasks, and vocations taken up by women.

7

Women's Work

The phrase "women's work" carries several meanings and innuendos to the modern ear. Both today and in the ancient world, certain tasks are primarily done by women. Two obvious ones come to mind immediately: midwifery and wet-nursing. Other jobs were done by both men and women, including trade and commerce jobs, cooking and baking, entertaining, and even fighting as a gladiator. Some jobs were reserved for men, including soldiering. What did women do in the ancient world? Most women were deeply invested in family life and raising children. Meals and clothing, soap and blankets, necessities of life often fell to the mother/wife to make, or to supervise slaves in their production. Women contributed to the family business, worked in the shop, labored in the fields, offered their services as midwives, wet nurses, house help. The poorer the woman, the less she traveled away from her home. Like most "average" or poor men of the day, a woman hoped to sustain the family through hard work and a bit of luck.

However, some women held jobs outside what we might call the "norm." Wealthy women had educational opportunities, and some studied philosophy. Other women were known to possess talents in the magical arts. Some were inventors. Roman women married to a high-ranking official often possessed extensive political clout. There is also the example of Cleopatra, who was ruler of Egypt in her own right and a key player in the high-stakes games of empire building.[1]

1. Sarah B. Pomeroy writes that Cleopatra "was not a courtesan, an exotic plaything for Roman generals. Rather, Cleopatra's liaisons with the Romans must be considered to have been, from her viewpoint, legitimate dynastic alliances with promises of the greatest possible

In previous chapters of this book, I often discuss issues based on religious categories: whether a woman is pagan, Jewish, or part of the emerging Christian sect. This has to do in part with my interest in discerning distinctive practices based on religious claims or affiliations. Yet this (somewhat) arbitrary classification should not blind us to the fact that religious attitudes can play little or no role in distinguishing behaviors. Instead, gender, class, and social status are more determinant of the options open to women. In many situations, a wealthy Jewish woman would have much in common with her wealthy gentile neighbor—luxurious clothes, home furnishings, slaves, quality food, entertainment opportunities—while poor gentile and Jewish women suffered the same anxieties over having enough food, keeping a house, and staying healthy.

This holds true for occupations as well. In most cases, work is viewed differently for men and women. As a rule, men gained (or lost) social prestige from their work; women's employment generally was not mentioned in epitaphs or portrayed in reliefs. Women did not gain (or were not given) much prestige for their work, perhaps in part because the majority of the tasks women did took place in the home, such as hairdressing, child care, and weaving. Often these tasks could be done by slaves, further devaluing the work. The tasks themselves did not garner honor, and thus few women identified themselves through their jobs. Moreover, a wife at leisure was a status symbol for her husband; however, in reality, only a few families could afford the luxury of a wife at ease. Thus we find conflicting messages circulated about women and work: they must be industrious in the home, recalling the ubiquitous praise of women's woolworking, but they also bring honor to their husband when they need not do any work to sustain the household. In sum, the sources reveal a multilayered landscape of activity and commerce done by both men and women.

Women's Work: Midwife and Wet Nurse

Qualifications for Midwives

Only a few areas of life were the exclusive domain of women, and perhaps none was as prominent as the birthing process led by the midwife. While male family members were likely close by and perhaps a male physician was near enough to give medical orders, the delivery event typically included only women. Often the midwife would care for the mother for several days after the birth, or longer if the midwife was a family slave.

Soranus, a physician from the early second century AD, discussed in great detail the qualifications for midwifery. Some seem commonsensical, such as the midwife having soft hands and a gentle heart and not being given to drink. He

success and profit to the queen and to Egypt" (Goddesses, Whores, Wives, and Slaves: Women in Classical Antiquity [1975; repr., New York: Schocken, 1995], 124).

also refuted certain generally accepted claims, for instance that a midwife must be young or must be a mother herself. And he recommended that the midwife be trained, perhaps by reading his manual. This suggests that at least some midwives were educated,[2] but Pliny the Elder's discussion of childbirth reveals that in many cases superstition and folk medicine carried the day. In these cases, the village midwife would have experiential knowledge of herbs but no formal education. Pliny recounts various treatments involving animal or plant parts and insects that were either ingested or applied to the body. For example, one remedy to aid childbirth was to stick a vulture's feather under the woman in labor, presumably under the birthing chair.[3] He also records that "midwives assure us that a flux, however copious, is stayed by drinking the urine of a she-goat, or if an application is made of her dung. The membrane that covers the new-born offspring of she-goats, kept till dry and taken in wine, brings away the after birth."[4]

What was the social status of the average midwife? Scholars are divided on the percentage of free or freed midwives compared with slaves, some suggesting that most midwives fell into the latter category. There is precious little epigraphic evidence of women identified as midwives, with only sixteen out of the thousands of Latin epitaphs collected specifying this occupation.[5] Of course, not every epitaph recorded the person's occupation, so it is unwise to draw firm conclusions about the number of midwives solely based on this sample. Within this small group, not all have their social status clearly marked, but perhaps nine were slaves of Caesar's house or of noble Roman families. Of these nine, only one died a slave; the others perhaps earned enough money to buy their freedom or were rewarded with manumission.

The Expense and Status of Midwives

Were midwifery services expensive? Probably a good midwife could earn a decent living. From a bit beyond the period under consideration, a marriage contract from the third century AD describes the husband providing forty drachmae for his wife's confinement; part of that sum would go to the midwife.[6] At that time, an ox driver made between thirty-four and forty-eight

2. A fourth-century BC Athenian epitaph commemorates Phanostrate, a midwife and a physician: "she caused pain to none, and all lamented her death" (Kaibel 45; Pleket 1). Translation in Mary R. Lefkowitz and Maureen B. Fant, *Women's Life in Greece and Rome: A Source Book in Translation*, 3rd ed. (Baltimore: Johns Hopkins University Press, 2005), 267.

3. Pliny the Elder, *Nat.* 30.44.

4. Pliny the Elder, *Nat.* 28.77 (trans. Betty Radice, LCL).

5. CIL VI.4458, 6325, 6647, 6832, 8192, 8207, 8947–49, 9720–25, 37810. For a translation of some of these epitaphs, see Lefkowitz and Fant, *Women's Life in Greece and Rome*, 267. See also previous note.

6. P.Oxy. 1273.33–34. For a discussion, see Valerie French, "Midwives and Maternity Care in the Roman World," in *Midwifery and the Medicalization of Childbirth: Comparative Perspectives*, ed. E. R. van Teijlingen et al. (New York: Nova Science, 2004), 53–62.

This terra-cotta relief from a second-century AD tomb near Ostia shows a midwife helping a woman give birth. An attendant supports the woman. (Photo courtesy of Werner Forman Archive, Ltd.)

drachmae a month, and a common laborer could expect about eight drachmae per month.[7] Moreover, it seems that midwives had access to provincial governors to dispute contracts for wages because they were viewed as part of the medical profession, or even as physicians.[8]

Evidence suggests that practices varied from east to west, with the latter having predominantly slave midwives. Such disparity is based in some measure on the relative wealth of Italy, especially Rome. They could afford to buy trained midwives to care for their families. In the eastern half of the empire, apparently, some women were able to obtain medical training that advanced them from a midwife (*maia*) to an obstetrician (*iatros gynaikeios*). For example, a husband and wife from Pergamum were a team of physicians. The husband praised his wife's beauty, wisdom, and chastity. "You bore me children completely like myself;[9] you cared for your bridegroom and your children; you guided straight the rudder of life in our home and raised high *our common fame in healing*—though you were a woman you were not behind me in skill."[10]

7. French, "Midwives and Maternity Care," 61n34.

8. *Digesta Justiniana* 50.13.1.

9. In this comment, the husband was saying that his wife was faithful to him. If she was with another man, the child born would resemble the lover, not the husband.

10. Pleket 20, italics added. For a translation, see Lefkowitz and Fant, *Women's Life in Greece and Rome*, 265.

In addition, there are gynecological tracts apparently written by women with Greek names. Such evidence suggests that in eastern regions, obstetrical care was viewed as a respectable profession in which a woman could earn a living, and even publish works used by male physicians.[11]

Yet the few physical images of the midwife suggest that society viewed their work differently from that of a male physician. The latter portrayal drew on iconography of either the Greek philosopher (seated, bearded, with the patient portrayed as smaller than the doctor) or the god Aesculapius. In the case of the midwife, however, we find in the Ostia relief pictured on the previous page that she is simply dressed, kneeling in front of her client.[12] In another example, a funerary stele from the second or third century AD, the woman is presented in a typical fashion and is simply standing holding a box.[13] The accompanying inscription reads "INI FII MEDICA," indicating her profession. "The small amount of evidence for the iconography of medical practitioners thus indicates that images of men and women did not share the same visual vocabulary, in spite of the equality described in the written sources."[14] Women doctors might be portrayed as matrons, but men's identities were enhanced by associations with the philosopher figure or the god Aesculapius.

Qualifications and Restrictions for Wet Nurses

Only women served as midwives, and of course, only women could be wet nurses. There is no evidence that bottle feeding was an option at this time. As with midwives, Soranus also wrote on the qualities of a good wet nurse. While he advocates maternal breast-feeding as the most "natural" and best-suited option for the nursling, he also cautions that breast-feeding might exhaust the mother, rendering her prematurely old. His description of a good wet nurse is instructive. A composite picture of his ideal wet nurse is a woman between twenty and forty years old, having had two or three births herself, with medium breasts, a strong build, an attentive and gentle demeanor, who is not given to drink and refrains from sex. Moreover, the woman should be a Greek, "so that the infant nursed by her may become accustomed to

11. French, "Midwives and Maternity Care," 55. Yet note the inscription from first-century AD Rome, which identifies Primilla as a physician who lived 44 years, thirty of those with her husband, Lucius Cocceius Apthorus. *CIL* VI.7581; *ILS* 7804. Translation in Lefkowitz and Fant, *Women's Life in Greece or Rome*, 264.

12. For a detailed discussion of the relief, see Natalie Boymel Kampen, "Social Status and Gender in Roman Art: The Case of the Saleswoman," in *Feminism and Art History: Questioning the Litany*, ed. Norma Broude and Mary D. Garrard (New York: Harper and Row, 1982), 70–71.

13. Stele of a doctor (Metz, Musée Archéologique). See Kampen, "Social Status and Gender," 70, 72.

14. Kampen, "Social Status and Gender," 70.

the best speech."[15] He also disabuses the notion that a boy's wet nurse must have birthed a boy, while a girl's wet nurse must have birthed a girl. "One should pay no heed to these people, for they do not consider that mothers of twins, the one being male and the other female, feed both with one and the same milk."[16]

Soranus's advice is echoed in the preserved contracts for wet nurses. In a legal document from Egypt (AD 187), a man contracts out his slave as a wet nurse to care for a woman's daughter for two years. For four hundred drachmae of silver, Tanenteris, the mother, employs the slave Sarapias to care for her daughter Helene.[17] In Egypt, two such contracts from 13 BC deal with a foundling (a child rescued from exposure). The slave owner in one instance is a man, and in the other, a woman. In each case, the wet nurse is represented by a male agent, either her husband or brother. The contracts stipulate a period of about eighteen months of nursing, at the woman's home, with three or four visits per month to the owner's home for inspection of the child. The first nine months are paid up front, and the remaining nine months are paid if the work has been judged satisfactory. The contracts state that the wet nurses may not drink heavily, nor have sex, nor nurse another child.

One of these contracts might have been made with a Jewish woman. The evidence for this comes from the names listed in the contract. Specifically, the contract between Marcus Aemilius and Theodote, daughter of Dositheos and wife of Sophron (both "Persians"), identifies the wet nurse and her father, the guarantor of the contract, and her husband with names akin to those used by Jews at this time. If this suggestion is correct, then this is an example of a Jewish wet nurse contracting with a gentile slave owner to care for his foundling baby girl.[18] Her contract states that she is not to lie with a man or conceive. Both her father and husband agree that Theodote will avoid intercourse for the eighteen months of her contract (or they willingly sign a contract they do not intend to live up to). Although a gentile man would have other socially acceptable alternatives for intercourse apart from his wife, the Jewish husband, at least in theory, was restricted from sexual activity outside of marriage.[19] In any case, the agreement meant that their marriage would not produce any children for at least two years. One could speculate as to whether their economic situation necessitated this option, or whether this occupation

15. Soranus, *Gyn.* 2.19. Translation by O. Temkin in Lefkowitz and Fant, *Women's Life in Greece and Rome,* 269.
16. Soranus, *Gyn.* 2.20. Translation by O. Temkin in Lefkowitz and Fant, *Women's Life in Greece and Rome,* 269.
17. P.Oxy. 91. Translation in Lefkowitz and Fant, *Women's Life in Greece and Rome,* 272.
18. *CPJ* 146; *BGU* IV.1106. Translation by A. Fuks in Ross S. Kraemer, ed., *Women's Religions in the Greco-Roman World: A Sourcebook,* rev. ed. (Oxford: Oxford University Press, 2004), 125.
19. One assumes the couple engaged in other sexual acts apart from intercourse.

was esteemed and sought after in their community. Probably either scenario represented historical reality.

The Expense and Status of Wet Nurses

Examining the preserved evidence, Keith Bradley finds that most wet nurses were either slaves or poor freeborn women. He points to Dio Chrysostom's remarks made at the turn of the first century AD that the job of wet nurse was reputable.[20] Both Juvenal[21] and Favorinus imply in their writings that wet nurses come from poor, free backgrounds. Favorinus laments that often the person chosen as a wet nurse is from a "foreign and barbarian nation . . . [whose] only qualification for the post is that of having milk."[22] Admittedly, his rhetorical flourish outruns his historical accuracy, but the implications of his words point to nonslave wet nurses. In contrast, the inscriptions preserved from Rome suggest that it was primarily slaves and freedwomen who served as wet nurses. These statistics mirror those of midwives: wealthy families in Rome had the financial ability to buy as slaves their wet nurses and midwives.

Wet-nursing cannot be understood in isolation from other important social and economic factors of the day, including the tremendous wealth available to the Roman elites, the great number of slaves (in Italy perhaps 33 percent of the population; in the rest of the empire, perhaps 10 percent), the *sine manu* marriage structure, divorce patterns, and maternal death from childbirth. The critics of those women who refused to breast-feed charged them (and their families) with materialism and vanity—vices that often accompany wealth. The influx of slaves into the economy allowed the wealthy more leisure time, and perhaps transformed once acceptable jobs into inferior ones. Moreover, specific family situations could drive the need for wet nurses. For example, a divorced woman from a licit marriage who gave birth to her former husband's baby had to surrender that child to the husband's family. In this case, a wet nurse would be essential. Again, if a woman died in childbirth, a wet nurse was called upon. We have only to look at the situation of Cicero's daughter Tullia to see both scenarios lived out. She was pregnant when she was divorced from her husband, and gave birth in her former father-in-law's home. Then she traveled to Cicero's house, where after one month, she died, likely of complications from childbirth. Her child survived only a few weeks, but

20. Dio Chrysostom, *Orationes* 7.114. See Keith R. Bradley, "Wet-Nursing at Rome: A Study in Social Relations," in *The Family in Ancient Rome: New Perspectives,* ed. Beryl Rawson (Ithaca, NY: Cornell University Press, 1986), 202–3.
21. Juvenal, *Sat.* 6.352–54.
22. Aulus Gellius, *Noct. att.* 12.1. Translation in Lefkowitz and Fant, *Women's Life in Greece and Rome,* 189.

during that time would have needed a wet nurse.[23] Given the alarmingly high infant mortality rate as well as the practice of infanticide or infant exposure, wet nurses were more or less in constant supply.

Women and Physical Labor

In the few snapshots of rural life in Italy and throughout the Roman Empire, we find women working the fields, caring for livestock, or overseeing those who do. In a fascinating look at life on the farm, Livy (late first century BC) includes a biography of a centurion named Spurius Ligustinus, a career military man.[24] He fought away from home for about twenty-two years, returning to his family between campaigns. His homestead was an acre of land upon which sat a hut, a gift from his father at marriage. Ligustinus married his cousin, his uncle's daughter on his father's side, and together they had eight children that lived to adulthood. For the most part on her own, the mother raised the children, provided food for them each day, tended the land, and gathered or chopped the firewood. Horace, a contemporary of Livy, describes approvingly the stern mother who prepares her sons to be good Roman soldiers and farmers by insisting on hard work at home. The boys must toil in the fields, chop firewood, and bring it to the house.[25] Notice that the sons perform the same tasks as their mother. A few women owned property or helped manage rural estates for the wealthy. One inscription remembers Valeria Maxima, who owned a farm in Italy (first century BC). She is memorialized in her epitaph as a mother, a farm owner, and the daughter of Valeria.[26]

Like Horace, Varro (116–27 BC) praised the physical strength and hardiness of rural women. He describes those women who look after the herdsmen watching the livestock in the mountains, claiming that the women are often not at all inferior to the men in working with the flocks. Not only can they look after the animals, but they can also cook food and keep the huts clean. And they do this all with nursing babies at their breast! This last claim reveals Varro's underlying argument. He means to shame contemporary urban women by comparing their pampered way of life with the tough, demanding reality of rural women's lives. He declares that "our newly delivered women who lie for days under their mosquito nets, are worthless and contemptible" compared to the woman from Illyricum (today part of the Balkans) who, when

---

23. Elaine Fantham et al. suggest "in 45 BCE Tullia died of postpuerperal complications after bearing a son who probably died within weeks" (*Women in the Classical World: Image and Text* [New York: Oxford University Press, 1994], 275).

24. Livy, *Hist.* 42.34.

25. Horace, *Carmina* 3.6.

26. *CIL* VI.3482. For a translation, see Lefkowitz and Fant, *Women's Life in Greece and Rome*, 209.

about to give birth, "steps aside a little way out of her work, bears her child there, and brings it back so soon that you would say she had not borne it but found it."[27] Varro belittles the real dangers of childbirth and romanticizes the strength displayed by women in rural life. Nonetheless, read with Horace and Livy, Varro completes the picture of rural women participating fully in the labors of farm life.

Urban life also had its share of demanding physical jobs, and women performed them alongside their male counterparts. A funerary inscription tells of a woman blacksmith who worked together with her husband, also a blacksmith (*ferrarii*).[28] Young girls were part of the working poor. "Viccentia, sweetest daughter, maker of gold nets, who lived for nine years and nine months," was likely occupied in making women's hair nets.[29] Similarly, Lysis, a *sarcinatrix* or clothes mender, died at eighteen; she was memorialized as thrifty and modest.[30] In the book of Acts, Priscilla is identified, along with her husband, Aquila, and Paul, as a tentmaker. This couple fits the pattern of married partners in towns working together in a family business. Tentmaking likely involved making awnings used as shade against the merciless Mediterranean sun as well as working with leather. The tools of the trade included curved needles, waxed thread, and awls to punch the holes for stitching.[31]

Business and Professional Women

Textiles and Clothing

Women often worked in domestic fields such as weaving and tailoring. While spinning wool was done by women in the home, the wool had to be finished before it could be made into clothes. Fullers took the homespun material and worked it so that it could be made into usable fabric to sew into clothing. Fullers also cleaned clothes; they were the ancient dry cleaners and laundry service. While fullers were typically male, there is one reference to a woman fuller in a papyrus from Oxyrhynchus (although the date is uncertain).[32] Aurêlia Rhachêl, daughter of Auan, mother of Irginês, identifies herself as

27. Varro, *De re rustica* 2.10.6–8. For a discussion and translation, see Fantham et al., *Women in the Classical World*, 267.

28. Sandra R. Joshel cites *CIL* VI.9398, which notes two groups of *colliberti* or freed slaves, the Titii and the Fannii, both of whose men and women worked as ironsmiths (*Work, Identity, and Legal Status at Rome: A Study of the Occupational Inscriptions* [Norman: University of Oklahoma Press, 1992], 141).

29. *CIL* VI.9213. Translation by Natalie B. Kampen, in Fantham et al., *Women in the Classical World*, 377.

30. *CIL* VI.9882. Translation in Fantham et al., *Women in the Classical World*, 377.

31. Jerome Murphy-O'Connor, *Paul: A Critical Life* (Oxford: Oxford University Press, 1997), 86–89.

32. P.Iand. 43. Cf. R. J. Forbes, *Studies in Ancient Technology* (Leiden: Brill, 1987), 4:88.

a fuller in this receipt in which she testifies to having done this work herself. She earned about one month's supply of grain, a princely sum. She did not write the voucher herself, for as indicated on the receipt, she was illiterate. We have no way to judge whether Aurêlia Rhachêl represented a sizable group of women, or whether she is the exception that proves the rule.

We find women tailors. Cameria Iarine, a freedwoman, dedicated a tomb to several men, including her patron, her patron's patron, and her husband (a freedman). All of them, including Iarine, apparently worked as a group in the same shop making fine clothing, as the epitaph commemorates these "tailors of fine clothing on Tuscan Street."[33] Women also worked in high-end businesses like dyeing. As Sandra Joshel notes, "Dyeing . . . required an extensive plant and expensive materials, and an individual dyer would have been inhibited from working on his or her own."[34] The book of Acts describes Lydia, the purple dyer from Thyatira. Her specific case will be discussed in chapter 9 (see also chap. 5), but one possible scenario is that she had numerous people, perhaps both slaves and freedpersons, working for her in this costly and laborious occupation. Lydia is not the only woman known by name from antiquity who was a dyer. Veturia D. l. Fedra was a freed dyer who paid for a tomb out of her own funds for herself, her patron, and her freedman husband, Nicepor.[35]

Moneylenders

Through the more than 150 records of a banker (male) named Jucundus, we know of fourteen women who received money as sellers from buyers who worked through Jucundus. For example, in AD 56, "Umbricia Januaria hereby attests that she received from L. Caecilius Jucundus 11,039 sestertii, less a percentage [1–2%] as his commission, for the auction of goods on her behalf."[36] Probably she was a freed slave of the fish-sauce merchant Umbricius Scaurus. While the actual receipt has only the woman's name, in the memorandum that accompanied it her male representative, Decimus Volcius Thallus, at her request verified the transaction.[37] In graffiti on a tavern's walls in Pompeii, a moneylender named Faustilla is mentioned as lending money with interest to a woman named Vettia.[38] Faustilla's name appears as well on the wall of the

33. *CIL* VI.37826. Joshel, *Work, Identity, and Legal Status*, 138.

34. Joshel (*Work, Identity, and Legal Status*, 135) worked with inscriptions from Rome (Latin) from the late first century BC to the late second century AD.

35. Joshel, *Work, Identity, and Legal Status*, 136.

36. *CIL* IV, supplement 1, 308–10. Translated by Natalie B. Kampen in Fantham et al., *Women in the Classical World*, 334–35.

37. For a description complete with drawings of this remarkable find, see August Mau, *Pompeii, Its Life and Art*, trans. Francis W. Kelsey (New York: Macmillan, 1907), 499–503.

38. *CIL* IV.8203. For a translation, see Natalie B. Kampen in Fantham et al., *Women in the Classical World*, 336.

private home of Granius Romanus, again lending money with interest.[39] In the first century AD, the senate passed a law preventing women from taking on or paying the debts of another person, or guaranteeing another's debt.[40] Women consequently were restricted in the social favors they could offer, for they could not stand as surety for another's debt. The motivation behind this law might have been to prevent a woman from taking on her husband's (or lover's) debt, thus protecting her family's interests.

Merchants and Vendors

Both Jewish and gentile women traded, bought, and sold all sorts of commodities.[41] For instance, waxed wooden tablets from the first century AD, gathered near Pompeii, describe a woman named Pactumeia Prima purchasing another woman, Tyche.[42] The ownership was contested, with A. Attiolenus Atimetus also claiming possession of the slave. The document notes that this dispute was settled out of court with Atimetus acknowledging Pactumeia's ownership. Both Pactumeia and Atimetus were present to witness the deal, which was recorded by C. Sulpicius Faustus. Also from the first century AD Pompeii, Julia Felix advertised a rental property. A graffito (AD 64–79) reads that she had available "an elegant bath suitable for the best people, shops, rooms above them, and second story apartments, from the Ides of August until the Ides of August 5 years hence, after which the lease may be renewed by simple agreement."[43] Julia Felix owned the largest piece of property in Pompeii, on which were public baths and extensive gardens used for entertainment (for a fee), as well as a wine shop and a take-out restaurant.[44] This property was located just across from the *palestra* or gymnasium and the amphitheater. Then as now, location is everything. Also in Pompeii, Asellina

39. *CIL* IV.8204. For a translation, see Natalie B. Kampen in Fantham et al., *Women in the Classical World*, 336.
40. J. A. Crook ("Feminine Inadequacy and the *Senatusconsultum Velleianum*," in *The Family in Ancient Rome: New Perspectives*, ed. Beryl Rawson [Ithaca, NY: Cornell University Press, 1986], 83–92) discusses the *senatusconsultum Velleianum* law, probably passed by Claudius or Nero.
41. Tal Ilan notes that "despite the unsuitability of this occupation for women according to the rabbinic ethical code, women did in fact work as shopkeepers, for certain laws deal specifically with this phenomenon" (*Jewish Women in Greco-Roman Palestine* [Peabody, MA: Hendrickson, 1996], 187). See *m. Ket.* 9:4.
42. *TPSulp.* 40 (= *TP* 28 + 105); see Jane F. Gardner, "Women in Business Life, Some Evidence from Puteoli," in *Female Networks and the Public Sphere in Roman Society*, ed. Päivi Setälä and Liisa Savunen (Rome: Institutum Romanum Finlandiae, 1999), 15–16.
43. *CIL* IV.1136. Translation by Natalie B. Kampen in Fantham et al., *Women in the Classical World*, 334.
44. See David Balch, "Rich Pompeiian Houses, Shops for Rent, and the Huge Apartment Building in Herculaneum as Typical Spaces for Pauline House Churches," *JSNT* 27.1 (2004): 27–46.

appears in several places on a tavern wall, suggesting that she owned it and made repairs to it after the AD 64 earthquake. Three other female names are found there as well, likely waitresses.[45]

Merchants had large establishments whose influence extended beyond their local neighborhoods. Cicero, in the first century BC, speaks approvingly of merchants because they do not involve themselves with retail, which Cicero thinks is a scam.[46] No reliefs have surfaced of women merchants, but we know from literature and inscriptions that they existed.[47] Suetonius remarks that "to the merchants he [Emperor Claudius] held out the certainty of profit by assuming the expense of any loss that they might suffer from storms, and offered to those who would build merchant ships large bounties, adapted to the condition of each: to a citizen exemption from the *lex Papia Poppaea*;[48] to a Latin, the rights of Roman citizenship; to freedwomen the privileges allowed to mothers of four children. And all these provisions are in force today."[49] Probably no reliefs were made of female merchants because wealthy women wanted a traditional public image, that of a proper, pious matron. "The ideology of gender division of labor was firmly entrenched even when reality daily violated it," remarks Natalie Boymel Kampen.[50]

Lower down the social ladder, vendors hawked their wares to potential customers. From Pompeii and Ostia (Rome's port city) several inscriptions and reliefs provide a glimpse of the marketplace. In a small marble relief a vegetable seller shows her wares on a trestle table, her right hand pointing proudly to her produce. She is dressed simply in a tunic and shawl, and her vegetables are carefully carved such that the zucchini and scallions are clearly identifiable.[51] A second marble relief from Ostia (pictured on the next page) is more elaborate in its depiction of a female poultry vendor. She stands in the middle of the picture, selling a piece of fruit to a male customer (perhaps a boy), with two other male customers standing at the left.[52] She is simply dressed with no elaborate hairstyle

---

45. *CIL* IV.7862–64, 7866, 7873.

46. Cicero, *De officiis* 150–51.

47. Kampen, "Social Status and Gender," 69.

48. These laws were established to promote marriage and encourage large families. A Roman male citizen was expected to produce three children, or face inheritance and tax liabilities. A Roman female citizen was released from tutelage if she produced three live births. See chapters 2, 3, and 4.

49. Suetonius, *Divus Claudius* 18–19 (trans. J. C. Rolfe, LCL).

50. Kampen, "Social Status and Gender," 69.

51. Ostia, Museo Ostiense, late second or early third century AD. The original location of this relief is unknown; it is unclear whether it was part of a tomb or a shop. For a detailed discussion, see Kampen, "Social Status and Gender," 62, 64–65.

52. Ostia, Museo Ostiense, late second or early third century AD. For a detailed discussion, see Kampen, "Social Status and Gender," 64–65. Kampen identifies the two men as customers, but I wonder if perhaps one man is a vendor, showing poultry to the other man, who may be holding a small dead animal. In either case, Kampen's point holds that the relief reveals a woman selling products to clients.

Marble relief from Ostia showing a female vendor (Photo courtesy of Erich Lessing/Art Resource, NY)

or stola.[53] Her counter is made of boards atop crates in which are held rabbits and chickens. On the left hangs poultry and game from a gibbet. On the far right, sitting on the counter, are two monkeys prepared to entertain potential customers. This small relief was likely designed to advertise their business.

Though both these reliefs date from the second or third century AD, their representations of female vendors match those of the first century AD found in Pompeii. Two paintings show female vendors, including one from Verecundus's dye shop. On the left doorpost of this dye shop is an image of a low table with indiscernible objects on it. Behind the table sits a woman who is touching the objects while a young child watches her. On the right doorpost, another image depicts dyers working and Verecundus himself showing off a finished cloth. These images are probably advertisements or representative of what happened in the shop.[54]

In sum, the iconography identifies saleswomen by specific poses, gestures, costumes, and hairstyles and distinguishes them both from their customers and from women of higher social status. The few surviving funerary inscriptions of female vendors support what appears in the reliefs. For example, a monument dedicated to Abudia Mengiste by her husband and former owner, M. Abudius Luminaris, declares that she sold grain at Rome's Middle Stairs,[55] while a second inscription notes that Aurelia Nais sold fish at the Warehouses of Galba.[56] Another inscription from Italy speaks of a woman manager of a shop (*officinatrix*).[57]

53. A stola is a "long and elaborate dress which identified the upper-class matron" (Kampen, "Social Status and Gender," 65). Roman female nobility at this time also wore elaborate hairstyles.

54. For a detailed discussion, see Kampen, "Social Status and Gender," 66–67.

55. *CIL* VI.9683.

56. *CIL* VI.9801.

57. Kampen, "Social Status and Gender," 66; Joshel, *Work, Identity, and Legal Status*, 212n25.

Unfortunately, the visual representations of saleswomen at work do not carry over into other occupations done by women. Many reliefs show male carpenters or masons or perfume makers. Women, however, are portrayed primarily in an allegorical or mythical context, and their activity is generally limited to fabric work such as spinning, weaving, or repairing cloth. The great temple of Minerva in Rome, for example, in its Minerva and Arachne frieze shows spinning done by mythical women as part of an allegory of the state. When wool baskets or spindles are present on funerary reliefs, they indicate female virtues of industry and modesty; they are not symbols of occupation. Why are female vendors the exception to the rule? Perhaps in most other cases, the jobs done by women for pay were also expected to be done at home for no pay. Women worked with fabric, cooked, and took care of children without pay in the home. But the vendor was different. "The occupation seems not to have had a traditional association with either sex, and may have granted the same degree of prosperity and independence to both sexes. Perhaps most important, however, is the fact that this was a public occupation which could not be mistaken for anything other than money-earning."[58]

There are two other situations in which working women are depicted: the lady's attendant and the prostitute. Reliefs depict the wealthy matron with her slaves doing her hair or attending to her toilette. The females working in the images announce the matron's wealth; they do not celebrate the tasks done by these women. In the Mishnah, the rabbis, in commenting upon a woman's uncleanness, assume that a lady's hairdresser is a legitimate profession.[59] They also suggest, however, that this job would be done by a slave,[60] which fits with the larger picture of duties performed by slaves. In an interesting aside, later rabbinic texts identify Mary Magdalene as a hairdresser.[61]

Women and the Arts

Male authors in the Greco-Roman period often spoke in reverent tones about the sixth-century BC poet Sappho, the creator of beautiful verse.[62] The preserved writings give testimony to her creative brilliance, and her style was

58. Kampen, "Social Status and Gender," 75.
59. *m. Kelim* 15:3.
60. *m. Qidd.* 2:3.
61. *b. Shab.* 104b. Tal Ilan discusses this: "the interpretation derives from another passage which mentions another woman who could be mistaken for Magdalene: 'Mariamme, the woman's hair-dresser' (*bHag.* 4b)" (*Jewish Women in Greco-Roman Palestine*, 188–89). For more on Mary Magdalene, see Matt. 27:56; Mark 15:47; Luke 8:2; 24:10; John 19:25; and the discussion in chapter 9.
62. Scholars are less confident today that they can speak definitively about Sappho's life and her loves, but the attention she gets, both ancient and modern, is a testimony to her skill as a poet.

especially influential in later love poetry. Following in her footsteps was the fourth-century BC poet Erinna, who displayed her own inventiveness and originality.[63] Her poem *The Distaff* is a lament for her lifelong friend Baucis who died shortly after getting married. In the poem, Erinna reminisces, "when we were young girls we sat in our rooms without a care, holding our dolls and pretending we were young brides."[64] In the first century BC, Sulpicia, daughter of Servius Sulpicius Rufus, wrote a few love elegies that were preserved by Tibullus. As did the male authors of her day, Sulpicia used a pseudonym for her lover, and berated him for his infidelity. "Let a toga'd whore and her wool-basket be of more importance to you than is Sulpicia, Servius' daughter. There are those who care about me, and their greatest worry is that I might lose my place to a nobody's bed."[65]

In the ninth century AD the Byzantine anthologist Photius described a woman historian, Pamphila of Epidaurus in Greece. Both the daughter and the wife of scholars, she wrote during the second half of the first century AD, composing thirty-three books on historical materials (*hypomnēmata historika*) and other works. She explained how she lived faithfully with her husband. After thirteen years of listening to his friends' discussions and reading books, she decided to collate the information. She organized it in a random manner, as she "thought a miscellany would be more enjoyable and attractive."[66] Photius editorializes that the style is simple because it was written by a woman.[67] If his information faithfully transmits a first-century setting, this woman had access to a library, she could read, and she was present at learned discussions that took place in her home. She was familiar with other works of history and made her own decisions about how to compose her volumes. Her works were cited by later historians and often were attributed to either her father or her husband.

Women's creativity was not limited to the literary arts. Pliny the Elder notes by name several women painters, some of whom were taught by their fathers.[68] He mentions a woman, Iaia (Laia or Lala) of Cyzicus, who never married; Pliny notes that her skills commanded a high price, more than most artists of the day. She painted both with a brush and with a stylus upon ivory, and did a self-portrait using a mirror. Pliny also refers to a woman, Olympias, who both painted and taught a painter named Autobulus. Inscriptions indicate women

63. Erinna eschewed tradition in presenting poems of lamentation: instead of the usual elegiac couplet or choral meter, she used the dactylic hexameter.
64. Translation by Marylin Arthur in Pomeroy, *Goddesses, Whores, Wives, and Slaves*, 138.
65. Tibullus, *Carmina* 3.16. Translation in Lefkowitz and Fant, *Women's Life in Greece and Rome*, 9.
66. Photius, *Bibliotheca* 175S 119b.
67. For a brief discussion, see Fantham et al., *Women in the Classical World*, 368–69.
68. Pliny the Elder, *Nat.* 35.40. For a translation, see Fantham et al., *Women in the Classical World*, 168.

involved in the jewelry trade,[69] including goldbeating and pearl setting. Several women, identified as goldbeaters, are paired with men. While it is entirely possible that these couples were married, Joshel cautions that "the bond expressed in their epitaphs was not marriage but that of shared work."[70]

Women were also trained as entertainers. A funerary inscription speaks lovingly of the child actress Eucharis who died at fourteen. Her patron, Licinia, who was likely a freedwoman from the Licinii family and a former actress herself, wrote a beautiful epitaph. It notes Eucharis's skill as a pupil of the Muses, of her dancing before nobles and in a Greek performance. "My patroness's love and care and praise are silenced by the pyre, and still in death. The daughter left her father to lament, the later born preceded him in doom. Twice seven birthdays lie with me engulfed in death's abode, and everlasting gloom. Please as you go pray earth lie soft upon me."[71] Women competed as athletes as well. Pausanias speaks of the Heraea games in which maidens raced for crowns of olive and statues dedicated in their honor.[72]

Though relatively uncommon, women also entertained large crowds as gladiators, fighting other women or male dwarfs.[73] Some women fighters were slaves, but Tacitus laments that during Nero's rule, not a few well-bred women embarrassed themselves by participating in the arena.[74] At the turn of the first century AD, Domitian seems to have arranged for women (and men) to fight at night under torchlight, which must have created a heightened sense of drama.[75]

Summary of the Average Woman's Work

Before examining the small but important subgroup of wealthy, educated women, I will sum up the findings so far. Women did almost every type of work that was done by men, with a few important exceptions: men did not work as midwives or wet nurses (or nurses, for that matter), and women were not soldiers or politicians. Women took care of the family farm, laboring in the fields or watching the herds. Women bought, sold, rented, and owned property. They ran businesses, employed staff, and owned slaves. They were artists, artisans, and vendors. The vast majority of women, freeborn or freed—those not fortunate enough to enjoy a wealthy lifestyle—did share one impor-

69. *CIL* VI.9435; Joshel, *Work, Identity, and Legal Status*, 134, 141.

70. Joshel, *Work, Identity, and Legal Status*, 142.

71. *ILLRP* II.803. For a translation (by Elaine Fantham) and discussion of the complete text, see Fantham et al., *Women in the Classical World*, 270.

72. Pausanias, *Graeciae descriptio* (Elis 1) 16.2–8. For a translation, see Kraemer, *Women's Religions*, 40–41.

73. Cassius Dio, *Hist. Rom.* 67.8.4. There is no evidence that women fought other men.

74. Tacitus, *Ann.* 15.32.3.

75. Suetonius, *Domitianus* 4.2.

These two female gladiators are identified by name as Amazon and Achillia, which may be their "stage" names. The marble bas-relief monument from first-century AD Halicarnassus (modern Turkey) could commemorate the women's freedom, as many slaves were granted their freedom if they fought well. But it might also indicate that their duel ended in an honorable draw, as signified by their helmets placed on the ground. The text above the women is open to interpretation. (Photo courtesy of British Museum/Art Resource, NY)

tant similarity with the upper crust: in both cases, women drew social status from their character, not their activity. Unlike men, who derived social esteem from their work, women gained social prestige from their virtues, which were promoted as being a faithful wife and mother, working diligently, and caring for the home. Saleswomen were the exception that proves the rule of gender stratification concerning work. Those women who identified themselves in inscriptions by their work generally presented themselves as part of a group of workers, including husband, patron, and slaves/freedmen.

When transferring this information onto a view of New Testament women, we should note several things. First, we must recognize the elite status of some women mentioned, such as Lydia, the dealer in purple cloth; in his interactions with her, Paul associated with the upper echelon of society. She likely had slaves and freedmen and women employed in her home and business. She probably exerted at least some influence within the city of Philippi, and perhaps also within her home city of Thyatira.

Second, we must imagine both men and women circulating in the marketplace as Paul preached the gospel. Saleswomen might pass by his shop on the way to their own, and Paul might have purchased his fruit and vegetables from women vendors. We should imagine Prisca working alongside Aquila and Paul in their tentmaking or leather-working. Perhaps Peter's wife sold the fish he caught. We must not imagine women, especially poor women (who with poor men made up the vast majority of the ancient world), tucked away in their homes, secluded from economic activity. Inscriptions, epitaphs, and visual art all suggest the active presence of women in the economy of the ancient world.

Activities of the Wealthy Woman

It was as true then as it is today: wealthy women have more opportunities for self-fulfilling activities and personal development. A few elite Greco-Roman women, often daughters of philosophers, chose to follow in their fathers' footsteps. In both gentile and Jewish elite circles, some women pursued the virtuous life of study and contemplation. Others sought a more general education or pursued the arts. Some women served their city as benefactors, providing money or influence to aid a constituency.[76] Women wrote poetry, gave lectures, financed fountains and colonnades. Women used their numbers to effect change in government laws[77] and to speak on behalf of unjust taxation.[78] In short, women with wealth contributed to the overall well-being of their cities, often in the same ways as did their elite male counterparts.

Yet not everyone praised women for their accomplishments. Ancient literature is peppered with snide comments or lengthy rants against women who speak in public. For example, the first-century BC Roman historian Sallust writes scathingly of a wealthy woman, Sempronia. He describes her as a notorious figure who excelled in the social arts but fell in with a political conspiracy for which she was censured. She was well educated in Greek and Latin literature, wrote verses, and had a good sense of humor and charm. But she apparently could "dance more adeptly than any respectable woman would have needed to" and cared little about her own modesty, such that Sallust declares, "her sexual desires were so ardent that she took the initiative with men far more frequently than they did with her."[79] Her crimes are those of "masculine daring," as she is accused of participating in civil unrest. Sempronia became a political whipping post for Sallust, who used her to further condemn a political enemy, Cataline, and his conspiracy in 62 BC, since Sempronia supported Cataline's bid for the consulship. Sallust further denigrates Cataline's character by claiming that other wealthy women of dubious behavior joined Cataline's cause. Sallust uses a familiar tactic to demean an enemy—accuse him of having women followers, especially licentious ones.

Educated Women and Female Philosophers

Sallust's description of Sempronia highlights the ambiguity many men felt concerning educated women. Sallust admitted that Sempronia had intellectual

76. For more on benefactors, see chapter 9.
77. For example, in 195 BC, women successfully protested the Oppian Law. See Livy, *Hist.* 34.1.
78. Hortensia spoke before the triumvirs at the forum against the planned tax on property owned by wealthy women, which persuaded the rulers to back down from their proposal. See Appian, *Bella civilia* 4.32–34.
79. Sallust, *Bellum catalinae* 25. Translation by Judith Peller Hallett in Pomeroy, *Goddesses, Whores, Wives, and Slaves*, 171–72.

talent, but tightly connected her education with sexual promiscuity. Charges of sexual misconduct are ubiquitous among descriptions of educated women, even some women labeled as philosophers. As such, evidence concerning female philosophers must be read carefully to tease out historical fact from diatribe. Joan Taylor, in examining women philosophers in Philo's description of the Therapeutics (*De vita contemplativa*), states that "most historical evidence is embedded in rhetorical material."[80] This caution is especially necessary when dealing with Sallust's diatribe or Juvenal's satires. The latter writes as much for entertainment and laughs as for historical accuracy, and so creates exaggerated pictures and even fantasies for his readers that might have little to do with the day-to-day world around them.

Taylor has categorized descriptions of female philosophers by male writers into several basic tropes, including woman as sexual partner, woman as comic character, the "bad" woman, woman as honorary male, and woman as model of virtue. Below we will look at how Plutarch, Musonius Rufus, and certain female Neo-Pythagorean philosophers[81] trumpeted philosophy as the avenue toward better (read: socially acceptable) wives and mothers. Daughters taught by their fathers are not viewed as creative thinkers in their own right, but as honorary males. They are depositories of their fathers' learning, to be dutifully passed on to their own sons. Authors might tout female members of a philosophical community to show that *even* women (who by nature are less virtuous, more emotional, less adept at the philosophical life) were changed for the better by the group. Female philosophers, either as individuals or as a group, are also labeled as sexually promiscuous, usually for two reasons: (1) the male author is attacking the male philosopher by accusing him of consorting with women; or (2) women philosophers seem "forward" or "bold" in their public demeanor, so the male author assumes that conduct as bold as, for example, public speech would naturally imply sexual availability.

Negative Views of Female Philosophers

Male authors and philosophers had plenty to say about women who chose to play on their field, and for the most part their opinions were negative. In

80. Joan E. Taylor, *Jewish Women Philosophers of First-Century Alexandria: Philo's 'Therapeutae' Reconsidered* (Oxford: Oxford University Press, 2003), 8. For more on reading between the biases in the ancient sources to discern historical truth, see the introduction above.

81. Pythagorus was a sixth-century BC philosopher whose school admitted men and women. Neo-Pythagoreans continued that tradition, but were socially conservative and promoted marriage as the chief goal and calling of a woman. "A woman must live for her husband according to law and in actuality, thinking no private thoughts of her own, but taking care of her marriage and guarding it. For everything depends on this" (Stobaeus, *Florilegium* 4.28.10; translation by Flora R. Levin in Pomeroy, *Goddesses, Whores, Wives, and Slaves*, 135; see also Holger Thesleff, ed., *The Pythagorean Texts of the Hellenistic Period* [Åbo: Åbo Akademi, 1965], 142–45).

general, Stoicism, the most popular and influential philosophical school in the Greco-Roman world, was quite conservative socially and supported gender hierarchy. Stoics' call for social equality extended only as far as questioning social distinctions among men. They encouraged women to marry and bear children. A prominent Stoic, Seneca (4 BC–AD 65), recalls his father's refusal to teach his mother philosophy because the former saw the enterprise as creating a bold and haughty woman. Seneca agrees in part with his father's sentiments but feels that her lack of education hindered her from dealing well with his exile.[82] Because Seneca felt women were naturally wild and passionate, he advocated philosophy as a way to rein them in.[83]

In a similar vein, Juvenal's invective reveals more about men's thoughts (or at least Juvenal's thoughts)[84] on proper society than any actual description of a woman's behavior, but his comments expose the dangers faced by women when they demonstrated their education. Juvenal paints a picture of a dinner party at which a woman speaks about Virgil and Homer: "she rattles on at such a rate that you'd think all the pots and pans in the kitchen were crashing to the floor or that every bell in town was clanging." He does not call her a philosopher, but rather contrasts her behavior with them; "she should learn the philosophers' lesson: 'moderation is necessary even for intellectuals.'" He whines that "there ought to be some things women don't understand," as he complains about their learning in public speaking, rhetoric, and the literary classics.[85]

Women who spoke in public were seen as invading male space, and were often ridiculed. As seen in Juvenal's tirade, not all these women claimed to be or were portrayed as philosophers; some were simply described as educated. At stake for some of these authors is the preservation of philosophy's reputation as defender of virtue (for example, Philo on the Therapeutics). To wear the mantle of philosopher a woman should be a "good" citizen, a proper house-keeper, a chaste wife. An educated woman might be bold and brash, but a truly philosophical woman supports the status quo. Thus, Musonius Rufus (a Stoic, discussed further below) and Plutarch (who was in part critical of Stoicism) argue for the education of women, but only as it promotes the philosophical values necessary for women to function in their homes and toward their hus-bands as deemed acceptable by society. Musonius Rufus confirms that some accuse female philosophers of being headstrong and bold because "they give up their households and go about with men and practice giving speeches, and argue and attack premises, when they ought to be sitting at home spinning

82. Seneca, *Ad Helviam* 17.3.
83. Seneca, *Epistulae morales* 2.14.1.
84. Though Juvenal disclaimed any allegiance to a particular philosophical school (*Sat.* 13.121), he owes much to the Stoic worldview.
85. Juvenal, *Sat.* 6.434–56. Translation in Pomeroy, *Goddesses, Whores, Wives, and Slaves*, 172.

wool."[86] He counters with two arguments: first, that both men and women are to continue their work for philosophical discussion, and second, that any philosophy worth its salt will reinforce the gender status quo. Musonius Rufus contends that daughters and sons should be educated in philosophy, but women should not be trained in the gymnasium (any more than men should be trained in spinning), nor will they display their learning through public speeches. Nature shows such behavior to be the exclusive domain of men. "I do not wish to say that it is appropriate for women to be very clear at speeches or to be very clever, for that would be unnecessary for women if they are indeed philosophizing *as women*."[87] Plutarch believes the husband must educate his wife so that she will avoid misdeeds and superstitions. "For if they do not receive the seed of a good education and do not develop this education in company with their husbands they will, left to themselves, conceive a lot of ridiculous ideas and unworthy aims and emotions."[88] Proper education done by father or husband avoided the major pitfalls many men saw with an educated woman, namely promiscuity and public brashness.

Juvenal's sentiments noted above, though grossly overstated for effect, do exhibit the hostility that many men carried toward educated women who spoke publicly. Equally significant is the fact that often a male writer attacked another man or philosophical school by charging that "their" women were promiscuous. For example, Cicero had no time for Epicureans, and one way he showed his contempt was by denigrating their women philosophers as mistresses and courtesans. An Epicurean named Metrodorus (ca. 330–277 BC) was associated with a woman named Leontium (possibly his wife), herself a student of Epicurus.[89] Cicero ridiculed her as a "little whore" who dared to write a treatise against Aristotle's student Theophrastus (who wrote in the fourth century BC). Never mind that she wrote Attic prose well, Cicero begrudgingly admits.[90] In fact, another antagonist indicted the entire Epicurean school as immoderate and uncontrolled in that they promoted a woman as their leader (*prostasia*).[91] In

86. Musonius Rufus, *Dissertationes* 3 ("That Women Too Should Study Philosophy"). Translation in Lefkowitz and Fant, *Women's Life in Greece and Rome*, 52.

87. Musonius Rufus, *Dissertationes* 4 ("Should Daughters Receive the Same Education as Sons?"). Translation in Taylor, *Jewish Women Philosophers*, 209–10 (italics original).

88. Plutarch, *Mor.* 138a–146a (= *Conj. praec.*). Translated by R. Warner in Lefkowitz and Fant, *Women's Life in Greece and Rome*, 184.

89. "Epicurus, the patron of pleasure (though Metrodorus his disciple married Leontium) says that a wise man can seldom marry, because marriage has many drawbacks" (Seneca, *De matrimonio* fr. 45, as quoted by Jerome, *Adversus Jovinianum* 1.48). Translation in "Nicene and Post-Nicene Fathers" (Second Series) vol. VI, *Jerome: Letters and Select Works*, ed. Philip Schaff and Henry Wallace (Cosimo Classics, 2007), 385. For a general discussion of Leontium, see Taylor, *Jewish Women Philosophers*, 202–5.

90. Cicero, *De natura deorum* 1.93.

91. Taylor, *Jewish Women Philosophers*, 203, citing Christian Jensen, "Ein neuer Brief Epikurs," in *Abhandlungen der Gesellschaft der Wissenschaften zu Göttingen Philologisch-Historische*

this way, women became weapons used to assault another man's philosophical fortress. Thus in the above example, Cicero was less concerned about Leontium per se, and more interested in condemning Epicureanism. He could further his goal by denigrating women associated with the group.

Positive Views of Female Philosophers

Though many authors saw female philosophers or even educated women as sexually promiscuous, others praised them. As noted above, Musonius Rufus promoted philosophical training for women, which, done correctly, would reinforce the status quo. He believed that both men and women should learn philosophy to become better citizens, because philosophical virtues reinforced social norms and promoted just deeds—in other words, philosophy taught people how to live admirably. He calls it "the science of living," knowledge that helps a woman both run her household and manage her slaves: "Now, wouldn't the woman who practises philosophy be just, and a blameless partner in life, and a good worker in common causes, and devoted in her responsibilities towards her husband and her children and free in every way from greed or ambition?"[92] He claims that a woman with philosophical training will be self-reliant, will love her children more than her own life, will breast-feed them,[93] will labor with her husband, and will even toil at jobs others might consider slave's work. Philosophy should make women more committed to their households and to upholding the family honor. A philosophy that makes a woman bold—as his critics charged—is hardly worthy of the name, but any true philosophy will encourage self-restraint, contentment, and the value of managing the household. Musonius Rufus's attitude is reflected clearly in Neo-Pythagorean writings authored by women. From the third century BC, Phintys, a member of the Pythagorean community in Italy, promotes this philosophy as the best way to achieve virtue, including the special female virtue of chastity. She admits that a woman should not be in the cavalry or work as a politician, but she believes the study of philosophy builds courage and justice, which are virtues all women should possess. "The mistress of the house and head of the household should be chaste and untouched in all respects."[94]

Though women were encouraged by some men to learn philosophy, they were barred from the social entitlements that accompanied learning. Philosophy

---

Klasse, 3/5 (Berlin: Weidmannsche Buchhandlung, 1933), 1–94. Jensen suggests that the criticism might come from Timocrates.

92. Musonius Rufus, *Dissertationes* 3. Translation in Lefkowitz and Fant, *Women's Life in Greece and Rome*, 51.

93. This curious mention of breast-feeding is another example of using breast-feeding as shorthand for a committed mother, as discussed in chapter 4.

94. Phintys, *De mulierum modestia* 2. Translation in Lefkowitz and Fant, *Women's Life in Greece and Rome*, 164 (see also Thesleff, *Pythagorean Texts*, 151–54).

was used as a tool to "tame" women's nature, to make them socially docile and compliant. Unlike their male relatives, women were discouraged from displaying their knowledge in the courts or at dinner parties. Instead, learning was touted as a way to reinforce the dominant position of men in public life and the quiet reserve of modest women.

Real Women Studying Philosophy

Behind the rhetoric, however, it is clear that real women studied philosophy. Several pieces of evidence secure this view. In a curious detail, the third-century AD Diogenes Laertius describes a scene from centuries earlier at the Stoic school where the famous Chrysippus learned under Zeno's successor, Cleanthes.[95] Diogenes writes that an older woman sat next to Chrysippus and observed that he wrote five hundred lines a day. Quite possibly this woman was a student as well.[96] Because this remark makes nothing of the gender of Chrysippus's fellow student, it seems quite probable that this is an accurate picture of a class setting where men and women studied philosophy together.

Diogenes also mentions Arete of Cyrene, a woman from the fourth century BC who wrote forty books and taught philosophy to one hundred and ten students.[97] She learned from her father, Aristippus, and was responsible for educating her son (also named Aristippus). Strabo says she was head of the school after her father's death. Arete broke no social taboos in her pursuit of philosophy because she was seen as a mouthpiece of her father. Further, by encouraging her son to pursue philosophy, she was teaching him to embrace the virtuous life. Arete is one of several women who were trained in philosophy by their fathers. The church father Clement of Alexandria, notes that in the fourth or third century BC, Diodorus (a Socratic Dialectician) taught his five daughters philosophy.[98] Clement's larger point is that *both* men and women are capable of great courage and virtue, including dying for one's faith. Thus he praises the modesty of Theano the Pythagorean, who when approached by a man sharply rebuked him. The man said, "Your arm is beautiful," to which she responded, "Yes, but it is not public."[99] Her philosophical training helped her avoid improper advances and secured her modesty. Finally, an inscription from Apollonia, Mysia from the second or third century AD reads,

95. Diogenes Laertius, *Vit. phil.* 7.181.

96. Taylor, *Jewish Women Philosophers*, 174. The Greek participle can be translated as one who attends the sick or one who attends a meeting or the gymnasium. The context suggests that this woman was present as Chrysippus worked, possibly also studying philosophy herself.

97. Diogenes Laertius, *Vit. phil.* 2.72, 86; see also Strabo, *Geographica* 17.3.22.

98. The Dialectical school focused on logical paradoxes and propositional logic. Diodorus Cronos was well known for his "master argument," which tries to prove that only the actual is possible.

99. Clement of Alexandria, *Stromata* 4.19.

"For Magnilla the philosopher, daughter of Magnus the philosopher, wife of Menius the philosopher."[100] Two women from the classical Greek period remained important figures for the study of women philosophers in the Hellenistic period. Diotima of Mantinea taught Socrates about love (erōs). Though scholars debate whether Diotima is a historical figure, some think it likely based on internal evidence within Plato's Symposium (ca. 385 BC). The discussion about erōs changes in the middle of the work. Initially, love is described as the path between mortal and immortal, but in the second half of the work, erōs is aligned with political wisdom. Perhaps Diotima's ideas were preserved in part but later modified.[101] The second woman, Aspasia, lived earlier, in fifth-century Athens. She was the partner/consort of Pericles, and also associated with Socrates. However, later traditions often branded her a whore. Plutarch describes Aspasia as Pericles' mistress, though he also declares that Pericles had a high regard for her as a philosopher and politician. Plutarch reports that Socrates came to visit her—clearly an honor—but in the same breath he accuses her of maintaining a house of ill repute.[102] Plutarch's comments offer another example of the prevalent opinion that women philosophers were also likely promiscuous.

Female Philosophy and Promiscuity

The primary reason many men believed female philosophers were promiscuous centered on the type of education necessary for achieving proficiency in philosophy. In most cases, the "school" was not part of public space such as the marketplace or temple, but was held in a private venue, and its members viewed one another as a community, even as a family.[103] This metaphor cut both ways for women. For rhetorical purposes, in presenting a philosophical school as a private group or family, a woman's modesty could be preserved much as it was in her own home. Yet the home was also the place where husband and wife shared a bed, and thus sex was part of the symbolic landscape. The teacher modeled before his students the virtuous life, thus there was much contact time between the teacher and student. This generated little gossip when students were men, but women who sought such an education risked slander because they were in contact with men outside their biological family.

The connection of learning and promiscuity is quite clear with the elite woman Hipparchia (born ca. 340–330 BC), the wife of Crates, a premier Cynic philosopher. The Cynics chose to live by nature and to eschew posses-

100. Pleket 30. Translation in Lefkowitz and Fant, *Women's Life in Greece and Rome*, 169.
101. Taylor (*Jewish Women Philosophers*, 186) suggests, "this slight dissonance may indicate that there is a real Diotima who taught a philosophy of erōs."
102. Plutarch, *Pericles* 24.4.
103. Taylor, *Jewish Women Philosophers*, 277.

sions, luxuries, and social conventions. They believed that if any private act was deemed virtuous then it would remain virtuous if done in public. They identified this virtue as "shamelessness" (*anaideia*). Hipparchia committed herself to the Cynic lifestyle and was adamant that she wished to marry Crates. Critics of the Cynic philosophy charge that Hipparchia and Crates lived in the *stoa* (covered public walkway in the marketplace) of Athens; a later tale has them having sex there in full public view.[104] She traveled with him, and spoke publicly at dinner parties.

Diogenes Laertius recounts an exchange she made with an antagonist, Theodorus, at a symposium. He was heckling her, and she responded with this syllogism: Premise 1: "Any action which would not be called wrong if done by Theodorus, would not be called wrong if done by Hipparchia." Premise 2: "Now Theodorus does no wrong when he strikes himself." Conclusion: "Therefore neither does Hipparchia do wrong when she strikes Theodorus."[105] Theodorus offered no reply to her superior, and comic, argument, but instead grabbed at her cloak. She remained undisturbed, as is fitting a Cynic philosopher. Given Diogenes' poor opinion of Cynics, we can probably trust his story about her learning and wit because that does not support his views.

A Case Study: The Therapeutrides (Female Therapeutics)

The connection between learned women and sexual promiscuity creates great tension in Philo of Alexandria's *De vita contemplativa*. In his study of a group of Jewish men and women who lived on the shores of a local lake, Philo is at pains to render the women philosophers as respectable, legitimate allegorists and students of Moses. The Mareotic Lake community studied scripture through an allegorical lens, wrote hymns, and worshiped God with their ascetic lifestyle. They represent for Philo the apex of theological reflection and simplistic life. All that he admires he finds lived out by this group, with one exception: the group is comprised of both men and women. As Taylor comments, "how could the *therapeutrides*, the female attendants of God, be presented in a way that would not only surpass the paradigms of good women philosophers but also conform to his own gender theory?"[106]

PHILO'S VIEW OF WOMEN AND THE "FEMALE"

Although the historical existence of this group has been questioned by a few scholars, many argue that Philo is writing about an actual group located in the region of Alexandria, Egypt. More difficult is determining the historical

---

104. See Musonius Rufus, *Dissertationes* 14.4; Apuleius, *Florida* 2.49.

105. Diogenes Laertius, *Vit. phil.* 6.97–98 (trans. R. D. Hicks, LCL). Cf. Lefkowitz and Fant, *Women's Life in Greece and Rome*, 167.

106. Taylor, *Jewish Women Philosophers*, 229.

accuracy of Philo's picture of the women in the group. Are they a figment of his fertile imagination, a rhetorical invention to further his polemical aims? Or does his description contain dependable information about Jewish women philosophers? Many scholars believe that careful scrutiny yields reliable data about wealthy Jewish women in first-century AD Alexandria, though they may disagree over details of that picture. This view is supported by the compelling argument that Philo clearly would prefer women not be part of the group. Their presence creates ideological problems for him, which suggests he would have little reason to create the Therapeutrides. He mentions them, therefore, because they were part of the community and he needed to explain why a group of philosophically minded Jewish men would be in a virtuous community that included women.

Particular aspects of Philo's view on women have been touched upon at various places above, but a brief summary of his attitudes will help frame his discussion of the Therapeutrides. Philo describes (elite) Jewish women as disdaining the public life for the domestic; they spend their days within the walls of their homes. He desires that the husband go to the synagogue, and upon returning home, instruct his wife.[107] In a few places, however, Philo reveals that Jewish women did venture beyond their four walls.[108] Important for our discussion is the emphasis Philo placed on women's seclusion in the home and their virtual absence from public life. To put a new spin on an old maxim, Philo believed women should be *not* seen and *not* heard. To that end he used clothing and physical structures (like homes or walled courtyards) to hide women from nonfamilial men. These same tactics are employed in his description of the women at Mareotic Lake.

We must also remember that Philo was deeply committed to the allegorical understanding of Scripture. One ramification of this attitude was his virtual noninterest in actual women and his obsessive concern with the feminine or "the female." He understood the soul as masculine and sense perceptions as feminine. He connected the mind with male and the irrational with female, but went a step further. Philo understood the human as composed of the mortal and the immortal, and then divided the mortal into male and female, but the immortal part of the human (that made in the image of God) was male. In his work *De opificio mundi*, Philo distinguishes between the "man" created in Genesis 2:7 and the male and female of Genesis 1:27. The latter is an "object of sense-perception . . . , consisting of body and soul, man or woman, by nature mortal."[109] The former is an idea, a type or a seal that is incorporeal and neither male nor female. As Judith Romney Wegner notes, "Philo's taxonomy of male and female as separate species enables him to discuss the relationship

107. Philo, *Hypothetica* 7.14; see also *Spec.* 3.169–71.
108. Philo, *Spec.* 3.174.
109. Philo, *De opificio mundi* 134 (trans. F. H. Colson and G. H. Whitaker, LCL).

between man and God without addressing the division of humankind into male and female."[110]

To best understand his description of these Jewish female philosophers, we must be alert to how Philo uses his allegorical approach and to his underlying ideology of women. Philo writes about the Therapeutic community in no small part to persuade the reader of his definition of "the good." His history is not an end in itself, then, but a way to further his own ideas on the supreme value of contemplation, virtue, and goodness. Taylor notes that the group has no autonomous voice, no chance to present a self-definition. In light of that, she suggests that we look for what she calls rhetorical dissonance in gaining an accurate picture of Therapeutrides.[111] In sum, Philo does not want to say much at all about these women at Mareotic Lake. It is up to the astute reader to discover what he wants to hide or downplay.

WOMEN IN *DE VITA CONTEMPLATIVA*

In his work *De vita contemplativa*, Philo starts with a general picture of contemplative philosophy's superiority and then turns to a specific discussion of the exemplary group outside the city, the Therapeutics. From this general overview, he focuses on the daily life of each philosopher in his hut. Up to this point, the reader has no idea that women are even part of the group. Not until Philo talks about the general meeting that takes place each seventh day does he note the presence of women.[112] At this assembly one side is reserved for men, the other for women, and a wall built halfway to the ceiling separates the two. "For even women, in accordance with their custom, are members of the congregation, because they have the same zeal and the same vocation." The half-wall allows for women to hear the speaker's voice but to maintain their modesty, according to Philo. He is at pains to describe this meeting place (*semneion*) as divided space before he mentions the presence of women. We have only Philo's testimony about the half-wall (to preserve female modesty). Elsewhere, he claims that synagogues were divided with a separate area for women, but neither archaeology nor other literature supports his assertion. It may be that he invented this half-wall to protect the honor of his beloved Therapeutic community from nasty slurs. Or perhaps he is reflecting the community's perspective on space. The term used for the room (*semneion*) in which the weekly meal is held is the same as that of the private study space in each member's hut. The group (or Philo) seems to image the weekly meal as an extension of their private studies, which they configure based on a household model.

110. Judith Romney Wegner, "Philo's Portrayal of Women—Hebraic or Hellenic?" in *"Women Like This": New Perspectives on Jewish Women in the Greco-Roman World*, ed. Amy-Jill Levine (Atlanta: Scholars Press, 1991), 46.

111. Taylor, *Jewish Women Philosophers*, 7, 12.

112. Philo, *Contempl.* 32–33.

Philo's first mention of women in the community, then, is done with an eye to preserving its male members' honor. That concern continues in his later descriptions of the women. Philo describes them as both mothers and virgins, which at first blush seems contradictory. But he invests each term with important metaphorical meaning as he walks a tightrope of public opinion about female philosophers. He must present these women as upstanding women of the community, as chaste, virtuous, and upholding the status quo. These two key social roles, mother and virgin/chaste wife, function as conceptual paradigms. Philo exploits the metaphorical meanings of these terms while he defends the behavior of the Therapeutrides as chaste, domestic mothers in the household of ideal philosophy.

How do Philo's Therapeutrides connect with the Jewish community within Alexandria? By taking seriously his claim that "most" of the women were aged virgins, it means that at least some of them were not virgins, but women who chose celibacy later in life. Second, if some were real virgins, they were apparently so raised by their families. This provides a window into at least a segment of wealthy Jewish families in Alexandria,[113] who apparently educated their daughters in the allegorical method and valued virginity as a choice their daughters could make.

Most scholars are satisfied merely with analyzing Philo's description of the Therapeutrides, but Taylor argues, convincingly I think, that the Therapeutrides point to the existence of other educated women who knew the Jewish law and its allegorical interpretation but did not embrace a contemplative lifestyle. Taylor also suggests that the Therapeutics drew from an established group of similarly minded Jewish philosophers living in Alexandria, Philo of course among them. Philo makes clear that the Therapeutics were already well versed in the allegorical method when they joined the Lake Mareotic community. Apparently they learned this approach in Alexandria. Moreover, Philo himself hints at a local Jewish woman philosopher when he speaks of seeking out Skepsis (which means "consideration").[114] Though many translators believe Philo is speaking metaphorically here, we recognize today both the biases of translators and the presence within Alexandria of Jewish and pagan women philosophers. Philo's Skepsis is quite possibly a real woman.

Therapeutic Rituals and Dress

On a final note, it is curious that Philo does not speak much about the women's dress, which was a typical way to recognize modest women.[115] Philo does not distinguish between men's and women's dress; instead, he describes

---

113. The fact that they were literate to such a degree suggests they derived from wealthy families. See Taylor, *Jewish Women Philosophers*, 94–95.

114. Philo, *Fug.* 55, 58.

115. Philo, *Contempl.* 38–39.

the uniform of the Therapeutics as a simple, sleeveless linen tunic to which can be added a heavy cloak. Philo's description matches nothing an elite woman would wear. On one hand, this may suggest that Philo is only describing the men's clothing. On the other hand, it may be that both men and women dressed this way, and because it does not fit general standards of propriety, he limits his discussion to a single reference. Philo follows up his sketch with a strong word on modesty, which he says is reflected by their dress, diet, and behavior. He spends more time portraying the debauched dress of boy slaves attending pagan banquets, depicting the clothes as revealing and erotic,[116] than he does reporting on the Therapeutics' dress, perhaps as a way to reinforce its simplicity—it is so basic, it needs only a brief description.

In one significant departure from their usual clothing, each community member dons "snow white raiment" like a priest for their seventh-week community celebration, the Sabbath of Sabbaths.[117] Both men and women eat from a special table that symbolizes the table of the shewbread of the temple. Philo includes that women are priests,[118] in that their souls are purified and their bodies are transcended, just like their male counterparts. The meal celebrates the members' victory of self-control (enkrateia) as they rejoice in their "sanctuary." No wall is necessary to separate men from women, for all present are purified souls who have shed, at least for the moment, the restrictions of the body. The Therapeutics, both men and women, symbolically understood as priests worshiping before God, celebrate throughout the night with hymns and dancing.

Unlike the seventh-day meal wherein gender distinctions play an important role in dividing space, in the Sabbath of Sabbaths festival, gender distinctions are minimized while the dichotomy between soul and body is exploited. For this day at least, the Therapeutrides celebrate as equals with their brothers. Yet Philo does not suggest that the women have become men and thus are equal. He does not use a dualism of the body/spirit to wipe away women's femaleness. Instead, it seems that as women they have an equally powerful role in the evening celebration. The reason women remain women in the ideology of the community rests in part on their understanding of the prophetess Miriam, Moses's sister. She is placed on equal footing with Moses as a leader of the people: Moses leading men, Miriam leading women, as interpreted from Exodus 15:1–21. Miriam provides the model of a female community member or leader: a prophetess, a composer and singer of hymns.

Exodus 15:20–21 indicates Miriam is a prophet and Aaron's sister (see also Num. 12:1–2). She plays the timbrel, dances, and leads the women in song. Her words noted in Exodus 15:21 closely follow the opening lines of

116. Philo, Contempl. 50–52.
117. Philo, Contempl. 66; see also 82.
118. Philo, Contempl. 66, 74, 82.

Moses's lengthy song previously stated in 15:1–18. For this reason, other traditions about Miriam, including Philo's own treatment, suggest that she merely repeated Moses.[119] But the Therapeutic community presents Miriam as a prophetess and composer of hymns of thanksgiving to God.[120] In other words, Miriam is a lot like the Therapeutrides. The Mareotic community expands on the Exodus narrative in another significant way. While the biblical text suggests that the choirs remained separate, and Philo supports this in his discussions of the text,[121] the Therapeutic community has a single choir: "men and women together, inspired by God, forming one chorus, sang hymns of thanksgiving to God their savior."[122] While Philo devalues Miriam as outward sense perception that has nonetheless been rendered pure, the Therapeutics see men and women's "thoughts and . . . speech [as] utterly noble."[123] After the banquet and celebration, each community member returns to their "customary trade and cultivation of philosophy,"[124] further reinforcing the picture of men and women participating equally in the task of allegorical interpretation.

In sum, the Therapeutrides reflect one possibility open to wealthy women who were capable of and interested in pursuing a dedicated life of contemplation and allegorical study. These women were supported by an affluent Jewish community in Alexandria that valued allegorical interpretation of the law. This segment of the Jewish population admired the contemplative life and allowed or even encouraged their daughters to remain virgins (or live celibate) if they so chose. It is highly likely that some or most of the women in this Alexandrian Jewish subgroup remained with their families and studied allegorically at home or with other like-minded scholars, much like Philo's fellow philosopher, Skepsis.

As we build a picture of Jewish women in other parts of the Diaspora and in Roman Palestine, we need to ask how influential these Alexandrian female philosophers were. Their high social status represented only a fraction of the general population. Education required money and leisure time, two commodities in very short supply among the working poor. Moreover, the allegorical approach (not unique to Philo) was roundly condemned by other prominent philosophers of the day. Yet because of their high status, these female philosophers might have presented ideals of female virtue and achievement that infused the social imagination.

119. Philo, De agricultura 80–82, declares that the two choirs sang the same hymn. He also calls Miriam the "purified outward sense."
120. An alternative Song of Miriam is preserved in fragmentary form in 4Q365 6a ii, 6c.
121. Philo, De vita Mosis 2.256–65.
122. Philo, Contempl. 87. Translation by Gail Paterson Corrington in Ascetic Behavior in Greco-Roman Antiquity: A Sourcebook, ed. V. Wimbush (Minneapolis: Fortress, 1990), 154.
123. Philo, Contempl. 88. Translation by Paterson Corrington in Wimbush, Ascetic Behavior, 154.
124. Philo, Contempl. 89. Translation by Paterson Corrington in Wimbush, Ascetic Behavior, 154.

Conclusion

There is no free lunch—so we hear. And that was true in the Greco-Roman world. Most everyone worked very hard to scrape by. Women and men worked side by side to provide for their families. Hard labor was the lot of most rural poor, with mothers and fathers out in their fields or caring for their flocks, building and repairing their homes, cutting firewood—the list was endless. The urban poor also struggled to earn a living. Women were shopkeepers, artisans, and skilled craftsworkers. Further up the socio-economic ladder, women were merchants, buying and selling, and loaning money. Women could be skilled artists whose works commanded a hefty sum. And women could be educated, even at the highest level as philosophers. With increased social visibility came increased social criticism. Women philosophers could be painted as virtuous or as promiscuous.

Amidst the numerous tasks and professions that occupied the people of the ancient Roman world, two jobs in particular were the sole reserve of men— that of soldier and politicians in the Roman Senate or as governors in the provinces.[125] Likewise, two occupations were done only by women: midwifery and wet-nursing. Unlike the exclusively male jobs that were highly valued, the exclusively female jobs, though honorable, carried little prestige. Perhaps this was because at least in the western half of the empire, and especially in Rome itself, these tasks were performed by slaves. As we will see in the next chapter, many of the jobs performed by free and freed women were also done by slaves, which may explain in part why so many women were not identified by their occupation. However, since many jobs that men performed were also done by slaves, this observation cannot be the only reason. Probably more important is the overarching social pressure to define women in relation to men, both in terms of family and in judging her moral character. That is, a woman was honored highly if she was a chaste wife—her virtue is defined relative to a male and the patriarchal value system. Said another way, in general, a woman was honored for who she was and how she behaved relative to a man, not for what she accomplished. Yet we have seen in this chapter that in reality, women accomplished many things, from the quotidian to the magnificent. On rare occasions, they received well-deserved acknowledgment, as in this first-century AD inscription from Lycia: "Antiochis, daughter of Diodotus of Tlos, awarded special recognition by the council and the people of Tlos for her experience in the healing art, has set up this status of herself."[126] But for most women their work was largely unheralded. This is especially the case for slaves and prostitutes, categories investigated in the following chapter.

---

125. In general, women did not hold public political offices; however, as we will see in chap. 9, some wealthy matrons did hold municipal city offices, probably based on their gifts to the city.

126. Pleket 12. Translation in Lefkowitz and Fant, *Women's Life in Greece and Rome*, 264.

8

Slaves and Prostitutes

A bill of sale from AD 142 reads: "Pamphilos . . . has bought in the marketplace from Artemidoros . . . a slave girl, Abaskantis, a Galatian by descent, about 10 years of age for the sum of 280 silver denarii."[1] Every society exploits and marginalizes a population segment. In the Roman Empire, the female slave was perhaps the most ill-used. Not only was her labor generally unrewarded, but her sexuality was subjugated and with it her honor compromised. Unlike male slaves who often were well trained and might gain both wealth and social respect, the female slave, unless she was a favored member of the imperial household or similar exalted family, often lacked marketable skills. She was locked into her domestic situation and sexually available both to her owner and those he (or she) permitted to have access to her. As she aged, her sexual appeal declined, and so did her earning potential. In contrast, her male co-slaves developed skills that increased in value over time. Though there are examples of freed female slaves who did well for themselves, the number of male slaves who achieved freedom and social prestige far outnumbers female slaves. In a culture that promoted chastity and modesty as its highest ideals for women, the slave was at the bottom of the social ladder.

The slave woman also served as a poignant symbol of defeat and despair. The "barbarian" woman as a chained captive of war, or clutching her infant in surrender, is a haunting image that recurs on coins and reliefs during the

---

1. For translation and discussion, see S. R. Llewelyn, ed., *New Documents Illustrating Early Christianity*, vol. 6, *A Review of the Greek Inscriptions and Papyri Published in 1980–81*, with R. A. Kearsley (North Ryde, Australia: Ancient History Documentary Research Centre, Macquarie University, 1992), 48–52.

Sestertius from the reign of Vespasian (AD 69–79) showing a seated female figure (representing Judea) mourning under a palm tree with a triumphal Roman soldier standing beside her (Photo courtesy of Michael F. Fitzpatrick)

imperial period. Captured women personified the defeated enemy, emasculating and shaming it by a portrayal of "its" women as war plunder, ready for slavery. Such images reinforced Roman ideology of the family in a perverse way, communicating that to destroy the enemy's women and children is to destroy the enemy completely by wiping out its next generation. Sadly, the conquered woman image is the most common depiction of real women on reliefs in the ancient world.[2] Perhaps best known of these commemorations of Roman victory are the Judea Capta coins. After the fall of Jerusalem in AD 70, Rome minted several similar coins trumpeting its victory in Judea. These coins depicted a Jewish woman, symbolizing the Jewish nation, often seated beneath a palm tree, weeping or in a position of mourning. In some cases, her hands are bound behind her back. In other coins, a large Roman soldier (perhaps recalling the general, and later emperor, Vespasian) towers over her with spear in hand.

     Another example comes from earlier in the first century. A court gemstone, the Grand Camée de France, depicts a seated Livia, the widow of Augustus and the mother of Tiberius, and below her a barbarian woman holding a child. As Natalie Boymel Kampen notes, "the barbarian woman with babe in arms signals the depth of defeat suffered by her society, just as Livia, [pictured] beneath her divine spouse and next to her ruling son, is the crucial line in the chain of enduring dynastic power."[3] This motif continued into the second century AD with the Septimius Severus Arch built in Leptis Magna commemorating a visit to his birthplace in North Africa.[4] In one relief, the triumphal proces-

2. Natalie Boymel Kampen, "Between Public and Private: Women as Historical Subjects in Roman Art," in *Women's History and Ancient History*, ed. Sarah B. Pomeroy (Chapel Hill: University of North Carolina Press, 1991), 233. "Real women" here refers to mortal, historical women as distinct from mythological women or goddesses.

3. Kampen, "Between Public and Private," 235. See photo of cameo on p. 134.

4. Relief of the Severan Arch of Leptis Magna, AD 206–9 (Museum of the Red Castle, Tripoli, Libya). For a discussion of this relief, see Kampen, "Between Public and Private," 224–32.

sional includes a female captive with a small child, while an older boy in front of her is being pulled away by a soldier. The scene is one of utter defeat and despair for the conquered and of absolute victory for Rome.

The power these visual images of defeat exerted over Rome's conquered people was enhanced by the common knowledge of a slave woman's perilous existence. Lowest on the social scale, by definition considered unchaste, the female slave had much to fear and little hope. Because the image of slavery is so powerful in the New Testament, and because a good number of Jewish and Christian women were themselves slaves, it is important to explore the life of the average female slave.

General Characteristics of Greco-Roman Slavery

Before the Civil War, a person visiting the South in the newly formed United States could distinguish easily between slave and free: skin color, education level, housing—all served to set apart black Africans from white Europeans. Was the same true in the Greco-Roman period? In most cases, the answer is no. Slaves were not distinguished by skin color, education level, or even where they lived. Their clothes resembled those of their poor freeborn neighbors, and they might live among them rather than in their owner's home. They could be better educated or more highly skilled and could have more wealth or better social connections through their owners than those freed or freeborn. They could form a type of marriage (see below) with children in a relatively stable family unit.

But they were still slaves. This disturbing reality holds in the legal and financial sense, but the social reality was much more nuanced. In the stratified, hierarchical society that was the Greco-Roman world, slavery was both an uncontested institution and an unstable one. That is, few people questioned the necessity of slavery—even slaves owned slaves. And a surprisingly large number of people owned slaves; even relatively poor families might have a slave or two. These slaves became part of the owner's estate and could be willed to heirs. From the first century AD, there is an account of three sons inheriting four slaves; they agreed to share the women's labor and their future children.[5] Evidence suggests that most female slaves were either born into that rank or were foundlings. Also, a free person was threatened with the possibility of becoming a slave if, for example, they were captured by pirates or conquered by the Roman army. A parent might sell a child into slavery, or expose an infant who was then raised by another as a slave. A person might receive slave status as a result of legal penalties, though the specific legal process for this is unclear.

5. P. Tebt. 2.407. Discussion in Jennifer A. Glancy, *Slavery in Early Christianity* (Minneapolis: Fortress, 2006), 10–11.

In no small measure, a slave was an object, an animal with a voice. Slaves were regularly flogged—a punishment illegal for a Roman citizen. Martial comments on the treatment given a slave who failed to prepare the master's dinner properly: "You say, Rufus, that your rabbit has not been cooked well, and you call for a whip. You prefer to cut up your cook, rather than your rabbit."[6] While he speaks with hyperbole here, we know that slaves could be branded, scarred, and made to wear identification collars. They could be hit and slapped by just about anyone. Slaves were vulnerable to verbal and physical abuse, though it was not the slave who was seen to be injured but the owner's dignity that was offended. Thus an attack on a slave was viewed as an attack on the owner. The social consequences, for example, of the apostle Peter slicing off the ear of the high priest's slave at Jesus's arrest are profound. From the wider social view, Peter directly insulted the high priest. Jesus's healing had the immediate effect of getting Peter off the hook; it may also reveal Jesus's concern for the plight of slaves.[7]

Slaves were vulnerable sexually as well. Both male and female slaves were sexually accessible to their owners, where they were often treated roughly. A first-century BC divorce petition put forward by a wife, Tryphaine, charges that her husband abused her, treating her as he would a slave.[8] Slaves were tortured before giving testimony and were pursued diligently if they escaped. The owner might offer a reward for the return of an especially prized slave. If slaves grew too sick or too old to work they might be abandoned by their owners. Emperor Claudius passed a law that such slaves, if they recovered, were granted their freedom. Moreover, the owner who killed an old or sick slave rather than provide care was condemned as a murderer. Since Hadrian about a century later made a similar law, it is unclear how diligently Claudius's provisions were enforced or how widespread such cases were.[9] It seems public sentiment was against owners who violently abused or abandoned their slaves, but the effectiveness of any public censoring of such behavior probably varied.[10]

Slave "Marriage"

Slave women could enter into a union with a man, although these were not licit marriages. Two slaves could cohabitate (*contubernium*) and would refer

6. Martial, *Epigrammata* 3.94. For a translation, see Jo-Ann Shelton, *As the Romans Did: A Sourcebook in Roman Social History* (New York: Oxford University Press, 1988), 177.

7. Only John 18:10 identifies Peter using the sword and identifies the slave as Malchus; cf. Matt. 26:51; Mark 14:47; Luke 22:50.

8. *BGU* IV.1105. For a discussion, see Glancy, *Slavery in Early Christianity*, 21.

9. Suetonius, *Divus Claudius* 25; Aelius Spartianus, *Hadrian* 18.7–11. For translations, see Shelton, *As the Romans Did*, 188.

10. For a careful description of the punishment given to slaves, see Keith R. Bradley, *Slaves and Masters in the Roman Empire: A Study in Social Control* (New York: Oxford University Press, 1987), 113–37.

to each other as husband and wife, however, the latter could not be charged with adultery, as her choice of sexual partners was ultimately determined by her owner. Of course, at any time the owners could separate these unions, but incentives fell on the side of keeping the pair together: they likely worked harder and were happier. Any children produced were the owner's property, and remained so even if the parents gained their freedom. The child would need to be redeemed just as would an adult slave.

Not only could a slave woman live in a contubernium but she could also be a concubine.[11] This term covers a range of meaning. In the literature, *concubina* might refer to a man's sexual liaisons outside of marriage (only women could be concubines). In a legal sense, a concubinage or *concubinatus* was a relationship wherein the man chose not to marry, or was unable to enter a licit marriage due to the inferior social status of the woman. Concubinage was not frowned upon as morally suspect, and a publicly declared concubine would have social stability. A widower might desire a concubine because he does not want his children to have a stepmother or share his wealth with any children that might come from this new relationship. A young man might take a concubine to avoid the duties of family until he reaches a more suitable age. An upper-class man would be unable to legally marry a freedwoman; *concubinatus* was the next best option.

The concubine was in a relatively secure position, especially if her partner was financially stable. She probably lived above her social station, but she had no claim on his property.[12] A concubine did not have the legal recourse granted a wife, including the protection against adultery. The man often gave gifts to his concubine. However, if the concubine became his wife, the law stipulated that any gifts given prior to the wedding were the woman's property. If the couple did not have a wedding, but the man decided that he did wish for them to be married, the issue of gifts becomes more complex because the date on which the concubine becomes a wife determines her claim on gifts. Moreover, any children born while she was a concubine were legally her children. If the man married another woman, it is unclear whether he needed to end the relationship with his concubine. No legal requirement existed, but perhaps social norms encouraged it.

If a slave couple had a child, he or she took the social status of the mother. If the mother was a slave when the child was born, the child was also a slave. If she was a freedwoman in an illicit marriage to a slave, the child was freeborn but illegitimate. If both the husband and wife were freed slaves and both were Roman citizens, then their children would be free citizens as well, and the father

11. Slave women in such a relationship were known as contubernales. For a general discussion, see Susan Treggiari, *Roman Marriage: Iusti Coniuges from the Time of Cicero to the Time of Ulpian* (Oxford: Clarendon, 1991), 52–54.

12. Susan Treggiari, *Roman Freedmen during the Late Republic* (1969; repr., New York: Oxford University Press, 2000), 212.

had the *patria potestas*. If only the mother was a freedwomen and a Roman citizen, her children were considered illegitimate and took their mother's *nomen*; the father had no legal rights over them. For example, two slaves might live in contubernium and then each gain their freedom and citizenship, at which point they could enter a licit marriage. Those children who were born while the parents were still slaves would keep their slave status and remain with the owner, while those born after the parents' freedom were considered freeborn. Of course, a slave couple could be separated and their children sold. An example of such complexity comes from the story of Antestia Glycera, a three-year-old girl who died. Her parents were slaves when she was born, and they were separated. By the time she died, both parents were free, as was the little girl, but each remained in a different household.[13] Slave unions often lasted a long time. In epitaphs of imperial slaves and freedmen, almost half of the unions lasted at least thirty years. Within this same group, female slaves usually "married" young, and over half died before they were thirty years old.

What would motivate slaves to enter in to contubernia? Probably the same reasons nonslaves entered marriage: companionship. Most slave unions were formed within their master's house. A male slave needed his master's permission to form a union with a slave from another household. Because any children from this union would be the property of the woman's owner, the male slave's owner had no incentive (other than perhaps garnering goodwill or rewarding his slave) of consenting to the match. To circumvent the owner's possible refusal a male slave might buy the female slave he desired. He might also buy one of his master's female slaves, thereby lessening the possibility she would be moved to another property owned by the master. Of course, anything or anyone owned by a slave was technically owned by his or her master. Slaves might also form unions to improve their social status. A male slave might "marry" a female slave of the household, with the hope that she would be freed sooner than he, especially if he is a valuable or skilled slave, one the owner would prefer to keep. Conversely, a man might seek his freedom, then free and marry a slave woman. This process took her from her owner's house to her new husband's house. Since the latter freed her he was considered her last owner and thus was owed loyalty much as any freed slave was obliged to their former owner.[14]

Though social climbing through marriage was acceptable for men, society frowned upon a free woman marrying a freedman, for that was below her so-

---

13. *CIL* VI.11924. For a discussion, see Beryl Rawson, "The Roman Family," in *The Family in Ancient Rome: New Perspectives*, ed. Beryl Rawson (Ithaca, NY: Cornell University Press, 1987), 24.

14. *CIL* I.1216 records such an event. The son of C. Caninius C. f. manumitted a slave, who then freed and married a slave girl (see also *CIL* I.1638). Treggiari (*Roman Freedmen*, 209) notes that "the *libertine* manumission of the wife by the husband rather than by the common owner presented the great advantage that she was free of legal obligations to a third party, since her husband became her patron."

cial station. Though a free woman might be drawn to a wealthy imperial slave because of his prestige and job security they could not form a licit marriage. However, she would be buried in his *familia* tomb, thus being associated with the imperial family. The slave would have the prestige a union with a freeborn woman offered. Only the slave's owner lost out because none of the children would be the owner's property. In AD 52, the senate therefore decreed that a free woman who united with a slave became a slave or freedwoman of her husband's owner. This law served the emperor by giving him the financial benefits of his slave's wife and offspring. Though a free woman might be attracted to form a union with a male slave, the reverse was not usually the case. Most female slaves did not marry above themselves, unless their owners chose to free and then marry them.

Manumission

If a slave was manumitted (freed), that freedom did not include self-determination. The freed slave was still under the *patria potestas* of his or her former owner. But the freed slave did acquire increased social prestige and honor, and usually Roman citizenship. Thus while the category "slave" was static, the people in that category could rotate in and out of it. As such, their social status also shifted, which agitated some Roman authors. Juvenal, for example, was a moderately well-off Roman who despised the wealthy freedmen and resented the upwardly mobile non-Romans, some of whom were slaves. He laments, "is a man to sign his name before me, and recline upon a couch better than mine, who has been wafted to Rome by the wind which brings us our damsons and our figs? Is it to go so utterly for nothing that as a babe I drank in the air of the Aventine, and was nurtured on the Sabine berry?"[15] Juvenal's whining reveals the social possibility that slaves and freedmen/women could amass a fortune if they had the right connections. Though this was more true of men, manumitted female slaves also had opportunities to gain wealth and social prestige.

The slave owner also had much at stake in a slave's manumission. Society looked favorably on those masters who freed their slaves, based on the prevailing Stoic ideal that a male slave could be his owner's moral equal.[16] Often it was financially or socially beneficial for the owner to grant the slave freedom. For instance, the owner might be unable to care for the slave due to financial reversals. Also, owners might manumit old or ill slaves, relieving themselves of the pecuniary burden of caring for them. These manumitted slaves were considered citizens and thus eligible for the corn dole meted out by the government in Rome. We do not know how many owners took advantage of this legal loophole, but Augustus sought to close it with orders that denied new

15. Juvenal, *Sat.* 3.81 (trans. G. G. Ramsey, LCL).
16. Cicero, *Paradoxa Stoicorum* 5; Horace, *Satirae* 2.7.75.

citizens access to the corn dole.[17] Or perhaps the owner granted freedom to
a hardworking slave as encouragement to the other slaves to labor harder for
such a reward. It might be that a slave was quite talented, and the social prestige bestowed on the owner for freeing that slave was motivation enough. The
gesture was ultimately self-serving, for the (former) owner now had another
client from whom to receive public honor. Moreover, at the freedman/woman's
death, the owner received a portion of their estate. An owner charged with a
capital offense might free his or her slaves to prevent their negative testimony.
Since as citizens they were protected from the torture typically inflicted on
slaves before they gave evidence, freed slaves would likely not incriminate their
(former) owners. Often owners would include in their wills the freedom of
their slaves. If this provision was made known to the slave, it could encourage
diligent service. Columella advises that a hardworking female slave who bore
three children might be rewarded with release from work, and a slave who bore
four children might be granted her freedom.[18] Perhaps the owner desired to
marry his slave woman, and so manumitted her. The *lex Aelia Sentia* restricts
a man under the age of twenty from manumitting slaves, except if he wishes
to marry his female slave. Larcia Horaea, for example, was granted freedom
for the express purpose of marrying her owner's son—the owner himself was
a freedman.[19]

The process for manumitting a slave was tightly regulated, involving a
representative of the state. If the owner's will stipulated the slave's freedom, it
was authorized by a magistrate. The owner and slave could also appear before
a magistrate or proconsul to declare their intentions. In the late republican
period, however, when manumissions became more frequent, informal methods
developed. In this case, the owner merely declared the slave free, often with no
witnesses present. Probably the owner's words were accompanied by written
confirmation. This more casual approach might be chosen if the slave was
dying and wished to be buried as a freedperson. Or perhaps no magistrates
were available to oversee the manumission. But with the informal process,
the slave was not granted Roman citizenship and any children remained the
owner's slaves. The quasi-legal status of the informal method created problems,
so probably during Augustus's reign freed slaves were guaranteed citizenship,
although they remained under the tutelage of their former owners. No matter what the specific circumstances, the manumission process was taxed at 5
percent of the slave's value. It is unclear whether the slave or the owner paid
this tax; probably each situation determined who paid it. For example, a slave
who bought his or her own freedom perhaps covered the tax as well.

17. Suetonius, *Divus Augustus* 42.
18. Columella, *De re rustica* 1.8.19.
19. *CIL* X.6009 (first century BC). For a translation, see Mary R. Lefkowitz and Maureen
B. Fant, *Women's Life in Greece and Rome: A Source Book in Translation*, 3rd ed. (Baltimore:
Johns Hopkins University Press, 2005), 165.

Slave Wealth and Prestige

How did slaves earn money? Technically, all that a slave had belonged to the slave's owner. But unofficially, slaves could earn wealth by working after hours or receiving gifts of appreciation. They circumvented the law stipulating that their earnings were devoted to their owners by employing the convention of *peculium*. This involved the head of the family setting aside for his child or slave (male or female) a part of the estate or property to be used as the recipient wanted. In the slave's situation, the owner might allow the slave to keep part of the earnings made in business transactions. While the money or property technically remained part of the owner's estate, in practice the son or slave (male or female) was given free rein. Slaves might bargain with their owners to use their *peculium* to buy their freedom.[20]

Slaves might also gain prestige through connections with their owners. In the ancient world the maxim "it's not what you know, but who you know" was true to a much greater extent than today in the West. Knowing someone important was the next best thing to being important yourself. Ironically, then, a slave might have more social power than a freeborn person if the slave was part of an eminent family. This holds true especially for male slaves of the imperial household. Emperor Claudius was notorious in the literature for bestowing wealth and power on his freedmen. For example, Marcus Antonius Pallas gained incredible wealth and became head of the imperial treasury (*fiscus*) under Claudius. Initially Pallas was the slave of Antonia, daughter of Mark Antony and Octavia and mother of Claudius. She manumitted him and probably also rewarded him with an estate in Egypt. Once manumitted, he placed her name (in the masculine form) in front of his own name, as was commonly done by freed slaves. Though freed, tradition held that he owed service to his former owner, and when she died, to her heir, in this case Emperor Claudius. A generation later, Pliny the Younger, viewing Pallas's elaborate funerary inscription set up by the senate, derogatorily referred to him as a slave even though he was a freedman. Jealous of his wealth and influence, Pliny complained that Pallas received the prestige due freeborn Romans, who were thus denied their rightful honor.[21]

Other imperial slaves drew on their skills to gain their freedom and used their social connections to amass wealth, including estates and villas, as well as slaves of their own. An epitaph from first-century AD Gaul declares the wealth of a certain Musicus Scurranus, slave and financial officer of Tiberius.[22]

20. Tacitus, *Ann.* 14.42; J. Albert Harrill, *The Manumission of Slaves in Early Christianity*, 2nd ed. (Tübingen: Mohr Siebeck, 1998), 154. See also Judith Evans-Grubbs, *Women and the Law in the Roman Empire: A Sourcebook in Marriage, Divorce, and Widowhood* (London: Routledge, 2002), 90, 144.

21. Pliny the Younger, *Ep.* 8.6.

22. *CIL* VI.5197. For a discussion, see Dale Martin, *Slavery as Salvation: The Metaphor of Slavery in Pauline Christianity* (New Haven: Yale University Press, 1990), 7–8.

When Scurranus died, his slaves dedicated an inscription to him with a partial list of his entourage, including a buying agent, a treasurer, a physician, several personal attendants, and two cooks. One woman's name, Secunda, appears at the end of the list, and no occupation is given—everyone knew what her responsibilities entailed. Apparently, through his business dealings and acumen, Scurranus amassed a fortune, though it was all under the umbrella of his master and patron, Emperor Tiberius. As evidenced by these examples, "slavery was arguably the most important channel through which outsiders entered the mainstream of Roman power structures."[23]

A stunning example of a slave's upward mobility is found in the story of Antonia Caenis. She began her career as a slave secretary to Antonia, the owner of Pallas noted above. She was given much responsibility and gained a reputation for business acumen. Cassius Dio approves of her faithfulness and writes about her sharp mind. "Her mistress Antonia, the mother of Claudius, had once employed her as secretary in writing a secret letter to Tiberius about Sejanus and had immediately ordered the message to be erased, in order that no trace of it might be left. Thereupon she replied: 'It is useless, mistress, for you to give this command; for not only all this but also whatever else you dictate to me I always carry in my mind and it can never be erased.'"[24] She was likely freed at the end of Tiberius's reign (AD 14–37), or at the beginning of Caligula's rule (AD 37–41), when her owner, Antonia, committed suicide. Probably during the reign of Tiberius, Vespasian fell in love with Caenis. At this point, Vespasian was years away from his emperorship. And though he continued his relationship with Caenis, he married a freeborn woman, Flavia Domitilla, and they had two sons, the future emperors Titus and Domitian, as well as a daughter, also named Flavia Domitilla. When his wife died at the end of Claudius's rule (AD 41–54), Vespasian behaved with Caenis as though they were husband and wife.[25] Of course, he could not enter into a licit marriage with her because of her former slave status. Caenis grew tremendously wealthy by negotiating and conferring political and religious offices. Cassius Dio writes that she had tremendous influence, "for she received vast sums from many sources, sometimes selling governorships, sometimes procuratorships, generalships and priesthoods, and in some instances even imperial decisions."[26] The suspicion was that Vespasian received a portion of her proceeds and so was content to look the other way. She wielded great power in her own right, and died in about AD 74 a very rich woman. Caenis's Cinderella story, however, was as rare as a fairy tale come to life.

Many female slaves earned money through sexual favors. An owner or an owner-approved lover might give gifts of appreciation to her. We know of one

23. Martin, *Slavery as Salvation*, 32.
24. Cassius Dio, *Hist. Rom.* 65.14 (trans. E. Cary, LCL).
25. Suetonius, *Vespasianus* 3.
26. Cassius Dio, *Hist. Rom.* 65.14 (trans. E. Cary, LCL).

Second-century AD
Roman mosaic showing
a slave woman pouring
wine from an amphora
into a pot on a stand
(Photo courtesy of
Alberto Fernandez/
Wikimedia Commons)

slave who received her freedom as a reward for her sexual services—and this from
the owner's wife! Scipio Africanus was fond of the slave girl and, upon his death,
his wife granted her manumission. Perhaps Scipio's wife wanted the girl out of
her sight, but it is just as likely that she was honoring the slave for her service.
It might also be the case that a lady's maid was tipped by her owner's lover as a
bribe to hold her tongue. Volumnia Cytheris, a wealthy freedwoman, probably
accrued her wealth through gifts from her influential lovers, including Mark
Antony, Brutus (who plotted against Julius Caesar), and Cornelius Gallus.[27]

Slave Women's Occupations

Slave women's duties often were the same as freedwomen's or freeborn wom-
en's tasks. They were "spinners, weavers, clothesmakers, menders, wetnurses,
child nurses, kitchen help and general domestics."[28] Women slaves served beer at
the beer shops, and were apprenticed to learn skills.[29] In Egypt, Thermuthion, a
slave girl of Platonis, was entrusted to a guardian who fed and clothed her and
took her to the instructor each day.[30] Female slaves worked as clerks and secre-

27. Sarah B. Pomeroy, *Goddesses, Whores, Wives, and Slaves: Women in Classical Antiquity*
(1975; repr., New York: Schocken, 1995), 198.
28. Pomeroy, *Goddesses, Whores, Wives, and Slaves*, 191.
29. Glancy, *Slavery in Early Christianity*, 42.
30. P.Oxy. 1647. Translation in Lefkowitz and Fant, *Women's Life in Greece and Rome*,
208.

taries for wealthy women. Slaves cut and dressed hair, folded clothes, and even held mirrors. They were readers, entertainers, flutists, masseuses. They might help manage their owner's country estate or perhaps travel with their mistress as she went about town, proclaiming her praises publicly. These slaves usually retained their slave status. Many of the inscriptions mentioning tradeswomen also indicate their freedwoman status, which suggests that they learned their trade as a slave and then upon gaining their freedom pursued their trade, often among a group of similarly trained former slaves. Frequently they continued working with their former patron and were able to purchase slaves of their own. Some occupations carried out primarily by women, such as attendant or bedchamber servant, could not be transferred to the public marketplace.

Prostitutes

In his *Satirae* 1.2.48, Horace comments on the ease with which a man bent on sex could satisfy his lust by paying for it with a freedwoman. While not all freedwomen were prostitutes, their status as former slaves, and thus probably sexually exploited, might have made them targets.

> There's safer sex at bargain rates—I'm talking
> About ex-slaves—the sort Sallustius
> Adores as madly as adulterers
> Adore some fellow's wife. Now he could pay
> A reasonable price for sex, in keeping with
> His means, and still be thought quite generous,
> Fair and good. He needn't let libido
> Disgrace and bankrupt him.[31]

For many slaves and freedwomen, and even a few poor freeborn women, physical labor involved selling their bodies as prostitutes. Such "work" was generally accepted in urban areas. Female infants exposed at birth might be raised as slaves and prostituted by their owners. These women served a clientele of slaves, freedmen, and poor freeborn men. These slaves often led a brutal life, so rough in fact that in Hadrian's day (early second century AD) it was an offense to sell a slave into prostitution without good cause. Of course, it might have been next to impossible for the slave girl to show she was unjustly sold into prostitution, but the law at least seems to show an awareness of the torments that might befall a slave prostitute.

Assessing the evidence for prostitutes and prostitution is difficult for several reasons. One important factor is the lack of precision among the sources. A

31. Translation by John Svarlien (http://www.stoa.org/diotima/anthology/horsat1.2.shtml [accessed April 15, 2009]).

A fresco from a Pompeii brothel, first century AD (Photo couresty of Wknight94/Wikimedia Commons)

slave woman providing sexual services might be considered a concubine when she is freed. In the literature, it can be hard to distinguish the idealized lover from a prostitute, at least as far as their behavior is concerned.[32] Images of prostitutes, along with dancers and actresses, in art carry heavy ideological weight. Moreover, prostitutes could be seen as proficient in the art of entertaining and lovemaking. Lumped together with prostitutes as sexually available were entertainers such as dancers, flutists, and castanet players, and particularly perfomers of pantomime who put on bawdy routines. Pantomime was second in popularity only to gladiatorial games. One renowned troupe was sponsored by Ummidia Quadratilla, a wealthy matron who died at the ripe old age of eighty. She had a theater built especially for her players, and they also performed their act in Rome. Pliny the Younger in his epistle to Geminius is concerned that her conduct threatens to tarnish the image of one of his protégés, the grandson of Ummidia Quadratilla.[33] She raised him and willed him two-thirds of her estate, earning Pliny's praise, but he was less enthusiastic about her "work." "She retained a set of pantomimes, whom she encouraged more than becomes a lady of quality. But Quadratus [her grandson] never witnessed their performances, either when she exhibited them in the theatre, or in her own house; nor did she exact his attendance."[34] Because the character of those performing pantomime so closely resembled prostitutes, Pliny was

32. See Natalie Boymel Kampen, *Image and Status: Roman Working Women in Ostia* (Berlin: Mann, 1981), 30n31, for a useful summary of the problem.
33. Pliny the Younger, *Ep.* 7.24.
34. Pliny the Younger, *Ep.* 7.24 (trans. W. Melmoth, LCL).

loathe to praise Quadratilla's troupe; however, her wealth and social status seemed to insulate her from direct condemnation.

Only one known epitaph classifies a woman as involved in prostitution. In this case, a freedwoman, Vibia Chresta, identifies herself as a procuress (female pimp) in a monument she established with her own funds for herself and her family. She claims that she did not defraud others in making her money.[35] Graffiti from tavern walls lewdly declared sexual conquests or adventures. One apparently popular figure was Primigenia, whose name is found on many walls in Pompeii. From the graffiti it seems she was quite lovely, and apparently an excellent lover—at least she seems to be in demand. In a note scratched on a wall in the neighboring town of Herculaneum, a freedman Hermeros of Phoebus asks her to visit him at the bank of Messius on Timinianus Street in nearby Puteoli.[36]

Where did prostitutes ply their trade? Certainly in brothels, but prostitutes also operated from their own homes, around the circus, theater, stadium, or at the baths, and apparently at the tombs and other outdoor locations. Martial speaks about an area in Rome, Subura, that seemed to have many prostitutes.[37] In Pompeii, however, seven out of the nine confirmed prostitutes' dwellings were architecturally attached to larger atrium homes. The entrances to these small cellae were from non-throughway streets, in isolated areas. The entrances were concealed from the grand entrances of the atrium home. Nevertheless the cellae were structurally part of the large atrium home, raising questions about possible relationships between the prostitutes and the homeowner. Were they his (or her) slaves who worked close to his home? Waitresses in taverns probably also served as prostitutes to interested patrons. For example, a man from the country brought his produce to the town market and stayed at the inn; his bill the next day included a "girl."[38]

Prostitutes and the Law

In some cases, prostitutes were protected by the law. In what must have been a harrowing experience, one prostitute, Manilia, refused to see her lover, Hostilius Mancinus, an aedile, one of the highest-ranking politicians in the city. He was probably drunk and did not take no for an answer, but tried to break down the door to her apartment building. She dropped a stone on his head, injuring him. He sued her before the tribunes, but she defended her actions by saying that Mancinus was dressed as though going to a party. The tribunes

35. CIL IX.2029. For a translation, see Lefkowitz and Fant, Women's Life in Greece and Rome, 212–13.
36. For a description and translation of the graffiti, see Joseph Jay Deiss, Herculaneum: Italy's Buried Treasure, rev. ed. (New York: Harper and Row, 1985), 147–48.
37. Martial, Epistulae 1.34; 3.82.
38. CIL IX.2689.

agreed that it was inappropriate for him to enter the apartment wearing a garland, for that made it clear he was not seeing her for official business of the city. They upheld her right to protect her dwelling from unwanted entry.[39] Most prostitutes were not so well connected in society. Nevertheless, indications are that for a lucky few, this work proved quite lucrative, either for the prostitute or for her owner (if she was a slave).[40]

In other cases, the law could work against a woman. During Emperor Tiberius's reign, a matron named Vistilia declared publicly that she was a prostitute to avoid being prosecuted as an adulterer. Tiberius was not amused. Vistilia was relying on an ancient tradition whereby a woman of noble birth could publish her name, confessing her infidelity. The public shame was deemed punishment enough. But in Tiberius's time, further punishment was meted out for adulterers. Not only was Vistilia condemned, but her husband, Titidius Labeo, was called on the carpet to explain why he did not immediately divorce his wife, as prescribed by the new laws. He pleaded that the full sixty days granted him by the law to prove her guilt had not yet elapsed, but his pleas fell on deaf ears. Vistilia was banished to the island of Seriphos.

Prostitutes who earned their living solely with their trade needed to register with the aedile.[41] Apparently each sexual encounter was taxed, which was paid by the prostitute herself, or by her pimp or the brothel owner. It was a money-making operation for many brothel owners, and even Emperor Gaius got involved. Suetonius recounts how Gaius Caligula devised new and punitive taxes: "on the earnings of prostitutes, as much as each received for one embrace; and a clause was added to this chapter of the law, providing that those who had ever been prostitutes or acted as panders should be liable to this public tax, and that even matrimony should not be exempt."[42] Graffiti from Pompeii indicates that a prostitute might earn two to sixteen asses (sixteen asses = one denarius), but the latter might be an exaggerated number.[43]

The Magical Arts and Prostitution

While the connection between magic and prostitution might seem farfetched, in the ancient world both shared common threads: love and women. The prostitute earned her living by courting lovers, and magic was often used to cause

39. The story is found in Aulus Gellius, *Noct. att.* 4.14, written about AD 180.

40. Pomeroy (*Goddesses, Whores, Wives, and Slaves,* 141) cites a tariff inscription from Egypt, ca. AD 90 (*OGIS* II.674), that requires a passport fee of 108 drachmae for a prostitute, but only 20 drachmae for other women. Was this fee indicative of social judgment against immorality, or did it indicate a prostitute's wealth? Perhaps the amount taxed a group rather than an individual.

41. See Tacitus, *Ann.* 2.85; Suetonius, *Tiberius* 35; Ulpian cited in *Digesta Justiniana* 25.7.1.2.

42. Suetonius, *Gaius Caligula* 40 (trans. J. C. Rolfe, LCL).

43. Pomeroy, *Goddesses, Whores, Wives, and Slaves,* 201.

a man or woman to fall in love. The use (or accusation) of magic was wide-spread throughout the Greco-Roman world, and both men and women were charged with applying magical arts. But certain women, especially prostitutes and, ironically, women among the highest echelons of Roman government, were most vulnerable to charges of using magic.[44] Prostitutes were usually accused of manipulating lovers, while charges of treason and treachery were leveled against nobility in addition to the charge of using magical arts.[45] Wives and mothers of senators and emperors played key roles in accusing and being accused of capital offenses done through magic. The varied literary evidence confirms the evidence from amulets and lead tablets, giving a rather coherent picture of what ancients thought about the magical arts.[46] Epigraphic evidence as well suggests that men and women feared magical arts and might explain circumstances as resulting from magic curses. For example, a soldier laments his wife's death with these words: "She [Ennia Fructuosa] did not receive the kind of death she deserved—cursed by spells, she long lay mute so that her life was rather torn from her by violence than given back to nature."[47]

Definition of Magic

Before going any further, a word about what constituted magic is in order. No modern consensus has emerged, but several recent discussions shed light on the issue. The sharp dichotomy between religion and magic, or science and magic, is rejected by most scholars in favor of a more nuanced position. Gender theory exposes the underlying issues of power that prompt accusations of magic. Men appear especially threatened when women perform magic because they thought women were unqualified to handle supernatural forces. It was thought that women were likely to get formulas wrong or gather the wrong items for spells. For example, in Apuleius's entertaining *Metamorphoses* (*The Golden Ass*), he is changed into an ass because his

44. That we know of proportionately more elite women charged with magic could be the result of how evidence was preserved. Most historians wrote almost exclusively about elite movers and shakers. And charges of magic were often leveled against political rivals, whether men or women. Both factors combine to suggest that more elite women than poor women could be accused of using magical arts.

45. Tacitus (*Ann.* 3.10–18; 6.26 [trans. Clifford H. Moore and John Jackson, LCL]) lists a total of thirty-nine women charged before the senate, of whom probably nine were charged with performing magical arts, seventeen were charged with treason, and eight with adultery. The three categories of charges often intermixed. A common theme throughout the cases is rivalry sprung from unregulated relationships, which is characteristic of charges of magic. See Elizabeth Ann Pollard, "Magic Accusations against Women in the Greco-Roman World from the First through the Fifth Centuries C.E." (PhD diss., University of Pennsylvania, 2001), 113.

46. *PGM* IV.296–334 contains a recipe for creating desire in a lover's object of affection.

47. *CIL* VIII.2756 (mid-second century AD). Translation in Ross S. Kraemer, ed., *Women's Religions in the Greco-Roman World: A Sourcebook*, rev. ed. (Oxford: Oxford University Press, 2004), 131 (cited in John G. Gager, ed., *Curse Tablets and Binding Spells from the Ancient World* [Oxford: Oxford University Press, 1992], 246).

lover, a maid in the service of a *maga* (female use of magical arts), used the wrong ointment. Elizabeth Pollard concludes that women took on male social characteristics as they performed magical arts, but because they were ill equipped for such roles, they became dangerous to society as they challenged social norms. "It is precisely a woman's perceived inability to dominate the summoned powers and carry through the penetrative force of some of the spells which renders her an inadequate subject of the ritual and makes her use of *magicae artes* so problematic and reprehensible to ancient contemporary commentators."[48]

Magic is socially deviant behavior, and charges of using magical arts were always negative. But this gets us no closer to what acts were specifically counted as magic. Here motive and intention were essential. Apuleius highlights this in his defense against the charge that he used magic, "a charge with which it is easy to create a prejudice against the accused, but which it is hard to prove."[49] Acts or incantations that twisted or parodied the Greco-Roman ideal of a matron—an obedient woman devoted to husband, children, and home—could be declared magical arts. Of course, prostitutes did not follow the social ideal of matronly behavior. They competed with other women for men, creating a potentially unstable social setting, which sociologists warn is a factor in charges of magic. Any variation in a lover's behavior, such as swapping one girl for another, could raise suspicion that magic was at the root of such change. The poets Tibullus and Propertius both believed that prostitutes could beguile men "by luring the moon from heaven and by performing rites on magical altar-fires."[50] Tibullus himself employs a wise woman/witch (*saga*) to gain the attention of his beloved. He also claims he has been bewitched by another *saga* to draw his affections toward the woman who engaged the *saga*. Propertius believes the prostitute works with herbs and makes the moon do what she wants; he implores her to make his Cynthia fall in love with him.[51] "What Propertius adds to our categories is the connection of prostitution with women's expertise in erotic rituals. Women with magical powers begin to be called *lenae* because of the frequency with which women's *magicae artes* are depicted as being used for erotic binding spells."[52] And yet in these depictions, and others, the prostitutes themselves do not perform magic. Instead, they seek out old women known to have those skills. Interestingly, prostitutes are not described as using magic to prevent pregnancies or procure abortions—problems that many prostitutes faced.

48. Pollard, "Magic Accusations against Women," 27.
49. Apuleius, *Apologia* 2.
50. Propertius, *Elegiae* 1.1.19–24. Translation in Pollard, "Magic Accusations against Women," 46. See also Tibullus, *Carmina* 1.5.41–60; Propertius, *Elegiae* 4.5.1–18.
51. Propertius, *Elegiae* 1.1.19–24.
52. Pollard, "Magic Accusations against Women," 47.

STORIES OF PROSTITUTES AND MAGIC

From the second century AD, Lucian's *Dialogi meretricii* (*Dialogue of the Courtesans*) supports Propertius's and Tibullus's picture of prostitutes and magic. In one story, the prostitute Glycera laments the loss of her soldier lover.[53] She tells her friend, Thais, that the man was lured away by his new lover, Gorgona. The latter's mother, Chrysarium, drugged him with her magic. This woman, who may not be Gorgona's biological mother but probably an older prostitute who took the younger girl under wing, could bring down the moon and fly at night, according to Glycera. Thais reminds Glycera that she pinched the soldier from another prostitute and assures her that she will soon have another steady lover. But Glycera resents Gorgona taking the soldier, and with him the money he gave her.

A similar fate befell Melitta, whose beloved Charinus believed her to be unfaithful and scorned her.[54] Her friend, Bacchis, recommends that she speak with him to straighten out the misunderstanding. But Melitta insists that this situation can only be solved by one of the old Thessalian women who know enchantments. Bacchis recommends one who comes from Syria, who helped her win back a lover. Bacchis goes into great detail about how the old woman created the potion and enacted the spell. The lover will have no choice but to return to Melitta, Bacchis confidently predicts. Moreover, the woman he is with now can be cursed if Melitta wants; all this for a fee of one drachma and a loaf of bread.

Ancient authors assign sexual aggression as characteristic of prostitutes, not proper matrons. But Pollard suggests that all women would be seen as "aggressive" when using spells to lure or keep their love, because the (male-dominated) social world organized sexual behavior into aggressive and passive domains. Perhaps no one more than Juvenal deplores the libidinous predispositions of women with their excessive and foolish activities. He resents women such as the female gladiator, Eppia, who move out of socially prescribed roles.[55] Women gladiators are especially problematic because they wield a sword, a man's weapon. Juvenal connects that type of usurped power with magical arts, citing incantations, poison, and the *hippomanes* as illegitimate weapons used to further women's insatiable lusts. [56]

---

53. Lucian, *Dialogi meretricii* 1. Translation by H. W. Fowler and F. G. Fowler, *The Works of Lucian of Samosata* (1905; repr., Whitefish, MT: Kessinger, 2006), 52–53. Also see Lucian, vol. VII (trans. M. D. Macleod, LCL).

54. Lucian, *Dialogi meretricii* 4.1–4 (trans. M. D. Macleod, LCL).

55. Juvenal, *Sat.* 6.103–14.

56. Many ancient authors refer to the *hippomanes*, a placenta membrane taken from a foal's head after birth. Pliny (*Nat.* 28.49.181–82) argues it could drive a stallion mad, while Virgil, Ovid, Propertius, Tibullus, and Juvenal note its use in love potions. See Pollard, "Magic Accusations against Women," 54n99.

Slavery in Judaism and Christianity

Female Jewish Slaves

What was the lot of a Jewish slave woman? If she was in a gentile house, gone was her freedom to worship God, to rest on the Sabbath, to eat only food prescribed in the law. If her owner was Jewish, she would have as much freedom to follow Jewish law as permitted by her owner. Like their gentile counterparts, these Jewish women were for the most part skilled in household tasks, or perhaps midwifery. Maybe their owner apprenticed them to learn a skill like weaving. Many of these women owned by gentiles were likely captured in war. Few would have been exposed and raised as slaves, if extant evidence is correct that Jews did not expose infants (see chap. 1). In all likelihood, their day-to-day existence would differ little from that of their fellow gentile slaves, including their sexual availability to gentile owners (less certain is the behavior of Jewish owners). Rabbis implicitly acknowledge this in their statements that a female infant slave who was freed by the time she was three years old could grow up and marry as a virgin.[57] They decreed this not because they felt she would not have been sexually handled at such a young age, but because they believed the hymen would grow closed again and she could be physically virginal when she married.[58] A Jew enslaved as a young girl would automatically be labeled a nonvirgin, even if she was one in the physical sense. Slavery presumed sexual activity.

Jewish Male Attitudes and Behaviors toward Female Slaves

In discussing sexuality and relationships, male Jewish authors were primarily interested in determining what constituted a licit marriage in the Jewish context and then promoting those behaviors that fostered their ideal. In general, characteristics would include monogamy between two Jews. The important historical question of how many Jews followed these prescriptions is difficult to determine; as we look at the literature, we are exploring primarily directives, not descriptions. With that important qualification in mind, within Jewish literature, including the rabbinic corpus, Jewish men overall were discouraged from having sex with female slaves.[59] In this, they are distinguished from gentile authors who allow (or advocate) sex with slaves (male and female) as an appropriate sexual outlet. Jewish authors, moreover, do not discuss sex with

57. *m. Ket.* 1:2; 3:1–2; *m. Nid.* 5:4; *b. Nid.* 43a.
58. Judith Romney Wegner, *Chattel or Person? The Status of Women in the Mishnah* (New York: Oxford University Press, 1988), 22–23.
59. For a comprehensive discussion about slavery within Judaism and Christianity within this time period, see Carolyn Osiek and Margaret Y. MacDonald, *A Woman's Place: House Churches in Earliest Christianity*, with Janet H. Tulloch (Minneapolis: Fortress, 2006), 105–17. For a helpful summary of slavery in the rabbinic corpus, see E. Leigh Gibson, *The Jewish Manumission Inscriptions of the Bosporus Kingdom* (Tübingen: Mohr Siebeck, 1999), 83–85.

male slaves, most likely because of the proscriptions against homosexuality that guided their views on sexual conduct.

In the Mishnah, sex with slaves is generally condemned.[60] Yet this begs the question of whether the context involves one's own slaves or that of another person. The specific case of *m. Ker.* 2:1–4 is instructive. In this section, the rabbis are commenting upon Leviticus 19:20–21, although the Mishnah does not cite specifically the biblical criterion that the slave woman is "designated for some other man." Instead, it talks generally about the restriction from having union with a slave woman—no qualification about whether the slave woman is owned by another or not. Since the rabbis do not always spell out everything in the biblical text but assume its presence in their argument, they may be assuming that the slave woman who has sexual union with a Jewish man belongs to someone other than the man in question. The subsequent comment in *m. Ker.* 2:5 may reflect on this qualification ("designated for some other man"), although it too does not use the phrase. Instead, it examines the status of one who has not yet been altogether redeemed, and discusses the status of one who is half bondwoman and half freedwoman. If *m. Ker.* 2:5 imagines the slave woman to belong to another man, then *m. Ker.* 2:1–4 prohibits a Jewish man from having sex with another person's female slave. In this the rabbis are in step with the broader Greco-Roman context.

However, a second interpretation is possible. The passage can be read such that two situations are discussed. In *m. Ker.* 2:2–3, then, the owner has sex with his own slave woman, while in 2:4 the bondwoman is owned by another. The rationale for this interpretation centers on the punishment meted out for behaviors. In the first case, the man is made to offer a single offering irrespective of how many times he has sex with the slave woman. This suggests a scenario where an owner has access to his slave woman and regularly has sex with her. In the second case the woman is punished with forty lashings, suggesting that she is in some sense liable for her misbehavior, which would hardly be the case if she was simply obeying her owner's wishes in engaging in sex.[61]

In a separate conversation in the Tosefta, *t. Hor.* 2:11 discourages taking a former slave as a wife, indeed suggests that a proselyte is better suited. The reason given is that the freedwoman would have been sexually accessible to the (male) owner (and presumably anyone to whom the owner offered her). *Sifra* 9.13 distinguishes between licit and illicit unions (understood as such within the Rabbinic community) in its discussion of whether a father can have

---

60. A word check for "slave-girl" or "the slave girl" or "slave girls" in the Mishnah resulted in thirty-five hits, with the term occurring several times in certain passages: *Eruvin* 5:5; *Yevam.* 2:5 (twice), 8; 7:5; 11:2; 16:7 (twice); *Ket.* 2:9; 3:1, 2, 7; 5:5 (twice); *Sot.* 6:2; *Gittin* 4:5; 7:4; *Qidd.* 2:3; 3:12, 13; *Bava Qamma* 5:4; *Eduyyot* 1:13; 5:6 (twice); *Avot* 2:7; *Zevahim* 5:5; *Bekhorot* 8:1; *Ker.* 1:3; 2:2, 3, 4, 5 (four times).

61. The punishment of forty lashes is in the category of extirpation, or expulsion from the community; see *m. Mak.* 3:15.

sex with his daughter-in-law. Not surprisingly, the rabbis follow the biblical injunction against this practice (Lev. 18:15; 20:12). However, they comment about whether the injunction would stand if the daughter-in-law was a slave woman or a foreigner, and conclude that the latter two categories are not applicable because they could not form a licit marriage with the son.

No further comment is made in the *Sifra* text about the slave woman because she is not relevant to understanding the specific biblical text. But in *m. Ker.* 2:4 (noted above), the discussion distinguishes typical illicit unions from the illicit union with a slave woman. In the former cases, intended violations are punished by extirpation.[62] But in the case of illicit union with a slave woman, the intended violations are dealt with through a guilt offering (which is less severe than extirpation).[63] Moreover, the culpable male is liable for one guilt offering no matter how many violations he commits. We should not conclude from this lighter sentence that the rabbis were uninterested in the Jewish male's sexual union with a slave woman. Rather, the rabbis were most concerned with preventing adultery, and sex with a slave woman was not that. Because the status of a wife is higher than that of a slave woman (which held true in gentile circles as well), the rabbis reflect a stronger punishment for those who sin against people of higher social status. Social rank also plays a role, though not necessarily a defining one, in Sirach, which warns young scribes to avoid any encounters with maidservants (Sir. 41:22). The Hebrew text of this passage identifies the slave woman as belonging to the reader, while the Greek translation (41:24 LXX) alters the pronoun to indicate another person's slave. Thus in the Greek, Sirach cautions a young scribal protégé against entangling himself in the sexual intrigues of a patron's house.[64] Was the translator influenced by the increasingly influential Hellenistic milieu, thus seeking to line up the text with the larger social conventions?

A final quotation should be highlighted. Hillel is credited with equating the number of maidservants with the amount of lewdness in a house.[65] One could understand him to be saying that more female slaves in the house meant more rampant sexual activity between them and their owners. However, in this same passage he remarks, "the more women, the more witchcrafts," and "the more male slaves, the more thievery." His comments reflect a standard negative stereotype against women and slaves. We cannot conclude that he was making a social comment about Jewish men's behaviors toward their female slaves, or about the specific acts of those women. He goes on to promote "the more

62. For most unintended illicit sexual violations a sin offering is required.
63. While the sin and guilt offerings are not definitively distinguished either in the biblical text or among the rabbis, usually the guilt offering presumes and necessitates that restitution is possible.
64. See Osiek and MacDonald, *A Woman's Place*, 106–7.
65. *m. Avot* 2:7.

study of the law, the more life," distinguishing the wise character of a Jewish man who applies himself to learning—the main goal of Hillel's teachings.

An emerging consensus suggests that Jews owned Jewish and/or gentile slaves and that they differed little from their gentile neighbors in their expectations and practices of slavery, with perhaps one caveat.[66] Ben Sira, Philo, and Josephus show a deep reverence for the biblical law, yet a surprising absence of any specific current applications of it in this case. Both Philo and Josephus (and the tannaitic rabbis) show a serious concern for Jews enslaved by gentiles. Could it be that while admiring the law and its potential within their community, they lacked either the will or the wherewithal to implement its requirements?[67] In the rabbinic material, the rabbis are adamant that a slave is a full human being, but the slave's status as property prevents a full realization of that humanity.[68] Slavery was subsumed under the larger category of the household within the Mishnah. The household members were categorized with the free (or freed) adult Jewish male in the defining role and having control over other household members, including women and slaves. It seems, then, that while good intentions perhaps materialized as compassionate treatment of slaves by Jews, no clear distinctions between Jewish and gentile masters can be drawn.

The reasoning behind this tentative conclusion is twofold. First, the institution of slavery was an economic structure that fluctuated based on geography and social situations; the institution did not rest on an ethnic or religious foundation. Second, the rabbinic evidence used to defend Jewish practices as distinct from those of their gentile neighbors might in fact suggest the opposite. It has been argued that Jews treated a Jewish slave differently (better) than they did a gentile slave. However, of the 129 passages that deal with the topic of slavery in the Mishnah, only 6 times are the categories of Hebrew or Canaanite (non-Israelite) slaves used; the other 123 times the Mishnah speaks of bondmen and freedmen.[69] In the 6 passages that distinguish between Jew and non-Jewish slave, the Mishnah is directly following the language of the biblical injunctions to illustrate legal principles, such as a slave's identification with his master, which cannot be shown using the category of bondman.[70] In the other 123 cases, when the rabbis are perhaps reflecting their own setting,

66. Dale Martin writes that the "slave structures of Jews in Palestine were not discernibly different from the slave structures of other provincials in the eastern Mediterranean" ("Slavery and the Ancient Jewish Family," in *The Jewish Family in Antiquity*, ed. Shaye J. D. Cohen, BJS 289 [Atlanta: Scholars Press, 1993], 127).

67. Gibson, *Jewish Manumission Inscriptions*, 93: "Thus, it seems that biblical law on slavery continued to be respected among some Jews but were [sic] not implemented."

68. Paul Virgil McCracken Flesher writes, "Sages do not portray him [a slave] as a sub-human 'monster,' that is, as something lacking the full rudiments of humanity" (*Oxen, Women, or Citizens? Slaves in the System of the Mishnah*, BJS 143 [Atlanta: Scholars Press, 1988], 37), a view that he contrasts with Aristotle's in *Pol.* 1.5–6.

69. Flesher, *Oxen, Women, or Citizens?* 35–36.

70. Flesher, *Oxen, Women, or Citizens?* 58–59.

they use the categories of bondman and freedman, consistent with the wider culture.[71] This meant that some Jews gained their freedom and were thus freedmen and freedwomen, and that some Jews, as former owners, enjoyed the praise of their freed men and women.[72]

Interestingly, both Josephus and Philo praise the Essenes for refusing to have slaves; by pointing to this divergent practice, they imply that the average Jew might in fact own slaves. Josephus lists a number of Jewish elite, including the high priest, who own slaves. Josephus states that the Essenes rejected slavery because it created injustice.[73] In a discussion about punishment for thieves, Josephus rails against a law put in place by Herod the Great, which sold the Jewish man into slavery and deported him. Josephus said this was too harsh because the living situation would cause them to compromise their religion.[74] In this same discussion, he notes that Jewish slaves are to be sold to Jews, not gentiles, because the Jewish law requires that a Jewish slave be free after six years of service. Because he is contrasting the uprightness of the Jewish people against the contempt for tradition that Herod the Great exhibited in his behavior, it is possible that Josephus is speaking here less as a historian and more as an apologist. Philo, a wealthy man, sees domestic servants as indispensable, "for the course of life contains a vast number of circumstances which demand the ministrations of slaves."[75] Philo wants Jews to own gentile slaves, so as not to burden someone from one's own ethnic background. And he suggests that Jews who own Jewish slaves should treat them as hirelings, not as slaves. Like Josephus, Philo cites the biblical injunction to free a Jewish slave after six years of service, but historians are unclear whether this rule was followed, and whether it was applied to women. If rabbinic sensibilities prevailed in a community, the woman would be unable to marry, which might put her at a financial or at least social disadvantage. But outside of rabbinic communities, things might be different.

Sexuality and Slavery in the New Testament

In the early second century AD, Pliny the Younger, governor of Bithynia, wrote to Emperor Trajan with a problem.[76] He wants to know what to do about

---

71. Martin writes, "We have no evidence—from inscriptions, papyri, or other texts—that this two-tiered slave structure [alleged by the Mishnah] ever actually existed outside the textual world of the rabbinic sources themselves, which are notoriously problematic for historical reconstruction of first century Palestine" ("Slavery and the Ancient Jewish Family," 116).

72. Martin, "Slavery and the Ancient Jewish Family," 113. Acts 6:9 speaks of a synagogue of freedmen in Jerusalem that spoke in opposition to the teachings of Stephen; assuming it is similar to other synagogues, freedwomen also participated in this assembly.

73. Josephus, *Ant.* 18.21.

74. Josephus, *Ant.* 16.1.

75. Philo, *Spec.* 2.123. Translation in Gibson, *Jewish Manumission Inscriptions*, 75.

76. Pliny the Younger, *Ep.* 10.96–97.

Christians: does he kill all accused of the crime, or allow them to recant? As part of his investigation, he interrogated two female deacons of the church who were also slaves. Following protocol, they were first tortured and then questioned. He says that he found no new information from them, but confirmed through their words that the Christian sect held depraved superstitions. Pliny's letter confirms what we find in the New Testament, that the church included slaves, perhaps a sizable percentage. And yet the sexual availability of female slaves (and male slaves) is not addressed. From the household codes in Colossians, as well as in 1 Peter and Ephesians, slaves are enjoined to obey their masters. In the Greco-Roman context, that would include accepting sexual advances and working as a prostitute.

Two questions immediately surface. First, did the New Testament authors share the Greco-Roman assumptions that labeled sex with one's slaves as "value neutral"? Second, is the slave morally culpable for sexual acts done in obedience to their owner's request? Neither question is answered directly and explicitly by the sources, while issues of authorship and provenance muddy the waters further. But we might find hints of Paul's opinions from other texts that address the issue indirectly. Specifically, 1 Thessalonians 4:3–6 and 1 Corinthians 5:1–7:40 might offer insight into at least some early communities' wrestling with issues of slavery and sexual immorality (*porneia*).

1 Thessalonians 4

In 1 Thessalonians, Paul charges his male readers to avoid sexual immorality by each "obtaining their own vessel." Both the verb and the noun are difficult to interpret, but it is clear (though modern translations skate over this) that Paul is concerned with men's sexual behavior, especially as it impacts wronging their brothers in the church. Interpreters generally assume Paul is arguing for men to marry, though the verb usually does not mean "to marry." Others argue that the verb should be interpreted as "control," while "vessel" should be understood as a euphemism for male genitals. In this case, Paul is urging the men to refrain from inappropriate sexual behavior, defined by most commentators as any activity outside of marriage. Because he does not state that explicitly, and because the gentile Thessalonians would not consider sex with slaves as inappropriate, some argue that Paul is recommending sex with one's slaves to avoid sex with another member's wife or other inappropriate behavior.[77]

This last suggestion falters in its foundational assumption that Paul accepted the gentile view of sexuality. The theory assumes Paul would consider an owner's intercourse with his slave from the lens of the institution of slavery, and thus as acceptable as asking the slave to cook a meal. But I suggest that Paul would view sexual actions through the lens of biblical restrictions, irrespective of whether the partner was a slave. Again, while a gentile male

---

77. Glancy, *Slavery in Early Christianity*, 62–63.

would seem to see nothing immoral about sex with his slave, it might also be presumptuous to assume that the Thessalonian Christians are unfamiliar with Jewish sensibilities. It does not appear, therefore, that 1 Thessalonians 4:3–6 encourages men to use their female slaves as sexual outlets.

1 Corinthians 5

A different matter is raised by Paul's discussion in 1 Corinthians 5 and the man with his father's wife. The man's activity is polluting the entire community, which must be purged of the contamination. Here a new concept is introduced, that of pollution. In this case, the church's acceptance of the man's behavior has created the pollution, and the remedy is for the church to denounce it and remove the offender lest by continual association others would be encouraged to act similarly. Why was the woman not expelled? Arguments from silence are always problematic. One might suggest that she was not a church member, and so was outside the community already. Another possibility is that she was a slave or freedwoman who had no authority to refuse the man's advances.[78] If the latter is the case, was she a church member? To answer yes is to assume that Paul did not hold her accountable as sinning because she had no way to refuse. In answering no, one is suggesting that Paul viewed a slave's participation in the owner's wishes as sexual immorality that banished them from the Christian community.[79]

The issue revolves in part around the concepts of pollution and sin. Does Paul consider a slave owner's sex with his female slave morally neutral? Though I do not think so, the advantage of this conclusion is that slaves who experience their owners' advances are not considered to have committed *porneia* or sexual immorality. However, the same conclusion can be reached if one assumes that for Paul *porneia* is the result of a decision (to sin). The pollution that comes from that act is erased or made clean through repentance. The second model fits better with Paul's overall understanding of the gospel message.

1 Corinthians 6

How could this idea be applied to 1 Corinthians 6:12–20? The prostitute is not the object of attention, but the man who purchased her services is. He is culpable because he sought out *porneia*, or an unacceptable sexual act (according to Paul). What can we assume about the prostitute? Most were slaves or freedwomen who still had to do their former owners' bidding. If we assume the woman was a member of the congregation, she was to be permanently banned from the church community (until she ceased her prostitution) because she was polluted, or she was not held liable for her actions because the real culprit was the owner who ordered her immoral (in Paul's mind) behavior. In this latter

---

78. Antoinette Clark Wire, *The Corinthian Women Prophets: A Reconstruction through Paul's Rhetoric* (1990; repr., Eugene, OR: Wipf and Stock, 2003), 74.

79. Glancy, *Slavery in Early Christianity*, 63–70.

case, Paul was not viewing the situation through the lens of pollution, but of sin, when determining the appropriateness of her participation in the church community. When Paul talks about sexual behavior, he speaks to those who have choices and who at times (such as the man in 1 Cor. 6) make the wrong choice. Those who have no choice, such as a believer who is married to an unbeliever, are not polluted or held liable for sinning when engaged in sex with someone outside the church (1 Cor. 7:14–16). The marriage relationship, even with a nonbeliever, keeps the believer pure and holy. I think the same line of thinking is applicable to those women (and presumably men) who were forced by their owners to have sex. So while prostitution in itself is unacceptable, those who are compelled to participate are not liable. Again, while intercourse outside marriage is unacceptable, slaves (male and female) are not pushed out of the church if they tolerate their owner's advances, as they are legally bound to do.

Conclusion

The reader might wonder why prostitution was discussed in a chapter on slavery. The primary reason for this placement is that the institution of slavery and the practice of prostitution were tightly interwoven within the fabric of the Greco-Roman world. They were often inextricably linked together, as seen in the imagination of social commentators such as first-century AD Dio Chrysostom, who presents the prostitute (*meretrix*) as also a slave, the two categories blurring into one. Dio's comment highlights the complexity of the issues, especially in discerning the definition of prostitution itself. The sexual economy of prostitution combined both the very personal (the sexual act) and the very public (economic activity). Prostitution was part of the trade and industry of a town or city, but the merchandise sold was that of a personal, intimate nature. The society accepted sexual activity with a prostitute as a legitimate male prerogative, thereby providing a steady stream of clients from which slave owners could profit. The sentiment expressed by Horace is revealing: he represents Cato the Elder as applauding with a "well done" the man who assuaged his lust with a prostitute (rather than with his wife).[80] Clearly the female prostitute was a social fixture.

The question of agency lurks in the background, as well as the asymmetrical relationship between humans that is implied in the sexual act conducted for money. Indeed it is precisely money that distinguishes prostitutes from mistresses or adulterous wives—though the latter two no doubt usually enjoyed gifts from their lovers. The mistress was defined completely by her sexuality because of the assumed choice made in forming a relationship with a certain man. Yet for the most part prostitutes had little say in the sexual encounter,

80. Horace, *Satirae* 1.2.31–32. Horace wrote in the first century BC.

for most prostitutes were slaves or were pimped by men who had legal control over them, such as fathers or husbands. Thus they were viewed primarily as economic tools used for profit by owners, human tools in the same sense as slaves. Said another way, in most cases, prostitution was one way that a slave's labor was capitalized upon by owners.[81]

No one romanticized the hard life of a prostitute slave. Nor do the ancient sources idealize the life of a slave in general. A chilling reminder is found on a fourth- or fifth-century AD human collar, inscribed by a Christian man about his slave: "I am the slave of the archdeacon Felix. Hold me so that I do not flee."[82] Jews, gentiles, and Christians owned slaves, and each community sought ways to control the excesses of the institution. Most accepted the institution of slavery, although a few ancient voices condemned it or at least its abuses. While no one doubts the harsh treatment endured by not a few slaves—the verbal and physical punishment and abuse meted out regularly—historians differ in how to weigh the evidence. Some suggest that slavery allowed for upward mobility in that freed slaves often rose in the social order. One need look no further than the imperial slaves and freed men and women to see evidence of this. Yet others note that slavery was a dismal life for most slaves, primarily because their position was so precarious, dependent upon the whims of their owners. Both angles are true insofar as they explain aspects of the evidence. But I suggest that we not allow the former reading to silence the latter—because while a few slaves might be fortunate enough to have decent owners or make strategic social advancements, clearly most were not that lucky.

Household slaves were generally integrated into the family to the extent that they interacted with them on a daily basis. Slaves could "marry" and have children, but those offspring were the owner's property. An owner might free his slave to take her as his concubine or give her to his son. Often slaves were born into a family, but others were foundlings, or were made slaves by being prisoners of war. A foundling might be raised to serve within the house or as a prostitute who worked from a brothel. An adult taken as a slave through war or piracy might be integrated into a family if she had a particular skill, such as midwifery. She might be trained to watch children or tend to her mistress. She might serve as a wet nurse in the family. Slave women worked alongside their male counterparts in all manner of activities. Slaves were ubiquitous in public places, such as the market, and participated (at times with restrictions) in religious festivals. Like male slaves, women could earn their freedom; however, because women were generally less skilled than male slaves, their earning potential was likewise decreased. This is not to say that no freedwoman was wealthy, only that

81. For a careful discussion of the issues, see Rebecca Flemming, "Quae Corpore Quaestum Facit: The Sexual Economy of Female Prostitution in the Roman Empire," *JRS* 89 (1999): 38–61.

82. For a discussion and translation, see Glancy, *Slavery in Early Christianity*, 9 and 158n1.

the number was far less than the number of wealthy freedmen. Upward mobility was a dream not universally realized, for either men or women slaves.

In the end, slave women were bound to another person and viewed as less than human, with few rights. Dio Chrysostom commented on the blindness of his age to the humanity of slaves. In a dialogue between a free man and a slave, the former looks down on the latter because of his slave status. The slave retorts that owners obtain slaves by three means—(1) inheritance or purchase, (2) slave women giving birth to slave children, and (3) prisoners of war. No one questioned the first two methods of enslavement, but for Dio, these were predicated on the third means. It is the last method that is actually the initial means of making slaves. And for Dio it is the most revealing, for it shows that by tracing ancestry back far enough, one would see that all men were free, until an illegitimate act of war condemned them to slavery. One born to a slave does have in his or her ancestry a free parent, and thus should not be condemned. "So we see that this earliest method, upon which all others depend, is exceedingly vulnerable and has no validity at all."[83] Dio Chrysostom's argument that undercuts the assumptions of difference between slave and free would have to wait centuries before society was ready to accept its wisdom.

In the highly stratified Greco-Roman world, status was everything; by that definition female slaves often had nothing. At the other end of the spectrum, wealthy patrons commanded respect and admiration from those they helped. In the following and final chapter, we explore the world of patronage—an institution that created numerous opportunities for women to receive honor and influence society.

---

83. Dio Chrysostom, *De servitude et libertate ii* (*Oratoria* 15) 26. For translation and discussion, see Glancy, *Slavery in Early Christianity*, 74.

9

Benefactors and the Institution of Patronage

As with any complex culture, the world of the Hellenistic period and the early Roman Empire offers mixed signals in its evidence of women's participation within the society. For example, wives are to be silent, yet they have a voice in religious festivals. Women should stay at home and spin wool, but many women are busy earning a living in the marketplace. Plutarch enjoins the wife to be seen only with her husband,[1] but numerous statues of women praise their public deeds with no mention of any man, husband, father, son, or brother. How do we reconcile such diverse images?

An essential institution, patronage, offers a key to unlocking this puzzle. Patronage, or public and private benefaction, grew and flourished at this time. This informal social code, enforced not by law but by the strength of social custom, drew its power from the honor/shame culture that permeated daily life in the Mediterranean world. In a spider's web of contacts between faithful clients and beneficent patrons, the wealthy expanded their influence by giving private donations and offering public benefaction, and with this blurred the lines between private home matters and the city's public, political realm.

The overlaying and interweaving of public and private in the institution of benefaction cannot be overemphasized in terms of women's history. During the classical Greek period, a sharp contrast was drawn between benefaction, such as building a temple or hosting a religious festival, and the public offices of magistrates who governed the city. But slowly in the Hellenistic period, and more quickly in the Roman Republic and Empire, public donations to

1. Plutarch, *Mor.* 139c (= *Conj. praec.* 9).

the city were described in familial language. Donors were called the father or mother of the city. Women who donated a gymnasium were described as chaste, honorable—language used by husbands when eulogizing their wives. The language of the home, in other words, controlled the expressions of public benefaction. Moreover, the positions of authority, such as magistrates, were given to those who provided needed services for the city, such as aqueducts or fountains. Benefactors expected (or were expected) to make good political and economic decisions on behalf of the city, for they had poured much of their own funds, and their own honorable reputations, into the city.

Furthermore, we must not forget the great social changes that resulted from Rome's success against Hannibal and the social upheavals caused by the mid-first-century BC civil wars. The constant turmoil shook the foundations of elite society. Women controlled their family's wealth as never before, with fathers, sons, and brothers off to war, exiled, or dead. But it was not simply that they had money; they also had the means to influence public policy with the evolving social system called *euergetism* (public benefaction). Seneca, the first-century AD Stoic philosopher, declared that patronage "constitutes the chief bond of human society."[2] The institution was based on reciprocity, the give and take between two people or groups. Often the term favor or grace (*charis*) was used to describe patronage, drawing on the three Graces, sisters who danced in a circle holding hands. Seneca explains that they dance thus because "a benefit passing in its course from hand to hand returns nevertheless to the giver; the beauty of the whole is destroyed if the course is anywhere broken, and it has most beauty if it is continuous and maintains an uninterrupted succession."[3]

Women Speaking before the Roman Senate

Patronage grew in unsettled times as Rome shifted from city-state to empire, and from a republic to imperial governance. For women, it seemed also to rise from the ashes of an amazing century of women's activity within the Roman courts. In the late second and first centuries BC, amidst the political and social convulsions that shook Rome, several women spoke to the senate or in the courts. The beginning of this era started with the repeal of the Oppian Law in 195 BC.[4] In what is probably the "most striking manifestation of women's power in the whole of Roman history," this demonstration opened a way for

2. Seneca, *De beneficiis* 1.4.2 (trans. J. W. Basore, LCL).
3. Seneca, *De beneficiis* 1.3.3–4 (trans. J. W. Basore, LCL).
4. This law enacted in 215 BC restricted women's finery in public and thus their abilities to highlight their wealth and family's honor. After 201 BC, with Hannibal's defeat, Roman men once again began to wear purple and display their wealth, but the Oppian Law prevented noble women from the same. The mass demonstration by elite Roman matrons before the senate was unprecedented. See Livy, *Hist.* 34.1–7.

individual women to defend themselves in court.[5] For example, Sempronia, the daughter of Cornelia and sister to the Gracchi brothers, at the beginning of the first century BC, gave testimony in the forum against a man, L. Equitius, who claimed to be the adopted son of her deceased brother Tiberius Gracchus. Her evidence, which Valerius Maximus notes was given honorably in keeping with her great family, convinced the jury.[6] About the same time, Fannia of Minturnae was divorced by C. Titinius. He kept the dowry, alleging that she was an adulterer. She defended herself in court, noting that he was fully aware of her past, and the judge agreed that he likely married her only to get his hands on the dowry.[7] As a third example, Hortensia spoke against the 42 BC plan of the triumvirs (Octavian, Antony, and Lepidus) to tax the fourteen hundred wealthiest women in Rome. In her famous speech to the triumvirs, she notes that in the past Roman women have been more than happy to donate their jewelry and finery to Rome for its wars against external enemies. But in this case, the issue is civil war, which Hortensia declares unworthy of the matrons' support. Moreover, the triumvirs are taxing dowry and property, with the result that the status of these women would sharply decrease.[8] Her speech persuades the leaders; even more important for our purposes, it was remembered as superior rhetoric.

About this same time, Cicero praises Laelia, daughter of politician and lawyer C. Laelius, for *elegantia*, or speaking with a lawyer's precision, which she likely learned from her father, who taught her the intricacies of Roman law. She was married to W. Mucius Scaevola. He was from a well-known family of lawyers and was Cicero's instructor in law. Cicero says that he was greatly impressed when he heard Laelia speak. Probably Cicero lived in their house, as was the custom of students, and so would have opportunities to converse with her.[9] Her father nominated her husband as augur even though he was the younger of the sons-in-law because he wanted to honor Laelia, who in his opinion deserved the job.[10] The college of augurs combined the role of priest, divining portends, with Roman law and politics; thus a politically astute and flexible legal mind was necessary for the office.

Though a scattering of women were praised for their eloquence and rhetorical abilities, in the end the senate and male pundits were unwilling to open the courts for women lawyers and orators. The defining moment was the career of Afrania, who at the turn of the eras prosecuted numerous cases, and whose

5. Richard A. Bauman, *Women and Politics in Ancient Rome* (New York: Routledge, 1992), 31.
6. Valerius Maximus, *Fact. dict. mem.* 3.8.6. He wrote during Tiberius's rule, early first century AD.
7. Valerius Maximus, *Fact. dict. mem.* 8.2.3. See Bauman, *Women and Politics*, 49–50.
8. Her speech is preserved by Appian, *Bella civilia* 4.32–33, composed in the second century AD. See also Valerius Maximus, *Fact. dict. mem.* 8.3.
9. Cicero, *De amicitia* 1.
10. Cicero, *Brutus* 101.

presence in the courts was finally rejected as immodest and unsuitable for the sex.[11] However unfortunate this turn of events might seem, the evidence of elite, educated women participating in the courts suggests that some families were educating their daughters and promoting rhetorical skills. Though one avenue of influence closed in the first century BC, a second opened—that of benefaction. In this new scenario, women continued to be politically influential and often were well educated. However, because the larger context of benefaction was nonlegal and rooted in the image of the *domus* (home), women were not seen as tramping on men's territories when they acted as benefactors.

Characteristics of Patronage

Patronage and the Courts

The patronage system was not grounded in law and the courts; however, the forces that undergirded patronage could be stronger and more rigid than any written law. Said another way, the power of patronage is found in the difference between knowing a law and knowing the judge who will enforce the law. Patronage meant that people with friends in high places got the limited resources available in the Greco-Roman world. The emperor's wife could be vastly more powerful than a senior senator, even though she could not vote or propose legislation, because she was on better terms with the supreme benefactor. Margaret Y. MacDonald makes a useful distinction between power and authority: the former gains acquiescence by others, while the latter is understood to be right or legitimate. Women in the Greco-Roman world had power even if they could not be a general or the emperor. They may have had supreme influence in running the empire or senate if they had power over a man who could make a decree or cast the vote. Livia, Augustus's wife, was a woman reputed to have as much power as her husband due to her influence with him. As MacDonald notes, "the female patron may be best understood as exercising power through the sphere of patronage with its network of clients and obligations."[12]

Patronage and the Honor/Shame Culture

Benefaction greased the wheels of the economy, so that any woman in business was also a part of the patronage system. Since Roman matrons were

11. Ulpian, a third-century AD Roman jurist, wrote that her conduct was unbefitting a woman, and the magistrates thereby restricted all women from representing another person in court, for that was a male function (cited in *Digesta Justiniana* 3.1.1.5). See also Valerius Maximus, *Fact. dict. mem.* 8.3. For a useful discussion of the evidence, see Bauman, *Women and Politics*, 45–52.

12. Margaret Y. MacDonald, *Early Christian Women and Pagan Opinion: The Power of the Hysterical Woman* (Cambridge: Cambridge University Press, 1996), 43.

present at banquets, they had informal access to the city's key players (both male and female) at every level. If patronage oiled the social wheels, then the honor/shame culture served as the engine that moved society along. Honor/shame mores should be contrasted with those of the Western culture of today. In the latter context, a person internalizes the values used to make a decision. In the former setting, a person looks to the wider society to evaluate whether particular conduct is becoming or suitable. While in the West we celebrate a person's independence and disdain for public opinion, such disregard for the opinion of one's social network would be unfathomable to the ancients. A person was held in honor because of the family's honor, or because of personal actions. For men honor was achieved by brave deeds, while for women honor was given for moral chasteness. In both cases, honor was received because the individual acted for the good of the society. The soldier was brave and protected the city; the wife was faithful and kept the family secure. Though there were differences in the sort of actions that brought honor for men and women, it was also possible for women to be praised for their (manly) courage, and men for their loyalty. The gendered differences in determining honor within the Greco-Roman culture are less important than a person's social status and wealth when looking at the patronage system.

Patronage and Friendship

Though repeatedly couched in the language of friendship, the patron/client relationship was almost always asymmetrical.[13] A patron might give a client money, food, an introduction to an important person, or advice. The client might reside in the patron's home. The patron might offer a low-interest loan to start a business or help the client find a spouse. The client was indebted to praise the patron publicly, for example, in the public greeting (*salutatio*) of the patron offered each morning at the patron's home. Often the client would praise the patron at the baths or as the patron traveled through the city. Patrons were expected to continue to support their clients, and clients were to remain loyal and provide whatever services the patron might require. A story about Herod the Great provides an interesting twist on the importance of loyalty in patronage. Herod sided with Marc Antony against Octavian, remaining loyal to his friend to the bitter end. After Antony's defeat, in a bold move he came before Octavian, now called Caesar Augustus. He did not hide his friendship with Antony; rather he promoted his loyalty to Antony as a virtue and pledged the same fierce devotion to Augustus. Luckily for Herod, Caesar accepted his pledge of fidelity.[14]

---

13. Thus true friends were *amici* while clients (*clientes*) were *amici minores* (Pliny, *Ep.* 2.6.2), *amici pauperes* (Pliny, *Ep.* 9.30), or *amici inferiores* (Seneca, *Ad Lucilium* 94.14).

14. Josephus, *Ant.* 15.6.6–7 (183); *B.J.* 1.20.1–2 (387).

Patronage, the Priesthood, and the Polis

Benefaction also happened at the city level: the local wealthy patron supported the city with public buildings, festivals, famine relief, or other benefactions. The people of the city were not each indebted to the patron individually; rather the community as a whole needed to praise the benefactor publicly with a statue, an inscription, special seats at games, or a ceremony offering a crown of gold or of olive branches. Elaborate tombs proclaimed the continuing glory of a deceased benefactor. Patrons did not necessarily live in the city they benefited; some wealthy patrons were citizens of several cities and made donations of temples or baths or funds for festivals in each of the cities.

Frequently benefaction was linked with the priesthood. During the Roman Republic, priests were often members of the senate; thus the priesthood was seen as a subclass of the magistracy. Upon taking office, the priest was to give a benefaction acknowledging his honored position. This "voluntary" payment (called a *summa honoraria*) usually took the form of a great feast lasting a few days, given mainly to his peers, thus reinforcing their elite status. In what has been called the "civic compromise," the aristocracy of Rome gradually absorbed the religious functions and offices of the ancient Roman king, and "at the end of a long political evolution, the 'civic compromise' produced its logical culmination, the Roman emperor."[15] With the rise of the Principate, the emperors used the priestly office to demonstrate their benefaction by giving these offices to their supporters, thus closely tying the priesthood with the political fortunes of the empire. The feast previously given by the new priest in appreciation of the honor bestowed upon him was changed under the emperors to a payment given to the emperor. For example, Gaius Caligula, in AD 40, inducted his wife and Claudius (who would be emperor after Gaius's death) into a newly established cult honoring Gaius as Jupiter Latiaris. Claudius could not pay the entire amount required and so put some of his property up for sale.[16] In this way, the *summa honoraria* became interwoven with imperial euergetism.

Not only in Rome, but throughout the empire, this pattern connecting wealth, beneficence, religion, and public office was repeated. For example, in Asia Minor at the turn of the eras, a certain Cleanax, son of Sarapion, proved to be a generous patron of the city of Cyme. An extant stele records that each new year (probably Augustus's birthday, September 23), Cleanax funded a huge festival with numerous sacrifices, giving wine, food, and entertainment to all the people of the city—citizen, noncitizen, and foreigner alike. He sponsored other festivals throughout the year as well. In doing so, Cleanax had the opportunity to demonstrate his generosity as well as his superiority

15. Richard Gordon, "From Republic to Principate: Priesthood, Religion and Ideology," in *Pagan Priests: Religion and Power in the Ancient World*, ed. Mary Beard and John North (Ithaca, NY: Cornell University Press, 1990), 197.

16. See Suetonius, *Divus Claudius* 9.2.

on the social scale. Religious benefaction was deemed selfless, for it was done for the benefit of the people; however, the gifts also served to increase political influence and capital. Euergetism makes possible a great display of wealth, without seeming to be self-serving. Cleanax's magnificent parties done on behalf of the gods were viewed as promoting self-restraint and so were above reproach. However, Richard Gordon perceptively notes, "duty is the most delicious disguise of self-interest."[17]

Though occurring a few centuries later during the time of Septimius Severus and Caracalla, a similar benefactor presented gifts to her town of Sillyon in Pamphylia. Menodora, daughter of a wealthy landowner, Megacles, was the public priestess of Demeter, the priestess for life for the city gods, and held the public offices of *dekaprotos*, *demiourgos*, and *gymnasiarch*. Like Cleanax, her priesthoods and civic offices are mixed together in the list, suggesting that people saw little distinction between them. Her benefactions were very similar to those of Cleanax: she gave money and corn to all the people and provided three hundred thousand drachmae in aid to children and orphans. But a closer look reveals that like all public benefaction, a prime motivation was the reinforcement of the social hierarchy and pursuit of honor. Her funds were not dispersed equally to all: a city councilor received eighty-six drachmae, while a citizen received nine drachmae, and a serf, three drachmae. The civic priesthood therefore blended euergetism with the propitiation of the deities to reinforce the current social order.

The grandest patron was the emperor himself. Nicolas of Damascus writes, "All people address him [as Augustus] in accordance with their estimation of his honor, revering him with temples and sacrifices across islands and continents, organized in cities and provinces, matching the greatness of his virtue and repaying his benefactions towards them."[18] Because Augustus's gift of peace was so impressive, his "clients" had to offer suitable responses, which included lauding him as divine. By doing so, they showed their loyalty, a key factor of the patronage system. If Augustus was the first great patron of the empire, his wife Livia was not far behind. By examining her benefactions we can trace the development of benefaction and note the political influence and social power it offered wealthy women.

Greco-Roman Gentile Women Benefactors

Empress Livia

Livia was the second wife of Caesar Augustus (he divorced his first wife, Scribonia, at the birth of their daughter, Julia). They married in 38 BC and

17. Richard Gordon, "The Veil of Power: Emperors, Sacrificers and Benefactors," in Beard and North, *Pagan Priests*, 230.
18. Nicolaus of Damascus, *FGH* 90 F 125. Translation in Simon R. F. Price, *Rituals and Power: The Roman Imperial Cult in Asia Minor* (Cambridge: Cambridge University Press, 1984), 1.

remained married until Augustus's death fifty-two years later. Livia survived until she was eighty-six years old, dying in the year AD 29. As with many public figures of the past, reliable historical information about Livia is scant, while rumors and innuendos abound. But all indications are that she was a leading benefactor; her vast personal wealth, coupled with her influence by way of her status as the emperor's wife, afforded her tremendous power throughout her life. Cassius Dio writes that in response to a question about her influence with Augustus, Livia answered that she was chaste herself, did whatever would please Augustus, stayed out of his affairs of state, and ignored his numerous dalliances.[19] Whether she said anything of the sort is unknowable, but it seems that at least one of these claims is not supported by her actions. She did indeed involve herself in the empire's affairs—as a benefactor. Cassius Dio writes of her generosity in giving dowries to certain senators' daughters, raising some of the senators' children, and even saving the lives of a few senators. She advanced the future Emperor Galba's career, naming him in her will,[20] and she brought up another future emperor's grandfather in her house; it was due to her influence that he had a place in the senate.[21] She was the chief priest of Augustus's cult[22] and was responsible to organize the annual games in his memory.[23] Because at Augustus's death she was the widow of a god, she was called the mother of the world (*genetrix orbis*) in the Roman provinces.

After Augustus's death, she had much influence over her son Tiberius. Cassius Dio notes that letters from him also included her name, at least at the beginning of his reign; furthermore, people writing to Tiberius included her name as well. She received members of the senate at her house, although she did not go to the senate, the military camps, or the public assemblies. But Cassius Dio declares that "she undertook to manage everything as if she were sole ruler."[24] In appreciation, the senate voted to make an arch in her honor, a tribute never before bestowed upon a woman. Sadly, it was never built because Tiberius, her son and emperor, resolved to take control of the project and then let it quietly go by the wayside. Livia was also to be called the mother of the country, *mater matria*, paralleling Augustus's *pater patriae*, but this honor had to wait until after Tiberius's death. Perhaps Tiberius was cautious about appearing to promote a dynasty, or perhaps he resented her favor in the eyes of so many; he did not attend her at her last illness, nor was he present at her

19. Cassius Dio, *Hist. Rom.* 58.2.
20. Suetonius, *Galba* 5.
21. Suetonius, *Otho* 1.
22. Cassius Dio, *Hist. Rom.* 56.46.1.
23. Tacitus, *Ann.* 1.73; Cassius Dio, *Hist. Rom.* 56.46.3.
24. Cassius Dio, *Hist. Rom.* 57.12. Translation in Roy Bowen Ward, "The Public Priestesses of Pompeii," in *The Early Church in Its Context: Essays in Honor of Everett Ferguson*, ed. Abraham J. Malherbe, Frederick W. Norris, and James W. Thompson, Supplements to Novum Testamentum 90 (Leiden: Brill, 1998), 325.

The monument Ara Pacis Augustae, south frieze, shows Livia, center, and her son Tiberius to her left. This monument celebrated Augustus's return from Gaul and Spain as well as the foundation of the imperial family with Livia a central figure as the mother of the future emperor. (Photo courtesy of Joe Geranio, Julio Claudian Iconograhic Association)

funeral. It fell to Emperor Claudius to deify Livia (his grandmother), who was then known as Diva Julia (based on Augustus's will, she was adopted into the Julian family, and was given the title Julia Augusta).[25] A cult celebrating her grew up in the Roman Empire.

Jews honored Livia as well. For example, she was a beneficiary in the wills of both Herod the Great and his sister.[26] Josephus tells the story of Livia's personal counsel to Salome to marry the man her father chose for her, Alexas. Livia (called Julia by Josephus) encouraged Salome in this direction for the latter's own advantage.[27] Philo, in his *Legatio ad Gaium*, offers high praise to the emperor's grandmother. He notes that Julia Augusta gave the Jerusalem

25. Interestingly, with the rise of the Principate, Roman women took on two names. During the Republic, a woman was known by her father's name (*nomen*), with a feminine ending. If the father was Julius, the daughter would be Julia. In imperial Rome, a woman gained a *cognomen*, such as Julia Agrippina or Julia Druscilla. See Bauman, *Women and Politics*, 7, who comments tongue in cheek that for this shift, "modern investigators are truly grateful."

26. For example, Yavneh was state land under Herod the Great, who willed it to his sister Salome, who in turn willed it to Livia, and so it became a holding of the imperial family (Josephus, *Ant.* 18.6; *B.J.* 2.9.1). See also Shimon Applebaum, "Josephus and the Economic Causes of the Jewish War," in *Josephus, the Bible and History*, ed. L. H. Feldman and G. Hata (Leiden: Brill, 1989), 259n11.

27. Josephus, *Ant.* 17.1.1.

temple gifts of golden vials and censers and many other costly items—and did all this with the realization that she would not be honored with a statue, as was the wider Roman custom. Philo commends her great wisdom, for she appreciated that which can be comprehended only by the intellect, not through the senses.[28]

Yet Livia's beneficence could also be portrayed as meddlesome and unwomanly. Tacitus depicted her as a ruthless, revengeful stepmother,[29] so that even when she did something kind, such as help her stepdaughter's daughter in exile, Tacitus is stinting in his praise. Moreover, he follows the common literary topos of disgruntled emperor and grasping empress or emperor's mother. Tacitus notes that Tiberius did not return to Rome for her funeral; the same sort of struggle is also described between Nero and his mother.[30] Suetonius cites a rather implausible reason for the family tension between Livia and Tiberius. Apparently, she asked him to grant a citizen the privilege of being on the jury lists. Such requests were commonplace and within the bounds of propriety; numerous inscriptions attest to the practice. Tiberius, however, was belligerent, saying he would only sign the form if it said he was doing so under orders from his mother. "Livia's power of patronage, a source of affection and regard for the empress, is thereby transformed into a sinister example of female presumption and an explanation for the emperor's withdrawal from the capital."[31]

The double-edged sword of public praise and condemnation struck both men and women in the imperial family, as well as the upper-crust elite senators. But the potential for misunderstanding and even vilification did not deter most people from participating in the patronage system. Indeed, one could not help but be a part of it, for society expected the wealthy to give and the clients or "friends" to receive and offer praise. Livia's example was copied by women throughout the Roman Empire. A few examples are worth noting as they highlight important aspects of patronage, including the public buildings as well as the personal influence promoted by the institution, especially as the system relates to women. The first examples come from Pompeii, a city whose tragic end, buried beneath the ashes of Vesuvius, became a blessing to archaeologists and historians.

Eumachia

At the time of Augustus, a woman named Eumachia was honored by the fullers of Pompeii with a statue and dedicatory base. The inscription reads:

28. Philo, *Legatio ad Gaium* 319–20.
29. Tacitus, *Ann.* 1.6.
30. Suzanne Dixon, *Reading Roman Women: Sources, Genres, and Real Life* (London: Duckworth, 2001), 111.
31. Dixon, *Reading Roman Women*, 111.

"To Eumachia, daughter of Lucius, public priestess, the fullers [dedicated this statue]."[32] Her benefaction to this important guild that worked in one of the leading industries of the city is noteworthy on several counts. The fullers were a powerful and important industry throughout the Mediterranean world and especially in Pompeii due to that region's sheep and wool business. In Pompeii, it seems that the fullers also had a hand in selling the final product, though that would not be the case in all cities. The fullers represented a very profitable business for the owner, and a source of tax revenue for the city. The trade guild had a monopoly on the clothing industry. It was also apparently an exclusively male guild, although there is at least one reference in the papyri to a female fuller.[33]

Eumachia's gift to the powerful guild highlighted her influence in the city. Her contribution included building a *chalcidicum* or vestibule serving as a statuary area, as well as a *crypta* or covered passageway, all with her own funds. The substantial building donated by Eumachia was located in the forum and was dedicated by Eumachia and her son to Concordia and to Pietas Augusta with an inscription written in large letters above the entrance.[34] In this way, she indicated her deep commitment to the reign of Augustus and his

Statue erected in honor of the fullers' patron Eumachia (Photo courtesy of Bianca Morganti and Daniel Lopes/flickr.com)

family. Such dedications were common during the period 7 BC to AD 12, promoted by Livia and her son Tiberius (soon to be emperor himself). For example, the Porticus Liviae in Rome was dedicated by Livia and Tiberius in

---

32. *CIL* X.813. Translation in Mary R. Lefkowitz and Maureen B. Fant, *Women's Life in Greece and Rome: A Source Book in Translation*, 3rd ed. (Baltimore: Johns Hopkins University Press, 2005), 159.

33. See chapter 7. As noted in that chapter, history does not always record for posterity the business activities of women. It would not be unwarranted, then, to suggest that women could and did participate in the fuller trade.

34. *CIL* X.811. The building has been dated to the reign of either Augustus or Tiberius.

7 BC to Concordia Augustus. Not coincidentally, Eumachia's building shares many architectural features with the Roman original.[35]

Empress Livia's well-known habits of benefaction fit the existing pattern of euergetism, even as they expanded it; Eumachia followed Livia's lead, which bolstered her prestige in Pompeii and linked her with the most powerful woman in the empire. Eumachia demonstrated her benefaction in several additional ways. For example, she built the largest extant tomb in Pompeii, which includes the inscription "Eumachia, daughter of Lucius, [built this] for herself and for her household."[36] She was married at one time to M. Numistrius Fronto, a *duovir* in AD 2/3 who probably died during his term.[37] No evidence suggests that she remarried, though Augustan law would have mandated she remarry unless she was over fifty, and perhaps she was, or possibly she received an exemption. Eumachia was influential apart from her husband or son. She used her wealth, gained through her father's brick-making business and a prestigious marriage, to promote her public honor in socially condoned ways, through service to the city as manifested through her euergetism.

What might an average day be like for Eumachia? Clients would greet her at the morning *salutatio*, praising her generous spirit and asking what tasks they might perform for her that day. Probably she owned her home (*domus*), likely a grand edifice, for Pompeii followed the style set in Rome of ostentatious self-promotion. Her house might take up most of a city block, but it would include small shops that paid rent to her. All day, her front door would stay open, while in the atrium (the first room one enters) slaves and clients mingled, along with her wealthy friends, for Romans did not differentiate sharply between public work areas and private space.

Mamia and Metrodora

Eumachia was not unique in Pompeii (or in the Roman Empire). Ten other women in this city were honored with the title *sacerdos publica*. This was an exalted position and linked the women with the public welfare of the city. According to Cassius Dio, the *sacerdotes* were elected by the people in public assemblies;[38] this practice goes back at least to the beginning of the Principate, in 27 BC.[39] From this we see the important public presence represented in this religious office. Their male counterparts who were priests of Augustus often

35. James L. Franklin, *Pompeis Difficile Est: Studies in the Political Life of Imperial Pompeii* (Ann Arbor: University of Michigan Press, 2001), 33, 41.

36. Translation in Lefkowitz and Fant, *Women's Life in Greece and Rome*, 160. There is some question as to whether Eumachia was buried in this tomb; see David W. J. Gill, "Acts and the Urban Élites," in *The Book of Acts in Its First Century Setting*, vol. 2, *Graeco-Roman Setting*, ed. David W. J. Gill and Conrad Gempf (Grand Rapids: Eerdmans, 1994), 116n72.

37. *CIL* X.892.

38. Cassius Dio, *Hist. Rom.* 37.1.

39. Ward, "Public Priestesses of Pompeii," 320.

held magisterial positions such as *duovir* and *aedilis*, the priesthood being a natural course to the higher public offices. There is no record of a female *duovir* or *aedilis*; however, a certain public priestess named Mamia, who built a temple to the genius of Augustus (probably with Augustus's permission) on her own property in the forum of Pompeii, was given a place of burial by decree of the decurions.[40] The latter group consisted of the local senate or municipal authorities who often gave such honors to magistrates. The tomb next to hers was for an Aulus Veius, who was *duovir* twice and *duovir quinquennalis* once. Like Mamia, he was buried at that spot by decree of the decurions.[41] We can only speculate whether Mamia, who was so highly honored at her death, held a magistracy position. Some historians suggest that women like Mamia and Eumachia had no political power because women could not vote. But by the time of the Principate, voting was less important because power was solidifying into the hands of a few. Popular assemblies lost power to those who were closest to the emperor. Clearly Eumachia and Mamia, priestesses in the Augustan cult, fit the profile of the prominent, influential citizen. Many inscriptions from Pompeii honor women with no mention of a husband, or mention first the woman's name and then her son's name. This suggests that women were not riding their husband's coattails to power or merely promoting their son's welfare.

In Asia Minor, there are more examples of the same behavior—women benefactors contributing to their cities and being honored for their services. Metrodora of Chios, an island just off the coast near Ephesus, was likely a Roman citizen as well as a citizen of Chios and lived during Nero's time. She was praised as a patron in part for building a large bath complex. She held important offices such as lifetime priestess of Aphrodite Livia, gymnasiarch (four times), and *stephanēphoros*, the highest-ranking city magistrate, who was honored by wearing a crown while in office. She was also distinguished in an inscription found in Ephesus; she spent large amounts of money on festivals and oil for the city games.[42]

The point to take away from these biographies is that women were present in public spaces. Statues of women abounded in the most prominent places in the city forum. Inscriptions praised their benefaction. Women served in the city magistracy. Clients publicly honored their works. In short, women of means in the ancient world had public influence and power, but not simply because they were wealthy. It was through the vehicle of euergetism—which allowed money to be lavished extravagantly on public works and programs but simultaneously was viewed as benefaction done with self-restraint—that women gained such

40. See *CIL* X.998.
41. *CIL* X.996.
42. For a detailed description, see R. A. Kearsley, "Women in Public Life in the Roman East: Iunia Theodora, Claudia Metrodora and Phoebe, Benefactress of Paul," *Tyndale Bulletin* 50.2 (1999): 189–211.

prominence. Euergetism extended the *domus* into the public, political sphere. Through its means, women could participate in the economic and political pulse of the city while remaining, in the eyes of the public, suitably modest matrons.

Jewish Women Benefactors and Gentile Women Benefactors to Jews

Everyone in the Mediterranean world participated to one degree or another in the patronage system. People depended upon their friends and family to open doors, provide start-up funds for a business, make introductions, smooth out conflicts—in short, to make life easier and more profitable. A network of relationships connected people, based on their family, their city of origin, their commercial interests, and their ties with those in political power. It is not surprising, then, that gentiles and Jews supported each other through the patronage system.

Julia Severa

One of the most well-known benefactors to a Jewish community is Julia Severa. Her specific connection to the community, however, is debated—was she Jewish, or put differently, would she have identified herself as Jewish? Was she a gentile sympathizer? Or was she uninterested in the religious claims of the synagogue and primarily concerned with advancing her honor by benefiting the local Jewish community?

The facts are minimal and open to interpretation: Julia Severa is named in connection with a building that, at the time of the inscription, was being used as a synagogue.[43] (The building is called an *oikos* or "house," which can refer to a synagogue.[44]) Three men are named as renovating the building, and the inscription's purpose is to describe their gifts. The benefactors are given a gold shield and the public honor of the inscription. The probable date of this inscription is sometime during the 80s or 90s AD, and most likely the building was constructed in the 50s or 60s.[45]

The vagueness, from our vantage point, of Julia Severa's relationship to the Jewish community has given rise to a number of theories. A minority argue that she was herself Jewish. However, another inscription notes that she was a high priestess of the local imperial cult during Nero's reign, and coins mark that she and her husband, Lucius Servenius Capito, were either archons (rulers)

---

43. *CIJ* 766; see also *MAMA* VI.264.

44. For the view that it may be a gentile association, see Stephen G. Wilson, *Leaving the Fold: Apostates and Defectors in Antiquity* (Minneapolis: Fortress, 2004), 62.

45. Paul R. Trebilco, *Jewish Communities in Asia Minor*, SNTSMS 69 (Cambridge: Cambridge University Press, 1991), 59.

or priests of the imperial cult, making it unlikely that she was Jewish. Others suggest that she was not connected in any way with the synagogue and that the inscription merely indicates that a certain building built by Julia Severa was currently in use by the Jews. But then why mention her name at all? Or why not make explicit in the inscription that "her" building had been sold or given to the Jews? At its most basic reading, the inscription suggests that Julia Severa at some point in the past had given this building to the Jewish community.

This invites a further question, namely whether Julia Severa was in some way a member of the Jewish community. Most likely she was not a Jewish proselyte, given her title as high priestess of the imperial cult in Acmonia. Nor need we speculate that she was an apostate Jew who nonetheless donated a building to the Jewish community.[46] Perhaps she was a God-fearer who desired to show her sympathies with the Jewish religion through a generous gift. We know that a number of gentiles in the Greco-Roman world found the synagogue inviting. But she may not have been interested in forming an attachment to the community other than one of patronage. Her gift of the building would have elevated her prestige within the city, adding to her already important civic role as *agōnothetēs* or leader of the city games. The few decades that likely passed until this inscription was made suggest that her beneficence continued to be appreciated by the Jewish community. This is not surprising since her name, and her husband's and son's names, continued to carry much weight. For example, her son was a member of the senate during Nero's reign and served in AD 73 as *legatus* to the proconsul of Asia. The Jewish community had a worthy "friend" and ally in Julia Severa.[47]

Tation

A similar magnanimous gesture was made a century or two later by Tation of Phocaea (a Greek colony in Ionia), the daughter of Straton, who donated a building (*oikos*) and courtyard to the Jews out of her own funds. The inscription indicates that she was honored by the community of Jews with a golden crown and a front seat or *proedria*, reserved for elders and patrons. As Tessa Rajak notes, "Crowns, shields, and front seats were . . . part of the basic cur-

46. The suggestion that Jews in Asia Minor were typically religiously lax and syncretistic is not, in my opinion, tenable. On Julia Severa as a Jewish descendent of Herod the Great, and also syncretistic, see F. F. Bruce, *The Epistles to the Colossians, to Philemon, and to the Ephesians*, New International Commentary on the New Testament (Grand Rapids: Eerdmans, 1984), 12–13.

47. Further possible evidence that Julia Severa is a gentile benefactor uninterested in the specific religious claims of the Jewish community is the possibility that one of the male donors commemorated in the inscription, Tyrronius Klados, was also a gentile pagan. Rajak and Noy argue that his title "*archisynagōgos* for life" is an honorary one, given in appreciation of his social benefaction. See Tessa Rajak and David Noy, "Archisynagogoi: Office, Title and Social Status in the Greco-Roman Synagogue," *JRS* 83 (1993): 75–93.

rency of so-called 'euergetism,' that reciprocal system of honors in exchange for benefactions which kept Greco-Roman cities going."[48] Her donation of a building to the Jews might be understood as an example of a gentile patron bestowing a generous gift to the Jewish community. But the rewards of her actions, namely having a front seat in the synagogue, suggest to some that she is a God-fearer or a Jew, for why would a pagan wish to be present at the festivals and Sabbath services of the synagogue?

In the end, it is impossible to determine which alternative is most accurate. Sadly, our knowledge about the ways Jews and gentiles might have interacted in a given city at a particular moment is very limited because the available evidence lacks the sort of depth required to draw a robust picture of such interface. But we can speculate. If Tation was a pagan, it is likely that the synagogue felt pleased with her presence, for her clout in the city lent to their community a particular status, which if nothing else protected the members from potential anti-Jewish sentiments. If she was a God-fearer, her position of privilege within the congregation might signal more than symbolic honor, giving her a voice among the others seated in the front. Since the Jewish community did not meet only for religious observances, it is entirely possible that as their patron, Tation was invited to a front seat during those meetings that had direct bearing on the Jewish community's relationship with the wider gentile population. Finally, if she was Jewish, this is an example of a Jewish woman placed in a highly significant role, sharing rewards generally given to leaders within the community. Specific duties related to her front seat are unspecified, but we should not rule out active leadership within the Jewish community, given the other leadership titles connected with Jewish women at this time (see chap. 6).

Fulvia and Helena, Queen of Adiabene

Josephus describes the interests of Fulvia a Roman woman, who embraced Judaism and was eager to benefit the temple (see chap. 5). She was swindled by four unscrupulous Jews who absconded with her temple donations. Josephus is ashamed that any Jew would act in such a despicable way, but his story reveals that gentile women proselytes might be inclined to benefit the Jerusalem temple.[49] Helena, Queen of Adiabene (a petty kingdom in northern Mesopotamia), converted to Judaism and decided to make a pilgrimage to Jerusalem. Once there, having been made aware of the plight of those hit by the severe famine, she provided food to the needy. Using her own resources, she sent her servants to Egypt to buy corn and to Cyprus for figs to distribute

48. Tessa Rajak, "The Synagogue within the Greco-Roman City," in *Jews, Christians, and Polytheists in the Ancient Synagogue: Cultural Interaction during the Greco-Roman Period*, ed. Steven Fine (New York: Routledge, 1999), 164.
49. Josephus, *Ant.* 18.81.

in Jerusalem. Pausanius notes that she built a magnificent tomb in Jerusalem.[50] The actions of both Fulvia and Helena are best understood within the institution of patronage. While in general the ancient authors had nothing but praise for benefaction and patronage, some prominent Jewish authors critiqued aspects of the system. Josephus, who speaks favorably about certain gentile patrons of the Jews, as well as Jewish worthies, decries in general the pride encouraged by the awards of silver and gold or crowns of olive branches.[51] He is quick to note that Jews do not make statues of the emperor (or any patron or ruler), nor do they put on elaborate funerals or erect fancy monuments in their honor.[52] Philo of Alexandria expresses dismay at the pride (*typhos*) that was so evident to him throughout the cities—including the golden crowns and purple robes extended to patrons. He suggests that Moses gave the law in the wilderness to avoid such conceit.[53] Jewish inscriptions confirm that most often Jewish patrons to the synagogue were remembered with inscriptions noting their titles, and perhaps a gold shield or a front seat in the synagogue.[54] It may be that in many cases, the community did not have the money to put up elaborate monuments, but it is also likely that the prohibition against statues and idolatry made Jews cautious when appropriating typical forms of public praise.

Women Benefactors in the Christian Community

Benefaction and patronage were essential to ancient society; gifts of buildings, money, food, and political or economic influence were expected and relied upon by the populace, whose personal and corporate duties required that they publicly honor their benefactors. This institution functioned within and between the gentile and Jewish communities. As we will see, the Christian community was no exception; both the Gospels and the Epistles yield evidence of women benefactors aiding the early church.

Phoebe and Julia Theodora

Phoebe is perhaps today the best known benefactor in the earliest Christian communities, based on Paul's commendation in Romans 16:1–2. She is noted as a deacon of the church of Cenchreae, the eastern port of Corinth on the Aegean Sea. More important is Paul's description of her as a *prostatis* of the

50. Pausanius, *Graeciae descriptio* 8.16.4–5.
51. Josephus, *C. Ap.* 2.217–18.
52. Josephus, *C. Ap.* 2.74, 205.
53. Philo, *De decalogo* 1.4–7.
54. Tessa Rajak, "Benefactors in the Greco-Roman Diaspora," in *Geschichte–Tradition–Reflexion: Festschrift für Martin Hengel zum 70*, ed. H. Cancik, H. Lichtenberger, and P. Schäfer (Tübingen: Mohr Siebeck, 1996), 1:312.

community and also of himself. The Greek term is best translated "patron" or "benefactor" based on epigraphic evidence. What is Paul implying in using this term, especially in relation to himself? To answer this question, it will be useful to draw on a contemporary inscription from Corinth that uses a related term to describe a local benefactor.

Julia Theodora was honored with five separate decrees in the mid-first century AD in Corinth. A stele records all five announcements, although likely they were not given at the same time.[55] The recipients of Theodora's largess hailed from her home area, Lycia in Asia Minor. Specific cities of Myra,[56] Telmessos, and Patara, as well as the federal assembly of the Lycians, sent their praise and appreciation in response to her generosity. They thanked her for her hospitality when she entertained traveling Lycians in her home, both private citizens and ambassadors. The decrees declare that not only was Theodora greatly to be praised, but the Lycians will also send a gold crown, to be used at her funeral when she enters into the presence of the gods. They also dispatched five minas[57] of saffron (a locally grown, valuable spice) for her burial and promised a portrait to be done with a gilt background.

JULIA THEODORA'S POLITICAL INFLUENCE

Julia Theodora provided political influence that aided some Lycian exiles in gaining the "friendship" of the Roman authorities.[58] The reason for their exile might be that in AD 43, Claudius incorporated Lycia as a Roman province, and things did not go smoothly for all involved. Julia Theodora may have intervened with Rome to mediate some disputes. It is also possible that the letters and announcements of her benefaction relate to AD 57 when the Lycian council charged a Roman ex-governor with extortion. They lost the case (though it is entirely possible that the governor was guilty), and those making the charges were exiled. Theodora might have interceded at this point. Whatever the specific circumstances that created the Lycians' need for benefaction, they praised her for her hospitality and mediating skills.

Unlike other benefactors noted above who built baths or donated oil for city games or hosted festivals, Theodora used her personal and political connections to benefit her countrymen in both political and economic ways. She is praised as being Roman, which likely means that she held Roman citizenship.[59] She was also a citizen of Corinth, as well as probably a city in Lycia.[60] It was not uncommon for wealthy people to hold citizenships in several cities.

55. *SEG* XVIII.143. For a helpful discussion of Julia Theodora, including the Greek and English translation of the stele, see Kearsley, "Women in Public Life," 191–98, 203–4.

56. Myra is mentioned in Acts 27:5.

57. One mina is about 500 grams.

58. *SEG* XVIII.143.52.

59. *SEG* XVIII.143.13, 22, 63, 67, 72.

60. *SEG* XVIII.143.17.

Citizenship would give Theodora added prestige and influence. She possibly traveled to Rome to intercede on behalf of the Lycians, as the term "authorities" (*hēgemones*) could refer to the Roman senate and perhaps a former governor of Corinth now residing in Rome.[61] But it is also possible that these Roman authorities are in Corinth; the term is frustratingly general. Perhaps Julia Theodora negotiated with them on behalf of her Lycian countrymen for commercial and political access to the city, especially its ports. Perhaps she met with Roman governors on their way to cities in the Lycian Federation, attempting to present the Lycian people in the best possible light.

Interestingly, no husband or son is mentioned in the decrees, which suggests that her influence and wealth were her own. Her heir, Sextus Julius, is also praised in the decrees, in part for imitating her devotion to the Lycians.[62] I will suggest below that Phoebe was also presented as a model for the Roman church to imitate.

Julia Theodora's Actions as Prostasia

Most important for this discussion, Julia Theodora is praised as the Lycians' *prostasia*, a cognate of the term used by Paul to describe Phoebe, *prostatis*.[63] The immediate context praises Julia Theodora for her hospitality and generous spirit supplying everything needed by the Lycian travelers and citizens. It seems plausible that Paul uses the cognate term with a similar intent: he praises Phoebe for the aid given to other Christians, perhaps with a specific eye to that help required of travelers. Paul was in need of homes to stay in during his ministry journeys, and his team as well as others likely sought the protection and security of resident sympathizers in each city they visited. The descriptor "benefactor" implies some wealth or influence, suggesting that Phoebe had a home large enough and wealth great enough to care for guests. Even more, as was the case with Julia Theodora, Phoebe likely had the social clout to help local and visiting Christians with any commercial, political, or social needs. For example, Paul worked while in Corinth. Did Phoebe introduce him to the leaders of the particular trade guilds important to Paul's job? Did she defuse any turmoil concerning his work or his religious claims? Did she know the governor, Gallio, or a member of his entourage, thereby smoothing out Paul's stay (or other Christians' experiences in Corinth)? Unfortunately we lack information to answer these questions. But Julia Theodora's example suggests that we could answer yes to any or all of the above.

---

61. *SEG* XVIII.143.5, 52. See Bruce W. Winter, *Roman Wives, Roman Widows: The Appearance of New Women and the Pauline Communities* (Grand Rapids: Eerdmans, 2003), 189–90.
62. *SEG* XVIII.143.55–56.
63. *SEG* XVIII.143.77; Rom. 16:2.

PHOEBE AS SISTER

What are the implications of Paul speaking of receiving benefits from Phoebe? Paul identifies Phoebe in three ways and in this order: as a sister (in Christ), as a deacon, and as a benefactor (Rom. 16:1–2). First and foremost, then, Phoebe is a member of the Christian community. She is "family" and thus has a special relationship with all other Christians. Her responsibilities to her family would include helping practically and financially as she is able. We saw above that wealthy patrons would build funeral monuments for their households, they would make loans to help freed slaves start a business, and they might serve as matchmakers or make political or commercial introductions to aide a family member. As a sister in the household of God, Phoebe would be expected to use her resources to better the lives of her brothers and sisters.

PHOEBE AS DEACON

Second on Paul's list, Phoebe is a deacon in the church of Cenchreae. This title has been hotly debated as to whether the office holder carried authority in the early church, and if so, how much. That argument seems to have grabbed onto the wrong end of the stick, imputing the characteristics of later church offices back into the first century. Instead, a careful examination of the *diakonia* word group suggests a sense of representation or agency.[64] That is, in calling Phoebe a deacon, Paul was identifying her as his agent or intermediary carrying his gospel message, or most specifically, his letter to the Romans. Paul asks the Romans to welcome or receive her in the Lord, using a verb commonly employed in diplomatic correspondence for receiving a messenger.[65] Paul speaks of himself in a similar vein a few verses earlier (Rom. 15:25, 31), referring to his "ministry" or *diakonia* to Jerusalem. He describes his assignment as an agent ensuring that the gifts from his churches make it safely to the saints in Judea. Again, to the Corinthians, he notes that both he and Apollos are *diakonoi*; they carry God's message and mediate God's word (1 Cor. 3:5).

A few other examples will help fill out the picture of Paul's meaning in referring to Phoebe as *diakonos*. When praising Stephanas and his household in 1 Corinthians 16:15–17, Paul describes them as devoted to the *diakonia* of the saints, here stressing their function as Paul's liaison with the Corinthian church, as well as perhaps their financial and organizational help in pulling

---

64. Carolyn Osiek and Margaret Y. MacDonald, *A Woman's Place: House Churches in Earliest Christianity*, with Janet H. Tulloch (Minneapolis: Fortress, 2006), 215. See Walter Bauer, Frederick W. Danker, F. W. Arndt, F. W. Gingrich, *A Greek-English Lexicon of the New Testament and Other Early Christian Literature*, 3rd ed. (Chicago: University of Chicago Press, 2000), 230: "service rendered in an intermediary capacity, mediation, assignment."

65. Margaret M. Mitchell, "New Testament Envoys in the Context of Greco-Roman Diplomatic and Epistolary Conventions: The Example of Timothy and Titus," *JBL* 111 (1992): 647. The verb in question is *prosdechomai*.

together the deputation that traveled to Ephesus and refreshed Paul's spirit. Similarly, Paul identifies Epaphras as a faithful *diakonos* (Col. 1:7), while in Colossians 1:23 Paul identifies himself as *diakonos*; in both instances the term suggests a bearer of a message—in this case, the gospel. When writing to Philemon (1:13), Paul uses the verbal form to describe his wish that Onesimus would serve as his *diakonos* "in the bonds of the gospel." This implies that Paul refers to Onesimus's function as going out for him in the interests of the gospel. Paul acted on behalf of the Macedonian churches in carrying their gift to Jerusalem; so too Onesimus would have the authority of Paul in promoting the gospel. Less likely is the sense that Paul was asking that Onesimus be his personal aide tending to his needs in prison. Tychicus as well is described as a faithful *diakonos* (Col. 4:7; see also Eph. 6:21). Not only does he take Paul's letter to the Colossian church, but he is also instructed to tell them (and the Ephesians) how Paul is doing and to encourage the churches. He acts as Paul's emissary, even as do Timothy and Erastus in Acts 19:22—all acted in Paul's name and with his authority.[66] In the case of Phoebe, then, Paul is likely stressing her role as go-between for the Corinthian churches and the Roman congregation, as well as her specific duty to carry Paul's letter, with his authority. She might also have business in Rome on behalf of her community in Cenchreae; Paul's note is too cryptic to draw any conclusions on this particular matter.

PHOEBE THE *PROSTATIS*

Third, Paul speaks of Phoebe as a *prostatis* or benefactor. She has benefited both the saints and Paul himself. The help she offered is not specified, but based on the praise given Phoebe's contemporary, Julia Theodora, the help could include hospitality in the fullest sense, such as housing and running interference for any social or political trouble generated by the gospel message proclaimed by Paul. If she is Paul's benefactor, that makes Paul her client. But he is recommending her to the Romans, which sounds as though he is her patron. Perhaps if we include in the equation the recipients of the letter—the Roman church—an answer to the dilemma emerges. In Romans 1:11–12 Paul is politely ambivalent about his role in relation to the Roman church. He speaks of giving them a spiritual gift, and thus positions himself as a benefactor, but then immediately qualifies himself as also wanting to receive from them a gift: their encouragement in the faith. In this Paul embraces the key aspect of patronage—reciprocity.

66. See John N. Collins, *Diakonia: Re-interpreting the Ancient Sources* (Oxford: Oxford University Press, 1990). The non-Christian use of the word group confirms that the root idea is that of a "go-between." "The words do not necessarily involve the idea of 'humble activity' at all, and never express the idea of being 'at the service of' one's fellow man. . . . The words do not speak of benefit either to the person authorizing the action or to the recipient of the action but of an action done in the name of another" (194).

If we look closely at his statement about Phoebe with this point in mind, we could argue that the Roman church is the patron in this exchange, and both Phoebe and Paul are "clients." In this sense, then, Paul is saluting another client, Phoebe, to his patron. He applauds her as a worthy client for the Roman church to take on, for she acted in a praiseworthy manner in her own context of Cenchreae. It is not clear that Paul is asking the Romans to offer her financial assistance. Paul may simply be requesting that they welcome her and facilitate her business in the city.[67] By lauding her, Paul is reciprocating her gift of aid (unspecified by Paul). A patron such as Phoebe could expect not only loyalty but even financial backing on occasion if the client had the means.[68] In promoting her, Paul raises his status as well—to be known by an important person is to be important yourself. Paul increases the status of the Roman church in portraying them as having two clients—a gracious move as he introduces himself to them. Finally, by divulging to the Roman church that he embraces the role of client, Paul opens the way for the Romans to become his patron for his journey to Spain.

PHOEBE, PATRONAGE, AND THE RECOMMENDATION LETTER

Another aspect of patronage comes into play here, that of the recommendation letter. Paul, in recommending Phoebe to the Romans, draws upon the customs and traditions of friendship in his day. In modern terms, friendship implies the association of equals, but in the ancient world, friendship, like patronage, usually involved a greater and lesser partner.[69] Status consciousness was ubiquitous within Roman society, extending into the realm of friendship. We should not assume, then, that in this recommendation Paul would be identifying Phoebe as his buddy. Specifically, he is telling the Romans that Phoebe is worthy of their attention because he can vouch for her character. Unlike today, when a recommendation usually addresses objective markers such as work habits or education, in Paul's time, the recommendation was based primarily on the person's character as evaluated by the recommender. The latter asked the recipient of the recommendation letter to trust his or her judgment.[70] A key test of anyone's friendship is their loyalty. Paul, in benefiting

---

67. We need not conclude with Efrain Agosto that Paul was asking for material support for Phoebe, and thus he must be using the term *prostatis* figuratively ("Patronage and Commendation, Imperial and Anti-imperial," in *Paul and the Roman Imperial Order*, ed. Richard A. Horsley [Harrisburg: Trinity Press International, 2004], 121).

68. Carolyn Osiek, "*Diakonos* and *Prostatis*: Women's Patronage in Early Christianity," *Hervormde Teologiese Studies* 61.1–2 (2005): 349.

69. For a critical examination of friendship in Paul's letter to the Philippians, see Joseph A. Marchal, "With Friends Like These . . . : A Feminist Rhetorical Reconsideration of Scholarship and the Letter to the Philippians," *JSNT* 29.1 (2006): 77–106.

70. Richard P. Saller, *Personal Patronage under the Early Empire* (Cambridge: Cambridge University Press, 1982), 109.

from Phoebe's patronage, was himself showing his loyalty to her by recommending her to one of his patrons, the Roman church. Paul commends Phoebe's actions so that the Roman church might act similarly toward her. She is not to be their benefactor, even as Paul is not their benefactor. Rather, the goal is reciprocity. This is not to downplay the important role that Phoebe played in Paul's ministry as his benefactor. Indeed, he asks the Romans in a rather oblique way to consider sponsoring him in his journey to Spain (Rom. 15:24). Rather, the sharp edge of the patronage system was blunted by Paul's vision that God is the ultimate Patron, and all Christians are his clients. Thus to place himself in the socially inferior role of client to the Romans is not threatening, for he is also on a mission from God, which counterbalances the social equation. So too with Phoebe—her benefaction does imply her socially superior status. But her role as emissary (deacon) for Paul and the church at Cenchreae mitigates the harshness of that asymmetrical relationship.

Lydia

Phoebe is not alone as an influential woman in Paul's churches. In Luke's presentation of Paul's ministries, both named and unnamed women serve as Paul's benefactors. For example, Lydia from Thyatira is a God-fearer (Acts 16:14) who joins the fledgling group after hearing Paul's preaching and welcomes Paul and his entourage into her home in Philippi (Acts 16:12–40).[71] She is known as a dealer of purple cloth, a business that generally earned a good living. Lydia, then, might be a well-born and prosperous commercial trader; the fact that she had a home large enough to accommodate Paul and his group, as well as the finances to care for their needs, suggests she was wealthy. Lydia's status as Paul's benefactor would make a leadership role in the church likely.

Not far from Lydia's home city of Thyatira, due north in the city of Aphrodisias was found a stele or pilaster with an inscription preserved on two sides listing men who had benefited the synagogue.[72] Almost half of the men are labeled *theosebeis* or God-fearers. A few were members of the group of ten that established this work and financed most of it, while others were *bouleutai*, holding an important office in the city's administration, one that required the holder to have extensive property, hold citizenship in the city, and participate in the public cults. Also among the men was a dealer in purple cloth, the same

---

71. For an extensive discussion of Lydia and God-fearers, see chapter 5.

72. Joyce Reynolds and Robert Tannenbaum, *Jews and God-Fearers at Aphrodisias: Greek Inscriptions with Commentary*, Proceedings of the Cambridge Philological Society, supplement 12 (Cambridge: Cambridge Philological Society, 1987). The inscriptions are generally dated to the late second or early third century AD, although some push the date for face *a* of the inscription into the fifth century AD.

commercial enterprise in which Lydia was involved. The Aphrodisias inscription supports the literary evidence that at least some wealthy gentiles gave gifts to the synagogue and were publicly recognized for their generosity. We cannot know whether some or all of the men noted on the inscription were attracted to Judaism, or whether their beneficence was guided by more social or political concerns. However, Lydia's benefaction of Paul and his group fits the picture sketched throughout the Roman Empire of gentiles' interest in the religious aspects of Judaism and synagogue life.

Elite Women Benefiting the Christian Community

Luke mentions elite female converts as well in Thessalonica, Beroea, and Athens (Acts 17:1–34). It may be that some of these women were kindly disposed to the synagogue, and the negative reaction by other Jews reflected frustration over the loss of a valued social ally. Highlighting the positive response by leading women is one way Luke presents the gospel message as respectable, or at least less threatening to the empire.[73]

Luke's interest in upper-class women's connections with the new sect and with the established synagogue is found as well in the works of Josephus.[74] The latter describes how aristocratic women attached to the imperial house interceded for Jews. Though he does suggest that a few of these women were Jewish sympathizers, it is clear that some functioned primarily as benefactors, especially using their political influence on behalf of the Jews. We have already noted the interest the Empress Livia took in Salome, Herod's granddaughter. Berenice, the mother of Agrippa I, was regarded highly by Antonia, the grandmother of Caligula, who lent money to Agrippa[75] and was instrumental in releasing him from prison when Caligula came to power.[76] The wife of Nero, Poppaea Sabina, used her influence to help liberate priests (including Josephus) taken to Rome in chains in AD 64. Interestingly, earlier she sided with the Jewish aristocracy against the procurator Festus (AD 60–62) and King Agrippa II when the latter built an addition to his palace that allowed him to see into the temple. In a tit-for-tat maneuver, the aristocracy built a wall to hide his vista, which also obstructed the Roman army's view, so Festus wanted the wall down. Poppaea Sabina pleaded with Nero for the wall to remain.[77] Josephus describes her as a God-fearer, but historians wonder if she is acting the part of the Jewish aristocracy's patron, using her political influence to benefit her clients in Jerusalem. Further suggesting this picture,

---

73. Osiek and MacDonald, A Woman's Place, 235.
74. See Shelly Matthews, First Converts: Rich Pagan Women and the Rhetoric of Mission in Early Judaism and Christianity (Stanford, CA: Stanford University Press, 2001).
75. Josephus, Ant. 18.164.
76. Josephus, Ant. 18.236.
77. Jospehus, Ant. 20.195.

she gave Josephus numerous gifts when he returned from Rome to Jerusalem in AD 64.[78] Of course Josephus might be exaggerating the affection and care these gentile women offered to Jews. But other sources confirm his story for the most part, so we can be fairly confident in their trustworthiness. Both Luke and Josephus might have overstressed the influence of patronage by wealthy gentile women to promote the political innocence of their respective groups, but the patronage was there nonetheless.[79]

Women Benefactors of Jesus

JOANNA

Women Christian benefactors were found not only in the Diaspora; in Palestine, Jesus enjoyed the patronage of a few women as well. Luke describes Mary Magdalene; Joanna, wife of Herod's steward Chuza; Susanna; and "many others" who provided for the group out of their own means (Luke 8:1–3). Because numerous books are devoted to Mary Magdalene's life and history,[80] we will focus more extensively on the lesser-known Joanna. Luke 8 reveals several things about Joanna. First, she and a number of other women accompanied Jesus and the twelve male disciples as they traveled throughout Galilee. Second, Jesus healed her of evil spirits. Third, she was the wife of Chuza, the steward of Herod Antipas. Fourth, she provided for the disciples out of her own funds. In Luke's Passion account, she is also present at the empty tomb (24:10).

Luke notes that Joanna traveled with the twelve male disciples throughout the general region of Galilee as Jesus preached and healed in various synagogues and open spaces.[81] What would it look like for men and women to travel together to various towns in Galilee and the surrounding area? It is common to gloss over this historical detail because it does not fit our imagined scenario of Jesus's ministry and women's roles within it. We might have a Hollywood image of Jesus and Mary Magdalene as generated in *The Last Temptation of Christ* or in *Jesus Christ Superstar*. If we do not follow Hollywood's sexualizing of Jesus's relationships with female followers, we might reconstruct Jesus's ministry relying heavily on rabbinic portraits of a

---

78. Josephus, *Ant.* 20.189–96.

79. Matthews writes, "Through highlighting Gentile noblewomen's support for their communities, these authors may be promoting the understanding of their respective communities not so much as 'foreign cults' but as political communities modeled to some extent on the Greek city or collegia" (*First Converts*, 64).

80. See, for example, Jane Schaberg, *Mary Magdalene Understood*, with Melanie Johnson-DeBaufre (New York: Continuum, 2006); Mary R. Thompson, *Mary of Magdala: What the Da Vinci Code Missed* (Mahwah, NJ: Paulist, 2006).

81. Kathleen E. Corley (*Private Women, Public Meals: Social Conflict in the Synoptic Tradition* [Peabody, MA: Hendrickson, 1993], 116) argues that Luke 8:1–3 stresses the authority of the Twelve and the mundane service of women.

"proper" rabbi, one who had no dealings at all with women.[82] Neither extreme is helpful. In looking closely at several historical details, I suggest that the Gospels, in speaking of women and men following a religious figure, reflect acceptable behaviors.

First, we should note that Jesus was teaching and healing in the predominantly Jewish area of Galilee. Hospitality was a key component of peasant life, and even distant relatives would readily offer one another food and housing. Female disciples, therefore, would have had little trouble finding shelter in village homes. In addition, it seems that many of the female disciples had male relations, such as husbands or sons, in the group. Thus they might be accompanied by a male family member, which respected the conventions in their culture. This suggests that Chuza was a member of the group. Though it is possible that Joanna is a widow once married to Chuza, mentioning his name suggests that he was alive during Jesus's ministry and at least sympathetic to it. Chuza's responsibilities would have made it difficult to travel with Jesus, but that does not preclude him having a sincere interest in Jesus's ministry. This would be especially true if Jesus healed his wife, as Luke recounts.

Second, women participated alongside men in other Jewish groups of this time. For example, Josephus tells of families living at Masada at the end of the disastrous First Revolt. Again, the early second-century AD Babatha archives were found in a cave that included letters of the loyal supporters of Simon bar Kochba. Was she a follower of his? Her stepdaughter's archive was also found there, suggesting a family tie. The "cave of horrors" with its numerous skeletons of men, women, and children witnesses to the involvement of entire families in the resistance movement. Fresh readings of the research and newly published manuscripts from Qumran challenge the status quo conclusion of only celibate males at Qumran.[83] The Rule of the Congregation (1QSa I, 4–11) and a highly fragmented liturgical text (4Q502) are explicit in their insistence on female participation in the group. They reveal the presence of women at all levels and at all ages. Not only did women travel with Jesus, they also came to hear him teach and to be healed.

Luke mentions that several women followed Jesus because he had healed them or cast out demons from them. Was Joanna or a member of her household ill, and Jesus healed them? Some speculate that the rich royal officer of John 4:46–54 is in fact Chuza. In this healing story, Jesus cures the man's son, and

---

82. Though there is useful information in his work, Joachim Jeremias's *Jerusalem in the Time of Jesus: An Investigation into Economic and Social Conditions during the New Testament Period* (trans. C. H. Cave and F. H. Cave [Philadelphia: Fortress, 1975], 359–76) suffers from an overconfidence in the historical veracity of rabbinic material (particularly talmudic) for reconstructing Jewish women's lives in first-century AD Judea and Galilee.
83. See chapter 6.

the latter's entire household believes in Jesus.[84] There is not enough information to determine what Jesus did specifically for Joanna, but presumably his actions greatly influenced her commitment to follow him and to provide funds for the group from her own resources.

Joanna's marriage to Chuza, a steward or financial administrator in Herod's court, suggests that she was a wealthy woman herself.[85] Most people married those of their own class and financial status. In the Roman Empire, married women could hold property and wealth apart from their husbands. Though Jewish women did not as a rule inherit from their fathers, they could receive gifts, and both mothers and fathers gave such deeds of gift to their daughters. In addition, a woman usually brought a dowry to the marriage. Most Roman marriages were *sine manu*; that is, the father did not transfer authority to the husband at the marriage.[86] This set-up allowed the wife's family to keep their money within their own family. The wife's dowry, then, belonged to her and her family. The husband could use the interest on the money, or benefit from the crops of the land as he wished, but the dowry amount returned to his wife at his death or in the case of divorce. Coming from an elite family meant that Joanna had access to education that many women (and not a few men) were unable to access. In all likelihood, she met important political and religious figures, was up-to-date on important news throughout the Roman Empire, and had opportunities to display leadership, even if it was to staff in preparing a banquet. In other words, Joanna was likely educated, erudite, and authoritative in demeanor.

Chuza was probably a Nabatean, from the country to the southeast of Judea in northwest Arabia. This group mingled with their neighbors in Judea; Herod Antipas's grandmother was a Nabatean, and he married a Nabatean princess. They practiced circumcision of young men, which meant that Chuza might have more readily converted to Judaism, having already undergone the procedure. It is likely that Joanna's family would insist on his conversion, if Josephus's stories about other wealthy women's family demands can be generalized.[87]

Certainly there is precedence for wealthy women supporting groups within Judaism. The Hasmonean queen Salome Alexandra favored the Pharisees over the Sadducees, and the wife of Pheroras (Herod the Great's sister-in-law) fol-

---

84. Chuza would not be the only member of Herod's court to join Jesus's followers. In Acts 13:1, the disciple Manaen is listed as one brought up with (therefore, a close companion or friend of) Herod the Tetrarch.

85. For the argument that Chuza was a poor slave or freedman with low social status, though with access to real funds, see Corley, *Private Women, Public Meals*, 111n13.

86. See the previous discussion in chapter 2.

87. For example, see Josephus, *Ant.* 20.2–4 (17–96) for the story of Queen Helene of Adiabene. See also Tal Ilan, *Jewish Women in Greco-Roman Palestine* (Peabody, MA: Hendrickson, 1996), 27–31.

lowed Pharisaic teachings and paid the Pharisees' fine when over six thousand refused to take an oath to Caesar. These women used their political power to protect the Pharisees, and both expected political support in return. In Joanna's case, however, it seems unlikely that she would expect Jesus to support her causes in the political arena. Nor could the tiny band following Jesus set up monuments to their benefactors, given their precarious situation and itinerant lifestyle. Moreover, patronage probably played out differently in the peasant and rural parts of Judea and Galilee than in the urban centers of Tiberias and Jerusalem. The average Jewish community would have involved itself in the patronage system by relying on the wealthy landowners to help with famine relief, to support its clients against legal judgments, and to provide funds for the temple. Hospitality, prominent within the patronage system, was also a crucial component of Judean and Galilean life.

JOANNA, PATRONAGE, AND *DIAKONOS*

Another way to examine this question of patronage is to look at the term used in Luke 8:3 to describe the women's benefaction. The root noun is *diakonos*, the same term used to describe Phoebe in Romans 16:1. This term has been understood to mean servant-like behavior, performing demeaning work for the sake of others and being socially subordinate. Those adhering to this interpretation see Joanna (and Mary and Susanna) as eschewing all her wealth as she became one of the itinerant members of Jesus's group. She embraces the demeaning role of servant in giving up her funds and her social prestige to join the Jesus movement.

However, as noted above, *diakonos* and its verbal form are tightly connected with the idea of serving under orders, or functioning as a go-between, an emissary. The term need not carry a sense of actions done by an inferior to their superior, nor does it necessarily entail demeaning activities. Rather, the term stresses that an act is based on the conviction that it was commissioned by another and must be carried out. Luke pushes for this latter understanding by noting that the women gave "out of their own resources," thus underlining the "purely profane sense"[88] of the phrase "they ministered to him." In a similar light, Acts 6:1–2 has the sense, not that the seven men chosen to help the community were preparing and serving food, but that they were administering the funds that allowed this service to take place. If this is a parallel text to Luke 8:2–3, then Joanna's actions are those of one who senses a commissioning to benefit Jesus and his group.

88. Collins, *Diakonia*, 245. He concludes, "In Christian writings, outside the table usage of the gospels . . . , the verb always signifies carrying out a task established either by God, by the terms of an ecclesiastical office, or by the authority of an apostle or by an authority within the community, in all cases with that special connotation of the sacred that characterises so much of its use in all senses and that of its cognates in non-Christian sources" (251).

This conclusion, however, still begs the question of her status. By using the verbal form of *diakonos,* was Luke suggesting that she gave up her status as a wealthy woman and the honor due her benefaction? Luke 22:25–27 is pointed to as a key passage, for here Jesus contrasts the euergetism of the gentiles with the one who serves, announcing that the latter is superior to the former in God's economy. The argument is that this text shows Jesus turning the patronage system on its head, reversing the status of poor and rich and at the same time arguing for a countercultural movement that disdained public honor.[89] The question is whether this "service" involves self-renunciation and promotes social paradox or is focused on Jesus as a waiter. John N. Collins concludes, "both the form of the word and the general context are thus telling us that we are presented with an image of Jesus as a waiter" and not a general description of service broadly speaking.[90] Note as well that Jesus speaks a few verses later (Luke 22:30) about these same disciples ruling from thrones in his kingdom. The reader is thereby cautioned against equating leadership and authority with the ruthless use of power ("as the gentiles do"; see 22:25).

Given the preponderance of evidence that the *diakonos* word group does not imply a low social status, it is quite likely that Joanna's gift to the group would not necessarily entail any particular statement about status reversal. That said, the term also does not suggest the goal of personal prestige. For example, Josephus talks about his surrender to Roman troops by stating that he was turning himself over to them based on God's will and was acting therefore as God's minister (*diakonos*).[91] There is no sense here of personal gain or glory. We should remember that the institution of patronage oiled the economic wheels, provided political security, and regulated the expectations of social interaction, lest all dissolve into chaos. The present task is not to decide whether patronage is "good" or "bad," nor is it to determine Luke's literary or theological schemas, but to draw a historical picture of women at this time, specifically in terms of patronage.

Patronage and Jesus's Teachings on Wealth and Honor

Those who suggest that Jesus turned the patronage system upside down are essentially substituting one form of honor for another. Rather than have a monument erected, the patron will have a jewel in their heavenly crown and a "well done" from God upon reaching their heavenly reward. The benefits

89. Richard Bauckham writes, "The radical reversal of status taught by Jesus and practiced in the community of his disciples is incompatible with the honor and status attributed to a wealthy benefactor by her beneficiaries" (*Gospel Women: Studies of the Named Women in the Gospels* [Grand Rapids: Eerdmans, 2002], 163).

90. Collins, *Diakonia*, 246. This is not to argue that *diakonos* never means slave or one who is last, but to caution that the term must be defined from the immediate context.

91. Josephus, *B.J.* 3.8.3 (354); 4.10.7 (626).

of patronage are delayed, but not eliminated; the responsibilities of benefaction are not removed, but reshaped. This may all be well and good, as long as one keeps women's equal participation in the revamped patronage system. In the institution of public benefaction, women had a socially acceptable voice. Those who would recast the system should take care that the new structure does not silence these women.

JOANNA AND JUNIA THE APOSTLE

Returning to the discussion of Joanna and her patronage, it has been argued that Joanna's high social status actually worked against her among the disciples, marginalizing her. To overcome this situation, Joanna gave up her wealth to be accepted among the group. Along with her wealth, she renounced her privileged position as a member of Herod's court when she began following Jesus and his itinerant group. While this reading rightly corrects previous readings ignoring that both women and men followed Jesus in his Galilean ministry, it might overstate Joanna's marginality within the group and her subsequent affinity with them. Joanna's education and life experiences would have likely made her comfortable with holding authority. Moreover, her control of at least some wealth suggests a person used to making important decisions. In most cases, these characteristics are valued by a group. Thus it is more likely that Joanna was not marginalized but was embraced by the group. She was not smeared for her previous connections to Herod's court;[92] rather, she was praised for choosing to side with God's people (as they understood themselves).

For several reasons I am hesitant to suppose that Joanna gave up her social rank or that others, within and outside the group, saw her as having little social prestige. First, a satisfying case can be made that with her connections to Herod Antipas's household, she protected Jesus during his ministry in Galilee and kept him safe from Herod's wrath. John the Baptist was not so fortunate, given that another woman active in Herod's court, Herodias, granddaughter of Herod the Great and Mariamme the Hasmonean, encouraged her daughter to request John's head on a platter. Second, Joanna might have been in a position to learn of Jesus's trial before both Antipas and the Sanhedrin—her social rank would have allowed her access to those in the know—and about the plans to execute Jesus early in the morning.[93] Finally, I wonder whether she could simply forget the breadth of learning, experiences, and opportunities, including social networks, afforded by her wealth. I suggest that the patronage system was still present in the Christian group inasmuch as Joanna could aid the disciples, not only in giving money, but in easing tight political situations and calling on her clients to help her new Christian "friends." Wealth and

---

92. Contra Bauckham, *Gospel Women*, 120.

93. Marianne Sawicki, "Magdalenes and Tiberiennes: City Women in the Entourage of Jesus," in *Transformative Encounters: Jesus and Women Re-viewed*, ed. Ingrid R. Kitzberger (Leiden: Brill, 2000), 199.

social position have a way of creating leadership opportunities that poverty robs from even the most gifted women (and men). How would this look if Joanna was also the Junia mentioned by Paul in Romans 16:7? There is no record in the biblical text of Joanna's activities after witnessing the resurrection. Richard Bauckham has proposed an interesting possibility: Joanna is Junia, the apostle commended by Paul in Romans.[94] According to Paul, Junia had a wonderful reputation among the apostles and presumably the churches as well.[95] If so, why do we know so little about her? Bauckham's theory suggests that we know more about her than we might previously have believed. He argues that Junia is the Latin name of the Hebrew Joanna. At first blush we might wonder why two names are used, but the New Testament is peppered with disciples who have two names, a Semitic one and a Greek or Latin one—the most famous is probably Saul whose Latin name was Paul. Other examples are Silas/Silvanus (also a Roman citizen; Acts 16:37); John (or Yehohanan) Mark (a common Latin praenomen; Acts 12:12, 25); Joseph Barsabbas/Justus (Latin; Acts 1:23). Some might have held Latin names from birth, while others chose names that sounded similar to their Semitic names but were easier for Latin and Greek speakers to pronounce.

Joanna's "station in life," rather than a concern over gender, might have played the biggest role in her being chosen as an apostle. In several cases, apostles came from privileged backgrounds that allowed them quality education, rhetorical skills, and an ease in leading others. Barnabas had property and sold it, giving all the money to the church. Paul was a Roman citizen and studied with the greatest Jewish minds of his day, certainly not something available to folks from the lower walks of life. If Joanna is Junia, then the background for this female apostle is a privileged one. This is not to suggest that she "bought" her position, but rather that the leadership requirements of an apostle would not have been easily gained by a poor woman. For example, Joanna/Junia would likely be fluent in both Aramaic and Greek, and perhaps Latin. Few Jewish women (or men) in Roman Palestine would have had such education.

Again, her role as benefactor established her as a person of social status; Joanna/Junia used the conventions of her day, exploiting the avenues open to her as benefactor to speak the gospel publicly without risking social condemnation upon her or the group. Doing "good" in the community through serving the gods or the less fortunate was quite in style in the ancient world. Joanna/Junia fit the role of religious benefactor and, as such, was not castigated by the general public, no more than were the male apostles for speaking publicly.

94. For more on Junia, see chapter 6.
95. Matthews (*First Converts*, 53), in her argument that Luke diminishes women in his own group while promoting pagan women, notes that Luke does not mention Junia or Phoebe and puts Priscilla after Aquila. Bauckham's argument, if correct, would weaken her claims.

If we remove patronage from the social equation, we take away the voice of some women; not only is their relative independence gone but so also is their place at the table of decision making.

MARY MAGDALENE, BENEFACTOR

We might gain a better appreciation for Joanna's benefaction by looking at another benefactor of Jesus, Mary Magdalene.[96] The two women are linked in Luke 8:1–3, as well as during Jesus's last days in Jerusalem, witnessing the Passion and the resurrection (Luke 24:10).[97] They are both healed by Jesus, which most likely led to their joining the group. But did they know each other before they were members of Jesus's group? Intriguing details, including their names, their need for healing, and their business activities, suggest that possibility.

As noted above, Joanna was likely from a wealthy Jewish Galilean family. During the time of Jesus's ministry, the Herodians and the Galileans were politically opposed to each other; moreover, earlier some Hasmoneans had moved from Judea into Galilee, setting up another rival group. In 38 BC Herod defeated Antigonus, a Hasmonean prince with eyes set on ruling Jerusalem, in the area surrounding Magdala. A decade later, in 29 BC, Herod murdered his wife Mary/Mariamme, a Hasmonean princess. Her name became very popular in the Galilee, perhaps as a gesture against Herod's rule.[98] It may be, then, that Mary's parents named her in part as a political statement against the Herodian house. Joanna's name comes from the Hasmonean John, so her family was probably pro-Hasmonean, sharing these sentiments with Mary's family. Since she had wealth enough to benefit Jesus and his male disciples, it may be that her family was wealthy. If so, it is entirely possible that Mary and Joanna knew each other because their wealthy families shared pro-Hasmonean political sentiments.

That we know her as Mary Magdalene, or Mary from Magdala, suggests that she traveled, for that moniker would hardly distinguish her among the townsfolk of Magdala; at home, she would be more likely known by her father's or mother's name. Mary might have traveled on business, either a family business or one that she built. Magdala (also known as Taricheae) was doing well economically in the early part of the first century AD, primarily due to its thriving salt fish export industry. Their products could be shipped across the Sea of Galilee to trade routes going north and east. Magdala was about

96. For an alternative view than that presented here, see Kathleen E. Corley, *Women and the Historical Jesus: Feminist Myths of Christian Origins* (Santa Rosa, CA: Polebridge, 2002), 27–52.

97. Paul's list of those who witnessed the resurrection does not mention any women by name, although women might be implied in his claim that five hundred people saw Jesus (1 Cor. 15:5–8). Some argue Paul is deliberately attempting to silence women. Another argument is that his primary focus is to compare himself favorably with the prominent apostles James and Peter.

98. Sawicki, "Magdalenes and Tiberiennes," 192.

three miles from Tiberias, the site of Herod Antipas's court; one could walk the distance in about an hour. Wanting to capitalize on trade, Herod Antipas built Tiberias even though Sepphoris would have been suitable for his court. He wanted to be part of the travel route to Jerusalem. People did not pass through Galilee if they landed at Caesarea Maritima. Those coming from the east would go down the eastern side of the Jordan, cross at Scythopolis (and thus not even enter Perea, also Herod's territory), then go south to Jericho and over the hills to Jerusalem. Herod wanted to give elite travelers a reason to cross the Sea of Galilee. Perhaps he employed Chuza to oversee entertainment and services for his elite guests. If so, it is likely that Joanna helped Chuza with his entertaining duties by paying special attention to the female guests, for it was acceptable for women to travel on pilgrimages with their husbands. Given the heavy traffic through Tiberias, it is quite possible that Mary Magdalene had business (and clients or patrons, or both) in the capital city.

Both Joanna and Mary are said to have been cured by Jesus; more specifically, Mary had seven demons cast out.[99] Speculation abounds as to what Mary's specific condition was, but I would argue against assuming that she was incapacitated by the illness or that it was caused by "the impact of the painful problems life can bring, particularly those special problems a woman faced in the Palestine of Jesus's day," such as the misogyny of Jewish men.[100] The reference to seven demons has led to an association of Mary Magdalene with the sinful woman in Luke 7:36–50.[101] Tradition has assumed that the woman who anoints Jesus in Luke 7 is a prostitute, but the text never identifies her as such.[102] In the parable of the prodigal son, Luke uses the specific term for prostitute (15:30). This implies that he could have been explicit about the unnamed woman if he intended to indicate that she was a prostitute. A close look at Luke's language reveals that he is connecting this sinful woman with the group of "tax collectors and sinners" (7:34) that Jesus (called a glutton and drunkard) is said to befriend.[103] The two women from Luke 7 and 8 are

99. It is possible that Luke uses the number seven figuratively here, to indicate that her situation was desperate. We do not know how the condition manifested itself.

100. Carla Ricci, *Mary Magdalene and Many Others: Women Who Followed Jesus*, trans. Paul Burns (Minneapolis: Fortress, 1994), 136. She continues with the improbable and anti-Jewish conclusion that Mary Magdalene likely felt suffocated by an inability to express herself, experienced pent-up frustrations at the lack of creative outlets and tensions from a repressed life force, all of which "finally upset the balance of her mind" (136–37).

101. The setting of the encounter Jesus has with the unnamed woman is important; it occurred at a meal. See chapter 2 for a discussion of public dining. Many scholars recognize the importance in Luke's Gospel of table fellowship and the symposium motif. Cf. Dennis E. Smith, "Table Fellowship as a Literary Motif in the Gospel of Luke," *JBL* 106 (1987): 613–38.

102. Corley, *Private Women, Public Meals*, 124–30, defends the identification of the sinful woman as a prostitute.

103. A similar passage in Matt. 21:31–32 reads "tax collectors and prostitutes," supporting the claim that Luke could have identified this woman as a prostitute had he wanted to.

conflated into a single person: a woman with a promiscuous past who is freed from her sinful ways by Jesus. Her sexually compromised history features in many portraits down through the centuries: she is young, beautiful, and seductive. Some go so far as to say that this composite "Mary" earned her wealth (the money she gave to Jesus and the male disciples) through prostitution. Such sentiments reveal a mind-set that is unable to imagine (or is unaware of) women holding occupations similar to men in the marketplace. Nor does such a position recognize that family wealth was often given to daughters. Others bolster their opinion that Mary was a prostitute by pointing to a reference in the rabbinic corpus that denounces the corruption of Magdala: the rabbis concluded that this sea port city was destroyed because of prostitution in its midst.[104] But there is no reason to assume that Mary was a prostitute just because her seaport town had prostitutes, any more than we should assume Prisca was a prostitute because she lived in Corinth.

Not only has Mary Magdalene been falsely connected to the sinful woman of Luke 7, but she has also been assumed to be the Mary of Bethany who anointed Jesus in John 11:2 and 12:3. The correlation is made through the gesture of anointing. Mary Magdalene carried spices to the grave to anoint Jesus's body, and Mary of Bethany anointed Jesus before Passion Week. In John 12:7, Jesus declares that the ointment Mary used is to be kept for the day of his burial, leading some to connect Mary Magdalene's visit to the grave with Jesus's words heard by Mary of Bethany. In one of the earliest witnesses to this conflation, Hippolytus writes in his *In Canticum canticorum* 25.6 that Martha and Mary were witnesses to the resurrection, and they are thus "apostles to the apostles, sent by Christ."[105] In this reference, Mary of Bethany, sister of Martha, is identified with Mary of Magdala.

Another account of Jesus being anointed before his death is found in Matthew and Mark, although in each case, the woman is unnamed (Mark 14:3–9; Matt. 26:6–13). If Jesus was anointed only once, then the unnamed woman in Luke 7 can be identified with Mary of Bethany, sister to Martha and Lazaras.[106]

---

104. See *y. Ta'anit* 4, 69c; *Midrash Lamentations* 2.2.4. The rabbinic material is from the talmudic period, reflecting at least the fourth century AD. Magdala (Migdol) is in a list of three cities destroyed by the Romans, the other two for their contention and witchcraft. The late date and standardized list of sins for the three cities lessen the historical value of these references in recreating first-century Magdala. For an overview of major issues, see Kitzberger, ed., *Transformative Encounters.*

105. Later Christian sources, including the *Epistle to the Apostles* 9 and the *Book of the Resurrection of Jesus Christ by Bartholomew the Apostle*, mention Martha present with Mary at the tomb.

106. For a careful survey of the church fathers' comments on Mary Magdalene, see Jane Schaberg, *Resurrection of Mary Magdalene: Legends, Apocrypha, and the Christian Testament* (New York: Continuum, 2004), 82–87. She notes that Tertullian might be the first to connect the sinful woman of Luke 7 with Mary Magdalene. In speaking about Mary's attempted touch of Jesus in John 20:17, Tertullian describes her as a sinner who had covered Jesus's feet with

And if one has already associated the unnamed woman of Luke 7 with Mary Magdalene, then Mary of Bethany must be Mary of Magdala. In AD 591, Pope Gregory the Great identified Mary Magdalene with the unnamed woman in Luke 7 and with Mary of Bethany.[107] He expounded that the seven demons were actually seven vices and that those vices would have been displayed in sexually promiscuous ways. With the exegetical stroke of pen, Pope Gregory reduced three women to one and removed from historical record the prominent place of Mary of Magdala's benefaction of the Jesus movement.[108]

Conclusion

It would be a mistake to suggest that public and private benefaction raised the level of all women throughout the Roman world. Just as false would be the claim that euergetism raised the level of all men at this time. But with the changing inheritance laws and the increased pressure on the wealthy to give generously to their clients and cities, wealthy, elite women had greater opportunities for political and social influence. Through the institution of patronage, both personal and public, women could access the halls of power and influence. Business arrangements could be made under the auspices of patronage: giving loans, receiving payments for loans, buying or renting property, assuming debt—all necessary for a business, and all possible for women within the culturally acceptable framework of patronage. The personal relationships that even today are so critical in business were open to women patrons. The morning *salutatio*, where clients greeted their patron at home, hoping for some benefaction, but also prepared to undertake any requested task, gave women patrons an insider's view of the city's politics and the means to influence its direction.

Women could promote their religious views in patronizing the local cult and pronounce their allegiance to Rome in serving in the imperial cult. This aid could take the form of festivals given to the entire city or only to honored citizens, or the construction or improvement of buildings. Priestesses assisted individual sect members and took on leadership responsibilities to advance the group's fortunes. And this was all done with society's moral approval, for women were using their wealth to further the common good. The increase in their own honor and prestige was the community's payment for such largesse. In the institution of patronage, status trumped gender; no shame was attached to men having women patrons.

Patronage allowed gentile and Jewish men and women to interact with common aims and goals. It provided opportunities for elite gentile women

---

kisses, bathed them with her tears, wiped them with her hair, and anointed them with ointment (*Adversus Marcionem* 4.18.9, 16–17).

107. Pope Gregory the Great, *Homiliae* 23.

108. The Orthodox tradition retains the three women as separate individuals.

to sponsor Jewish causes and allowed Jewish women a voice in their Jewish community or in the larger political arena. Benefaction provided the platform for gentile and Jewish women interested in the Jesus movement to publicly contribute to its welfare. The female benefactors would have a voice and an authoritative role in the community, granted to them without consideration of gender. For all its faults (noted by the ancients themselves), the institution of patronage was in many respects gender-blind. As such, it allowed a freedom of movement at most social levels for women to participate in the social, economic, and political environment without any cultural condemnation. Thus while a woman might otherwise be stigmatized for speaking or acting publicly on economic, religious, or political matters, a patroness had liberty to exercise her ideas and interests with society's blessings.

Conclusion

Virginia Woolf noted that "for most of history, Anonymous was a woman." She perceptively identifies the struggle in rebuilding the history of women: while evidence suggests they were doing significant things, so often when we try to put flesh on the figure, it seems like dressing a ghost—the form lacks substance.

Yet still the hints intrigue, the echoes tease the investigator. If directed at this project, Woolf's comment might read instead, "in much of history, women are

From a dining room in third-century AD Sepphoris, this mosaic of an anonymous woman has been dubbed "Mona Lisa of the Galilee." (Photo courtesy of George Kalantzis/Wheaton College)

anonymous." This book was a small attempt to bring to life and light women of the Greco-Roman period. We examined family, religious activities, jobs and vocations, and the system of patronage that, like glue, held the social order together. We looked at real women, individuals who cared for children, bought and sold property, worshiped at festivals, worked to make ends meet. At the beginning of the project, somewhat discouragingly, the more information I gathered, the less coherent and consistent the picture of real women appeared. On the one hand, some data insisted that women were passive, reclusive, and apolitical, while other material highlighted women's capabilities in leadership and public service. How does one make sense of material that points in opposite directions? I suggest below at least two lines of approach.

Prescriptive versus Descriptive

First, I recommended that we distinguish carefully between evidence that is prescriptive and paradigmatic and evidence that is descriptive. Much of ancient literature was composed from an androcentric perspective mandating normative behavior and attitudes. The patriarchy of the day fed vindictive satires and nasty invectives against uppity women who dared to tread in a man's domain. This material was exposed as reflections of male authors' attempts to regulate, control, and create social order and construct the male gender. Therefore, besides normative literature, we looked at private letters, inscriptions, business receipts, and archaeological remains such as statues, votive offerings, and art. While these sources do not offer a direct, immediate perception of historical reality, they present a cogent rebuttal to the idealized literary portrait of the genus "woman."

We have seen that women were active in their families, raising children and educating them. Women braved the real risks of childbirth, dangers as tangible as those seen by soldiers on the battlefield, and many lost their lives in the process. Both Jewish and non-Jewish mothers actively participated in their adult children's lives, contributing to their daughters' dowries or their sons' political ventures. Marriages were often held together by mutual love and respect. Most marriages of the day followed the *sine manu* model, wherein the wife retained control over her property; the husband did not take over his wife's assets but did control the proceeds. Women carried their dowry into marriage, and retained that wealth whether the marriage ended with divorce or the death of their husband. Divorce was an option open to both men and women, although Jewish women were perhaps less likely or able to divorce their husbands. Overall, women with a sizable dowry had the increased independence that wealth brings. Moreover, a matron's status greatly impacted her place in society. A wealthy freedwoman might have more social clout than a poor free woman. A woman's autonomy was usually circumscribed by her father, guardian, or tutor, who in varying degrees served as her representative in key legal transactions and in court.

Not only were women's lives occupied by responsibilities in the home, but women also participated in the religious activities of the larger community. Women joined religious groups and held titles of authority. Depending upon the individual sect, women functioned as priestesses sacrificing to the deity and managing the festivals. Women ventured on pilgrimages, offered votives and prayers for loved ones, and joined men in active veneration of the gods/God, donating funds for sacrifices. Jewish women with excellent educations participated in the Therapeutics, reading scriptures and composing hymns in devotion to God. Their withdrawal from society is markedly different from the lives of the Vestal Virgins, who were right in the middle of Rome's political and military activities; they kept the flame of Rome's future security burning. The range of options available to women drawn to the religious was extensive.

Patronage

Second, I argued that social location was paramount in sorting through the dissonance and disparate practices and beliefs. Specifically, I noted that the institution of patronage structured society and offered platforms for women's public participation in the life of the ancient city. With the practice of public and private benefaction, women gained access to centers of influence and persons of power. As a patron, a woman received public honor; with that came the expectation of privilege and respect. The system of benefaction allowed women autonomy to express their support of particular events (such as city festivals), or work projects (aqueducts or road paving), or religious groups (donating a mosaic floor for a temple). Statues of female benefactors decorated the public places—markets, temples, baths, and fountains—to honor those women who enriched the city.

The social currency of the day was public honor shown in statues, plaques, honorary seats in assemblies, and elaborate tombs. Women patrons were given all such public honors, praised simultaneously for their matronly, chaste deportment and their generous public giving. Patronage extended the household into the public sphere, blurring the boundaries of both and allowing women a respectable place at the table of civic movers and shakers. Benefaction downplayed the gender of the giver. So long as the benefactor could be thought of as a mother of the city or daughter of a cult, she was shielded from public charges of unwomanly character.

Moreover, benefaction crossed ethnic lines, such that both Jews and gentiles participated in this informal but pervasive social institution. It penetrated religious groups, trade guilds, and village life. It fostered business deals, bolstered friendships, and created intricate social networks. It gave women opportunities to grow a business, influence legal decisions, affect a religious group, and shape the political landscape. It allowed for both men and women to sponsor projects that furthered their reputations and also benefited others. In essence, euergetism provided a context in which to think about women as other than the opposite of (and less than) men.

Expanding Our Imagination

As we examined the everyday life of women, we saw that rural women worked alongside men in caring for their animals, building their homes, and feeding their families. Slave women did all manner of work required in the home and in the marketplace; many worked as prostitutes. While I do not suggest an egalitarian paradise during the Greco-Roman period, I hope I encouraged the reader's imagination to think beyond the stylized snapshots of ancient women sequestered in cramped homes, barefoot and pregnant. I am not sanguine enough to think that we can recover women's actual voices, but I remain confident that echoes of their heartaches and successes are recoverable.

It is perhaps surprising to the modern reader to see that women were active in the commercial world as merchants, vendors, artisans, and shopkeepers. Women populated the marketplace, selling, buying, and loaning money. Women worked as midwives and wet nurses, as doctors, writers, and philosophers. They composed verse and wrote stories. Women enjoyed the Roman banquet and the baths. A few spoke in court—persuasively, as in the story of Hortensia. Repeatedly we have seen how women overturned social expectations or upended biased customs to further their purposes. Hortensia defied traditional mores that demanded women keep silent by speaking publicly to the triumvirs. Yet she called on accepted social customs of familial honor to bolster her case. She was remembered as eloquent and just, and served as a positive symbol for women's public involvement.

That Was Then, This Is Now

Of course, studying figures from the past is exciting in its own right, but usually we are more interested in those historical persons who in some way help inform our present. The past so often determines the future. This is the case today for many Jews and Christians who understand or legitimate their beliefs and practices about women based on the customs and laws preserved from the ancient past. Getting the historical story right and the facts correct therefore plays a large part in current debates about women's proper behaviors and attitudes. Apart from confessional interests, many men and women are concerned that setting the record straight about the experience of women in history is a necessary step in creating a better future for modern societies.

Conclusion

Faulty, unreflective historical claims serve contemporary ideologies and agendas; this book is a small attempt to present real, historical women and their busy, productive, messy, and heartbreaking existences. In so doing, it opens the door to creative reflection on current practices and attitudes; it shines a new light on modern biases and perhaps offers better solutions to impasses surrounding gender issues in the church and our communities today. I offer a few modest observations about the possible impact a robust understanding of ancient women's lives might have in discussions today about women's roles in religious communities and society at large.

First, and perhaps most importantly, we must exercise more imagination to repopulate the ancient landscape with women. Otherwise, we fail to include women as active members of the polis or a rural town; we assume that only men were writing, drawing, buying, selling, building, cleaning, and doing all the other jobs upon which society depends. We have to reboot our imagination with regard to who filled the ancient streets, because women were everywhere, present publicly at all social levels. They were present at dinner parties, at the baths, in the marketplace as buyers and sellers, and in the highest levels of city government as benefactors. As we construct our own social and religious communities, we might ponder the reality that ancient women demonstrated interest in the significant trends and discussions that energized their culture. But we cannot forget that many also suffered the social biases against foreigners, or struggled as a slave. Certain doors remained closed—those of the senate and of the military. Indeed, some women fared much better than some men, but overall, because at the highest levels men made the decisions, women as a group had fewer opportunities for self-expression than did men.

For those who study the New Testament, the fact that women were present in most communal venues entails a reassessment of who would have heard a missionary preacher like Paul or Peter speak to market crowds. Women were present alongside men in public places—women from a wide swath of society, including slaves and wealthy patrons. Such a realigned vision offers an opportunity to reflect on the challenges faced by the early church concerning not only gender but also racial and social diversity. And it allows the contemporary church to examine its own record.

Second, we have to appreciate that women held both official and unofficial titles and positions of power. Women retained titles of importance in religious sects and in city government. Accompanying these titles were the honor and social status granted to patrons. The informal system of patronage was all the more powerful because it was unregulated by the courts. The ramification of this reality is that men in the ancient world knew women who had power over them, who had greater social prestige, and who could be called upon to grant favors. This holds true for all communities, including Jewish and emerging Christian communities. Patronage, social status, and wealth often trumped gender as the most important social category.

Patronage, of course, was then and is now a double-edged sword. To those who have wealth, it opens doors for increased influence and opportunities for helping one's community. But to those who lack the means, it places them in a dependent posture; poor men and women were alienated from the corridors of power and prestige. Thus while patronage allowed some women great influence, is this an appropriate avenue to take in bolstering women's status today? Ironically, the very system that allowed such freedom for some women in the ancient world strikes many of us today as anathema. Instead, we cling to the conviction that individuals can pull themselves up by their bootstraps. However, this adage often downplays the social forces that hinder women's pursuit of a better job or lifestyle. And so many of us admit the truth of this modern-day proverb: "It's not what you know; it's who you know." Thus I find myself in the uncomfortable position of praising the ancient patronage system because it allowed some women real social and religious influence. But I am unable to promote the institution wholeheartedly because far too many women (and men) remained at the mercy of other's favors in their client role.

Third, we should note that in Greco-Roman society women controlled their own funds and finances, unlike so much of later history in the West (such as Victorian England). Wives controlled their dowry and could own and will property. This meant that women had their own funds to sponsor business ventures or religious communities. Such women could pursue education, and some were quite learned. As is true today, those with means influenced their surroundings. This should alert us to the active role that women played in shaping groups, because their funds impacted the contours of the city or religious community that they sponsored. We can no longer envision women as passive recipients. They had opportunities to affect and change their local milieu or even the world stage, not simply by using their money, but also by using their education to interact with and discuss the pressing issues of the day.

For those exploring the New Testament, this reality must be factored into any description of discipleship: some women were capable of theological discussion and had the means to sponsor the group. We should expect that Jesus, Paul, and traveling missionaries (which included women) met educated women with strong business acumen and effective community influence. Ironically, women's lack of participation in church politics and leadership hierarchy in later history has led some to argue that the way forward is to go back to the model of the first-century church. I do not imagine, however, an egalitarian utopia in the early church. Communities negotiated the question of female participation based on local situations—for example, whether wealthy women were members of the church and whether the female followers of Jesus had much if any education. Some of their answers might appear sexist by our standards, assuming we have understood their injunctions correctly. Understanding the cultural and social world of these women (and men) allows us to critique that world, and perhaps to critique our own. As we do so, it offers us an opportunity to think more deeply about the subtle (and explicit) forms of sexism (to say nothing of racism) endemic to the ancient culture and, sadly, to our own. But knowing history allows us to avoid repeating its mistakes and to build on its successes.

In short, as we dialogue today about the role of women in society and in the synagogue and church, about women in political leadership and the "glass ceiling," about a woman's role in family and community, we would do well to have an accurate picture of those women who walked these paths before us. Women in the world of the earliest Christians offer us a portrait of possibilities.

Bibliography

Agosto, Efrain. "Patronage and Commendation, Imperial and Anti-imperial." In *Paul and the Roman Imperial Order*, edited by Richard A. Horsley, 103–23. Harrisburg: Trinity Press International, 2004.

Allen, Prudence. *The Concept of Woman: The Aristotelian Revolution, 750 B.C.–A.D. 1250*. 2nd ed. Grand Rapids: Eerdmans, 1997.

Applebaum, Shimon. "Josephus and the Economic Causes of the Jewish War." In *Josephus, the Bible and History*, edited by L. H. Feldman and G. Hata, 237–64. Leiden: Brill, 1989.

Bagnell, Roger S., and Raffaella Cribiore. *Women's Letters from Ancient Egypt, 300 BC–AD 800*. Ann Arbor: University of Michigan Press, 2006.

Balch, David L. *Let Wives Be Submissive: The Domestic Code in 1 Peter*. Society of Biblical Literature Monograph Series 26. Chico, CA: Scholars Press, 1981.

———. "Rich Pompeiian Houses, Shops for Rent, and the Huge Apartment Building in Herculaneum as Typical Spaces for Pauline House Churches." *Journal for the Study of the New Testament* 27.1 (2004): 27–46.

Bauckham, Richard. *Gospel Women: Studies of the Named Women in the Gospels*. Grand Rapids: Eerdmans, 2002.

Bauer, Walter, Frederick W. Danker, F. W. Arndt, F. W. Gingrich. *A Greek-English Lexicon of the New Testament and Other Early Christian Literature*. 3rd ed. Chicago: University of Chicago Press, 2000.

Bauman, Richard A. *Women and Politics in Ancient Rome*. New York: Routledge, 1992.

Beard, Mary. "Re-reading (Vestal) Virginity." In *Women in Antiquity: New Assessments*, edited by Richard Hawley and Barbara Levick, 166–77. New York: Routledge, 1995.

Belleville, Linda. "Ἰουνιαν . . . ἐπίσημοι ἐν τοῖς ἀποστόλοις: A Re-examination of Romans 16.7 in Light of Primary Source Materials." *New Testament Studies* 51 (2005): 231–49.

Bickerman, Elias. "Two Legal Interpretations of the Septuagint." In *Studies in Jewish and Christian History, Part 1*, 201–13. Leiden: Brill, 1976.

Bohak, Gideon. *Joseph and Aseneth and the Jewish Temple in Heliopolis*. Society of Biblical Literature Early Judaism and Its Literature 10. Atlanta: Scholars Press, 1996.

Bradley, Keith R. *Slaves and Masters in the Roman Empire: A Study in Social Control*. New York: Oxford University Press, 1987.

———. "Wet-Nursing at Rome: A Study in Social Relations." In *The Family in Ancient Rome: New Perspectives*, edited by Beryl Rawson, 201–29. Ithaca, NY: Cornell University Press, 1986.

Branham, Joan. "Bloody Women and Bloody Spaces: Menses and the Eucharist in Late Antiquity and the Early Middle Ages." *Harvard Divinity Bulletin* 30.4 (2002): 15–22.

Brooten, Bernadette J. *Women Leaders in the Ancient Synagogue*. Brown Judaic Studies 36. Atlanta: Scholars Press, 1982.

Brouwer, H. H. J. *Bona Dea: The Sources and a Description of the Cult*. Leiden: Brill, 1989.

Bruce, F. F. *The Epistles to the Colossians, to Philemon, and to the Ephesians*. New International Commentary on the New Testament. Grand Rapids: Eerdmans, 1984.

Camp, Claudia V. "Understanding a Patriarchy: Women in Second Century Jerusalem through the Eyes of Ben Sira." In *"Women Like This": New Perspectives on Jewish Women in the Greco-Roman World*, edited by Amy-Jill Levine, 1–39. Atlanta: Scholars Press, 1991.

Charlesworth, James H., ed. *Old Testament Pseudepigrapha*. 2 vols. Garden City, NY: Doubleday, 1983–85.

Cohen, Shaye J. D. "Menstruants and the Sacred in Judaism and Christianity." In *Women's History and Ancient History*, edited by Sarah B. Pomeroy, 273–99. Chapel Hill: University of North Carolina Press, 1991.

Cole, Susan Guettel. "New Evidence for the Mysteries of Dionysos." *Greek, Roman and Byzantine Studies* 21 (1980): 223–38.

Collins, John N. *Diakonia: Re-interpreting the Ancient Sources*. Oxford: Oxford University Press, 1990.

Corley, Kathleen E. *Private Women, Public Meals: Social Conflict in the Synoptic Tradition*. Peabody, MA: Hendrickson, 1993.

———. *Women and the Historical Jesus: Feminist Myths of Christian Origins*. Santa Rosa, CA: Polebridge, 2002.

Corrington, Gail P. *Ascetic Behavior in Greco-Roman Antiquity: A Sourcebook*. Edited by V. Wimbush. Minneapolis: Fortress, 1990.

Cotton, Hannah M., and Ada Yardeni. *Aramaic, Hebrew and Greek Documentary Texts from Naḥal Ḥever and Other Sites, with an Appendix Containing Alleged Qumran Texts*. Discoveries in the Judean Desert 27. Oxford: Clarendon, 1997.

Crawford, Sidnie White. "Mothers, Sisters, and Elders: Titles for Women in Second Temple Jewish and Early Christian Communities." In *The Dead Sea Scrolls as*

Background to Postbiblical Judaism and Early Christianity, edited by James R. Davila, 177–91. Leiden: Brill, 2003.

Crook, J. A. "Feminine Inadequacy and the *Senatusconsultum Velleianum*." In *The Family in Ancient Rome: New Perspectives*, edited by Beryl Rawson, 83–92. Ithaca, NY: Cornell University Press, 1986.

Deiss, Joseph Jay. *Herculaneum: Italy's Buried Treasure*. Rev. ed. New York: Harper and Row, 1985.

Dixon, Suzanne. "Family Finances: Terentia and Tullia." In *The Family in Ancient Rome: New Perspectives*, edited by Beryl Rawson, 93–120. Ithaca, NY: Cornell University Press, 1987.

———. *Reading Roman Women: Sources, Genres, and Real Life*. London: Duckworth, 2001.

———. *The Roman Family*. Baltimore: Johns Hopkins University Press, 1992.

———. *The Roman Mother*. Norman: University of Oklahoma Press, 1988.

———. "Sex and the Married Woman in Ancient Rome." In *Early Christian Families in Context: An Interdisciplinary Dialogue*, edited by David L. Balch and Carolyn Osiek, 111–29. Grand Rapids: Eerdmans, 2003.

Edwards, Catherine. *Politics of Immorality in Ancient Rome*. Cambridge: Cambridge University Press, 1993.

Engels, Donald. "The Problem of Female Infanticide in the Greco-Roman World." *Classical Philology* 75.2 (1980): 112–20.

Epp, Eldon Jay. *Junia: The First Woman Apostle*. Minneapolis: Fortress, 2005.

Evans-Grubbs, Judith. "Hidden in Plain Sight: Expositi in the Community." Paper presented at the Fifth Roman Family Conference: Secrets de familles, familles secrètes: Mémoire et identité familiales, Université de Fribourg, June 15, 2007.

———. *Women and the Law in the Roman Empire: A Sourcebook in Marriage, Divorce, and Widowhood*. London: Routledge, 2002.

Fagan, Garrett G. *Bathing in Public in the Roman World*. Ann Arbor: University of Michigan Press, 2002.

Fantham, Elaine, Helene Peet Foley, Natalie Boymel Kampen, Sarah B. Pomeroy, and H. A. Shapiro. *Women in the Classical World: Image and Text*. New York: Oxford University Press, 1994.

Feldman, Louis H., and Meyer Reinhold, eds. *Jewish Life and Thought among Greeks and Romans: Primary Readings*. Minneapolis: Fortress, 1996.

Ferguson, Everett. *Backgrounds of Early Christianity*. 3rd ed. Grand Rapids: Eerdmans, 2003.

Flemming, Rebecca. "Quae Corpore Quaestum Facit: The Sexual Economy of Female Prostitution in the Roman Empire." *Journal of Roman Studies* 89 (1999): 38–61.

Flesher, Paul Virgil McCracken. *Oxen, Women, or Citizens? Slaves in the System of the Mishnah*. Brown Judaic Studies 143. Atlanta: Scholars Press, 1988.

Forbes, R. J. *Studies in Ancient Technology*. Vol. 4, *The Fibres and Fabrics of Antiquity*. Leiden: Brill, 1987.

Fotopoulos, John. *Food Offered to Idols in Roman Corinth: A Social-Rhetorical Reconsideration.* Tübingen: Mohr Siebeck, 2003.

Franklin, James L. *Pompeis Difficile Est: Studies in the Political Life of Imperial Pompeii.* Ann Arbor: University of Michigan Press, 2001.

French, Valerie. "Midwives and Maternity Care in the Roman World." In *Midwifery and the Medicalization of Childbirth: Comparative Perspectives*, edited by E. R. van Teijlingen, G. W. Lewis, P. McCaffery, and M. Porter, 53–62. New York: Nova Science, 2004.

Gager, John G., ed. *Curse Tablets and Binding Spells from the Ancient World.* Oxford: Oxford University Press, 1992.

García Martínez, Florentino, and Eibert J. C. Tigchelaar, eds. *The Dead Sea Scrolls Study Edition.* 2 vols. Grand Rapids: Eerdmans, 1997–98.

Gardner, Jane F. "Women in Business Life, Some Evidence from Puteoli." In *Female Networks and the Public Sphere in Roman Society*, edited by Päivi Setälä and Liisa Savunen, 11–27. Rome: Institutum Romanum Finlandiae, 1999.

Gardner, Jane F., and Thomas Wiedemann. *The Roman Household: A Sourcebook.* New York: Routledge, 1991.

Gibson, E. Leigh. *The Jewish Manumission Inscriptions of the Bosporus Kingdom.* Tübingen: Mohr Siebeck, 1999.

Gill, David W. J. "Acts and the Urban Élites." In *The Book of Acts in Its First Century Setting.* Vol. 2, *Graeco-Roman Setting*, edited by David W. J. Gill and Conrad Gempf, 105–18. Grand Rapids: Eerdmans, 1994.

Glancy, Jennifer A. *Slavery in Early Christianity.* Minneapolis: Fortress, 2006.

Gordon, Richard. "From Republic to Principate: Priesthood, Religion and Ideology." In *Pagan Priests: Religion and Power in the Ancient World*, edited by Mary Beard and John North, 179–98. Ithaca, NY: Cornell University Press, 1990.

———. "The Veil of Power: Emperors, Sacrificers and Benefactors." In *Pagan Priests: Religion and Power in the Ancient World*, edited by Mary Beard and John North, 201–31. Ithaca, NY: Cornell University Press, 1990.

Graham, Harvey. *Eternal Eve.* Garden City, NY: Doubleday, 1951.

Gray, Patrick. "Abortion, Infanticide, and the Social Rhetoric of *The Apocalypse of Peter.*" *Journal of Early Christian Studies* 9.3 (2001): 313–37.

Grossman, Maxine L. *Reading for History in the Damascus Document: A Methodological Study.* Studies on the Texts of the Desert of Judah 45. Leiden: Brill, 2002.

Harland, Philip A. *Associations, Synagogues, and Congregations: Claiming a Place in Ancient Mediterranean Society.* Minneapolis: Fortress, 2003.

Harrill, J. Albert. *The Manumission of Slaves in Early Christianity.* 2nd ed. Tübingen: Mohr Siebeck, 1998.

Harris, William V. "Child-Exposure in the Roman Empire." *Journal of Roman Studies* 84 (1994): 1–22.

———. "The Theoretical Possibility of Extensive Infanticide in the Graeco-Roman World." *The Classical Quarterly* 32.1 (1982): 114–16.

Hopkins, Keith. "Contraception in the Roman Empire." *Comparative Studies in Society and History* 8.1 (1965): 124–51.

Horsley, G. H. R., ed. *New Documents Illustrating Early Christianity.* Vol. 1, *A Review of the Greek Inscriptions and Papyri Published in 1976.* North Ryde, Australia: Ancient History Documentary Research Centre, Macquarie University, 1981.

Ilan, Tal. *Integrating Women into Second Temple History.* Peabody, MA: Hendrickson, 2001.

———. *Jewish Women in Greco-Roman Palestine.* Peabody, MA: Hendrickson, 1996.

———. "'Man Born of Woman . . .' (Job 14:1): The Phenomenon of Men Bearing Metronymes at the Time of Jesus." *Novum Testamentum* 34 (1992): 23–45.

———. "Premarital Cohabitation in Ancient Judea: The Evidence of the Babatha Archive and the Mishnah (*Ketubbot* 1.4)." *Harvard Theological Review* 86 (1993): 247–64.

Inowlocki, Sabrina. "Wisdom and Apocalypticism in *Aseneth.*" Paper presented at the Society of Biblical Literature Annual Meeting, Toronto, Canada, November 2004.

Instone-Brewer, David. *Divorce and Remarriage in the Bible: The Social and Literary Context.* Grand Rapids: Eerdmans, 2002.

———. "1 Corinthians 7 in the Light of the Jewish Greek and Aramaic Marriage and Divorce Papyri." *Tyndale Bulletin* 52.2 (2001): 225–43.

———. *Techniques and Assumptions in Jewish Exegesis before 70 CE.* Tübingen: Mohr Siebeck, 1992.

Isaksson, Abel. *Marriage and Ministry in the New Temple: A Study with Special Reference to Mt. 19.13–12 and 1 Cor. 11.3–16.* Lund: C. W. K. Gleerup, 1965.

Jefferies, Daryl F. *Wisdom at Qumran: A Form-Critical Analysis of the Admonitions in 4QInstruction.* Piscataway, NJ: Gorgias, 2004.

Jensen, Christian. "Ein neuer Brief Epikurs." In *Abhandlungen der Gesellschaft der Wissenschaften zu Göttingen Philologisch-Historische Klasse, 3/5,* 1–94. Berlin: Weidmannsche Buchhandlung, 1933.

Jeremias, Joachim. *Jerusalem in the Time of Jesus: An Investigation into Economic and Social Conditions during the New Testament Period.* Translated by C. H. Cave and F. H. Cave. Philadelphia: Fortress, 1975.

Joshel, Sandra R. *Work, Identity, and Legal Status at Rome: A Study of the Occupational Inscriptions.* Norman: University of Oklahoma Press, 1992.

Kampen, Natalie Boymel. "Between Public and Private: Women as Historical Subjects in Roman Art." In *Women's History and Ancient History,* edited by Sarah B. Pomeroy, 218–48. Chapel Hill: University of North Carolina Press, 1991.

———. *Image and Status: Roman Working Women in Ostia.* Berlin: Mann, 1981.

———. "Social Status and Gender in Roman Art: The Case of the Saleswoman." In *Feminism and Art History: Questioning the Litany,* edited by Norma Broude and Mary D. Garrard, 63–78. New York: Harper and Row, 1982.

Kearsley, R. A. "Women in Public Life in the Roman East: Iunia Theodora, Claudia Metrodora and Phoebe, Benefactress of Paul." *Tyndale Bulletin* 50.2 (1999): 189–211.

Kitzberger, Ingrid Rosa, ed. *Transformative Encounters: Jesus and Women Reviewed.* Leiden: Brill, 2000.

Klauck, Hans-Josef. *Ancient Letters and the New Testament: A Guide to Context and Exegesis.* With Daniel P. Bailey. Waco: Baylor University Press, 2006.

Köstenberger, A. "Ascertaining Women's God-Ordained Roles: An Interpretation of 1 Timothy 2:15." *Bulletin for Biblical Research* 7 (1997): 107–44. Reprinted in *Studies on John and Gender: A Decade of Scholarship*, chap. 14. New York: Peter Lang, 2001.

Kraemer, Ross S. *Her Share of the Blessings: Women's Religions among Pagans, Jews, and Christians in the Greco-Roman World.* Oxford: Oxford University Press, 1992.

———. "Jewish Mothers and Daughters in the Greco-Roman World." In *The Jewish Family in Antiquity*, edited by Shaye J. D. Cohen, 89–112. Brown Judaic Studies 289. Atlanta: Scholars Press, 1993.

———. "Jewish Women in Rome and Egypt." In *Feminism in the Study of Religion: A Reader*, edited by Darlene M. Juschka, 223–27. New York: Continuum, 2001.

———, ed. *Maenads, Martyrs, Matrons, Monastics: A Sourcebook on Women's Religions in the Greco-Roman World.* Philadelphia: Fortress, 1988.

———. "Monastic Jewish Women in Greco-Roman Egypt: Philo Judaeus on the Therapeutrides." *Signs* 14 (1989): 342–70.

———. "Typical and Atypical Jewish Family Dynamics: The Cases of Babatha and Berenice." In *Early Christian Families in Context: An Interdisciplinary Dialogue*, edited by David L. Balch and Carolyn Osiek, 130–56. Grand Rapids: Eerdmans, 2003.

———. *When Aseneth Met Joseph: A Late Antique Tale of the Biblical Patriarch and His Egyptian Wife, Reconsidered.* New York: Oxford University Press, 1998.

———, ed. *Women's Religions in the Greco-Roman World: A Sourcebook.* Rev. ed. Oxford: Oxford University Press, 2004.

Kroeger, Richard Clark, and Catherine Clark Kroeger. *I Suffer Not a Woman: Rethinking 1 Timothy 2:11–15 in Light of Ancient Evidence.* Grand Rapids: Baker Books, 1992.

Lefkowitz, Mary R., and Maureen B. Fant. *Women's Life in Greece and Rome: A Source Book in Translation.* 3rd ed. Baltimore: Johns Hopkins University Press, 2005.

Levine, Lee I. *The Ancient Synagogue: The First Thousand Years.* New Haven: Yale University Press, 2005.

———. "Synagogue Leadership: The Case of the Archisynagogue." In *Jews in a Graeco-Roman World*, edited by Martin Goodman, 195–213. Oxford: Clarendon, 1998.

Levinskaya, Irina A. *The Book of Acts in Its First Century Setting.* Vol. 5, *Diaspora Setting.* Grand Rapids: Eerdmans, 1996.

Levison, Jack. "Is Eve to Blame? A Contextual Analysis of Sirach 25:24." *Catholic Biblical Quarterly* 47 (1985): 617–23.

Lewis, Naphtali, Yigael Yadin, and Jonas C. Greenfield, eds. *The Documents from the Bar Kokhba Period in the Cave of Letters.* Judean Desert Studies 2. Jerusalem: Israel Exploration Society, 1989.

Lightman, Majorie, and William Zeisel. "Univira: An Example of Continuity and Change in Roman Society." *Church History* 46.1 (1977): 19–32.

Lindsay, W. M., ed. *Sexti Pompei Festi De verborum significatu quae supersunt cum Pauli epitome.* Inscriptiones Latinae Liberae Rei Publicae II.803. 1913. Reprint, Hildesheim: Georg Olms, 1965.

Llewelyn, S. R., ed. *New Documents Illustrating Early Christianity.* Vol. 6, *A Review of the Greek Inscriptions and Papyri Published in 1980–81.* With R. A. Kearsley. North Ryde, Australia: Ancient History Documentary Research Centre, Macquarie University, 1992.

MacDonald, Margaret Y. *Early Christian Women and Pagan Opinion: The Power of the Hysterical Woman.* Cambridge: Cambridge University Press, 1996.

———. *The Pauline Churches: A Socio-Historical Study of Institutionalization in the Pauline and Deutero-Pauline Writings.* Cambridge: Cambridge University Press, 2004.

Marchal, Joseph A. "With Friends Like These . . . : A Feminist Rhetorical Reconsideration of Scholarship and the Letter to the Philippians." *Journal for the Study of the New Testament* 29.1 (2006): 77–106.

Marks, Susan. "Jewish Weddings in the Greco-Roman Period: A Reconsideration of Received Ritual." PhD diss., University of Pennsylvania, 2003. Forthcoming from Georgias Press.

Martin, Dale B. *The Corinthian Body.* New Haven: Yale University Press, 1999.

———. "Slavery and the Ancient Jewish Family." In *The Jewish Family in Antiquity,* edited by Shaye J. D. Cohen, 113–29. Brown Judaic Studies 289. Atlanta: Scholars Press, 1993.

———. *Slavery as Salvation: The Metaphor of Slavery in Pauline Christianity.* New Haven: Yale University Press, 1990.

Matthews, Shelly. *First Converts: Rich Pagan Women and the Rhetoric of Mission in Early Judaism and Christianity.* Stanford, CA: Stanford University Press, 2001.

Mau, August. *Pompeii, Its Life and Art.* Translated by Francis W. Kelsey. New York: Macmillan, 1907.

Maxfield, Valerie A. "Soldier and Civilian: Life beyond the Ramparts." In *Birthday of the Eagle: The Second Augustan Legion and the Roman Military Machine,* edited by Richard J. Brewer, 145–64. Cardiff: National Museums and Galleries of Wales, 2002.

McGinn, Thomas A. *The Economy of Prostitution in the Roman World: A Study of Social History and the Brothel.* Ann Arbor: University of Michigan Press, 2004.

McGrath, James F. "Was Jesus Illegitimate? The Evidence of His Social Interactions." *Journal for the Study of the Historical Jesus* 5 (2007): 81–100.

McKnight, Scot. "Jesus as *Mamzer* (Illegitimate Son)." In *Who Do My Opponents Say That I Am?* edited by Scot McKnight and Joseph B. Modica, 133–63. London: T&T Clark, 2008.

Mitchell, Margaret M. "New Testament Envoys in the Context of Greco-Roman Diplomatic and Epistolary Conventions: The Example of Timothy and Titus." *Journal of Biblical Literature* 111 (1992): 641–62.

Modica, Joseph B. "Jesus as Glutton and Drunkard." In *Who Do My Opponents Say That I Am?* edited by Scot McKnight and Joseph B. Modica, 50–75. London: T&T Clark, 2008.

Mulroy, David. "The Early Career of P. Clodius Pulcher: A Re-examination of the Charges of Mutiny and Sacrilege." *Transactions of the American Philological Association* 118 (1988): 155–78.

Murphy-O'Connor, Jerome. *Paul: A Critical Life*. Oxford: Oxford University Press, 1997.

Netzer, Ehud. *The Architecture of Herod, the Great Builder*. With Rachel Laureys-Chachy. Texts and Studies in Ancient Judaism 117. Tübingen: Mohr Siebeck, 2006.

Neusner, Jacob. *Development of a Legend: Studies on the Traditions concerning Yoḥanan ben Zakkai*. Leiden: Brill, 1970.

Nielsen, Inge. *Thermae et Balnea: The Architecture and Cultural History of Roman Public Baths*. 2 vols. Aarhus, Denmark: Aarhus University Press, 1990.

Osiek, Carolyn. "*Diakonos* and *Prostatis*: Women's Patronage in Early Christianity." *Hervormde Teologiese Studies* 61.1–2 (2005): 347–70.

Osiek, Carolyn, and David L. Balch. *Families in the New Testament World: Households and House Churches*. Louisville: Westminster John Knox, 1997.

Osiek, Carolyn, and Margaret Y. MacDonald. *A Woman's Place: House Churches in Earliest Christianity*. With Janet H. Tulloch. Minneapolis: Fortress, 2006.

Peterlin, Davorin. *Paul's Letter to the Philippians in the Light of Disunity in the Church*. Leiden: Brill, 1995.

Pollard, Elizabeth Ann. "Magic Accusations against Women in the Greco-Roman World from the First through the Fifth Centuries C.E." PhD diss., University of Pennsylvania, 2001.

Pomeroy, Sarah B. *Goddesses, Whores, Wives, and Slaves: Women in Classical Antiquity*. 1975. Reprint, New York: Schocken, 1995.

———. "Infanticide in Hellenistic Greece." In *Images of Women in Antiquity*, edited by Averil Cameron and Amélie Kuhrt, 207–22. 2nd ed. London: Routledge, 1993.

Porten, Bezalel, and Ada Yardeni. *Textbook of Aramaic Documents from Ancient Egypt*. 2 vols. Jerusalem: Hebrew University, 1986.

Price, Robert M. *The Widow Traditions in Luke-Acts: A Feminist-Critical Scrutiny*. Atlanta: Scholars Press, 1997.

Price, Simon R. F. *Rituals and Power: The Roman Imperial Cult in Asia Minor*. Cambridge: Cambridge University Press, 1984.

Rajak, Tessa. "Benefactors in the Greco-Roman Diaspora." In *Geschichte–Tradition–Reflexion: Festschrift für Martin Hengel zum 70*, edited by H. Cancik, H. Lichtenberger, and P. Schäfer, 1:305–22. Tübingen: Mohr Siebeck, 1996.

———. "The Synagogue within the Greco-Roman City." In *Jews, Christians, and Polytheists in the Ancient Synagogue: Cultural Interaction during the Greco-Roman Period*, edited by Steven Fine, 161–73. New York: Routledge, 1999.

Rajak, Tessa, and David Noy, "Archisynagogoi: Office, Title and Social Status in the Greco-Roman Synagogue." *Journal of Roman Studies* 83 (1993): 75–93.

Rawson, Beryl. "The Roman Family." In *The Family in Ancient Rome: New Perspectives*, edited by Beryl Rawson, 1–57. Ithaca, NY: Cornell University Press, 1987.

Reynolds, Joyce, and Robert Tannenbaum. *Jews and God-Fearers at Aphrodisias: Greek Inscriptions with Commentary*. Proceedings of the Cambridge Philological Society, supplement 12. Cambridge: Cambridge Philological Society, 1987.

Ricci, Carla. *Mary Magdalene and Many Others: Women Who Followed Jesus*. Translated by Paul Burns. Minneapolis: Fortress, 1994.

Richlin, Amy. "Carrying Water in a Sieve: Class and the Body in Roman Women's Religion." In *Women and Goddess Traditions in Antiquity and Today*, edited by Karen L. King, 330–74. Minneapolis: Fortress, 1997.

Roller, Matthew B. *Dining Posture in Ancient Rome: Bodies, Values and Status*. Princeton: Princeton University Press, 2006.

Rowlandson, Jane. *Women and Society in Greek and Roman Egypt: A Sourcebook*. Cambridge: Cambridge University Press, 1998.

Saller, Richard P. *Personal Patronage under the Early Empire*. Cambridge: Cambridge University Press, 1982.

Satlow, Michael L. *Jewish Marriage in Antiquity*. Princeton: Princeton University Press, 2001.

———. "Reconsidering the Rabbinic *ketubah* Payment." In *The Jewish Family in Antiquity*, edited by Shaye J. D. Cohen, 133–51. Atlanta: Scholars Press, 1993.

Sawicki, Marianne. "Magdalenes and Tiberiennes: City Women in the Entourage of Jesus." In *Transformative Encounters: Jesus and Women Re-viewed*, edited by Ingrid R. Kitzberger, 181–202. Leiden: Brill, 2000.

Schaberg, Jane. *Mary Magdalene Understood*. With Melanie Johnson-DeBaufre. New York: Continuum, 2006.

———. *Resurrection of Mary Magdalene: Legends, Apocrypha, and the Christian Testament*. New York: Continuum, 2004.

Schiffman, Lawrence H. *Reclaiming the Dead Sea Scrolls*. Philadelphia: Jewish Publication Society, 1994.

Schottroff, Luise. *Let the Oppressed Go Free: Feminist Perspectives on the New Testament*. Louisville: Westminster/John Knox, 1993.

Schuller, Eileen M. "Women in the Dead Sea Scrolls." In *The Dead Sea Scrolls after Fifty Years: A Comprehensive Assessment,* edited by Peter W. Flint and James C. VanderKam, 2:117–44. Leiden: Brill, 1999.

Schultz, Celia E. *Women's Religious Activity in the Roman Republic*. Chapel Hill: University of North Carolina Press, 2006.

Shelton, Jo-Ann. *As the Romans Did: A Sourcebook in Roman Social History*. New York: Oxford University Press, 1988.

Smith, Dennis E. *From Symposium to Eucharist*. Minneapolis: Fortress, 2003.

————. "Table Fellowship as a Literary Motif in the Gospel of Luke." *Journal of Biblical Literature* 106 (1987): 613–38.

Smith, Jonathan Z. *Imagining Religion: From Babylon to Jonestown*. Chicago: University of Chicago Press, 1982.

Standhartinger, Angela. "Women in Early Christian Meal Gatherings: Discourse and Reality." Translated by Martin and Nancy Lukens-Rumscheidt. http://www.philipharland.com/meals/AngelaStandhartingerWomeninMeals.pdf (accessed April 15, 2009). Paper presented at the Society of Biblical Literature Annual Meeting, Philadelphia, PA, November 2005.

Staples, Ariadne. *From Good Goddess to Vestal Virgins: Sex and Category in Roman Religion*. New York: Routledge, 1998.

Stegemann, Hartmut. "Some Remarks to 1QSa, to 1QSb, and to Qumran Messianism." *Revue de Qumran* 17 (1996): 479–505.

Strange, James F. "Ancient Texts, Archaeology as Text, and the Problem of the First Century Synagogue." In *Evolution of the Synagogue: Problems and Progress*, edited by Howard Clark Kee and Lynn H. Cohick, 27–45. Harrisburg, PA: Trinity Press International, 1999.

Taylor, Joan E. *Jewish Women Philosophers of First-Century Alexandria: Philo's 'Therapeutae' Reconsidered*. Oxford: Oxford University Press, 2003.

Thesleff, Holger, ed. *The Pythagorean Texts of the Hellenistic Period*. Åbo: Åbo Akademi, 1965.

Thompson, Mary R. *Mary of Magdala: What the Da Vinci Code Missed*. Mahwah, NJ: Paulist, 2006.

Trebilco, Paul R. *Jewish Communities in Asia Minor*. Society for New Testament Studies Monograph Series 69. Cambridge: Cambridge University Press, 1991.

Treggiari, Susan. "Divorce Roman Style: How Easy and How Frequent Was It?" In *Marriage, Divorce, and Children in Ancient Rome*, edited by Beryl Rawson, 31–46. Oxford: Clarendon, 1991.

————. *Roman Freedmen during the Late Republic*. 1969. Reprint, New York: Oxford University Press, 2000.

————. *Roman Marriage: Iusti Coniuges from the Time of Cicero to the Time of Ulpian*. Oxford: Clarendon, 1991.

Ward, Roy Bowen. "The Public Priestesses of Pompeii." In *The Early Church in Its Context: Essays in Honor of Everett Ferguson*, edited by Abraham J. Malherbe, Frederick W. Norris, and James W. Thompson, 318–34. Supplements to Novum Testamentum 90. Leiden: Brill, 1998.

————. "Women in Roman Baths." *Harvard Theological Review* 85.2 (1992): 125–47.

Wassen, Cecilia. *Women in the Damascus Document*. Academia Biblica 21. Atlanta: Society of Biblical Literature, 2005.

Wegner, Judith Romney. *Chattel or Person? The Status of Women in the Mishnah*. New York: Oxford University Press, 1988.

————. "Philo's Portrayal of Women—Hebraic or Hellenic?" In *"Women Like This": New Perspectives on Jewish Women in the Greco-Roman World*, edited by Amy-Jill Levine, 41–66. Atlanta: Scholars Press, 1991.

Wilson, Stephen G. *Leaving the Fold: Apostates and Defectors in Antiquity.* Minneapolis: Fortress, 2004.

Winter, Bruce W. *Roman Wives, Roman Widows: The Appearance of New Women and the Pauline Communities.* Grand Rapids: Eerdmans, 2003.

Wire, Antoinette Clark. *The Corinthian Women Prophets: A Reconstruction through Paul's Rhetoric.* 1990. Reprint, Eugene, OR: Wipf and Stock, 2003.

Witherington, Ben, III. *Women in the Earliest Churches.* Cambridge: Cambridge University Press, 1991.

Wolters, Al. "IOYNIAN (Romans 16:7) and the Hebrew Name Yĕḥunnī." *Journal of Biblical Literature* 127 (2008): 397–408.

Young, Robin Darling. "The 'Woman with the Soul of Abraham': Traditions about the Mother of the Maccabean Martyrs." In *"Women Like This": New Perspectives on Jewish Women in the Greco-Roman World*, edited by Amy-Jill Levine, 67–81. Atlanta: Scholars Press, 1991.

Index of Scripture and Other Ancient Writings

341

Index of Subjects